INDIAN WARS
of
NEW ENGLAND

VOLUME I

Herbert Milton Sylvester

HERITAGE BOOKS
2008

HERITAGE BOOKS
AN IMPRINT OF HERITAGE BOOKS, INC.

Books, CDs, and more—Worldwide

For our listing of thousands of titles see our website
at
www.HeritageBooks.com

A Facsimile Reprint
Published 2008 by
HERITAGE BOOKS, INC.
Publishing Division
100 Railroad Ave. #104
Westminster, Maryland 21157

Copyright © 1910 Herbert M. Sylvester

— Publisher's Notice —
In reprints such as this, it is often not possible to remove blemishes from the original. We feel the contents of this book warrant its reissue despite these blemishes and hope you will agree and read it with pleasure.

International Standard Book Number: 978-0-7884-1041-3

TO MY WIFE

THE INSPIRER AND LOVING CRITIC

OF ALL MY LABORS

I AFFECTIONATELY DEDICATE

THIS WORK

PREFACE

"THE Compiler of an History can challenge little to himself but methodizing his Work, the Materials being found ready to his Hand; Diligence in gathering them together, and Faithfulness in improving them, is all that is upon the point required of him; in both which I have endeavoured to make good what the Profession I have now taken up obliges me unto."

An Advertisement to the Reader,
Hubbard's "Indian Wars."

AN ADVERTISEMENT TO THE READER

IN this relation of the conflict between the English settler and the New England aborigine, the author leaves the field of ethnologic investigation to the more curious and speculative student. After the Relations of the Jesuits, and of Ventromile, Lincoln, Kidder, Leland, Higginson, and O'Brion, there seems very little to be added of a people who ceased to exist a century and a half ago, and whose origin and history are involved in obscure tradition prior to the advent of Waymouth and Champlain.

The origin, especially, of the New England Indian is a matter wholly of conjecture. His annihilation, however, is an historic fact. It is with the finals of his savage activities, in which the Levitical concept was observed to the letter, that the author is compelled, by the historic areas to be surveyed, to be content.

LIST OF AUTHORITIES

THE author of "The Indian Wars of New England" acknowledges his indebtedness to the following authorities in the preparation of his work, for which he desires to give the proper credit: —

Acadiensis
Adams, *Portsmouth*
Banvard, *Pilgrims*
Barry, *History of Massachusetts*
Baylie, *Old Colony*
Belknap, *New Hampshire*
Bodge, *Narragansett*
Bourne, *History of Wells and Kennebunk*
Bouton, *Lovewell's Fight*
Bradford, *Plymouth*
Caverly
Charlevoix, *Canada* (Shea)
Cheever, *Puritans*
DeForest, *Indians of Connecticut*
Dexter, *Church's King Philip's War*
Drake, *Book of the Indians, Old Indian Chronicles*
Freeman, *Civilization and Barbarism*
Frost, *Book of the Colonies*
Higginson
Hubbard, *Indian Wars, History of New England*
Hutchinson, *Letters*
Jackson, *Early Settlers*
Johnson, *Deerfield*
Lechford, *Plain Dealing*

INDIAN WARS OF NEW ENGLAND

Leland, *Algonquin Legends*
Lincoln, *Abenake Language*
Lithgow-Douglass, *Dictionary of Indian Names*
Maine *Historical Collections*
Morton
Neale, *Puritans*
O'Brion, *Abenake Language*
Palfrey, *History of New England*
Parkman
Penhallow, *Indian Wars*
Pierce, *Indian History and Genealogy*
Purchas
Rogers, *Rangers*
Sewall, *Papers*
Thacher, *Plymouth*
Trumbull, *Indian Wars*
Ventromile, *Abenake Language*
Willis, *History of Portland*
Winsor, *Memorial History of Boston*
Winsor, *Narrative and Critical History of America*
Winthrop, *Letters*
Wood, *New England Prospect*
Young, *Chronicles*

Consulting both original and contemporary sources, the author does not claim to have discovered anything new after the lapse of centuries, but he has endeavored to give some shape to the disheveled data of numerous chroniclers, whose relations seemed to him to be mostly matters of place, with neither beginning nor end, and in some instances, apparently, of very little accomplishment or value. In "The Indian Wars of New England,"

LIST OF AUTHORITIES

as herein chronicled, a complete, continuous, and chronological relation of a century of Indian warfare is for the first time offered to the historical student. The only apology the author has to make is his surprise at the amount of rubbish that has been garbed as history and mounted upon the pedestal of alleged erudition.

SUB-TITLES

TOPOGRAPHY OF INDIAN TRIBES
THE EARLY SETTLER AND THE INDIAN
THE PEQUOD WAR
WARS OF THE MOHEGANS

FOREWORD

TO the student of Indian history of the early New England period the catalogue of the librarian would allow one to infer that the ground had been already preëmpted by Mr. William Hubbard and some other well-known writers upon the savage tragedies of the early New England days, whose labors are more famous for being a quaint reflection of the times than for comprehensive treatment of the subject at hand. Without Mr. Drake's labors, allied to those of Church and Belknap, the earlier story would be a meager one. It is to these authors one goes with assurance and infinite satisfaction, and one feels safe in accepting them as authorities upon the matters of which they write. Mr. Hubbard, who is most tedious in his narrative, leaves one at the threshold of Mr. Penhallow's "Relation," which brings one to the verge of 1726; while Mr. Palfrey's consideration of the events which limit the scope of the present work is general rather than subjective. Unquestionably, Mr. Palfrey offers very little of the conflicts of the English settler with the Indians. His objective was a "History of New England," to which the depredations of the savages were necessarily incidental. With Gardener's "Pequod Wars" and Church's "Philip's War" is ushered in a decade of peaceful

INDIAN WARS OF NEW ENGLAND

years, the termination of which leaves one upon the threshold of a most sanguinary conflict which broke out anew in 1688, and in which the stage of activities was shifted from the purlieus of Mount Hope[1] to the northern boundaries of New Hampshire and eastward about the marshes of old Scarborough and the islands of Merry-meeting Bay.

Isolate attacks were made upon the Connecticut River settlements at the outset; but with the destruction of Hadley and Deerfield, and one or two towns in the Hudson River Valley, the settlers along the coast of Maine and about the Piscataqua bore the brunt of the terror and devastation which everywhere followed in the wake of the savage allies of the French whose outposts at Norridgewock and Pentagoët afforded the Jesuit, Ralé, and the son-in-law of Madockawando, St. Castin, ample seclusion in which to foment and perfect their plots under the guiding hand of Frontenac, whose great labor was the progress of New France and the extension of its domain as far to the west as Albany and the country about the Hudson and Iroquois, and as far south as New York. From 1677 to 1685 the Indians had been peaceable. There were mutterings of a storm along the uplands of the Scarborough lands, where lived Henry Jocelyn and the Algers.

---

[1] Mount Hope is supposed to be a corruption of Montaup. Banvard, *Plymouth and the Pilgrims*, p. 215.

FOREWORD

It broke and passed with a half-dozen savage butcheries, in which the Algers paid the penalty of their greed of land and their ungenerous attitude toward their savage grantors. Jocelyn had been made a captive by Mugg, the Saco sachem, and released. An exchange of captives was made, and the Scarborough settlers turned to the tilling of their acres anew, while Scottow began the building of his fort. Frontenac had been recalled. Denonville had superseded him, and, in the whirl of events, Frontenac, who was hanging about the court of Louis XIV., then at the zenith of its brilliancy, needy and out of kingly favor, pushed by influential friends and a wife whose subtle intriguing was to prove of service to her ambitious husband, was about to see his fortunes mended.

Frontenac had his faults. He was fiery and headstrong; but he was as keenly active and energetic, and of an unconquerable vitality. Denonville proved to be a bitter disappointment to his master, and the king was not wholly unmindful of Frontenac, to whom he had presented a "gratification" of 3,500 francs. Letters from Denonville betrayed the desperate state of affairs at Quebec. In his need the king determined to restore Frontenac to the dignity of which he had stripped him seven years before. He summoned Frontenac into his presence and, remarking that it was his belief that the charges which had led to his recall were unfounded, he added, "I send you

INDIAN WARS OF NEW ENGLAND

back to Canada, where I am sure that you will serve me as well as you did before; and I ask nothing more of you."[1]

Frontenac was in his seventieth year. It was Denonville's plan to carry the war into the English colonies. His plan was accepted by the king in a modified form, but one which made the wished-for results more doubtful. New York was the objective-point, the immediate conquest of which was decided upon. The raids upon Cascoe and the towns to the south along the coast, the devastation of the New Hampshire border, and the destruction of Schenectady were almost simultaneously accomplished by the three war parties sent out respectively from Montreal, Three Rivers, and Quebec. This was in 1690. In this year Pemaquid was destroyed; Salmon Falls as well. The trail of the savage wound through the woods of old York; and everywhere in its wake were the smokes of burning cabins and the stark figures of the settlers, dead and mutilated, almost across their own thresholds.

This was twelve years after the ending of King Philip's War, the beginning of an era of savagery that has been paralleled nowhere in the history of civilization.

Hubbard's story is perhaps sufficient, so far as it goes; yet here at the second coming of Frontenac

---

[1] Goyer, *Oraison Funèbre du Compte de Frontenac.*

FOREWORD

began a new era of savage barbarities that were to extend through a half-dozen Indian outbreaks, at the instigation of the French, and which were to cover a span of two generations with all the demoralization of flame and bloodshed. And while the author has it in mind to go back to the beginning of things colonial, he hopes he may be able to add something of interest to the narrations that have gone before, and which have found many interpreters whose stories have been perpetuated in reprints, which of itself is but an added proof that the author need to make no apology for the work he has undertaken. The material is abundant. In the main it is veracious. The difficulty seems to be in the matter of selection so as not to over-burden the work with that which takes on some color of value more from local tradition than from its actual importance as a record of the so-called lean days, and at the same time to enable the impartial reader to realize unconsciously the historical truthfulness of the events portrayed. The story is told chronologically, as one would unwind a strand of yarn from its reel. If the author's notes at times seem to be somewhat *in extenso*, it is because he has preferred to offer them to the reader under the color of a personal comment, rather than as a part of the text, thus avoiding that disposition to digression which, while it illuminates, is apt to impair the directness of the relation.

The interest of the author in Indian lore, or,

INDIAN WARS OF NEW ENGLAND

more particularly, Indian history as related to the early settlements of New England, has been crystallized somewhat in his story of the Pioneer Settlements of the Maine Coast— a relation which terminated with the closing years of the peace following the death of King Philip. With the completion of this work the author hopes to have paid his debt of admiration to the sturdy characteristics of his forefathers, and as well to have afforded to others some inspiration to continue the investigation here begun. It is the story of a great and significant drama, the stage-settings of which are the green woods of the wilderness,—their somber shadows and ominous silences by day, and their horde of voiceless terrors

"When Night's black mantle covers all the world,"—

a mingling of tragedy and romance, in which Fate severed the thread of the French power upon the continent of North America at the inevitable moment, but at what cost to the New World dwellers upon the English frontiers of 1688 and 1759 can never be estimated.

THE AUTHOR.

TOPOGRAPHY OF INDIAN TRIBES

TOPOGRAPHY OF INDIAN TRIBES

FROM the nature of the two races it was inevitable that, on the part of the English, there should be a contemptuous indifference to the red man; while on the part of the latter it was as inevitable that in time the spirit of hatred and vengeance should replace the courteous generosity of the great Massasoit and his contemporaries, Samoset and Canonicus. The English settler, as typified in the Puritan,—who, by the way, is not to be confounded with the Separatists of the Plymouth Colony,—was the antithesis of the aborigine of the New World.[1] To the Puritan the Indian was a

---

[1] The term "Puritan," as a generic appellation of the English who comprised the settlements from Cape Cod to Cape Ann, is misleading. The terms "Pilgrim" and "Puritan" by many writers have been used interchangeably, as if their religions and politics were identical. The terms are not synonymous. The Puritans were of the Established Episcopal Church; yet while they retained this connection, they were self-appointed reformers of its doctrines and practices. They yielded to the supremacy of the king as the head of the Church, whose articles of faith they accepted, while protesting against certain alleged abuses with which they claimed it was infected. Laboring for the eradication of the same as a process of internal purification, they were known as Puritans. Governor Winthrop was the head of this particular cult.

The Plymouth people were *separated* from the Established

INDIAN WARS OF NEW ENGLAND

heathen, without rights or privileges, and he was treated accordingly.

The Indian was among the rudest of the aboriginal races. His language was untameably rugged;

Church. They were non-conformists, disputing the domination of the civil and ecclesiastical powers in matters of conscience, especially that interference which would make it compulsory upon them to observe a form of worship which, according to their belief, was offensive to God. They claimed entire freedom of conscience. Their ultimate act was secession from the parent body, to become known as Separatists.

There was a wide difference in their religious beliefs and practices from those of the Puritans. When they left English Plymouth for the New World they left it as pilgrims, and they became Pilgrims, indeed. As the settlers of Plymouth, they are properly designated as the Pilgrim Fathers. They were of a proscribed sect. They were without a charter, protection, or encouragement. Even their New World destination was controverted by a trick of which they were ignorant. They were the sport of circumstance.

Discounting the Weston settlement at Wessagusset (1623-24); passing over the coming of Captain Wollaston to Merry Mount, now Quincy, the resort of that "Lord of Misrule," Tom Morton (1625); the Puritan régime begins with the coming of John Endicott to Salem (1629). Governor John Winthrop came over the next year, at which time William Blackstone lived a hermit life on the west slope of Beacon Hill, while Thomas Walford was at Mishawam (Charlestown). Samuel Mavericke was at East Boston. All these settlers, from Wessagusset to Salem, were known as "the planters." This was the soil in which Governor Winthrop was to sow the seed of Puritanism, the embryo of an ultra-religious and political commonwealth.

TOPOGRAPHY OF INDIAN TRIBES

so was his environment. It was, as well, singularly deficient, finding expression in unintelligible gutturals and grunts. While his ear was touched with solace of tuneful notes,— harmonious sounds such as make up a strain of music,— his own song was no more than a monody, a succession of notes strung upon a single line, to make up a series of wild chromatics as colorless as the air that bore them upon the hearing of others. To him the essence of music was vociferation, punctuated by unearthly yells and wild whoops. Of melody and rhythm, unless indicated by the genuflexions of their bodies as they swayed to and fro in their burial ceremonies, interpolated with chants pitched in low, weird key or shrilling with wild despair, they knew nothing except, perhaps, in its most rudimentary character.

They had no literature,— no arbitrary signs which in combination might be interpreted into cogent meaning,— only such rude hieroglyphics as they were wont to inscribe on the bark of the birch, or the skins of animals taken in the chase,— figures of beasts and birds and of their own kind traced with a bit of charcoal, a symbolical writing which they understood, a rude scrawl in pantomime.[1] They were picture-writers and, to a limited

---

[1] It is recorded, after the first foray by the English upon the Norridgewocks where the Jesuit Ralé had his little chapel, an Indian paddling down the Kennebec in his canoe came

INDIAN WARS OF NEW ENGLAND

degree, they understood the use of the ocherous earths and the juices of certain plants and tree-rinds which yielded them brilliant pigments and dyes. They were exceedingly fond of bright colors. The Indian's eyes, his ears, and even his finger-tips were unerring interpreters. By day or night he traversed the forest with sure footsteps. The stars were his compass; and when the stars were obscured he read the bark of the trees with a glancing touch. The leaves at his feet betrayed the stranger who had trespassed upon his domain, and with a nose as keen as that of a fox he scented danger at a far distance. His nerves of hearing were as delicately adjusted as the finest constructed seismograph. As if nature had taken him under her special protection, she had endowed him with the keenest of outward sensibilities, as she had the deer, and the animals who preyed upon it.

The Indian was limited even in his traditions, all of which were supernaturally improbable. His traditions of the origin of his race suggest the

---

upon a bit of birch bark upon which was pictured the death of the priest. Ralé was supposed to have been killed in the attack on the Norridgewock village, but, singularly enough, got away. The picture-writing was a news-bulletin; but in this case it proved a canard. It remained for Lieutenant Jacques, in the Moulton raid, to send the bullet home to the heart of Ralé, considered by the English to be the arch-conspirator and instigator of the fiendish butcheries perpetrated by his savage followers.

TOPOGRAPHY OF INDIAN TRIBES

Darwinian theory,— that it was evolved from the animal kingdom. Some singular traditions prevailed among the Abenake, which were handed down from father to son, after the fashion of the Sagas of the Norsemen.[1]

---

[1] The Rev. Mr. Heckwelder, whom Baylie, in his *History of New Plymouth*, alludes to as a "modern missionary," relates an interesting tradition concerning the origin of the Indians of the north Atlantic coast, including the tribes along the St. Lawrence. The tradition had its origin among the Delawares (Leni Lenape), and is certainly plausible; and while the author does not follow Heckwelder literally, the relation here given, while considerably abbreviated, is close enough.

The story is, the Leni Lenape nation came from the west beyond the Na-me-esi-Sipu [Mississippi]. Crossing the Great River, they came to the country of the Alligwe, from which nation we have the word "Alleghany." On their way, however, to the Great River they fell in with the Mengwe [Iroquois], who, like themselves, were migrating to the eastward to find a land that suited them. Crossing the Mississippi, they were confronted by the Alligwe, a gigantic race who understood the arts of war and who had regularly constructed fortifications. The Leni Lenape wished to settle in their domain; but when the Alligwe saw the great numbers of the Leni Lenape they attacked the latter with an intent to destroy them, so fearful were they of being absorbed by this strange people.

The Mengwe, who had been passive spectators of this hostile interference, offered to join forces with the Leni Lenape and compel a passage of the Alligwe country if, after conquering the country, they should be allowed to share it with the Leni Lenape equally, to which the latter at once

INDIAN WARS OF NEW ENGLAND

As to the arts, they were primarily workers in stone, as their implements readily indicate. At Sabino, at the mouth of the Sagadahoc River, are indications that there was once at that place a primitive factory where were fashioned stone axes,

---

agreed. They immediately attacked the Alligwe with their combined forces, and, after many years of warfare, overcame them and compelled them to flee across the Great River into the further west. The conquerors divided the country, the Mengwe choosing the region about the Great Lakes and their tributary waters, while the Leni Lenape occupied the lands further south. Being at peace with each other, these two nations increased with great rapidity. Another migration then took place, the more adventurous Lenape crossing the Alleghanies to follow the Susquehannah to the great bay of the Chesapeake, keeping on to the Delaware River, still exploring eastward through the Schegichbi [New Jersey] country, until they came to the Hudson River. They found these countries uninhabited. Returning home with the news, the Leni Lenape migration began in greater force, and settlements were made on all four of the great rivers,— the Delaware, Potomac, Hudson, and Susquehannah. The Delaware country was the center of their possessions; but more than half the Leni Lenape pushed still further east to settle on the Atlantic. They became the three great tribes of The Wolf, The Turkey, and The Turtle. The latter called themselves the Unamis. The Turkey took the tribal name of Unalatchgo. As their tribes multiplied, they extended out beyond the River of the Mohicans [the Hudson], the Wolf totem belonging to the Minci [Monseys]. Their council-fire was at Minisink.

From these and the body of the Delawares sprung other tribes, grandchildren of the parent nation. These, choosing to live by themselves, spread over that part of the country

TOPOGRAPHY OF INDIAN TRIBES

and gouges with which they hollowed out portions of trees, which were shaped into the rude vessels that answered to their necessities. Quantities of stone relics have been found at that place, and not far away are the shell-heaps of Damariscotta,

---

known as the Eastern States. As the years went on, new families were generated, until the whole Atlantic country was peopled by the descendants of the original Leni Lenape.

During this time the Mengwe had increased until they had filled up the country about the Great Lakes and had extended their habitations along the St. Lawrence until they again came in contact with their old allies, the Leni Lenape, through their descendants, which became a cause of hostility. The trouble terminated, the Mengwe nation established its superiority over the Leni Lenape and became known as "The Five Nations."

This tradition is contracted from Baylie's direct quotation of Heckwelder, who is regarded by him as somewhat credulous and liable to be imposed upon by Indian narrators. Nothing is imputed to Heckwelder, if he gave the tradition as he received it. In matters of tradition it is difficult to trace the origin; but Heckwelder offers this particular narration as a certain indication of the common origin of the Atlantic tribes of New England extending southward to Virginia. Heckwelder's contention — or assumption — has some support from the notable similarity of their dialects with that of the Delawares; also the radical difference which was apparent between the languages of the Delawares and the Iroquois.

Baylie's *History of the Pilgrims*, p. 33.

It strikes the author of this work that the question of the initial race from whence sprung the Indians of North America is yet open to debate.

which have given rise to much discussion as to their origin, so extensive are these deposits.

They were superstitious, believing in dreams like the ancients of the days of Nebuchadnezzar, and as well in incantations. Every tribe had its medicine-man, who was consulted upon important occasions. Their worship was crude and unintelligible, except that they acknowledged the power of a good spirit, whom they addressed as their "Manitou," as well as that of another, an evil spirit, who inhabited the air about them — an invisible atom of malevolence whom they were always endeavoring to appease through their medicine-man. This spirit was the instigator of everything that was bad, and to it were ascribed all their misfortunes in war and of the chase. They seemed to have no comprehension of the human agency by which communities guide their affairs. The benignity of the Manitou was their constant solicitude. When things went wrong with them Manitou was asleep, or on the chase somewhere in the Happy Hunting-grounds of the Indian's Hereafter.

They had no permanent living-place; no home. Their perpetuation of the memory of their dead was by heaping up an occasional tumulus of dirt. They erected no monuments, unless one instance may be mentioned as existing on the eastern bank of Taunton River.[1] There has recently been dis-

---

[1] This stone is known as Dighton Rock. Upon it is traced a

TOPOGRAPHY OF INDIAN TRIBES

covered in the bed of a stream in the town of Solon, Me., a shelving ledge, for the great part of the time under water, upon which are some curious rock-tracings. Like those on Dighton Rock, they are uninterpretable. Other stones of a similar character are to be seen elsewhere about New England — notably, a boulder at Damariscotta, and as well, at Manana, a bit of rock in the sea adjacent to Monhegan. In their writing, arrow-heads,

---

multitude of strange hieroglyphics to which, as yet, no key has been discovered. The tracings are evidently a work of regular design. It has become famous by reason of its projection into the controversy of the Norse Occupation and the discovery of the coast of New England by Leif, the son of Erik the Red. Bjarne, son of Herjulf, had been driven by adverse winds south of Greenland, by reason of which he came upon a strange country at three separate times before he was able to head his ship back to Iceland. This was about the year 990. Following Bjarne, Leif headed his ship toward Greenland and then sailed south until he came to a pleasant country to which he gave the name of Leifsbudir, afterward called Vinland, by reason of the grapes which grew there in abundance. In 1002 Thorvald, a brother of Leif, came hither. About 1008 Thorfinn Karlsefne came over with three vessels. He had with him one hundred and sixty persons. His object was to establish a colony at Vinland. Three years later the settlement was abandoned. Other and later voyages took place, but they are all the subject of oral tradition. Professor Rafn essayed to interpret the mystery of Dighton Rock. He accepts the inscription as undoubtedly of Norse origin. Other scholars have agreed with him. Mr. George Bancroft styles the Sagas, which were first printed

INDIAN WARS OF NEW ENGLAND

flints, and charred coals were used by these untutored sons of the wilderness. The thin rind of the birch was the Indian's letter-paper. Upon it were transcribed the symbols within which the meaning of their messages was concealed, a veritable cipher to the uninitiate. Between the various tribes the means of conveyance of these messages was by a runner, a young Indian whose wind and sinew were equal to the arduous strain of a journey of days and nights through the pathless forest, possibly; though from east to west and to the southward along the coast were well-worn trails which might be termed primitive highways. It was by these bits of bark and the pictures on them that they convened their council-fires, where, with much silence, amid the wreathings of fragrant tobacco-

---

in 1837, "mythological in form and obscure in meaning." The Danish antiquaries accept them as legitimate. The rock is located some seven miles from Taunton, in Asson-neck, now the town of Berkely. It is, at low-water line, some nine or ten feet across at its base; it is about four feet high, of smooth face which slopes to the water.

It was discovered by the English in the days of Cotton Mather, whose description of it was published in the transactions of the Royal Society. It has been a Chinese puzzle to the antiquarian. It is evidently of an origin utterly without the scope of the Indian of North America. It has given rise to the most singular vagaries, and by some has been ascribed to the Phœnician navigators. Whatever it may stand for as a vestige of a once existing race, its antiquity is more remote, possibly, than as yet has been accorded it.

TOPOGRAPHY OF INDIAN TRIBES

smoke, they reached the ultimatum of their debate.

While it has been asserted that the savage had no literature, it is true that in the wigwams of the Abenake were not infrequently found collections of hieroglyphic writings, if they might be so classed, which consisted of bits of bark, stones, and other object-records. Their medicine-men had scrolls of bark upon which were singularly uncouth tracings of incantations which they were wont to read to the sick. The Micmacs were adepts in the art of picture-painting; and while the Abenake may not have practised it to so great an extent, it was something they were wont to use not infrequently to convey information to others. It was a picture-vocabulary, some specimens of which are preserved among the writings left by Father Ralé. It was as if the understanding was to be appealed to through the vision.

The moon was the Indian calendar. It was a weather prognosticator. A watery moon foretold snow or wet; a reddish one indicated high winds. It was prophetic of cold, when the rivers would be covered with ice and the snow would be deep in the woods. It foretold as well the bursting of the spring buds. The simples that grew in the woods were the source from which their pharmacy was supplied. There was healing in the trees, as the scurvy-stricken followers of Jacques Cartier, much to their relief, found at Stadaconé, a little palisado

INDIAN WARS OF NEW ENGLAND

on the banks of the St. Charles, where he wintered in 1535, the prey to inaction and the rigorous climate of a Canadian winter, amid a savage and inhospitable people.[1]

The Indian, half animal himself, knew the language of the wild creatures of the wilderness woods, many of which they adopted as the totems of their tribes, and as well revered for the benefits derived from them in food and clothing. They talked with the moose through the hollows of their hands, with the owl and the crow. The beaver taught them the lesson of industry at their very wigwam doors. They spun their thread from the roots of the spruce; the rushes of the swamps gave them their mats; the hide of the deer, their bowstrings. They thatched the roofs of their huts and fashioned their canoes from the bark of the birch, the elm, or the oak. Nature was their literature, unabridged and unexpurgated. The summer days

---

[1] Parkman, *Pioneers of France in the New World*, p. 217.

Cartier had made his second voyage to the St. Lawrence (1535). He wintered at Stadaconé. With the opening of the next year, 1536, a malignant scurvy afflicted his little company of adventurers. Twenty-five died, leaving less than a half-dozen to care for the sick. The prospect was annihilation for the entire party. Cartier met a savage who had not long before been prostrated with the scurvy, but who appeared to be in perfect health. Questioning him as to what had brought about this miraculous healing, the latter told him of a certain evergreen, the "ameda," a brew of the leaves of which was most efficacious. Cartier, obtaining the simple,

TOPOGRAPHY OF INDIAN TRIBES

were their paradise, while the winter, with its snow-smothered silences, was a period of hibernation, when to eat and sleep was their single solace. Inured to exposure, often on the verge of famine, the Indian was a stoic of the extreme type. His philosophy was that of endurance at the expense of all fancy or imagination, in the creative sense. Child-like, yet subtle; hospitable, yet treacherous; forbearing, yet revengeful; loyal, yet impressionable, he was as fickle as the winds. To his friends, his heart was in his hand. To his enemy, he was the quintessence of all that was crafty, cruel, and vindictive.

If the Indian was anything, in matter of degree he might be classed among the mystics. Whatever was beyond his immediate comprehension became at once a source of either fear or admiration. More an impressionist than either analyst or logician, to him the mystery of the Jesuit ritual was like mist upon the waters. It was a visual perception rather than a revelation. It remained for Eliot to locate the spiritual pulse of the savage.

A creature of perfect vitality and of equally fine nervous organism, he was apparently insensible to exposure to the elements[1] or to the pain inflicted

---

made a brew of which his men drank freely, so that in six days all were on the road to health.

Parkman says, "The wonderful tree seems to have been a spruce, or, more probably, an arbor-vitæ."

[1] It was on March 16, 1621, that Samoset made his appear-

INDIAN WARS OF NEW ENGLAND

by his enemies. His accuracy of ear, of scent, of touch, was a part of nature's phenomena. Wild, uncouth, he was one of nature's mosaics, as were the wild things that dropped to his unerring arrow. As a type, to the European he was an exceptional, original, unexpurgated. As a human problem, he was wholly unreducible. His acquaintance with civilization was the first step toward his utter extinction as a race. Once inoculated with the poison in the white man's cup, his moral and physical deterioration was like that of a forest tree stricken with an irreparable decay.

Apparently the Indians of southern New England were of a higher intellectual order, possibly by reason of their living in larger communities and because their trade in wampum brought them in contact with the tribes still further south. The two great tribes of that part of New England which bordered on Long Island Sound were the Pequots and the Narragansetts. While the latter sustained traditions of singular interest, the savages along the coast bordering on the Gulf of Maine were more rude in their habits and customs than either

---

ance at Plymouth. Mourt says he was naked, with "only a leather girdle about his waist, with a fringe about a span long." Drake makes mention that it was very cold weather; and Mourt adds, "We cast a horseman's coat about him." Samoset remained at Plymouth five days. When he went away, Mourt says, "We gave him a hat, a pair of stockings and shoes, a shirt, and a piece of cloth to tie about his waist."

TOPOGRAPHY OF INDIAN TRIBES

the Delawares or the Iroquois. These two great Indian powers were located south of the Hudson. The Pequots and Narragansetts were both notable tribes. They were the mint-masters — the makers of wampum for their savage neighbors.[1] As manufacturers of wampum (and they were adepts in the art), these two tribes became wealthy and influential. At the time of the coming of the Plymouth settlers they were at the zenith of their power. Traders in a commodity over which they exercised a monopoly, they acquired an ascendency in the councils of the Indians to the eastward which ceased only with their practical extinction.

Other tribes, whose ingenuity and industry availed them little or nothing, other than a meager subsistence gained from the chase, or the cultivation of the open places in the wilderness which they made their habitat, were undergoing unconsciously the inevitable decay common to lack of

---

[1] Wampum, or wampumpeag, was made from the shell of the "quahag," one of the largest of the clam species. These shells were susceptible of a high polish, and were colored. They were attached, in varicolored patterns of unique and curious design, to strips of cloth originally woven of fine roots, or a vegetable fiber which resembled cotton, and later to strips of cloth obtained from the English. Those of a bluish tint were most esteemed. Among the savages, wampum was used in the place of precious metals, of which they seemed to have little or no knowledge, but which were not uncommon among the tribes further to the south or west.

INDIAN WARS OF NEW ENGLAND

stimulus to the attainment of larger creature comforts and the seeking out of new gratifications. The savage of the northern New England coast was, while of a magnificent physique, in all his tendencies animalistic; his natural desire was solely the satisfying of his stomach and the sustaining of his energies by the slothfulness of sleep. On the opposite, his acquired tastes were but a few steps from actual debauchery. He was akin to the dweller in the hollows of trees, the damp recesses of rock-shadowed caves: a half-naked solitary, as it were, nomad in all his instincts, obtaining by violence what could not otherwise be had peaceably; an individual apart from the other world races. Singular as it may seem, crediting the Indian with these untoward characteristics, he was still most kindly and generous in his hospitality,[1]

---

[1] After the first winter at Plymouth, with the coming of the warm weather the neighboring Indians began to frequent the seashore for lobsters and fish. While they were in the way of becoming an annoyance to the settlers (for the savages were apt to go wherever they could get anything to eat), the settlers treating them with kindness, they hung around the settlement until it was decided to send an embassy to Massasoit with a request that he prohibit the continuance of this drain upon their slender resources. Stephen Hopkins and Edward Winslow were appointed ambassadors. Squanto, who had long before been kidnapped by Hunt and sold as a slave in Spain,— to be afterward released and sent to England, whence he was returned home,— went along as interpreter. Their gifts to Massasoit were a red coat and a copper

TOPOGRAPHY OF INDIAN TRIBES

sharing his last morsel with an accepted guest, or even a stranger; giving up his couch of skins and even his wigwam to those whom chance or purpose had thrown in his way.

Contemptuous of labor, that was for the squaw, for whom they had an even deeper contempt. To call an enemy a *woman* was a species of contumely unequalled by any other epithet in their limited vocabulary. In conflict they were ferocious, subtle, and treacherous, seeking the cover of fences and trees, and rarely ever showing themselves in the

---

chain. When Massasoit was arrayed in his red coat Hopkins and Winslow delivered their message, which was that they wished to pay for the kettle and the corn they had taken in the winter; and they went on to say that, as their crops were uncertain, and not having much other food, they would be unable to extend to his people the same hospitality in the future as they had in the past, though they would still be pleased to do it if it were in their power. Their request to Massasoit was that he suffer none of his people to come to the settlement, *except those who had skins to trade.* If, however, he wished to come himself, or have some particular friend, they would be glad to entertain them as heretofore. That they might not be imposed upon, they suggested that he send the copper chain with his friend or messenger as the credential of representation. After the business of the meeting was over pipes and tobacco were brought. So poor was Massasoit that he had nothing to offer them for supper. His guests expressed a desire to remain over night. In one part of the wigwam was a rude bed of plank, but a few inches from the ground, which was covered with a coarse mat. One end of this plank platform was given to the visitors, while the sagamore and

INDIAN WARS OF NEW ENGLAND

open, unless in overpowering numbers. Their modes of torture were of the most satanic ingenuity; yet, with all their indifference to the weaker sex of their tribes, their respect for the chastity of their women was inviolable. Friend or foe, they never forgot a benefit or forgave an injury.[1]

The Indian has been described as of tall, angular, and generally stalwart physique; but in that respect he was subject to the same variations in stature as other races. An acquaintance with the western Indians of to-day bears out the assumption.

---

his wife slept at the other end. Two other Indians were to be accommodated, who, during the night, so crowded the Englishmen that they got but little sleep, and so were more weary in the morning than when they lay down. For breakfast they had two large fish which Massasoit had secured with his arrows in the early morning. This was the first food the ambassadors had eaten for a day and two nights. Kindliness was in Massasoit's heart, but his larder was not stocked with abundance. Massasoit told them he was sorry he could not give them better entertainment.

Banvard, *Plymouth and the Pilgrims*, p. 54.

[1] The Nausets never forgave the English for the dastardly act of Hunt in kidnapping a considerable number of that tribe, whom he had decoyed aboard his vessel and carried to Spain, where they were sold as slaves. John Billington, a "vicious lad and a great plague to the colony," strayed away. A party was sent out after him. The searching-party spent the night at Cummaquid [Barnstable Harbor], at which place they met a squaw who was then reputed to be a hundred years of age. When she saw the Englishmen she became greatly excited, weeping "excessively." Asking her

TOPOGRAPHY OF INDIAN TRIBES

In peace and plenty his physiognomy was calmly mild, if not pleasantly suggestive. In anger or unrest his features were as shifty as the sea in a whipping gale. As an expression of savagery, they were demoniac. They were at once brave, timid, detesting falsehood in others, and again courting it; haughty and insolent with those of inferior rank or power, they were most humbly docile in the presence of their superiors in strength and influence. The mood of the savage was kaleidoscopic. It varied, like that of a child, with every circumstance. What he might have become had the New World remained a sealed book to the Old is problematical. The inference is that in the long years

---

what so affected her, she replied that when Captain Hunt was at that place she had three sons who went aboard his vessel to trade, and he had carried them away captive to Spain. The Nausets, who were settled at what is now Eastham, were never fully gained over to the English interest, such was their deep and abiding hatred of the white race. They never forgot or forgave Hunt, or his people. This unfortunate event occurred in 1614, or six years before the coming of the *Mayflower*.

Banvard, *Plymouth and the Pilgrims*, p. 57.

It was at this place the English were attacked upon their second venturing from the *Mayflower*, when they went to spy out the land (Dec. 6, 1620). It is worthy of note that their first reception at the hands of the natives was one of hostility (Drake's *Indian Wars*, p. 11). At their first landing the natives ran away. Their traditions of the white men were not reassuring.

INDIAN WARS OF NEW ENGLAND

to be unfolded they might have evolved into traders and explorers, and have taken the initial step, as have some of the races of the Orient, toward a more complete civilization. They might, on the other hand, have fallen a prey to the natural decadence incident to a people without cohesion or high moral purpose, of which they had neither.

Their mode of living was of the rudest sort. Through the secret recesses of the wilderness were the scattered villages of the different tribes. In New England they were to be found bordering on the shores of the ocean where fish were to be readily taken, and in the middle country, about the Great Lakes or along the rivers which led from them outward to the sea. The squaws were the tillers of the soil, accomplishing what they could with their rude implements of stone or wood; while the men, with their bows, their arrows flint-headed or tipped with the claws of the eagle, and their axes of stone curiously sharpened, were off on the chase or engaged in an occasional foray against some aboriginal enemy. After the war against King Philip closed they were more gregarious in their habits, living in sequestered villages, as those at Pentagoët, Norridgewock, and Pigwacket, from which places they issued under the direction of the French in organized bands to leave a trail of devastation wherever they passed.

They knew little or nothing of metals, although the tribes about the Great Lakes, in what has now

TOPOGRAPHY OF INDIAN TRIBES

become the great copper-producing country, were reputed to have utensils of that metal. Copper knives have been found, of Indian origin, of a singularly fine temper, as well as copper vessels, artistically fashioned, which were indicative of such at one time being in quite common use. It is possible that the Indians of the Middle West had their knowledge from the tribes still further south, who were not ignorant of the ceramic arts, and whose acquaintance with the more precious metals is well assured.

The New England tribes had no domestic animals; but they were well acquainted with the culture of maize, of beans, and of squashes and "pumpions." Tobacco was cultivated among all the tribes, even into western Maine;[1] but, lazy and improvident, they were more often than not on the verge of famine, when the snare and the arrow were made to supply their slender larder. The

---

[1] The seed of the *Nicotania Rustica*, probably. The plant has greenish yellow blossoms. It grows wild in old fields in some parts of the North, a relic of cultivation by the Indians. Roger Williams says: "They take their *Wuttamaoug* (that is a weake Tobacco) which the men plant themselves, very frequently; yet I never see any take so excessively as I have seene Men in Europe. . . . They say they take Tobacco for two reasons; against the rheume which causeth the toothake, which they are impatient of; secondly, to revive and refresh them, they drinking nothing but water."
R. I. Hist. Coll., vol. i., pp. 35, 55.

woods abounded with deer, and the streams with fish. Wild fowl in large numbers were to be found wherever there were feeding-grounds about the inland ponds, except in the severer months of the winter season, when everything was under an embargo of snow and ice. Amid all this natural plenty the Indian was wont to feel the sharp pangs of hunger as the price of his indolence, when his only resource was sleep and absolute inaction.

Whatever there was of cohesion among the various tribes was the result of intimidation. They had no body politic; no code of laws; no axis about which their common interest might revolve. Each tribe had its sachem, who ruled independent of outside interference, between whom and the medicine-man the honors were about equally divided. Their tribal divisions were almost innumerable. In what are now known as the Provinces the Micmacs, who were a part of the great Armouchiquois, had their roaming-grounds. At the mouth of the St. Croix River was the Passamaquoddy tribe. West and south along the coast, up and down the Penobscot, were the Tarratines. Westward, halfway to the headwaters of the Kennebec, at Norridgewock, was a branch of the Sokoki. Lower down that river were the Kennebequi. Over on the Androscoggin was another contingent known as the Androscoggins. On the Presumpscot were the Ammacongins, while along the headwaters of the Saco were the Pigwackets. These formed the great

TOPOGRAPHY OF INDIAN TRIBES

Abenake family, the Pigwackets being akin to the Norridgewocks and known as the two Sokoki settlements in Maine.

Passing over the territory of New Hampshire into the Plymouth country, and following the shore to Long Island Sound, one is in the land of the Pequots, once a powerful and aggressive people, of which Sassacus was the chief sachem. He had his settlement upon a commanding eminence in what is now Groton. His settlement was enclosed in a stout stockade; for he was most thoroughly hated and detested by his neighbors. He was the most powerful sachem of the surrounding tribes, and the Pequots, unlike the other tribes, lived compactly. They were feared, as they were disliked; for they were for the greater part of the time at war with the Narragansetts. They dominated the Mohegans, of whom they exacted a tribute. About the time of the coming of the English, Uncas, who was of the royal family, rebelled against Sassacus. Uncas was not without some influence, having married a daughter of Tatobam.

The English came early in contact with Sassacus and his Pequots, who, feeling secure in their power, treated the former with great disdain and not infrequently with undisguised contempt. Actuated by his hatred for Sassacus, once hostilities had broken out between the English and the Pequots, Uncas immediately espoused the cause of the English, and a war ensued that culminated in the extinction of the Pequot race, the remnant finding its way to the country of the Mohawks, who, with savage philosophy, failed not to take advantage of the opportunity to pay off old scores, which they improved by severing Sassacus's head from his body.

This act of the Mohawks is suggestive, especially in matters of comity with their savage neighbors. In war the Indian was the epitome of ferocity, unrelenting in his cruelty. Skulkers ordinarily, when fighting at bay they were desperately brave. Victorious, they were drunken with delight, which Parkman describes as a "ferocious ecstasy." In their torturing of captives they were fiendish in their ingenuity. They burned their victims at the stake, scalping them alive, sticking their bodies full of splints of flaming pitch-pine, or using them as living targets for the hurtling knife or tomahawk. They beheaded them to carry the heads home as trophies to their squaws, who, with these gory evidences of battle slung about their necks, joined in the dances of the victors about the helpless captive.[1]

Champlain mentions an instance in his second encounter with the Iroquois, in the year 1610, which took place on the banks of the St. Lawrence, near the mouth of the Richelieu River, when the

---

[1] Parkman, *Pioneers of New France*, p. 359.

body of one Iroquois captive was drawn, quartered, and eaten by his Montagnais allies.[1]

The squaws, and even the children — boys and girls — took part in these inhuman orgies. The Abenake were not unlike the more northern tribes, yet it is assumed that with them burning at the stake was more infrequent. A solitary instance is recorded by St. Castin, which took place at Pentagoët. Indian or pale-face, however, the scalp was taken. Stretched and hung up to dry against the interior walls of the wigwam, they were so many insignia of individual prowess. The more scalps a savage could show, the more weighty his influence in the deliberations of the council-fire.

The victim at the stake was challenged to sing his death-song, which, while being a relation of his

---

[1] Cannibalism was not uncommon among the North American tribes. Parkman is of the opinion such was very rarely a conspicuous event. He attributes it to a spirit of revenge or ferocity; sometimes to a religious practice, as with the Miamis, among whom existed a secret society — a religious fraternity of man-eating savages.

To eat the heart of an enemy, especially if he were brave, was held to impart the same quality to the eater, which was in a way a traditional proverb among the savages. Hunger among the rovers of the winter woods was appeased by their eating of their own kind As one contemplates the ways and the manners of this untutored people, it must be remembered that they were responsible to no higher authority than their individual appetites and passions; that all their instincts were colored by the atmosphere of their surroundings.

INDIAN WARS OF NEW ENGLAND

former victories over his captors, was as well a diatribe against their cowardice in war and their unimportance as a people. It was a monologue of taunts and cutting epithets, calculated to arouse the fury of his captors to the highest pitch, when his death-cry was drowned in a bedlam of frenzy on the part of his tormentors.

Before the fires were lighted the captive was usually scalped,[1] to the accompaniment of yells and whoops of unrestrained delight. It was a gala occasion, in which all the pent brutalism of the tribe found vent, an excess of sheer bloodthirstiness which was kept up to the point of physical exhaustion.

In the wars with the English the scalping-knife, which was usually of French manufacture, and the tomahawk generally sufficed; possibly because, after slaking his vengeance, the savage aggressor's

---

[1] Note to Parkman's *Pioneers of New France* is here quoted: "It has been erroneously asserted that the practice of scalping did not prevail among the Indians before the advent of the Europeans. In 1535 Cartier saw five scalps at Quebec, dried and stretched on hoops. In 1564 Laudonnière saw them among the Indians of Florida. The Algonquins of New England and Nova Scotia were accustomed to cut off and carry away the head, which they afterwards scalped. Those of Canada, it seems, sometimes scalped dead bodies on the field. The Algonquin practice of carrying off heads as trophies is mentioned by Lalemant, Roger Williams, Lescarbot, and Champlain."

TOPOGRAPHY OF INDIAN TRIBES

paramount idea was to get away from the scene of his butchery without detection. The smoke of the burning cabin rising above the woodland pointed the savage trail in the pathless air.

Implacable toward his foe, his only approach to mercy was to offer his captive the gauntlet. Women and children taken captive were usually adopted into the tribe, especially if they were young, comely, and in good health. They had, however, no use for the old, the sick, or the frail. A babe in arms was apparently their special aversion.

Running the gauntlet was an even greater torture than outright death. It was a race for life between a double file of all the able-bodied members of the tribe, as well as the squaws and children, in which blows from war-clubs, tomahawks, and knives were rained down upon the shoulders and head of the captive, his body bent to ward off the assault and to elude, if possible, the death-blow which awaited him at every step. Even if the captive escaped into the wilderness, his wounds were worse, possibly, than the stake; for, weaponless and exhausted, he was perhaps not only broken physically, but face to face with starvation and the wilder denizens of the woods, with only the sun or the stars to guide him to safety. Such were these "peasants and paupers of the forest."

The Narragansetts were of Rhode Island. Canonicus was their sachem, and, like Massasoit and Samoset, he was possessed of a most noble nature.

INDIAN WARS OF NEW ENGLAND

He liked the English, and was especially kind to Roger Williams, to whom he was princely in his generosity, giving him the whole of what is now Providence County, and to the Hutchinson settlers the island of Rhode Island. His nephew, Miantonomoh, was of like character and manly spirit. Some writers have endeavored to cast the odium of the savagery that marked the later generations of the Indian upon that race; but the English were the original trespassers, beyond cavil. In those early days there were nowhere three greater souls than those of Samoset, Massasoit, and Canonicus. It would be difficult to match them among the English whom they received so generously, and to whom, out of their poverty, they gave so much.

On the eastern edge of the Narragansetts lived the Wampanoags, whose habitat was in that section now known as Bristol. Massasoit was of this tribe.

East and north of the Narragansetts, as well, were the Pokonokets. In fact, that was the generic title by which all the cognate Indian tribes about the Plymouth settlement were known.

Massasoit was beloved of all these people, whose home was at Pokonoket.[1]

The son of Massasoit was Metacomet, after

---

[1] Pokonoket, or Pawkunnawkut, is now included in the town of Bristol, R. I. The English early gave it the name of Mount Hope, corrupted from the Indian, "Mon-taup," the

TOPOGRAPHY OF INDIAN TRIBES

Massasoit's death better known as King Philip. Owing to the plague which visited this nation shortly before the coming of the Plymouth people, its fighting force was reduced to less than sixty men. Prior to the plague the Pokonokets had been a powerful nation, boasting some three thousand warriors, who were generally allied to the Massachusetts, forming a combination over which the Narragansetts were unable to prevail.

This plague was a most disastrous event. All the way from Canada to Long Island Sound the tribes were grievously stricken and decimated. Had the plague not occurred as it did, the English would have been driven into the sea. The forces which the French were able to call to their aid would have been increased by thousands, and the schemes of Denonville and Louis XIV. might possibly have become a reality.

In the locality of Plymouth and Bristol the country was practically depopulated.

Among the shore tribes were the Pocassetts, whose habitat was in the Swanzy, Somerset, Rehoboth, and Tiverton district. Corbitant was the

---

origin of which is obscure. It is a sightly eminence which affords a beautiful view of Providence, Warren, Bristol, and the surrounding country.

For a description of this picturesque locality, see Drake's *Book of the Indians*, p. 16; Alden's *Coll. Epitaphs*, vol. iv., p. 685; Stiles, *Notes to Church's History of King Philip's War*, p. 7.

INDIAN WARS OF NEW ENGLAND

sachem of this tribe, and he was not over-friendly to the English. The unfortunate Weetamoo succeeded him, to whom has been credited much of the incentive that led Philip to conspire against the English, which the death of Alexander may be said to have accelerated. The romantic story of Weetamoo will preface the relation of the causes that led up to the outbreak of King Philip.[1]

The Saconets were the aboriginal occupants of the neighborhood of Little Compton. In King Philip's War they were governed by the queen-sachem Awashonks. The Namaskets were located in the vicinity of what is now Middleborough; and

---

[1] Weetamoo was the widow of Alexander, and squaw-sachem of the Pocassetts. Alexander was Philip's brother. She was drowned in August, 1667, while making the effort to escape from her pursuers across the Tetticut River on a raft of boughs. Her body was found in Mettapoisett. Some of the settlers cut off her head and placed it upon a pole in Taunton, where it was at once recognized by the Indians who had been taken prisoners by the English, and who "made a most horrid and diabolical lamentation, crying out that it was their queen's head." By reason of the death of Alexander, who, she believed, had been poisoned by the English, she opposed the latter bitterly. Mather said, "She was next to Philip, in respect of the mischief that hath been done."

As indicative of the spirit of the English about this time, Dr. Increase Mather is quoted as speaking of the death of some of Philip's followers at Narragansett: "We have heard of two and twenty Indian captains slain, all of them brought down to hell in one day."

TOPOGRAPHY OF INDIAN TRIBES

the Nausets at Eastham, on Cape Cod; the Mattachees at Barnstable; the Monomoys at Chatham; the Saukatucketts at Mashpee; and the Nobsquassetts at Yarmouth.

The Massachusetts were located about Boston Bay, and were once a great tribe; but in 1630 they counted hardly a hundred.[1] The Massachusetts sachem was chief of the Wessagussets, Pankapogs, Nonantums, Nashuas, Neponsets, and a portion of the Nipmucks. Their territory lapped against that of the Pokonoket sachem Massasoit on the south, the Nipmucks on the west, and the Pawtuckets on the north and east. The territory of the Pawtuckets extended from Salem on the south to the north of the Merrimac River as far as Portsmouth, and to the Nipmucks on the west, taking in Essex, part of Middlesex, and a part of New Hampshire, including the Pennacooks, Agawams, Naumkeags, Piscataways and Accomintas, the Newichawannocks, and a few other minor families.[2]

The Nipmucks were a widely scattered people whose habitat was to the westward of the coast tribes. They were usually collected in families,

---

[1] Roger Williams says that "the Machusetts were called so from the blue hills." In the vocabulary of Indian words, by Rev. John Cotton, the definition of Massachusetts is, "an hill in the form of an arrow's head." Drake says, "If any man knew, we may be allowed to suppose that Roger Williams did."

[2] See Godkin.

INDIAN WARS OF NEW ENGLAND

being always exposed to the danger common to a lack of unity. Baylie is of opinion that had the English not appeared to colonize the country the Nipmuck would have been absorbed into the life of the surrounding tribes, and thus would have lost identity.

West of the Hudson were the Mohawks. The tribes west of the Pequots and east of the Hudson River were tributary to the Mohawks. The Nipmucks in the Connecticut country had been annexed to the Pequots. At Hadley and Springfield were two small tribes, in a way unimportant, the sachem of the Hadley tribe being the son of the Springfield sachem. In the Berkshires the Indians may be said to have had no villages.

At Mattabesick [Middletown] was the sachem Sowheag. The Podunks were at East Hartford. Other tribes kept to the shore of the Sound, like the Wongungs at Chatham; the Nehanticks, Lyme; the Memunkatucks at Guilford; the Wopowags at Milford; Paugessetts at Derby; and Quinipiacks at New Haven. Dr. Trumbull estimates these Connecticut tribes at five thousand, of which number about one fifth were warriors;[1] that there were altogether in Connecticut, at the advent of the English, from fifteen thousand to twenty thousand

---

[1] DeForest says: "Trumbull, from whom wiser things might have been expected, seems to have been actuated by an unreflecting disposition to magnify as much as possible

TOPOGRAPHY OF INDIAN TRIBES

Indians. It was the most densely populated of any territory of similar extent in North America north of Mexico.

Along the Sound was an abundance of fish; the soil was fertile and responsive; the climate was equable; and the occupants of this territory were prosperous, powerful, and, in point of comparison with other tribes to the eastward, wealthy. Outside of the Pequots, the Indians on the Connecticut River gave the English slight trouble. They lived in constant fear of the Mohawks and were anxious for the friendship of the English, in whom they saw their only hope of security.

The Mohawk was the buccaneer of the Hudson Valley. His normal condition was to be mixed up in a quarrel. His greatest delight was to despoil his savage neighbor. Every year the Mohawks made up several parties of marauders, who were dispersed in different directions in search of their prey. Their favorite method of attack was by

---

their importance and numbers. In his account of the different tribes he usually, if not invariably, selects the largest known estimates, and introduces them into his narrative without the slightest attempt at reasonable criticism."

DeForest, *History of the Indians of Connecticut*, p. 44.

"We shall probably make a liberal estimate when we allow twelve hundred warriors for the whole State, and six or seven thousand individuals for its entire aboriginal population."

DeForest, *History of the Indians of Connecticut*, p. 48.

INDIAN WARS OF NEW ENGLAND

ambush. In their forays they made an exception of the English, whom they never disturbed or molested, meet them as they would, armed or unarmed; also of the "praying" or converted Indians. They made war only upon their own kind. To them, at that time, the English bore a charmed life.

Such was the disposition of the aborigines along the coast of the Gulf of Maine and up the Sound toward the mouth of the Hudson River, at least during the first generation of the settlements. It was with the tribes south of the Merrimac the English settler had to deal until the breaking out of St. Castin's War in 1690, when, with the exception of a few isolated attacks south of the Piscataqua and in the direction of Albany, the theater of activities was transferred to Maine. With the death of Philip, and the subjugation of his allies, the settlers of Massachusetts, Connecticut, and Rhode Island lived in a condition of comparative safety.

The following quaint and curious description of the Indian, as the early colonists about Massachusetts Bay found him, was written by Thomas Lechford, of "Clements Inne, in the County of Middlesex, Gent." Lechford was the first law-practitioner of early Boston. He says: "They [the Indians] are of body tall, proper, and straight; they goe naked, saving about their middle, somewhat to cover their shame. Seldome they are abroad in the extremity of Winter, but keep in their *wigwams*, till necessity

TOPOGRAPHY OF INDIAN TRIBES

drives them forth; and then they wrap themselves in skins, or some of our English coorse cloath: and for Winter they have boots, or a kind of laced tawed-leather stockins. They are naturally proud, and idle, and given much to singing, dancing, and playes; They are governed by *Sachems*, Kings; and *Saggamores*, petie Lords; by an absolute tyrranie. Their women are of comely feature, industrious, and doe most of the labor in planting, and carrying of burdens; their husbands hold them in great slavery, yet never knowing other, it is lesse grievous to them. They say *English* men much foole, for spoiling good working creatures, meaning women. And when they see any of our *English* women sewing with their needles or working coifes, or such things, they will cry out, Lazie *squaes!* but they are much kinder to their wives by the example of the *English*. Their children they will not part with upon any terms to be taught. They are of swarthy complexion and tawny: their children are born *white* but they bedawb them with oyle, and colours presently. They have all black haire, that I saw.

"In times of mourning, they paint their faces with black lead, black, all about the eye-brows, and part of their cheeks. In time of rejoicing they paint red, with a kind of vermilion. They cut their haire of divers formes, according to their Nation or people, so that you may know a people by their cut; and ever they have a long lock on one side of their heads and weare feathers of Peacocks, and such like, and red cloath, or ribbands at their locks; beads of *wampom-peag* about their necks, and a girdle of the same, wrought with blew and white *wampom* after the manner of checker-work, two fingers broad about their loynes: Some of their chiefe men goe so, and pendants of *wampom*, and such toyes in their ears. And the women, some of the chiefe, have faire bracelets, and chaines of *wampom*. Men and women of them come confidently among the *English*. . . . They have *Powahes*, or Priests, which are witches, and a kind of Chirurgions, but some of them are faine to be beholding to the *English* Chirurgions. They will have their times of *powaheing*, which they will of late have called Prayers, according to the *English* word. The *Powahe* labors himselfe in his incantations, to extreme sweating and wearinesse, even to extacie. The *Powahes* cannot work their witchcrafts, if any *English* be by; neither can any of their incantations lay hold on, or doe any harme to the *English*, as I have been credibly informed. The *Powahe* is next to the King or *Sachem*, and commonly, when he dyes, the *Powahe* marries the Squa *Sachem*, that is, the queene. They have manie wives; they say they commit much filthinesse among themselves. But for every marriage the *Saggamore* hath a fadome of *wampom*, which is about seven or eight shillings value. Some of them will attend diligently to anything they can understand by any of our Religion, and are very willing to teach their language to any

TOPOGRAPHY OF INDIAN TRIBES

English. They live much better and peaceably for the *English:* and themselves know it, or at least, their *Sachems,* and *Saggamores* know so much, for before they did nothing but spoile and destroy one another. They live in *wigwams,* or houses made of mats like little hutts, the fire in the midst of the house. They cut downe a tree with axes and hatchets, bought of the *English, Dutch,* or *French,* & bring in the butt-end into the *wigwam,* upon the hearth; and so burne it by degrees. They live upon parched corne, (of late they grind at our *English* mills,) Venison, Bevers, Otters, Oysters, Clammes, Lobsters and other fish, Ground-nuts, Akornes, they boyle all together in a kettle. Their riches are their *wampom,* bolles and trayes, kettles, spoones, bever, furres and canoes. He is a *Sachem* [whose wife] hath her clean spoons in a chest, for some chiefe *English* men, when they come on guest-wise to the *wigwam.* They lye upon a mat, with a stone, or a piece of wood under their heads; they will give the best entertainment they can make to any *English* comming amongst them. They will not taste sweet things, nor alter their habit willingly; onely they are taken with tobacco, wine, and strong waters; and I have seene some of them in *English* or *French* cloathes. Their ordinary weapons are bowes and arrowes, and long staves or halfe pikes, with pieces of swords, daggers, or knives in the ends of them: They have Captaines, and are very good at a short mark, and nimble of foot to run away. Their manner of fighting is most commonly all one style. They are many in number, and worship *Kitan*, their good god, or *Hobbamocco*, their evill god; but more feare *Hobbamocco*, because he doth them most harme. . . . Among some of these Nations, their policie is to have two Kings at a time; but, I thinke, of one family; the one aged for counsell, the other younger, for action. Their Kings succeed by inheritance."[1]

---

[1] Lechford, *Plaine dealing, or Newes from New-England* (London, 1642), pp. 49–52.

Third Series, *Mass. Hist. Coll.*, vol. iii., pp. 102–105.

John Josselyn, *Two Voyages to New England* (London, 1675), pp. 123–140.

Vide Reprint in Third Series, *Mass. Hist. Coll.*, vol. iii., pp. 293–305.

THE EARLY SETTLER AND THE INDIAN

THE EARLY SETTLER AND THE INDIAN

OF the English occupancy of New England, the years between 1675 and 1760 may well be regarded as the most important in the formative period of colonial history. While the decade following the coming of the *Mayflower* was pervaded with resultant potencies, it was hardly more than the suggestive initial which marked the opening of the first chapter of a story destined to lead in the history of nations.

As an indent at the beginning of this historical paragraph the picture is one of tragic interest. Its foreground is a mere handful of self-exiled humanity; isolate; shelterless almost; with an impoverished larder and, as against the voiceless threat of impending and unknown perils, apparently impotent. Over their heads was the roof of a ship's deck — a ship anchored in a strange sea under the lee of a strange and unexplored country. Its background is a like strange wilderness of foreboding silences, whitened with a rime of snow and sleet. Its low horizon, grimly, inhospitably gray, is suggestive of a sinister prophecy. As colorless as this particular moment appears, it is tinged with the invisible rose of an unheralded daybreak before which the aboriginal mystery, as old as the Skrellings of the Norse Sagas, is eventually to disappear.

INDIAN WARS OF NEW ENGLAND

If the landing of William Bradford and his little company of Separatists — the unconscious nucleus of an entirely new political principle, the germ of a new statehood the fundamental tenet of which was absolute freedom of conscience — was the beginning of a New World epoch, the unheralded advent of Samoset among the Plymouth settlers and the rude embassy of Massasoit together were the landmark from which was to be reckoned the displacement of the aborigine from his birthright and the consequent deterioration of his proffered friendship to the English into secret — and finally open — hostility. The Plymouth people were kindly and temperate in their treatment of the savage when it did not cost them overmuch, though, after their English fashion, they discouraged his familiarities. Stranded upon the rugged shores of Massachusetts, threatened with starvation, put upon short rations at times, the unwritten law of Plymouth was — self-preservation. Unfamiliar with the comity of their savage neighbors, they often trespassed upon the rights of these unsophisticated children of the forest, but not always intentionally. Had the later comers been as kindly-intentioned and forbearing toward the Indians as were the settlers at Plymouth, as expressed through Winslow in his dealings with them, the story of Philip's treachery might have found no occasion for a narrator. The Puritan, however, was of a different pattern and of coarser weave.

THE EARLY SETTLER AND THE INDIAN

With the coming of the Puritan began the encroachments of the settler upon the prescriptive rights of the Indians, the absorption of their hunting-grounds, their maize-fields, and the streams that supplied them with their fish. The Puritan was a trader, with a trader's conscience. The Englishman made his superior civilization the apology for his slender honesty with the aborigine.[1] If the Indian had any prescriptive rights, they were

---

[1] The first letter of instruction to Governor Endicott from the New England Company contained the following: "And above all, we pray you be careful that there be none in our precincts permitted to do any injury, in the least kind, to the heathen people; and if any offend in that way, let them receive a correction. . . . And for the avoiding of the hurt that may follow through our much familiarity with the Indians, we conceive it fit that they be not permitted to come to your plantation but at certain times and places, to be appointed them. If any one of the salvages *pretend* right of inheritance to all or any of the lands granted in *our patent*, we pray you endeavor to purchase their title, that we may avoid the *least scruple of intrusion* [italics the author's]."

Young's *Chronicles*, p. 159.

Young says, in a note, "The first President Adams, being asked his opinion concerning the treatment of the Indians in New England, replied that he believed that it had been just. 'In all my practice at the Bar,' said he, 'I never knew a contested title but what was traced up to the Indian title.'"

Naturally that would be the result, and while the distinguished gentleman quoted may be safe in his statement, it proves nothing. It is a well-known fact that the king *was the source* of almost all New England titles.

ignored. If the Indian gave a deed of his lands to the English, it was by an instrument of which he had no comprehension, the consideration for which was a pittance — a something to tempt the appetite of the savage, which ranged from strong waters to pumpkins. The Puritan took shelter behind these conveyances, and divers historians have been at great pains to establish the fact that the Indians were compensated for their lands, when the fact remains that the poor savage was a modern Esau who parted with his birthright for a mess of pottage — and poor pottage at that.[1]

When the Pilgrims were drawing up their compact of government in the cabin of the *Mayflower*, in Cape Cod Harbor, they were unaware that the Great Patent of New England had been created under the hand of the king, by which the shore be-

---

[1] Robin Hood, a sachem of the upper waters of the Sagadahoc River, deeded a large tract of land on the Sasanoa, a stream rich in historic associations, for a hogshead of corn and a few pumpkins.

In March, 1640, the Norwalk Indians sold a large part of their territory to one Roger Ludlow, of Fairfield, Conn. The conveyance comprised all the land between the Norwalk and Saugatuck Rivers. Its depth into the country was as far as a man could walk from the sea in a day's span. The consideration for the deed was "eight fathoms of Wampum, Six Coats, ten hoes, ten hatchets, ten scissors, ten *jewsharps*, ten fathoms of tobacco, three kettles of six hands about, and ten *looking-glasses* [italics the author's]." The deed was signed by Mahackemo and four of his tribe.

THE EARLY SETTLER AND THE INDIAN

fore them had been erected into the County of Devon, with Plymouth as its shire town, and by which certain English land promoters were to "plant, rule, and govern New England." The *Mayflower* compact created no body politic. It gave no legislative or judicial powers to those associated under it. Its strongest obligation was the common consent; yet it was of the highest moral character, else it could not have endured, as it did, for a decade. Probably its saving salt was the devoutly religious practice and feeling which directed the habits of the community, where each member was upon a footing of the most perfect equality.

In 1630, when Allerton[1] had obtained from the council larger powers than those of the Pierce patent, which had passed into the hands of the Merchant Adventurers (a trading company, without political power), was established the source of all the titles to land in New England. The original

---

[1] Isaac Allerton was at one time the richest man in the colony; was assistant, 1621, and sole officer for three years under the government. His wife dying soon after landing, he married Fear Brewster, daughter of Elder William; she dying, 1633, he married again. He passed his later years at New Haven, and died there, 1659, insolvent. He was an energetic man and had pushed his enterprises as far as the Penobscot River, where he established a trading-station with the Indians.

Savage, *Gen. Dict.*, vol. i., p. 38.
Leyden, *MSS. Record.*

right to the soil was founded solely upon occupation. The English found it without inhabitants,— what they termed a wilderness,— and to them occupation was the strongest title they could acquire.[1]

They had as well full and free consent from Massasoit, as the sachem governing the territory within the limits of which they proposed to erect their homes.[2] They interfered with no native right. Fishing and hunting were as free after as before their coming, and the English believed there was an abundance of both for their maintenance. However specious the premise of the writer who finds himself impelled to apologize for the self-aggrandizement of the first-comers to New England, the fact remains that these processes of historical justification are mere afterthoughts. The

---

[1] Higginson mentions the plague which visited the Indians some "twelve years since,"— he must have been writing about 1630,— so there were "very few left to inhabit the country. The Indians are not able to make use of the one fourth part of the land; neither have they any settled places as towns to dwell in; nor any ground as they challenge for their own possession, but change their habitation from place to place."

Young's *Chronicles*, p. 556.

[2] Dexter, in his note, *Mourt*, 91, says that Massasoit "sold much land to the English at various times, and always scrupulously, and most honorably, kept his treaty agreements with them."

Also, Church's *Entertaining Passages*, p. 38; Drake's *Book of the Indians*, pp. 81-92.

THE EARLY SETTLER AND THE INDIAN

title was in the savage by right of prior occupancy, — an occupancy covering untold years,— and was to pass into the hands of another and alien race by that process of absorption which the strong ever exercise over the weak. If it was not by acts of overt subjugation, it was by methods sufficiently allied to that principle. With the coming of the "planters" who began their settlements about Boston Harbor no pretext was allowed to pass unimproved for a quarrel with the natives, who in every controversy with the English found themselves worsted. Like the redoubtable Captain Miles Standish, the English went about with the traditional chip on their shoulders, nor were the savages long in interpreting this attitude as inimical to their interests, vested or otherwise.[1]

The story that runs down through the seventeenth century and well into the eighteenth covers a series of tragic vicissitudes. The relation is one of treachery on the part of the English, with adroit

---

[1] Francis Higginson, a reverend divine of New England in 1630, in a little book of twenty-five pages, "Printed at London at the Signe of the Blew Bible in Green Arbor, 1630," says of the Indians: "For therein dealing with us, we neither fear them, nor trust them; for forty of our musketeers will drive five hundred of them out of the field." He adds, "We use them kindly, they will come into our houses sometimes by half a dozen, or half a score, at a time when we are at victuals, but will ask or take nothing but what we give them." Young's *Chronicles*, p. 259.

instigation and Jesuit interference on the part of the French; and on the part of the Indian, the climax of savage duplicity and cruelty, fiendish butchery and annihilation.

Outside of the settlement at Plymouth, the quest of the English adventurer primarily was fish and furs. He marked his first footholds with a trading-station. He came loaded with knives, axes, and trinkets of trifling value, glass beads and cheap cloths of brilliant colorings, which he exchanged for peltry. Captain John Smith was at Monhegan in 1614, and relates that, for trifles, they got "near 11,000 beaver skins, 100 martin, and as many otters, the most of them within a distance of 20 leagues." Hunt, who accompanied him, remained behind; but instead of a ship-load of peltry, he had "betrayed four and twenty of those poor savages aboard his ship, and most dishonestly and inhumanly, for their kind usage of me and all our men, carried them to Malaga; and there, for a little private gain, sold these silly salvages for rials of eight." Smith goes on to say that "this vile act kept him ever after from any more employment to those parts." Smith practically robbed the Indian of his merchandise, while Hunt robbed him of his freedom.

The memory of the savage, where his wrongs were concerned, is proverbial, and it is pertinent right here to allude in passing to the several kidnapping episodes which began with the adventurous

THE EARLY SETTLER AND THE INDIAN

Verrazano. Incidentally, they throw a side-light upon the savage disposition to hostility against the actual settler when he made his advent among them, which is not only their justification, but a matter of self-defence.

Verrazano was here in 1524. He made an extended voyage along the coast. One finds this in Foster's narration of that adventure. Baylie locates Verrazano's point of contact with the neighboring country as somewhere along the Connecticut shore. Foster says: "Twenty of his [Verrazano's] men landed and went about two leagues up into the country. The inhabitants fled before them, but they caught an old woman who had hid herself in the high grass, with a young woman about 18 years of age. The old woman carried a child upon her back, and had, besides, two little boys with her. The young woman, too, carried three children of her own sex. Seeing themselves discovered, they began to shriek, and the old one gave them to understand, by signs, that the men were fled to the woods. They offered her something to eat, which she accepted, but the maiden refused it. This girl, who was tall and well-shaped, they were desirous of taking along with them, but as she made a violent outcry, they contented themselves with taking a boy away with them."

Eleven years later Jacques Cartier was at the St. Lawrence River. Donnacona was sachem of the tribes in that locality. He received Cartier hospitably, a kindliness which Cartier repaid by kidnapping him and carrying him away to France, where the savage soon after died.

In 1605 Weymouth sailed into the mouth of the Sagadahoc River. We will let Sir Ferdinando Gorges tell the story. He says that Weymouth, "falling short of his course [in seeking the Northwest passage], happened into a river on the coast of America called Pemmaquid, from whence he brought five of the natives." Returning to England, Weymouth sailed into the harbor of Plymouth, then under Gorges's jurisdiction. Three of these savages were Nahanada, Skittwarroes, and Tisquantum. Gorges says, "These I seized upon. They were all of one nation, but of several parts, and several families. This *accident* [italics the author's] must be acknowledged the means, under God, of putting on foot and giving life to all our plantations." History does not record that at that time the English had any plantations in North America.

Shortly after 1606 a vessel was fitted out and despatched under Henry Chalons. Its destination was the New England coast. He had two of Weymouth's savages along. He was captured by the Spaniards. Assacumet, one of the savages, was recovered, and possibly the other.

Before the news of Chalons's capture was had in London another vessel was fitted out at Bristol, as a reënforcement to the Chalons expedition, with

THE EARLY SETTLER AND THE INDIAN

Martin Prin as master. Dehamda and Skittwarroes, two of the kidnapped savages, accompanied him.[1] They returned to England with Prin. The following year, 1607, these two savages acted as pilots for the first New England colony. They went into the mouth of the Sagadahoc with the English, to return at the first opportunity to their tribes. The Sagadahoc settlement was abandoned the following spring and the locality deserted by the English until the Smith expedition of 1614, after which it is probable there was a fishing-settlement at New Harbor on Pemaquid Point, these waters being almost constantly frequented for the great stores of codfish which they contained, as many as fifty fishing-vessels being here at one time.

In 1611 Captain Edward Harlow was at Monhegan, where he kidnapped three Indians, one of whom escaped. Sailing to the southward, they came to an island then known to the savages as Nonono. Here Harlow captured another savage. Sailing down to Capawick (Martha's Vineyard),

---

[1] The savage Dehamda is undoubtedly the Nahanada of the Sagadahoc country. The spelling of the Indian names by the early historians is somewhat uncertain. It has been questioned whether the Tisquantum mentioned in connection with Weymouth's voyage was the Squanto who acted as the interpreter of the sachem Massasoit in his interviews with the English. The dates given put the matter in some doubt. Drake is inclined to believe in their identity.
See Drake, *Book of the Indians*, p. 4.

he captured two others, Epanow and Coneconum, and then, with these five unfortunates, he hoisted sail for home. Epanow — or Epenewe, as Gorges calls him — returned with Captain Hobson in 1614. Hunt, who had kept Captain Smith company over, was the last to leave the region of Monhegan.

Sir F. Gorges records: "While I was laboring by what means I might best continue life in my languishing hopes, there comes one Henry Harley [Harlow] unto me, bringing with him a native of the Island of Capawick, a place seated to the southward of Cape Cod, whose name was Epenewe, a person of goodly stature, strong and well-proportioned. This man was taken upon the main [by force], with some 29 others by a ship of London that endeavored to sell them for slaves in Spaine, but being understood that they were Americans, and being found unapt for their uses, this one of them they refused, wherein they exprest more worth than those that brought them to the market, who could not but known that our nation was at that time in travel for setling of Christian colonies upon that continent, it being an act much tending to our prejudice, when we came into that part of the countries, as it shall further appear. How Captain Harley came to be possessed of this savage, I know not, but I understood by others how he had been shown in London for a wonder. It is true (as I have said) he was a goodly man, of a brave as-

THE EARLY SETTLER AND THE INDIAN

pect, stout and sober in his demeanor, and had learned so much English as to bid those that wondered at him, Welcome, Welcome; this being the last and best use they could make of him, that was now grown out of the people's wonder. The captain falling further into his familiarity, found him to be of acquaintance and friendship with those subject to the Bashaba, whom the captain well knew, being himself one of the plantation, sent over by the lord chief-justice [Popham], and by that means understood much of his language, found out the place of his birth."

Epanow found Assacumet here in London. Planning to escape, in their longing for the wilderness, they showed a great astuteness, and a keener intellect than that with which they had been credited. Their first effort was to discover the motive of the English in going over to the new country in their great ships. That in their possession, they exercised their cunning in playing upon the avaricious disposition of the English by telling their jailers they knew where there was gold in abundance, at the same time expressing their willingness to lead them where it was to be found. It was to be had among the sands of Capoge, an island off the coast of Cape Cod, as well as along the dunes of the Cape itself.

When Captain Hobson sailed away from England, in 1614, Epanow, Assacumet, and Wanape kept him company. Once they were anchored in familiar waters and his kin were gathered about the ship in their canoes, Epanow effected his escape. Gorges mourned the event: "And thus were my hopes of that particular [voyage] made void and frustrate." Captain Thomas Dermer was over here in 1619. He went ashore at Martha's Vineyard to trade with the savages. Epanow was there. There was a fight in which several of the savages were killed. All of Dermer's men who were ashore, according to Morton, were likewise killed, except the one who "kept the boat." Epanow made a special effort to capture Dermer; "But the [captain] himself got on board very sore wounded, and they had cut off his head upon the cuddy of the boat, had not his man rescued him with a sword, and so they got him away." Tisquantum, or Squanto, was with Dermer at this time. These kidnappings, brought down to the time of the beginning of the Plymouth settlement, to the savages of the different tribes up and down the coast were more than a tradition. The victims of these nefarious practices were again on their own ground awaiting the opportunity to retaliate.

The Pilgrims were to come near the end of the following year.

One can imagine the savage Nahanada, Epanow, and Squanto as they gathered about their wigwam fires, Ingram-like, relating the stories of their wanderings, and of the strange peoples and stranger things they had seen in their captivities — tales as

THE EARLY SETTLER AND THE INDIAN

strange to them as the tales of the Thousand and One Nights have seemed to the present-day reader. Squanto was a good story-teller, and no doubt his auditors were lost in amaze, and felt their hearts chill with strange fear as they saw the hull of the adventurous Englishman, growing larger and ever larger, upon the horizon of the Great Waters.

Anticipating somewhat the outbreak that came in 1675 between King Philip and the colony of Massachusetts Bay, the intercourse of the settler with the Indian, always of shifting color and aspect, lends to the events that marked the first days at Plymouth, and that accumulated through the growing years, including the Pequot troubles of 1637, a cumulative interest.

The relation of the happenings that led up to the treachery of Philip and his annihilation, and that ten years later betrayed the ambitious schemes of Louis XIV., is a mingling of savage vindictiveness and French diplomacy. If the savage proved an apt pupil, his English neighbor was no less an adept in the unwisdom of dishonesty, and in catering to the animal propensities that found their first victim amid the silence and isolation of Richmond's Island, off the mouth of the Spurwink River, a tide stream that breaks apart the Scarborough marshes. George Richmon came here first. He may be regarded as a contemporary of the Plymouth settlement. He had a trading-station on the island, where he built a small vessel. The occupancy

INDIAN WARS OF NEW ENGLAND

passed quite early from Richmon into the possession of Walter Bagnall. Bagnall was an acquaintance of Thomas Morton's, and it was here Morton spent some portion of his time after his difficulty with the purists of Plymouth. Bagnall was murdered by the savages, and his trading-house burned. It was the first instance of its kind in the history of the settlements.[1]

---

[1] Bagnall was a dark-visaged man, of scant principle, who robbed the Indians, in his trade with them, unmercifully. He had incurred their suspicion and hatred. He sold them rum, got them drunk, and then paid them what he pleased. Squidrayset is supposed to have been the ringleader in the crime, no doubt instigated by his knowledge of the kidnappings by the English on either side of his domain. The event happened some eight years after the settlement of Plymouth [Drake gives the date October, 1631. It must have been one or two years earlier]; but so far was Richmond's Island to the eastward, and so notorious was Bagnall's character, that no particular importance was attached to the event. An English sloop touched at the island a month later; but the English found only a heap of ashes and a few charred bones. Two years later this island passed into the possession of Edward Trelawney, an English merchant who sent over one John Winter (1630-31) as his agent. Winter was no less unprincipled than Bagnall, except that he cloaked his greed somewhat. That he did not share the fate of Bagnall is possibly owing to the fact that he had at his back a company of sturdy servitors, who were amply supplied with muskets, ammunition, and even more formidable gunnery. Winter did not live to see the onslaught of Mugg upon the Scarborough settlers, which was contemporary with the conflict of 1675.

THE EARLY SETTLER AND THE INDIAN

The easternmost point of English contact at the beginning of the Plymouth settlement was at Pemaquid, and it is more than probable that there was a small resident English population at New Harbor. If there was, it is evident that its contingent had no annalist who regarded its occupation as of sufficient importance to inspire a record of its meager incidents of living. That such do not exist affords no presumption against such an inference; for negative proof is sometimes most convincing. That was Samoset's domain, whose friendliness to the English was evidenced in his generosity to Brown, to whom he gave a conveyance, around 1628, of most ample proportions. In nobility of character, Samoset was the equal of Massasoit; and in natural intelligence, greatly his superior.[1]

---

[1] Samoset is the John Somerset who affixed his sign-manual, a rudely-drawn bow and arrow, to a conveyance to John Brown of a large tract of land in Bristol, Me. He was the sachem of the Pemaquid country and the original proprietor of all the lands in that extensive domain. He was a friend of Levett, who built a house in Casco Bay, the first house-builder within the Maine province. He entertained Levett at Capemanwagen, now known as Southport, Me., in 1625. His deed to Brown bore also the signature of Ungongoit. It is noted as being the earliest deed made by a savage to the white man. Samoset was living as late as 1653; for in that year he sold land to William Parnall, Thomas Way, and William England. That he was very aged at that time is certified by the tremulous hand with which he affixed for the last time, probably, the sign of the hunter's bow and

INDIAN WARS OF NEW ENGLAND

Whenever the English conscience had to do with the Indian, it was singularly dormant.[1] If the

arrow. He was not alive at the breaking out of King Philip's War. He was a whole-souled gentleman, kindly, generous, pacific, and a staunch friend of the white man. He loved John Brown as a brother, and John Brown always treated Samoset with the utmost consideration. When the other houses of the settlers were destroyed about Pemaquid by the savages, Brown's was untouched.

Maine Hist. Soc. Coll., vol. v., pp. 186–193.

Sewall's *Ancient Dominions of Maine*, p. 102.

[1] An excerpt is here given from *Plymouth Colony Records*, vol. vii., p. 195:

"1674–5. Att the Court of his Matie holden att Plymouth 2 March. 2^{cond} March, 1674,

Before Josias Winslow   John Freeman
       John Alden   Constant Southworth
       William Bradford   James Browne, and
       Thomas Hinckley   James Cudworth.
              Assistants, etc.

..... "Robin, of Massachusetts, Ralph and Sampson, of Nobscussett, Indians, in the right of theire wives, the daughters of Napoitan, Indian Sachem, deceased, complaineth of much wronge doñ unto them by reason of sundry English men unjust possession and detaining of sundry lands belonging to the said complainants, which were the lands of Napoitan aforesaid, and not by him sold unto them, the said lands lying between Bound Brooke and Stony Brooke, in the constablewick of Yarmouth and in p̃ticular complaines against John Winge, in an action on the case, to the damage of fifty pounds for his possessing and detaining wrongfully from them a p̃sell of the said lands, whereupon hee hath built, fenced and otherwise improved."

This action was *non-suited*.

THE EARLY SETTLER AND THE INDIAN

Indian was to be Christianized, it was at the expense of his patrimony. On the one hand was the proselytism of Eliot; on the other, the bulldozing characteristic of Miles Standish, and land-piracy — a harsh recapitulation of the English attitude toward the Indian, but, nevertheless, comprehensive. The Indian's vast domain of virgin forests and leaping waters was appropriated by an alien power which issued at will its royal land-grants, without care or consideration of those whose primary rights were legitimate, and incontestably well-founded.

The English took up the best places along the seashore, as they took the best of everything the savage had to offer. The greed of commerce was everywhere pushing at his elbow. His fishing and hunting grounds were impoverished to fill the Englishman's purse, else they were sequestered by a jealous occupation. While the Indian was silent under intense provocation, the Englishman was as instant to resent interference with his trinkets of perhaps trifling value, and as well his assumed rights of realty, as he was indifferent to the prescriptive rights of the aborigine.[1]

---

[1] "Sometime after the Plymouth people had been to Nauset to purchase some corn and not being able to remove the whole of it, returned again for the balance." This was in 1622. The amount purchased was eight hogsheads of corn and beans. "Standish went to bring the corn left at Nauset [and, as usual, gets himself into difficulty with the Indians]. One

INDIAN WARS OF NEW ENGLAND

While the traditions of the Anglo-Saxon have been accepted as standing for a well-ordered liberty, and an observance of the rights of the individual, on the virgin soil of New England they found their liveliest expressions in the absorption of land areas: a process of deglutition in which the rights of the original owner were utterly ignored. Nor were the times without their secret machina-

---

of Aspinet's men happening to come to one of Standish's boats, which being left entirely without guard, he took out a few trinkets, such as 'beads, scissors, and other trifles,' which when the English captain found out, 'he took certain of his company with him, and went to the sachem, telling him what had happened, and requiring the same again, or the party that stole them,— *or else he would revenge it on them before his departure;'* and so he departed for the night, *'refusing whatsoever kindness they offered* [italics the author's].' However, next morning, Aspinet, attended by many of his men, went to the English, 'in a stately manner,' and all the 'trifles;' for the exposing of which the English had ten times as much reprehension as the man for taking them."

Drake, *Book of the Indians*, p. 13.

Standish was inclined always to be rather truculent. Drake says he exercised more power in the Plymouth Colony than the governor himself. He was a military man whose experience in the Low Countries especially fitted him to deal with savages. He was, despite all the laudatory writings of the so-called hero-worshippers, something of a savage. No one who has ever written of him has credited him with either a predominating intellect or a superabundance of moral principle. He was, undoubtedly, the man for the time and the place — the bully, by proxy, for the community.

THE EARLY SETTLER AND THE INDIAN

tions and diplomacies, in which Winthrop was a past-master. The Indian was a heathen, to be despoiled without mercy. While to the English he could show no recorded title to his holdings in realty, a vast and unexplored domain which offered inexhaustible riches in furs and possibly in precious metals, the latter fell back on Biblical precedent as an apology for his indiscriminate trespassing upon a weaker people. His understanding grew only as his wrongs accumulated, and he bided his time with a marvellously unobtrusive patience.

If Massasoit was unsuspicious, at the advent of the white stranger, that his unbidden guest was to plunge his people into involuntary pauperism, if he was too generous of himself and his belongings, his simplicity was not shared by any member of his family. Alexander, Weetamoo, and Philip were wiser in their generation than Massasoit. Impelled by the finality of events, Philip appealed to the court of last resort to the savage. He was gifted with a prophetic eye. The Pequots were annihilated. The English were occupying everywhere. The privileges of his own people were being curtailed with every rising sun. That he lost his suit was inevitable, because he was subject to the fatalism that always crowds the weaker to the wall. The least the English could have done was to make the people whose lands they took their wards. As drastic as these lines may seem by way of criticism, as distasteful as they may appear, they are nevertheless

INDIAN WARS OF NEW ENGLAND

deserved, if history is to be written to the plummet of the truth; for the Indian was never at any time the debtor of the Puritan settler. He was a target not only for the Puritan bullets, but as well for the prayers of the Puritan clergy, who were wont to give thanks when the English bullet did its work especially well. Increase Mather was notably fervent in thanksgiving upon these occasions.[1]

The Indian was the unfortunate victim of every avaricious whim of the white man, who scrupled

---

[1] The Puritan was an iconoclast in all things which, from the Puritan point of view, were un-Puritan, which as well comprehended his attitude toward the aborigine. His religion was one of repression. Like the traditional face of this austere individual, it was thin, angular, and joyless. At home, on English soil, toward the Established Church he was diplomatic, though inclined to open criticism of its integrity.

It was different with the Pilgrim, who, ignoring the established faith, — a declaimer against its practices, to become a downright secessionist along spiritual lines, courting persecution in the garb of an exile, — eventually became the persecutor of others whose religious practices differed from his own. While the shores of Massachusetts Bay offered new and untried experiences, he accepted them with a phenomenal fortitude, and even exaltation.

The first labor of the Pilgrim and Puritan was the erection of a little State — an oligarchy of laymen. Citizenship was probationary, if not altogether selective. The Anglo-Saxon *folk-mote* had become a judicial commune, before which tribunal the aspirant for civic rights and privileges was placed on trial. Conscience was yoked to dogma. A code of personal conduct was inaugurated never contemplated under

THE EARLY SETTLER AND THE INDIAN

not to plunder him of his peltry or his corn, as the occasion offered. One of the first things done by the Plymouth people when they happened upon a cache in which the savages had stored their crop of corn was to help themselves to its contents, carrying away even the kettle which had been used for its partial protection; and all without a thought of the toil that had produced it, or of the need of its owner. When they ate it they asked God's grace upon it, with never a query as to their savage

---

the broadest interpretation of the Charter of Runnymead. Individual belief was put under bonds for good behavior, to become the like bond-servant of a restrictive tenet. The Church of the Puritan was made the bailee of temporal and spiritual development along lines as austere, as rugged, as the wind-blown coast along which the Puritan planted his roof-tree. His nature, as wrought out by his environment in conjunction with his religious teaching, was harsh and unelastic. His desire for acquisition was the response to an imperative demand — *self-preservation.*

So, the foothold of the first settlers was at the expense of a consideration of the equitable rights of others, notably the aborigine. With the close of the first decade after the landing at Plymouth and the occupation of ancient Shawmut, the Puritan character had found its groove, and a half-decade later had established its policy, and was moving along lines of definite direction and effective purpose. Under the velvet hand of John Winthrop, the Massachusetts Bay Colony became the foundation of the New England confederacy, which finally developed into a political power with which the Mother Country was unable to cope. The liberalism of the present century is a regenerated Puritanism.

INDIAN WARS OF NEW ENGLAND

neighbor. From the beginning, almost, the Indian was a creature to be made drunk, and despoiled after he had been debauched.

It needed two generations of the white man to educate the Indian; more than sixty years of English intercourse, such as it was, to precipitate a conflict, which, to have been successful on the part of the savages, should not have been so long delayed.[1] It was a conflict for extermination, which was to continue, after a desultory fashion, beyond the middle of the following century. It was under the shadow of Mount Hope (Mon-taup) that the jealous and intriguing Philip, whose hatred of the English was fanned by the unfortunate Weetamoo, invoked the ultimate extinction of his race, which was practically accomplished less than a century

---

[1] There was a conspiracy as early as 1623, between Peksuot, Wittuwamet, and perhaps Iyanough, to rid themselves of the English. Massasoit had been approached by the conspirators and, declining to engage in these machinations against the settlers, charged Hobomok to warn them of their danger. Massasoit designated the Indians of Nauset, Paomet, Sacconet, Mattachiest, Manomet, Agowaywam, and the island of Capawack. Winslow says Massasoit advised them "to kill the men of Massachuset, who were the authors of this mischief." Miles Standish, who had a good nose for such matters and who was not averse to the smell of powder, "was to make his party good against the Indians." It was 23d March, 1623, "a yearly court day" at the Plymouth settlement. After due deliberation, war was declared against the Massachusetts Indians, and hostilities were to be carried

THE EARLY SETTLER AND THE INDIAN

later within the depths of a Maine wilderness. The knell of the Indian was sounded on the shore of Lovewell's Pond with the death of the Pequaket sachem, Paugus.[1]

It is of interest in this story to follow the Plymouth people through the early years of their intercourse with their savage neighbors. The story should be taken in its entirety, which is given with great fulness in Mourt's *Relation*,[2] in which all

---

into the enemy's country. Standish at once started for Wessagusset, where, by a device, he lured Peksuot and Wittuwamet and two other savages into a cabin along with as many of his own men, whereupon the fight commenced which resulted in the killing of all four of the Indians, without special injury to the Standish party. Describing the event, Winslow says: "But it is incredible how many wounds these two panises [Peksuot and Wittuwamet] received before they died, not making any fearful noise, but catching their weapons, and striving to the last."

[1] This fight was known as the Battle of Lovewell's Pond. It took place at the mouth of Battle Brook, in what is now Fryeburg, Me. It is a beautiful sheet of water, and a place of much historic interest. This was the end of the Pigwacket tribe, the only remnant of which was the old squaw Moll Locket, who lived here until her death. The tradition is that after a time Moll's husband came back from Canada bringing another squaw with him, which Moll resented. Moll and the strange squaw at once engaged in a fight as to which of them should have the man. Poor Moll was vanquished, and the victor carried her savage paramour off in triumph.

[2] Dexter says, in his note to *Mourt*, p. 98, that "Edward Winslow was almost necessarily the author of that part of

writers upon this period have placed implicit dependence. Much is to be gleaned from Bradford and Winslow. From what they have left as to their intercourse with the Indians, one can readily follow the attitude of the savages toward these people, and as readily trace out the causes which led up to a complete alienation of interests, and finally to open hostility. After the Puritans came, the situation was in a way of being more complicated, by reason of the cold-blooded commercialism which entered into all of their transactions with these unfortunate people. Thomas Morton paved the way for the degradation of the Indian as he pursued his revelries at Merry Mount, which were hardly more than a series of debaucheries in which the Indians, men and women, took a lively part. Merry Mount was a sore spot to the Plymouth people, who finally succeeded in arresting Morton and sending him to England for trial. Nothing was done with the matter there, for a year later Morton was again at Boston.

---

the *Relation* [*The Journey to Pokonoket*], as it was written by a participant in the Journey. There are several verbal correspondencies with the avowed works which endorse the supposition."

Young, in his *Pilgrims*, regards the *Relation* as the work of Mr. George Morton, *Mourt* being a corruption of the surname. Drake ascribes the authorship of the work to several of the company at Plymouth. He takes Mourt to be the publisher's name; but upon what ground he

THE EARLY SETTLER AND THE INDIAN

The eleventh of November, 1620, the *Mayflower* came to anchor in the Plymouth offing. Morton's *Relation* records: "Munday, the 13. of *Novomber* [O. S.], we vnſhipped our Shallop and drew her on land, to mend and repaire her, having bin forced to cut her downe in beſtowing her betwixt the decks, and ſhe was much opened with the peoples lying in her, which kept vs long there, for it was 16. or 17. dayes before the Carpenter had finiſhed her; our people went on ſhore to refreſh themſelues, and our women to waſh, as they had great need; but whilſt we lay thus ſtill, hoping our Shallop[1] would be ready in fiue or sixe dayes at the furtheſt, but our Carpenter made flow work of it, ſo that ſome of our people, impatient of dleay, defired for our better furtherance to travaile by Land into the Coun-

---

does not explain. He accepts the suggestion of *Judge* Davis that Richard Gardiner was the author; how that conclusion is arrived at originally, we know not. Drake admits, however, that, as a relation of the early settlement of "any country, there never was a more important document." It was printed in 1622, in London.

The author is of the opinion, from the continuity of style and construction, that *Mourt's Relation* is the work of a single author, and is inclined to Morton as the Plymouth annalist.

[1] "They having brought a large shalop with them out of England, stowed it in quarters in ye ship, they now gott her out & sett their carpenters to worke to trime her up; but being much bruised & shattered in ye shipe wth foule weather, they saw she would be longe in mending."

Bradford, *History of Plymouth Plantation*, p. 80.

INDIAN WARS OF NEW ENGLAND

trey, which was not without appearance of danger, not having the Shallop with them,[1] nor meanes to carry provifion but on their backes to fee whether it might be fit for vs to feate in or no, and the rather becaufe as we fayled into the Harbour, there feemed to be a river opening it felf into the maine land; the willingnes of the perfons was liked, but

---

[1] It was an inclement season, and there was more comfort on ship than on shore, there being no shelters up for their convenience; neither was there any timber cut from which such shelters could have been constructed. There were one hundred to be set ashore who were to begin the Plymouth Colony. They must have been the opposite of "impatient" of delay, except as they might desire to know somewhat of the bleak coast before them. The truth of the matter was, Captain Jones had made port, from his point of view, and was anxious to discharge his cargo. Baylie says, "The master of the ship and the crew, continuing their importunities, the pilgrims resolved to commence their settlement without delay."

History of New Plymouth, p. 52.

"But what heard they daly from ye m^r & company? but y^t with speede they should looke out a place with their shallop, wher they would be at some near distance; for ye season was shuch as he would not stirr from thence till a safe harbor was discovered by them wher they would be, and he might goe without danger; and that victelle consumed apace, but he must & would keepe sufficient for them selves and their returne [to England]. Yea, it was muttered by some that if they gott not a place in time, they would turne them & their goods ashore & leave them."

Bradford's *History of Plymouth Plantation*, p. 96.

THE EARLY SETTLER AND THE INDIAN

the thing it felf, in regard to the danger was rather permitted then approved, and fo with cautions, directions, and inftructions, fixteene men were set out with every man his Mufket, Sword, and Corflet under the conduct of Captaine *Miles Standish*,[1] vnto whom was adioyned for counfell and advife, *William Bradford, Stephen Hopkins,* and *Edward Tilley.*"

In tracing the genealogy of events that make up the story of the troubles which, though not always apparent between the English and the

---

[1] "Myles Standish is supposed to have been born at Duxbury Hall, near Chorley, in Lancashire, some twenty-three miles N. E. from Liverpool, in 1584; served as a soldier in the Low Countries; became interested in the Pilgrims, and joined them, though not one of their church; brought over only his wife, Rose, who died a month after the landing; he next married Barbara ———, who is supposed to have come in the Ann, in 1623. He was constantly engaged in the public service; was Assistant nineteen years; went to London for the colony in 1625, returning the following Spring. About 1631 he settled on Captain's Hill, in Duxbury, on condition at first of moving into Plymouth in the winter time that they may the better repair to the worship of God; there he died $\frac{3}{13}$ Oct., 1656, aged 72. He named, in his will, four sons,— Alexander, Miles, Josiah, and Charles,— and a deceased daughter, Lora."

Mourt's *Relation* (Dexter's note), p. 14.
Savage, *Gen. Dict.*, vol. iv., p. 162.
Plymouth Colony Records, vol. xii., p. 6.
N. E. Hist. and Gen. Reg., vol. v., pp. 335–338.
Winsor's *History of Duxbury,* p. 320.

INDIAN WARS OF NEW ENGLAND

Indian, were always in a way existent, one must needs begin at the inception of their relations. No act on the part of either is unimportant. For that reason this story of Mourt of the first venture from the deck of the *Mayflower* into the woods of Cape Cod becomes the natural point of contact, historically, of approach to a clear understanding of those occurrences insignificant, possibly, at the time, but of cumulative influence through a half century of comparative inaction on the part of the Indians against their white neighbors. It was a silent influence, yet none the less effective.

It was the fifteenth of November, O. S.,[1] 1620. They were put ashore in accordance with their arrangements made on the ship. Started on their explorations, their first discovery of any importance was made when they had gone about a mile

---

[1] The calendar was corrected by Pope Gregory, 1582. His correction was not adopted by the British Parliament until 1751, when it was directed that eleven days in September, 1752, should be retrenched, and the third day of the month reckoned as the fourteenth. This was denominated New Style, or the Gregorian account. The year was made to commence on the first day of January instead of, as formerly by the Old Style, on the twenty-fifth of March. Old Style, or the Julian year, is so called from Julius Cæsar, who regulated the calendar about forty years before Christ. Before the Gregorian change there was more or less confusion of dates, oftentimes as to whether January, February, and a portion of March closed the year or began the new one.

Gregory dropped ten days from the Julian Calendar, as

THE EARLY SETTLER AND THE INDIAN

inland. "They espyed five or sixe people, with a Dogge, comming towards them, who were Savages, who when they saw them ran into the Wood and whisled the Dogge after them."

Bearing weapons, the English set after them to overtake them, but it was a vain pursuit. If one is

---

has already been suggested. The reason for so doing was the supposition in the Julian Calendar that the length of the year was 365 days, 5 hours, 48 minutes, and $45\frac{1}{2}$ seconds. Therefore the civil year was 11 minutes and $14\frac{1}{2}$ seconds longer than the solar. In one hundred and thirty years this difference would amount to a whole day. At the coming of 1582, this anticipation of the equinox amounted to ten days, which brought the happening of the vernal equinox on the eleventh of March instead of the twenty-first, as it would have done had the Julian Calendar conformed to the course of the sun. These ten days were dropped to even up the civil year with the solar year. To preserve the integrity of the calendar after that, it was ordered that three days should be dropped every 400 years, which was nearly equivalent to one day for each cycle of 130 years. Instead of suppressing one day for every 130 years, it was thought better to make the correction in leap year only, by which computation there were left 365 days to each common year. Before that every 100th year was a leap year; but it was ordered by Pope Gregory that every 400th year, only, should be considered as leap year, and the other centurial years as common years, the year 1600 being retained as leap year. Making 1700, 1800, and 1900 to be common years, as they would have been by O. S., the error incident to the odd time is corrected. By this, Dec. 11, 1620, O. S., is Dec. 21, N. S., a difference which is perennial. For that reason Dec. 21, 1620, is the true day of the landing of the Pilgrims.

INDIAN WARS OF NEW ENGLAND

inclined to comment on this proceeding, the conclusion is that it was a most indecorous overture. The pursuit lasted for a space of "about ten miles."[1] They followed the savages by the "trace of their footings." From Mourt one would glean that this first Indian hunt was terminated only by nightfall. Setting their watch, they waited until the following morning, when, like so many hounds, they again took up the trail of the savages, but fruitlessly, which was undoubtedly a great disappointment to Captain Miles Standish, who liked the smell of powder and the noise of conquest. The principal event of that day was the discovery of some ancient corn-fields of the savages and some old mats which covered what was undoubtedly an Indian grave, which they inspected with more curiosity than respect. They kept their course, as they thought, toward their ship, which led them into some "new stubble," off which the Indians "had gotten Corne this yeare." A little further on, they came into the stubble of another corn-field where had been a house; also they found "a great Ketle, which had been some Ships ketle and brought out of Europe."[2]

---

[1] Dexter's *Mourt*, p. 16.

[2] About 1617 "a French ship was cast away at Cap-Codd, but ye men gott ashore, & saved their lives, and much of their victails & other goods."

Bradford, *History of Plymouth Plantation*, p. 98.

Bradford adds that the Indians killed all but three or four,

THE EARLY SETTLER AND THE INDIAN

Under a heap of sand, which they dug open with their hands, they found "a little old Basket full of Faire *Indian* Corne." They dug still deeper and found "a fine new Basket full of very faire corne of this yeare, with some 36. goodly eares of corne, some yellow, and some red, and others mixed with blew, which was a very goodly sight: the Basket was round, and narrow at the top, it held about three or foure Bushels, which was as much as two of us could lift up from the ground, and was very handsomely and cunningly made; But while wee were busie about these things, we set our men Sentinell in a *round* ring, all but two or three which digged up the corne.[1] We were in suspence what

---

using the survivors worse than slaves, two of them being redeemed by Captain Dermer.

[1] The placing of the "Sentinells in a round ring" was a significant performance. It was probably a case of conscience, not unlike that which prompted them to apologize one to another by saying they would make their plundering good to the savage owners of the corn if they could "come to a parley with them." The English began their career at Plymouth by plundering the natives of the fruits of their toil, violating their sepulchers, and robbing them of their utensils. Afraid of interruption at their surreptitious occupation, their desire for acquisition, whetted to a keen edge by the sight of that "*little old Basket full of Faire Indian Corne,*" undoubtedly suggested a barrier of sentinels. The only excuse possible for this outrageous trespass is the possible danger they might be in from starvation, once the *Mayflower* had turned her prow toward England; but, unsatisfied with this accom-

to doe with it, and the Ketle and at length, after much consultation, we concluded to take the Ketle, and as much Corne as we could carry away with us; and when our Shallop came, if we could find

plishment, they had it in mind to prosecute their search at another time for more of the savages' provender.

The early settlers followed the custom of the Indian in keeping such of his crops as were to be wintered in excavations in the ground. The author has within his own recollection two or three cellars which were dug into the dry hillside and walled up with rough stone, pointed with clay from some neighboring meadow. They were common before it became the general custom to dig cellars for their houses.

As for the Indians, one finds this in Force's *Tracts*, vol. ii., v., p. 30, *New English Canaan:* "Their Barnes are holes made in the earth, that will hold a hogshead of corne a peece in them. In these (when their corne is out of the huske and well dried) they lay their store in greate baskets (which they make of Sparke) with matts under about the sides and on top: and putting it into the place made for it, they cover it with earth; and in this manner it is preserved from destruction or putrifaction; to be used in case of necessity, and not else."

Freeman says, "The ears had been doubtless reserved by the Indians for seed."

Civilization and Barbarism, p. 28, foot-note.

The same custom has always prevailed among the New England farmers to select their seed ears as they husked, on which they left a few husks by which they were braided into trusses and hung in the cool, dry places about the farmhouse beyond the reach of mice and squirrels. The early settler attended the agricultural school of the savage, whose methods hold good to this day.

THE EARLY SETTLER AND THE INDIAN

any of the people, and come to parley with them, we would give them the Ketle againe, and satisfie them for their Corne, *so we tooke all the eares and put a good deale of the loose Corne in the Ketle for two men to bring away on a staffe; besides they that could put any into their Pockets filled the same;* the rest we buried for we were so laden with Armour that *we could carry no more.*"[1]

Not finding their way to the ship, as they had anticipated, they were again overtaken by the darkness, whereupon they built a barricade and set their guard as the night before.[2] The following day they got back to the *Mayflower.* Bradford takes occasion to remark, "And so like ye men from Escholl carried with them of ye fruits of ye land, &

---

[1] The italics are the author's. The question, "*Did the Pilgrims Wrong the Indians?*" in the *Congregational Quarterly*, vol. i., pp. 129–135, being a justification of the Pilgrims, has this: "This was indicative of the spirit of fairness with which the Pilgrims of Plymouth always acted towards the aboriginal owners of the soil."

Any *right* "spirit of fairness" would have impelled the Pilgrims to leave the corn *as they found it.* In honesty, there was no other way. But their leader was a graduate of the Wars of the Low Country, where plunder was a soldier's pay. No amount of specious deduction, no veneer of heroics framed in a series of lean days, can change the fact. The white man was the cupidious oppressor of the Indian from the *first.*

[2] Bradford describes this shelter: "So they made them a barricado (as usually they did every night) with loggs, staks,

INDIAN WARS OF NEW ENGLAND

showed their breethren; of which, & their returne, they were marvelusly glad, and their harts incouraged.

"After this, ye shalop being gott ready, they set out againe for ye better discovery of this place, & ye m^r. of ye ship desired to goe him selfe, so ther went some 30. men, but found it to be no harbor for ships but only for boats; ther was allso found 2. of their houses covered with matts, & sundrie of their implements in them, but ye people were rune away & could not be seen; also ther was found more of their corne, & of their beans of various collours. The corne & beans they brought away, purposing to give them full satisfaction when they should meete with any of them (as about some 6. months afterward they did, to their good contente)."[1]

& thike pine bowes, ye height of a man, leaving it open to leeward, partly to shelter them from ye could wind (making their fire in ye middle round aboute it), and partly to defend them from any sudden assaults of ye savages, if they should surround them."

Bradford, *Plymouth Plantation*, p. 84.

[1] The only recompense the English made for the corn and beans of which they possessed themselves during the forages of the preceding November seems to have been the return of the kettle to Massasoit filled with peas, which was very pleasing to the sachem. This incident was consummated upon Massasoit's first visit to the Plymouth settlers, about the 22d of March, 1621, which was a few days after the first appearance of Samoset.

THE EARLY SETTLER AND THE INDIAN

Bradford continues: "But the Lord is never wanting unto his in their greatest needs; let his holy name have all ye praise." This proceeding on the part of the Pilgrims was a spoiling of the Egyptians, and to them justified by Biblical precedent.

On this second foray they found another place "like a grave, only it was bigger and longer than we had seen. It was also covered with boords, so we mused what it should be and resolved to digge it up." What blunted sensibilities these adventurers — for such they had become among these wilderness woods — must have possessed in this disturbing and despoiling of these strange resting-places of the dead, which should have been sacred to any but a barbarian! These English had no compunctions, and so they kept on with their digging, without respect to the traditions or the feelings of the people who had here performed the last rites in accordance with their customs. There was certainly nothing of a propitiatory character toward the native in this desecration.

Mourt goes on: "We found first a Matt, and under that a fayre bow, and ther another Matt, and under that, a boord about three quarters [of a yard] long, finely carved and painted, with three tines or broches [a broche is a spit on which meats are roasted; the description being suggestive of a trident, as if the deceased had been a sailor] on the top like a Crowne; also betweene the Matts we

INDIAN WARS OF NEW ENGLAND

found Boules, Trayes, Dishes and such like Trinkets; at length we came to a faire new Matt, and under that two Bundles, the one bigger, and the other lesse, we opened the greater and found in it a great quantitie of fine and perfect red Powder, and in it the bones and skull of a man. The skull had fine yellow haire[1] still on it, and some of the flesh

---

[1] Thomas Morton, who was such a thorn in the side of the Plymouth Colony, mentions some Frenchmen who were captured by the savages anterior to the settlement at Plymouth. He says: "It fortuned some yeares before the English came to inhabit at new Plimoth in New England, that, upon distast given in the Massachusets Bay by Frenchmen, then trading there with the natives for beaver, they set upon the men, at such advantage, that they killed manie of them, burned their shipp, then riding at anchor by an island there, now called *Peddock's Island*, in memory of *Leonard Peddock* that landed there, (where manie wilde anckies [some sort of animal] haunted that time, which hee thought had been tame,) distributing them unto five sachems which were lords of the severall territories adjoyning, they did keep them so long as they lived, only to sport themselves at them, and made these five Frenchmen fetch them wood and water, which is the generall worke they require of a servant. One of these five men outliving the rest, had learned so much of their language, as to rebuke them for their bloudy deed: saying that God would be angry with them for it; and that he would in his displeasure destroy them; but the salvages (it seems, boasting of their strength) replyed, and said, that they were so many that God could not kill them."

Morton's *New Canaan*, pp. 22, 23.

Captain John Smith has the same story.

THE EARLY SETTLER AND THE INDIAN

unconsumed; there was bound up with it a knife, a packneedle, and two or three old iron things. It was bound up in a Saylers canvas Casacke [coarse frock, or blouse] and a payre of cloth breeches; the red Powder was a kind of Embaulment, and yeelded a strong, but no offensive smell; It was fine as any flower. We opened the lesse bundle likewise, and found some of the same Powder in it, and the bones and head of a little childe, about the leggs, and other parts of it was bound with strings, and bracelets of fine white Beads; there was also by it a little Bow, about three quarters long and some other odd knacks; we brought sundry of the pretiest things away with us, and covered the Corps up againe."[1]

---

[1] What a meanly base and thoroughly contemptible proceeding, which in these days would be punished as an inexcusable vandalism! Standish, the captain of the band, may be considered as somewhat calloused; but for Carver, Bradford, Winslow, and others of the conscience of the new settlement to allow themselves to become parties to so execrable an enterprise is difficult to understand. What the natives may have thought of the matter is only conjecturable. It was iconoclastic to a degree, and smacks of a heathenism on a par with the marooning of a hundred poor sailors at Pamlico by the English buccaneer, Hawkins, in 1567.

The Indian had a great veneration for the burial-places of his people. The mat upon which the deceased died, his dish out of which he was wont to eat and drink, were placed upon his grave. No Indian would meddle with them; for they were consecrated to the use of the dead, and if they should be taken

INDIAN WARS OF NEW ENGLAND

Comment is needless, and it is no wonder they felt moved to surround themselves at night with a barricado, and as well to post sentinels. It is to be apprehended that the bold Captain Standish might have been the moving spirit in this ghoulish curiosity.

While they were speculating, some one and some another, as to the former pretensions of the occupant of this grave, "two of the Saylers, which were newly come on the shore, by chance espied two houses [wigwams], which had been lately dwelt in,

---

away the departed spirit might be compelled to go naked and hungry in the other world.

Key, *Mass. Hist. Coll.*, vol. iii., p. 237.

Washington Irving says: "Indians are remarkable for the reverence which they entertain for the sepulchers of their kindred. Tribes exiled for generations from the former abode of their ancestors, have been known to turn aside from the highway, and guided by wonderfully accurate tradition, have crossed the country perhaps for miles, to some locality, — perhaps hill, buried in woods, where the ashes of their tribe were originally deposited, and have there passed hours in silent meditation.

"'In early records may be seen that planters at Passongesit having defaced monuments of the dead, and plundered the grave of a Sachem's mother of some skins with which the grave had been decorated, the Sachem, influenced by sublime and holy feeling, gathered his men and addressed them in simple and pathetic language of filial piety and Indian eloquence.' We may not quote his whole speech, but the gist of it is, that he dreamed his mother came and reproached him for allowing the desecration."

THE EARLY SETTLER AND THE INDIAN

but the people were gone. They having their peeces, and hearing nobody entered the houses, and tooke out some things, and durst not stay, but came again and told us; so some seven or eight of us went with them, and found how we had gone within a slight shot of them before."

Mourt goes on to describe what they found in the houses, adding, "Some of the best things we tooke away with us, and left the houses standing as they were, for it was growing towards night and the tyde almost spent, we hasted with our things downe to the Shallop, and got aboard that night, intending to have brought some Beades and other things to have left in the houses, in sign of Peace, and that we meant to truck with them, but it was not done by meanes of our hastie comming away from Cape Cod, but so soone as we can meete conveniently with them, we will give them full satisfaction."

Always throwing a sop to their consciences, the Pilgrim marauders never found opportunity, by any record of the transaction we have seen, to make their promises good, even to themselves. The expedition which they contemplated in order to square their consciences—for it is evident they were possessed of some sensing of the law of *meum et tuum*—never was accomplished. The return of the kettle taken in the first expedition, a modicum of peas for the bushels of corn appropriated, a scarlet "horseman's coat," and a copper chain, all of

INDIAN WARS OF NEW ENGLAND

which went to Massasoit, proved the limit of the restitution on the part of the English. This apparently was their contribution to the "good contente" of the savages.[1]

On the sixth day of December, O. S., following, the English set out upon an exploring expedition which led them into Wellfleet Bay. Of this company were Carver, Bradford, Standish, Winslow, and six others. Their errand was to find, if pos-

---

[1] Baylie says, on the occasion of the visit of the English to the Nausets on account of the Billington boy straying away, they finding him there: "The English performed an act of justice by making ample satisfaction for the corne which they had taken away during the preceding year."
Baylie, *History of New Plymouth*, p. 78.

The only mention Mourt makes of the matter is: "And one of those whose Corne we had formerly found, we promised him in restitution & desired him either to come to Patuxet (Plymouth) for satisfaction, or else we would bring them so much Corne againe, hee promised to come, wee used him very kindly for the present."
Dexter's *Mourt's Relation*, p. 115.

Bradford says: "Those people also came and made their peace; and they gave full satisfaction to those who corne they had found and taken when they were at Cap-Codd."
Bradford, *History of Plymouth Plantation*, p. 124.

Nothing appears after this to show that any of the Nausets went to Plymouth "for satisfaction." Bradford's narrative is by implication. He was writing of what occurred at Nauset. Mourt is direct, and while Mourt is almost photographic in detail, Bradford is often disappointingly meager.

[102]

THE EARLY SETTLER AND THE INDIAN

sible, a more satisfactory place whereon to lay the foundations of their settlement. Landing, they built a barricado, for it was almost night when they reached land, setting their sentinels as usual. Some four or five miles away they discovered the smoke of a camp-fire "which the savages made that night." In a cul-de-sac of the bay they found parts of a dead grampus which had been cast up on the shore. The Indians had begun to cut it up; but upon discovering the English approaching, they had taken a hurried departure. The English followed their trail where the savages had "strucke into the woods by the side of a pond." Instead of savages, or even a wigwam,[1] they found a field that had at some time been set to corn; also a "great burying-place one part of which was incompassed with a large Palizado, like a church-yard." Afterward, they came to some wigwams that seemed to

---

[1] "Their houses are verie little and homely, being made with small Poles pricked into the ground, and so bended and fastened at the tops and on the sides they are matted with Boughes, and covered on the Roofe with Sedge and old Mats."
New England Plantation, Force, vol. i., xii., p. 13.

"Their doore is a hanging Mat which being lift up, falls downe of it selfe."
Roger Williams, *R. I. Hist. Coll.*, vol. i., p. 51.

Another description of an Indian interior is of a "lodgehouse:" "Their lodging is made in three places of the house aboute the fire they lye upon plancks commonly aboute a foote or 18. inches above the ground raised upon railes that

have been sometime abandoned, and some mounds that were suggestive of hidden treasures of corn. Mourt says they found "two baskets of parched acorns hidden in the ground, which we supposed had been Corne when we beganne to digge the same."[1]

Finding their way back to the shore, they built a barricade of logs. Seeing their boat safely drawn up in the creek, they settled themselves for the night. About midnight they were aroused from their slumbers by a strange noise, a "great and hideous cry," whereat the sentinels gave the alarm. They turned out the guard, which meant everybody in the party. Mourt says, "So we bestirred

---

are borne up on forks they lay mats under them, and Coates of Deares skinnes otters beavers Racownes and of Beares hides, all which they have dressed and converted into good lether with the haire on for their coverings and in this manner they lye as warme as they desire."

New English Canaan, Force, vol. ii., v., p. 20.

Vide Gookin and Roger Williams, *1 Mass. Hist. Coll.*, vol. i., p. 150.

R. I. Hist. Coll., vol. i., p. 50.

As to Indian wigwams see, further, *R. I. Hist. Coll.*, vol. i., pp. 47–51; Force, vol. ii., v., pp. 19, 20; *Mass. Hist. Coll.*, vol. i., p. 149; Schoolcraft's *Indian Tribes*, etc., vol. ii., p. 63, etc.

[1] "Akornes also they dry, and in case of want of Corne, by much boyling they make a good dish of them: yea sometimes in plentie of Corne doe they eate these acornes for a noveltie."

Roger Williams, *R. I. Hist. Coll.*, vol. i., p. 90.

THE EARLY SETTLER AND THE INDIAN

ourselves and shot off a couple of Muskets, and noyse ceased."

At daylight they were up and at their devotions. Some had taken their muskets to the boat, or had dropped them on the sand under some of their extra clothing (there being but four of the party who had their weapons by them), to be in greater readiness to get away. Those who were carrying the armor to the boat, when they had returned to get their breakfast, were suddenly surprised by "a great and straynge cry," which they recognized as the same by which they had been alarmed at midnight. One of the party who was somewhat away from the barricado came running, his feet shod with fear and his lips tremulous with the cry of "Indians! Indians!" A flight of arrows cut the air,[1] while the English made a scramble to regain their muskets on the sands. The redoubtable Standish, "having a snaphance [a flint-lock] ready," made a shot at the Indians who were making a sharp encounter with those who had run to the boat, as if to prevent them from regaining their

---

[1] Johnson, in his *Wonder-working Providence* (*2 Mass. Hist. Coll.*) has this: "Now the Indians, whose dwellings are most neere the water-side, appeared with their Bowes bent and Arrowes on the string, let fly their long shafts among this little company, whom they might soon have enclosed, but the Lord otherwise disposed of it, for one Captaine Miles Standish having his fowling-peece in a redinesse, presented full at them, his shot being directed by the provident Hand of the

INDIAN WARS OF NEW ENGLAND

muskets. Successful in gaining their weapons, they opened fire from the boat. The tide of the battle was turned, at least so soon as one whom the English took to be the leader of the attacking party was wounded. The Indians faded away as silently as they had come, and Mourt says: "Wee followed them about a quarter of a mile, but wee left sixe

---

most high God, strook the stoutest sachem among them in the right arme, it being bent over his shoulder to reach an arrow forth his Quiver, as their manner is to draw them forth in fight, at this stroke they all fled with great swiftnesse through the Woods and Thickets, then the English, who more thirsted after their conversion than destruction, returned to their Bote without receiving any damage."

Mr. Dexter, in a note to Mourt's *Relation*, says that Johnson gives "no clue to his authority for this statement." Dexter questions it.

Bradford, who was an eye-witness, does not mention Standish particularly, but says, "In ye mean time, of those that were ther ready, tow muskets were discharged at them, & 2. more stood ready in ye entrance of ther randevoue, but were commanded not to shoote till they could take full aime at them."

History of Plymouth Plantation, p. 103.

"Samoset afterwards informed the Pilgrims that these were *Nauset* Indians, and that their hostility was occasioned by the fact that 'one Hunt' had previously deceived them, and stolen some of their tribe, and sold them for slaves."

Dexter's note, Mourt's *Relation*, p. 54.

The sachem Chikkataubut was the instigator of this attack. Of the graves found by the Plymouth settlers, which they opened and rifled with their usual disregard of right and

THE EARLY SETTLER AND THE INDIAN

to keepe our Shallop, for we were carefull of our business; then wee shouted all together severall times, and shot off a couple of muskets and so re-

---

decency, one contained the body of the *mother* of this sachem. Over the body was set a stake. Two large bear-skins, sewed together and hung to the stake, were spread over the ground. These were appropriated by the English and taken away. When the sachem learned of the despoiling of his mother's grave he complained to his people and demanded immediate vengeance. He was undoubtedly present at the attack at Nauset, and may have been the one who was wounded.

Drake, *Book of the Indians*, p. 44.

There is no mention of the bear-skins in Mourt's *Relation*.

We find Chikkataubut's alleged harangue to his people, whom he was inciting to attack the English, in Morton's *New English Canaan*, pp. 106, 107. Here it is:

"When last the glorious light of all the sky was underneath this globe, and the birds grew silent, I began to settle, as my custom is, to take repose. Before mine eyes were fast closed, me tho't I saw a vision, at which my spirit was much troubled, and trembling at that doleful sight, a spirit cried aloud, 'Behold! my son, whom I have cherished; see the paps that gave thee suck, the hands that clasped thee warm, and fed thee oft; canst thou forget to take revenge on those wild people, that hath my monument defaced in a despiteful manner; disdaining our ancient antiquities, and honorable customs. See now the sachem's grave lies like unto the common people, of ignoble race defaced. Thy mother doth complain, implores thy aid against this theivish people new come hither; if this be suffered, I shall not rest in quiet within my everlasting habitation.'"

See account of the desecration of this particular grave, taken from Mourt, on p. 97 of this work, *ante*.

INDIAN WARS OF NEW ENGLAND

turned: this wee did that they might see wee were not afrayed of them nor discouraged." He notes that they picked up eighteen arrows; that they were headed with "brass, others with Hartshorne, & others with Eagles' clawes."[1] Their coats, which hung in the barricado, were "shot through and through." They named the locality the place of *The First Encounter*. In the light of subsequent events, this incident may be taken as prophetic.

The settlement of new Plymouth was established. Every man built his own house, and as soon as it was ready for occupancy he left the ship and set up his household goods on shore. They had finished their storehouse, and much of their property — muskets and munitions of offence and defence — were there stored. The common house, for that was their designation of it, in some unknown

---

[1] No mention is here made of what seems to have been the commoner arrow-heads of the Indian usage. Perhaps the Cape Indians were not able to get flints for their arrow-heads so readily as the more easterly tribes. They do not mention finding the flint arrow-heads. It was a matter of skill to mount a flint-headed arrow.

See Schoolcraft, *History of Indian Tribes*, vol. iii., p. 467.

Hutchinson notes that after the English came the savages pointed their arrows with brass, fastening them to a small stick six or eight inches long, so fashioned that it could be inserted into the end of the pithy elder which they "bound round to strengthen it."

History of Massachusetts, vol. i., p. 411.
Mourt, p. 55.

THE EARLY SETTLER AND THE INDIAN

manner caught fire, but was saved. They charged it to the Indians. Two days after, on February 16, an alarm was raised by reason of one of their number seeing a party of Indians while he was out after game. A meeting of the settlement was called, and military orders were established. Miles Standish was chosen captain, and to him was given full authority in military matters.

From this, on to the same day of the following month, the savages had kept away from the Plymouth people. On that day, however, they were surprised by the unheralded advent among them of a solitary Indian, whose first word to them was, "Welcome!" Mourt says, "He very boldly came all· alone and along the houses straight to the Randevous, where we intercepted him, not suffering him to goe in, as undoubtedly he would, out of his boldness, hee saluted us in English, and bad us well-come, for he had learned some broken English amongst the Englishmen that came to fish at Monchiggon, and knew by name most of the Captaines, Commanders, & Masters, that usually come." As no improvement can be made on the relation of Mourt, his account is given verbatim. He continues his description of the great Samoset:[1] "He was a man free in speech, so farre as he could expresse his minde, and of seemly

---

[1] Samoset was the sachem of a tribe of Indians who had their habitat about the Sagadahoc River, and perhaps to the

INDIAN WARS OF NEW ENGLAND

carriage, we questioned him of many things, as he was the first *Savage* we could meete withall; He sayed he was not of these parts, but of Morathiggon [Monhegan], and one of the *Sagamores* or *Lords* thereof, and had beene 8. moneths in these parts, it lying hence a dayes sayle with a great wind, and five dayes by land; he discoursed of the whole Country, and of every Province, and of their *Sagamores*, and their number of men, and strength; the wind beginning to rise a little, we cast a horse-

---

eastward. He was a great man among his people, and a great friend of Brown, who may be regarded as the English pioneer of the Pemaquid country. He gave Brown a deed of a very extensive tract of country, which included a large part of the Pemaquid peninsula, of which in these days Bristol may be regarded the most important town. The deed was acknowledged before Abraham Shurts, who has been called the father of American conveyancing. The jurat which appears in the modern conveyance is practically, word for word, as it appears in Samoset's deed to Brown. When the Indian troubles broke out in Maine, and the cabins of the settlers were involved in one common devastation, Brown's dwelling was undisturbed. It was not long after this generous gift to Brown that Samoset disappears from local history. What became of him, or how or where he died, is involved in obscurity. He was the Chesterfield of his people, a wholehearted, great-souled savage. But perhaps one ought not to call him a savage, for he was more civilized than some of the English with whom he came in contact. He stands out among the men of his time with a marvellous distinctness. For a review of his character see Sylvester's *Pemaquid, Maine Pioneer Settlements*, vol. iv., pp. 186–196.

THE EARLY SETTLER AND THE INDIAN

man's coat about him, for he was starke naked, onely a leather about his wast, with a fringe about a span long, or little more; he had a bow & 2 arrowes, the one headed, and the other unheaded; he was a tall straight man, the haire of his head blacke, long behind, onely short before, none on his face at all; he asked some beere, but we gave him strong water, and bisket, and butter, and cheese, & pudding, and a peece of a mallard, all which he liked well, and had been acquainted with such amongst the English; he told us the place where we now live, is called, *Patuxet*,[1] and that

---

[1] "Patuxet"— elsewhere as Savage (Appendix to Winthrop, vol. ii., p. 478) gives it, "Patackost" ("Patackoset?") — is probably of a different derivation from "Pawtucket;" i.e., "at the little falls." "Petuhqui," or "Puttukque," signifying "round," is a common element in Indian nomenclature, as a preface of "rock," "hill," etc. John Smith (1616) gives the name "Accomack" as the Indian name for Plymouth shore (*3 Mass. Hist. Coll.*, vol. vi., p. 119). It undoubtedly had its name from some of the neighboring Massachusetts tribes: perhaps tribes further north or east, to whom the country around Cape Cod might have been designated as the "land beyond," or "on the other side of the bay." Cotton gives it the name of "Ompāum." What Indian he ever knew he is credited with picking up among the natives of that particular locality (*3 Mass. Hist. Coll.*, vol. ii., p. 232). Dexter suggests that the name is of later origin — that it may have been applied to the place as the capital, or great gathering-place, of the colony, signifying "place of tribute," or of "acknowledging sovereignty." These are rather fanciful derivations, which go to show how strenuously one will sometimes strive for the unattainable.

Mourt, Dexter's edition, p. 83.

INDIAN WARS OF NEW ENGLAND

about foure yeares agoe, all the Inhabitants dyed of an extraordinary plague, and there is neither man, woman, nor childe remaining, as indeed we have found none, so as there is none to hinder our possession, or to lay claime unto it; all the afternoone we spent in communication with him, we would gladly have beene rid of him at night,[1] but he was not willing to goe this night, then we thought to carry him on ship-boord, wherewith he was well content, and went into the Shallop, but the winde was high and water scant, that it could not returne backe: we lodged him that night at *Steven Hopkins* house, and watched him; the next day he went backe to the *Massasoits*, from whence he sayed he came, who are our next bordering neighbors: they are sixty strong, as he sayth."

Saturday morning following, the English gave Samoset a knife, a bracelet, and a ring, and he left them, promising to bring some of the Massasoits [Wampanoags] with some furs, as Mourt says, "to trucke with us."

---

[1] This does not lead one to infer that the spirit of hospitality was equal to the pretensions of the Plymouth settlers. They were evidently over-suspicious, else they were poor judges of character. Samoset's quiet and gentlemanly approach should have disarmed them at once. Even when he was housed under Hopkins's roof they set a watch upon him, which in any other Indian would have aroused a deep resentment. Samoset was too noble to entertain any feeling of that sort, and repaid their treatment, at best of the perfunctory sort

THE EARLY SETTLER AND THE INDIAN

Samoset came back to them the following day, and with him "five other tall proper men, they had every man a Deeres skin on him, and the principall of them had a wild Cats skin, or such like, on one arme; they had most of them long hosen up to their groynes, close made; and aboue their groynes to their wast another leather, they were altogether like *Irish*-trouses; they are of complexion like our English Gipseys, no haire or very little on their faces, on their heads long haire to their shoulders, onely cut before, some trussed up before with a feather, broad wise, like a fanne, another a fox tayle hanging out: These left, (according to our charge given before) their Bowes and Arrowes a quarter of a myle from our Towne, we gave them entertaynment as we thought was fitting them, they did eate liberally of our English victuals, they made semblance unto us of friendship and amitie; they song & danced after their maner like Anticks; they brought with them in a thing like a Bowcase (which the principall of them had about his wast) a little of their Corne pownded to Powder,

---

(the underlying motive was to use him as a go-between to the Wampanoags, that they might engage in some sort of dicker with that tribe), by making them acquainted with the great Massasoit, to whose friendship they were most deeply indebted for the opportunity to perfect their little commonwealth. This relation, in which Bradford coincides, does not show a very broad sense of humanitarianism.

which put to a little water they eate;[1] he had a little Tobacco in a bag, but none of them drunke (smoked) but when he listed, some of them had their faces paynted black, from the forehead to the chin, foure or five fingers broad; others after other fashions, as they liked; they brought three or foure skins, but we would not trucke with them at all that day (Sunday), but wished them to bring more, and we would trucke for all, which they promised within a night or two, and would leave these behind them, though we were not willing they should, and they brought us all our tooles againe which were taken in the Woods,[2] in our mens absence, so because of

---

[1] "*Nókechick*, a parch'd meal, which is a readie very wholesome food, they eate with a little water, hot or cold; I have travelled with neere 200 of them at once, neere 100 miles through the woods, every man carrying a little *Basket* of this at his *back*, and sometimes in a hollow *Leather Girdle* about his middle, sufficient for a man for three or four daies. With this ready provision, and their Bow and Arrowes, they are readie for War and travell at an houres warning. With a *spoonfull* of this *meale*, and a *spoonfull* of water from the Brooke, have I made many a good dinner and supper."
Roger Williams, *R. I. Hist. Coll.*, vol. i., p. 13.

[2] Some tools which the settlers left in the woods where they had been at work were taken by the Indians. Samoset said the Nausets, who were at the southeast of the Plymouth settlement, were ill-affected against the English. It was among these people that Thomas Hunt, master of a ship in Captain Smith's company, made his infamous kidnapping raid. These were sold as slaves in Spain. The *Brief Relation*

THE EARLY SETTLER AND THE INDIAN

the day we dismissed them so soone as we could. But *Samoset*, our first acquaintance, eyther was sicke, or fayned himselfe so, and would not goe with them, and stayed with us till Wednesday morning: Then we sent him to them, to know the reason why they came not according to their words, and we gave him a hat, a payre of stockings and shooes, a shirt, and a peece of cloth to tie about his wast."

Another interruption by the Indians occurred that same day, the savages making signs of defiance; but they disappeared when Captain Standish and another, with their muskets, appeared, along with two other of the settlers who were unarmed, who kept them company, in answer to their challenge. The following Thursday, a "very fayre warme day," about noon, Samoset, and Squanto, the only native of Patuxet,[1] made their appearance at the settlement. Squanto could

---

of the President and Council for New England states that "the friars, when it was found whence these slaves were come, took some of them and instructed them in the Christian faith. Some got over to England and proved of great service to Gorges and others."

Mass. Hist. Coll., vol. xix., p. 6; vol. xxvi., pp. 58, 61, 132.

[1] Squanto (Squantum, Tisquantum, Tasquantum) was, as Dexter says, undoubtedly one of the five Indians who were kidnapped and taken to England by Capt. George Weymouth in the mid-summer of 1605, when he left the mouth of the Sagadahoc, as he set out on his return voyage to that country.

[115]

INDIAN WARS OF NEW ENGLAND

speak English, and told the English that Massasoit "was hard by, with *Quadequina* his brother, and all their men. They could not well express in English what they would, but after an houre the

---

He (Squanto) may have come back to America and have been kidnapped a second time by Hunt. There is some confusion as to the times of these occurrences, and the narrative of his adventures is somewhat confusing.

This was his first appearance to the English. He at once assured them of his friendship and established himself as their interpreter. He was ambitious, inclined to meddle, not always veracious, and, in his relations to Hobomocko, something of an Iago. He was a born mischief-maker, a self-constituted ward-heeler in the crude politics of his race.

Mourt says he was the only remnant of the Patuxet tribe to survive the plague, which is possibly due to his being out of the country. For a time he dwelt in Cornhill, London, with Master John Slaine, merchant. This plague was somewhat extensive in its ravages. Its eastern limit was in the Kennebec wilderness. Its southern limit was Narragansett Bay. It began in 1617, and prevailed some three years. It was nearly abated in 1619. The savages, in their account of it, say the Indians died so fast "the living were not able to bury the dead." It is related that when the English came the bones were strewn upon the ground. This Squanto was a plotter, and forfeited his life in 1622 by conspiring to destroy that of Massasoit. Massasoit demanded Squanto, that he might punish him; but the English regarded him as invaluable to their interests, and protected him, thereby repudiating the second article of their treaty with Massasoit. Out of respect to the English, Massasoit would not seize the conspirator without their consent. Massasoit offered the English his beaver-skins for Squanto, and sent his own knife for the cutting off of Squanto's head and hands, which were to be

THE EARLY SETTLER AND THE INDIAN

King came to the top of an hill over against us, and had in his trayne sixtie men, that wee could well behold them, and they us: we were not willing to send our governour to them, and they [were] unwilling to come to us, so *Squanto* went againe unto him, who brought word that wee should send one to parley with [them], which we did, which was *Edward Winslow*, to know his mind, and to signifie the mind and will of our governour, which was to have trading and peece with him. We sent to the King a payre of Knives and a Copper chain, with a Iewell in it. To *Quadequina*, we sent likewise a Knife and a Iewell to hang in his eare, withall a pot of strong water,[1] a good quantitie of

---

brought to him. For some time after, Massasoit, wearied by the pretences of the English in the matter, seemed to frown on the latter, as they complained.

Squanto was the pilot in the voyage to Boston Bay in the autumn of 1621. It was he who advised robbing the Nanepashemets of the furs they offered for sale. Drake credits him with being a spy on the English in the interest of Corbitant, the Nauset sachem. If it were so, they were doubly duped when they permitted Squanto to escape his just deserts at the hands of Massasoit. The English kept their treaties when it was for their interest; when it was an indifferent matter they were great sticklers for justice. It made a difference with them whose bull was gored.

Drake's *Book of the Indians*, pp. 10, 13, 18, 21, 39.

[1] With all the fine conscience of the Pilgrims, barring the manners and customs of the times, the present of a "pot of strong water" to an unsophisticated savage, while it may

INDIAN WARS OF NEW ENGLAND

Bisket, and some butter, which were all willingly accepted: our Messenger made a speech unto him, that King James saluted him with words of love and Peace, and did accept of him as his Friend and Alie, and that our Governour desired to see him and to trucke with him, and to confirme a Peace with him, as his next neighbor: He liked well of the speech and heard it attentively, though the Interpreters did not well express it; after he had eaten and drunke himselfe, and given the rest of his company, he looked upon our messengers sword and armour which he had on, with intimation of his desire to buy it, but on the other side, our messenger showed his unwillingness to part with it: In the end he left him custodie of *Quadequina* his brother, and came over the brooke, and some twentie men following him, leaving all their Bowes and Arrowes behind them. We kept six or seven as hostages for our messenger; Captaine *Standish* and master *Williamson*[1] met the King at the brooke with a halfe a dozen Musketiers, they saluted him and he them, so one going over, the one on the one

---

have been a most hospitable act, was from the appetite for drink which not long after began to possess the Indian, and which changed his character in many respects, as well as his fortunes, not only a reprehensible but an unfortunate courtesy.

[1] The name Williamson does not appear in the list of the Pilgrims. It is probably an error. John Williams had died previous to this. Dexter regards it as a misprint.

THE EARLY SETTLER AND THE INDIAN

side, and the other on the other, conducted him to an house then in building, where we placed a greene Rugge and three or foure Cushions, then instantly came our Governour with Drumme and Trumpet after him, and some few Musketiers. After salutations, our Governour kissing his hand, the King kissed him, and so they sat downe. The Governour called for some strong water, and drunke to him, and he drunke a great draught that made him sweate all the while after, he called for a little fresh meate, which the King did eate willingly, and did give his followers. Then they treated of Peace, which was;

"1. That neyther he nor any of his should injure or doe any hurt to any of our people.

"2. And if any of his did hurt to any of ours, he should send the offender, that we might punish him.

"3. That if any of our tooles were taken away when our people were at worke, he should cause them to be restored, and if ours did any harme to any of his, wee would do the like to them.

"4. If any did unjustly warre against him, we would ayde him; If any did warre against us, he should ayde us.

"5. He should send to his neighbor Confederates to certifie them of this, that they might not wrong us, but might be likewise comprised in the conditions of Peace.

"6. That when their men came to us, they

should leave their Bowes and Arrowes behind them, as wee should doe with our Peeces when we came to them.[1]

"Lastly, that doing thus, King Iames would esteem of him as his friend and Alie: all which the King seemed to like well, and it was applauded of his followers, all the while he sat by the Governour he trembled for feare: In his person he is a very lustie man, in his best yeares an able body, grave

---

[1] Upon the application of Massasoit and his son, this "Auncient league and confederacy" was renewed by the Plymouth Court, Sept. 25 (O. S.), 1639.
Morton, *New England Memorial*, p. 112.
Plymouth Colony Records, vol. i., p. 133.

With Massasoit this was a sacred compact, and one most conscientiously adhered to and observed during his lifetime. In the year 1632 he was attacked by the Narragansett Canonicus. Captain Standish, with his English soldiers, made a summary ending of this conflict, though Massasoit expected a serious war. On this occasion he changed his name to Owsamequin.

Miantonomoh had, in some way, obtained possession of a portion of Massasoit's domains, so that the Commissioners of the United Colonies in the autumn of 1643 ordered that "Plymouth labor by all due means to restore *Woosamequin* [Massasoit] to his full liberties, in respect to any encroachments by the Nanohiggansetts, or any other natives; so that the properties of the natives may be preserved to themselves, and that no one Sagamore encroach upon the rest as of late: that *Woosamequin be reduced to those former terms and agreements between Plymouth and him.*"

Massasoit had already sold much of his lands, and prac-

THE EARLY SETTLER AND THE INDIAN

of countenance, and spare of speech: In his Attyre little or nothing differing from the rest of his followers, only in a great Chaine of white bone Beades about his necke, and at it behinde his necke, hangs a little bagg of Tobacco, which he dranke (smoked) and gave us to drinke; his face was paynted with a sad red like murry,[1] and oyled both head and face, that hee looked greasily: All his followers likewise, were in their faces, in part or in whole paynted, some blacke, some red, some yellow, and some white, some with crosses, and other Antick workes, some had skins on them,[2] and some naked, all tall strong men in appearance: so after all this was done, the Governour conducted him

---

tically all, before he died. He was living in 1662 and after the death of his son Alexander. He may have died that year. The actual time of the event is uncertain. Hutchinson follows Hubbard, giving 1656 as the year of Massasoit's decease. He is clearly in error. He was alive in 1661, when Uneko attacked one of his villages, killing some of the Wampanoags and carrying others away captive.

Records, United Colonies.
Drake's *Book of the Indians*, pp. 25–27.

[1] A dark red; *vide*, Latin, *morum*, mulberry. "A princely color."

[2] "They make shooes of Deeres skinnes, very handsomely and commodious, and of such deeres skinnes as they dress bare, they make stockings that comes within their shooes, like stirrop stockings, and is fastened above at their belt which is about their middell. . . . Those garments they always put on when they goe a hunting to keepe their skinnes from

INDIAN WARS OF NEW ENGLAND

[Massasoit] to the Brooke, and there they embraced each other and he departed."[1]

We have been thus minute in following Mourt

---

the brush of the Shrubbs, and when they have their Apparrell one, they look like Irish in their trouses, the Stockings join so to their breeches."
Morton's *New English Canaan*, Force, vol. ii., v., p. 22.

[1] It is on this part of Cape Cod that Sir Francis Drake landed in 1586. Probably Massasoit was not then born. Capt. John Smith credits Drake with giving New England its name, in his description of the country after his voyage of 1614. Massasoit makes no mention of seeing other English here before the coming of the Plymouth settler. Neither Gosnold (1602) nor Dermer's coming in 1619 seems to have any place in his recollection. Dermer says he found a place which had been inhabited, but nothing more. Massasoit's silence is inexplicable if he had met Dermer, as one would infer from the latter's letter of Dec. 27 (O. S.), 1619, to Samuel Purchas. Dermer writes: "When I arrived at my savage's (*Squanto's*) native country, (finding all dead) I travelled alongst a day's journey, to a place called *Nummastaquyt*, where finding inhabitants, I despatched a messenger a day's journey farther west, to Pocanokit, which bordereth on the sea; whence came to see me two kings, attended with a guard of 50 armed men, who being well satisfied with that my savage and I discoursed unto them, (being desirous of novelty) gave me content in whatsoever I demanded; where I found that former relations were true. Here I redeemed a Frenchman, and afterwards another at Masstachusit, who three years since escaped shipwreck at the north-east of Cape-Cod."

Drake makes this extract from Davis's notes to *Morton*. See Drake, *Book of the Indians*, p. 18.

THE EARLY SETTLER AND THE INDIAN

for the reason that in detail he is almost photographic, and as well that in his *Relation* is found the key to much that for the lack of his story would seem somewhat obscure. The hostile meetings, though unimportant, comparatively, between the English and the neighboring savages, punctuate Morton's, or Mourt's, story with a like savage suggestion. As initial movements, the records by both Mourt and Bradford are of tragic importance. In no way can one obtain so vivid a picture of the days immediately following the debarkation from the *Mayflower* as by taking their story in the original.

Massasoit had made his visit of state. He had taken away with him a good impression of the newcomers; his friendship was to become a valuable asset in their adventurous enterprise; nor did the English value it at its present worth, else they had been more hospitably forbearing. From the human point of view, the Indian, as a man, was always to be taken at a usurious discount by his English neighbors. It was a policy-game with the latter, in which the savage invariably scored a blank; a sort of rude diplomacy in which the versatile treachery of the savage was no match for steel-hardened astuteness and alert perspicuity, both of which were the logical sequences of an Anglo-Saxon heredity. From the very nature of the case, the aborigine was *doomed*.

The Plymouth people, sometime in the latter

INDIAN WARS OF NEW ENGLAND

part of June of this year, or, it may have been, in the early days of July, went to Pokonoket[1] to visit Massasoit, who received them with every manifestation of delight. Two days of Massasoit's meager fare was the limit of their endurance of savage hospitality, and they returned to Plymouth. It was about this time that a boy known as John Billington, whose father afterward was the subject of the first public execution at Plymouth, was lost in the woods. He was out after berries and lost his way, to finally become located at Nauset. Thither the English went after him. They set out from Plymouth in their shallop, and when they had come into Cummaquid [Barnstable] harbor

---

[1] "Pokonoket" ("Pakonokick," "Pawkunnawkutt," etc.), unless greatly corrupted, can be derived only from *pohkenai* or *pogkeni*, "dark," and *ohke*, "land" or "place." This is directly opposed, in its literal or primary signification, to "wampan-ohke." Eliot has, for "brightness, but . . . in darkness" (*Isa.* lix., 9), "*wompag, gut . . . pohkenahtu.*" The origin of the name is open to conjecture. "Wampan," signifying, primarily, "white" or "bright," was used figuratively for the dawn, and the region of light, "the east." *Pohkenai*, "dark," may have been, and very probably was, similarly used for the place of sunset, "the west;" though it is not found in that sense in Eliot or in Roger Williams. If so, "Pokonoket" would be the "west country" to the Plymouth tribes, as the "east country" of the Narragansetts. Or the name may be of local origin — from the color of the soil, the obscurity of the forest, or other suggestion of darkness.

Dexter's *Mourt*, p. 102, note.

THE EARLY SETTLER AND THE INDIAN

they dropped anchor.¹ Here they were met by some of the Nausets. Taking four of the savages into their shallop to be retained as hostages, they went ashore to have an interview with Iyanough, the sachem of Cummaquid, by whom they were at once joined on their further voyaging to Nauset, where the Billington boy was detained. They sent Squanto overland to Aspinet, the Nauset sachem, to demand young Billington's peremptory return. This accomplished, they returned to Cummaquid, having "established a firm peace with the Indians of that region."

It was during this voyage they learned, probably through Squanto, who in some manner was kept well-informed of the attitude of the neighboring tribes toward the English, that the Narragansetts had attacked Massasoit, killed some of the Wampanoags, and taken Massasoit away as a captive. It was about this time that Hobbomok, a chief captain of Massasoit's, and a savage of great integrity and personal bravery, attached himself to the English.²

---

¹ The expedition to Nauset was undertaken between the end of July and the middle of August.

Prince, *New England Chronicles*, vol. ii., p. 107.

² Hobbomok was a celebrated Paniese, or war-captain, also a trusted favorite of Massasoit. He is credited by the English as holding Massasoit to their interests more closely than the latter would have consented had Hobbomok been

Reaching Plymouth, they also learned that Corbitant, an inferior sachem under Massasoit, was at Namasket for the purpose of arousing the Wampanoags of that section against the English.[1] Anxious for the fate of Massasoit, Squanto and Hobbomok set out at once for Namasket. They gained the village quietly, but were discovered by Corbitant, who attacked the wigwam where they

---

otherwise disposed. It was through Hobbomok the English learned that the Massachusetts were inclined to enter into an offensive alliance with the Narragansetts against them. He as well fathomed the duplicity of Squanto, which was later more than once made apparent. He informed the people at Plymouth of Squanto's double-dealing, and Winslow writes: "Thus by degrees we began to discover Tisquantum [Squanto], whose ends were only to make himself great in the eyes of his countrymen by means of his nearnesse and favor with us, not caring who fell, so he stood."

It was Squanto who put the Plymouth settlement into great alarm with the report that the Narragansetts were coming with Massasoit to destroy the settlement. It was Hobbomok's wife who had been sent to Pokonoket privately and who there made the discovery of Squanto's plot, for which Massasoit demanded of Winslow that he deliver Squanto to him for punishment. Winslow says, "For these and like abuses, the governour sharply reproved him [Squanto], yet he was so necessary to and profitable an instrument, as at that time we could not miss him."

Drake's *Book of the Indians*, pp. 38, 39.
Winslow's *Journal*.

[1]Corbitant lived at Mettapoisett. He was much like Philip

THE EARLY SETTLER AND THE INDIAN

were lodged. Corbitant was especially incensed against Squanto by reason of his intimacy with the Plymouth people, and threatened him with his knife. While Squanto was struggling for his life Hobbomok escaped and made his way directly to Plymouth with the news that their interpreter had undoubtedly been killed by Corbitant. Standish

---

in his character and disposition,— cruel and treacherous; and he also held the English in contempt and hated them as intruders, and was ready for any enterprise which would result in their destruction or injury. He held no intimacies with them, nor wished for their friendship. He was openly discourteous when in their company, and made no pretense of concealing his enmity.

In 1621, mid-year, he was mixed up in a conspiracy with the Narragansetts to accomplish the overthrow of Massasoit. He liked not the latter's friendly intimacies with the English. He determined to get Squanto and Hobbomok out of the way, when the road would be clear to operate against Massasoit, who, though mild and equable in his disposition, was in his prime and not easily to be overborne. After the sortie upon his village by Standish and the rescue of Squanto (who was supposed later to have had some relations with Corbitant inimical to the interests of the Plymouth settlers), which was a foretaste of the energetic action likely to follow any interference with the English interests, the Nauset sachem swallowed his choler and curbed his ambition for war in so far that he made his appearance at the Plymouth settlement on September 13, the same year,— just thirty days after his capture of Squanto,— confessed his error, and made his peace.

Drake's *Book of the Indians*, p. 28.

at once made up a war party of fourteen,[1] and, setting out in the rain through the woods towards Namasket, under the guidance of Hobbomok, they broke into the Indian village in the deep of the night and made an immediate attack, searching the wigwams for Squanto, to discover him at last, uninjured. In the mêlée three of Corbitant's people were wounded. Corbitant himself succeeded in escaping. Standish, assuming that the story of the capture of Massasoit was true, notified those of the Nausets who remained in the village that if Massasoit was not returned at once, and unharmed, or if Corbitant should incite the Wampanoags to further insurrection, the English would destroy him. They very considerately took the wounded Indians with them to the Plymouth settlement, where they were soon healed and sent back to Mettapoisett.

This summary action on the part of the English had the proper effect. It was made to appear that the story of Massasoit's capture and the foray of

---

[1] Mourt gives the number of men sent on this expedition as ten: "On the morrow we set out ten men Armed."
Relation, Dexter's edition, p. 120.

Winslow says, "Whereupon it was resolved to send ye Captaine & 14 men well armed, and to goe & fall upon them in ye night."
Journal, p. 125.

After the summary disposition of Wittuwamett and Peksuot at Wessagusset, by Standish, Corbitant is lost in obscurity.

THE EARLY SETTLER AND THE INDIAN

the Narragansetts was only a rumor. Whether the sore went deeper than the surface, the touch of Standish at Nauset sufficed to sear it.[1]

The report of this incident reached the ears of the Narragansett sachem, Canonicus, who at once despatched a messenger to the English in the interests of peace. The savages were not so much intimidated by the muskets of the English as they were by the occult powers which they believed them to possess. The people at Plymouth were credited with being in collusion with evil spirits, and having the power, through their God, to bring upon the Indian any misfortune, even to their destruction, at will.[2]

---

[1] This agreement was the result of the raid on Nauset:
"September 13, Anno. Dom., 1621.

"Know all men by these presents that we, whose names are underwritten, acknowledge ourselves the loyal subjects of King James, King of Great Britain, France and Ireland, defender of the faith &c. In witness whereof we have subscribed our names and marks as followeth.

Ocquamehud,	Nattawahunt,	Quadequina,
Caunacone,	Corbitant,	Huttamoida,
Obbatinua,	Chikkatabak,	Appanow."

Drake, *Book of the Indians;* also Morton.
Bradford's *Journal.*

[2] To avert possible calamity which the English might send against them, the Massachusetts tribe and the savages of some others "got all the Powows [medicine-men and conjurors] in the country, who, for three days together, in a horrid and devilish manner did curse and execrate them [the

INDIAN WARS OF NEW ENGLAND

They remembered the plague with a singular terror; and, as well, the fact that it followed closely upon the heels of the prophecy and death of the French sailor who a few years before had unfortunately fallen into their hands, and through them was reduced to a state worse than slavery. The Plymouth people had heard much of this tribe that was situated along the shores of Boston Bay, and whose roaming-grounds extended even to the Piscataquis River; for the Massachusetts were a tribe with traditions. They were not friendly to the English, but indulged in many hostile threats which had come to the ears of the Plymouth Colony. The latter determined to explore the country; and so it happened, after the submission of Corbitant and his fellow conspirators, that in the same month of September Captain Standish, with a force of twelve white men and three Indians, Squanto being one of the latter, left Plymouth just

---

English] with their dismal conjurations, which assembly and service they held in a dark and dismal swamp. Behold how Satan labored to hinder the Gospel from coming into New England!"

Mourt's *Relation*.

In those days the settler was about as cracked over some things as was the poor savage over others. They were not unlike the savage in that to what they failed to understand they attached mysterious and supernatural qualities and powers. It was the imagination, abnormally developed, of a conscience-ridden people.

THE EARLY SETTLER AND THE INDIAN

before midnight on an ebb tide, hoping to reach Massachusetts Bay by break of the following day.[1] The light wind and their miscalculation of the distance so retarded their voyage that they did not reach Thompson's Island until late in the afternoon. At this place they dropped anchor. The following morning, early, they pulled up their anchor into the shallop and bore away toward what is now the northern part of Quincy, which came to take on the name of Massachusetts Fields, which it bore for many years. They had not only come to spy out the land, but to make friends with its people, who were then but the remnant of a once powerful tribe. The plague was here, as elsewhere.

On the edge of this plain, where that tribe had its common meeting-place, they beached their craft opposite the Squantum headland, amid a mingling of marsh and sandy shore. Here they found a little heap of lobsters which the Indians had collected, and, true to the rough traditions of the times, the voyagers from Plymouth at once forestalled the savages by making their morning meal off the succulent crustaceans. Starting on their tour inland, they met an Indian woman on her way after the lobsters. Standish had the grace, however, to tell her what had become of the lobsters, and gave her some slight token by which her

---

[1] The distance from Plymouth to Boston Harbor was, by water, about forty-four miles.

INDIAN WARS OF NEW ENGLAND

disappointment was appeased, so that she afterward showed them the way to the sachem of her people, Obbatinewat, who at once essayed to guide them up the Mystic at the other side of the bay, where they hoped to find the widow of Nanepashemet, the squaw-sachem of the Massachusetts tribe.

Finding no one at the mouth of the Mystic, they spent that night on their shallop. The following morning they in part pushed forward into the country now known as Medford and Winchester. From the chronicles of the Pilgrims one finds the date to have been October first, (N. S.), and one can imagine the glory of the autumn woods and the mellow atmosphere that kept them company. After a journey of some three or four miles they came upon an Indian village, deserted, according to the narration. A little farther on into the deepening wilderness they came upon the deserted wigwam of Nanepashemet, and in a near-by swamp his rude stockade. "In the midst of this Pallizade stood the frame of an house, wherein being dead he lay buryed."[1] Not long before the landing of the Pilgrims the Tarratines had swooped down from the Penobscot country and Nanepashemet and his tribe had paid the penalty of their isolation. Rock Hill, Medford,[2] is supposed to have been the scene

---
[1] Dexter's *Mourt's Relation*, p. 127.

[2] An Indian skeleton was exhumed in West Medford, Mass., Oct. 21, 1862, a short distance S. E. from Mystic

THE EARLY SETTLER AND THE INDIAN

of this foray upon the sachem of the Massachusetts Indians.[1]

The queen-sachem had not waited for Standish and his men; for they found only the poles of recently dismantled lodges, among which they came across a heap of corn under a mat. Coming

---

Pond, which, partly because there was with it a pipe with a copper mouthpiece, it was thought might be Nanepashemet's.
Proceedings Mass. Hist. Soc., December, 1862.

Nanepashemet is said to have been at one time the most powerful sachem of New England. He resided at Lynn until "the great war of the Taretines," in 1615. He then retreated to Medford, where he built him an house on Rock Hill. He was killed by the Tarratines in 1619.

Roger Williams, Key, etc., *R. I. Hist. Coll.*, vol. i., p. 110, says: "Nanepashemet was the Wampanoag for 'Moone God.'"

Brooks's *History of Medford*, p. 72.
Newhall's *History of Lynn*, p. 35.
Shattuck's *History of Concord*.

His [Nanepashemet's] house was not like others, but "a scaffold was largely built, with pooles and plancks some six foote from the ground, and the house upon that, being situated on the top of a hill."
Dexter's *Mourt*, p. 127.

The date of this expedition is fixed by both Bradford and Prince as Tuesday, Sept. 18-28, 1621.

[1] The sachem of the locality was Obbatinewat. He was tributary to Massasoit, though of the Massachusetts. He complained of the Tarratines, who lived to the east along the Penobscot River and were accustomed to come hither almost every year about the time of harvest and take away their

to another stockade, they sent out two of the Indians who had come along with them to show them the way, who found not far away a knot of Indian squaws about a pile of corn which they had evidently brought hither in their flight from the Standish party. Although terror-stricken at the approach of the whites, the friendliness of Standish prevailed, and the women were not long after entertaining the strangers with an appetizing repast of boiled cod and such other native delicacies as their limited larder allowed. By dint of persuasion one Indian, "shaking and trembling for feare," was induced to meet the palefaces; and, though he promised them his furs, he was silent as to the whereabouts of the queen-sachem. Squanto suggested the plundering of these confiding savages, urging, "They are a bad people, and have often threatened you!" But Standish turned a deaf ear to Squanto; and so friendly had the squaws become that they kept Standish company back to his boat, where they "sold their coats from their backs, and tied boughs about them, but with great shamefacedness, for," as the relation continues, "indeed they are more modest than some of our English

---

corn. It was on one of the incursions of the Tarratines that Nanepashemet was killed. So fearful were the Massachusetts of this section that they were continually wandering from place to place, to avoid their dreaded enemy.

Freeman, *Civilization and Barbarism*, p. 35.

THE EARLY SETTLER AND THE INDIAN

women." Before noon of the following day Standish had returned with a small stock of furs and a regret that the Plymouth Colony "had been ther seated."[1]

Allusion is here made to this first noted exploration of Boston Harbor, as the English made another visit hither some eight months later under the auspices of a London merchant, Mr. Thomas Weston, whose intercourse with the savages was not of so pacific a character as had been that of Standish.

Weston's party came down the North Shore in an open boat, possibly from Pemaquid way, in the mid-days of May, 1622. There were ten of them, and their object was the establishment of a trading-post somewhere along the coast adjacent to the Plymouth settlement, with which enterprise, commercially, Weston had been connected. His interest was wholly speculative, aroused by the glowing reports which Capt. John Smith had brought back from his numerous voyages to the New World. Smith had been in Boston Harbor, possibly. In his map of New England he had suggested its most important river, which the savages declared penetrated "many days journeys the entrails of that country." This visit of Smith's was in 1614, and according to his account of the locality the French had been here even earlier than himself, and had stripped the natives of their barter, so that he found

---

[1] Bradford's *Plimoth Plantation*, p. 105.

their stores of furs utterly depleted. After the coming of Smith other French came here to trade for furs, only to lose their ship, their scalps, and their freedom; for the savages surprised them at anchor off Pettuck's Island, burning their vessel and either killing the crew or carrying them into savage captivity. Years after, pieces of French money were found in Dorchester ground. Other French came, but left no relation of their visits. Some were shipwrecked; but the stories are mostly those of tradition.[1]

Weston accepted the Leyden exiles as a means to an end, but he profited little from his connection with the Plymouth settlement. So far as the English partners of the Plymouth interest were concerned, the venture was a financial failure, which Weston decided was due more to "weeknes of judgement, than weeknes of hands." He rather roughly informed the Plymouth folks that they had been more inclined to discourse and argumentation among themselves than to improving their opportunities for trading. He as well terminates his connection with these people, who, to him, seem to deal more in words than in any other commodity. Weston sold his interest in the Plymouth venture

---

[1] Pratt, *Relation, 4 Mass. Hist. Coll.*, vol. iv., p. 489.
Morton, *New English Canaan*, chap. 3.
Savage, *Winthrop*, vol. i., p. 59, note.
Bradford, *Plimoth Plantation*, p. 102.

THE EARLY SETTLER AND THE INDIAN

to the Merchants Adventurers Company, to evolve another scheme in which the "family" was to be eliminated, and getting together the toughest and roughest of human material for his new adventure, which was to become the initial movement for the settlement of the lands about Boston Harbor, and in the near future was to arouse the further animosity of the Indians and possibly imperil the security of the little colony at Cape Cod.

It was on the occasion of Winslow's temporizing with the messengers of Massasoit who had come to the settlement to demand the surrender of Squanto, or, in lieu of the *corpus*, his head and hands to carry back to their sachem, that a fishing-boat was discovered in the offing of the harbor. Squanto had conspired against Massasoit. His messengers were becoming importunate. Winslow was in a dilemma. If he refused to give Squanto into the custody of the messengers he was repudiating his treaty of the year before with Massasoit. If he acceded to their demands he was possibly losing an invaluable servant. The sail out on the waters of the bay was a plausible excuse for delaying his decision. It might be a party of French, and he told them he had heard rumors of designs by that nation against the English, and that the Indians were to help them. He desired them to wait; but, unable to conceal their rage and disappointment, they turned from him and disappeared into the woods to make their way back to Poko-

INDIAN WARS OF NEW ENGLAND

noket, their first mission to the English under their treaty a failure.[1] The English were punctilious in their exactions of the Indians' promises; as to their own, they did as suited their convenience. The Plymouth settlers remind one of the famous parable of the unjust steward.

The boat coming into the harbor was from Monhegan. It had come from one of Weston's fishing-vessels there engaged in taking fish about Penobscot Bay. It was in May of 1622 (O. S.) and the colony was out of provisions. They had no bread; no fish-hooks. The season for sea-fowl had passed. They were digging their sustenance from the mud of the clam-flats. Physical debilitation and increasing discouragement were the results. In this impoverished condition they were found by the crew of Weston's shallop, which had brought along seven passengers from the fleet of thirty

---

[1] Thacher, in his *History of Plymouth*, gives a very full relation of this incident, but makes no comment. See p. 46.

Drake says that the delay in acceding to the demands of Massasoit's messengers for Squanto, whom, for their respect for the English, they would not seize, "was occasioned by the appearance of a boat in the harbor which the governour *pretended* might be that of an enemy, as there had been a rumor that the French had meditated breaking up the settlement of the English in this region. This, however, was doubtless only a pretence, employed to wear out the patience of his unwelcome visitors."

Drake, *Book of the Indians*, p. 22.

THE EARLY SETTLER AND THE INDIAN

vessels about Monhegan, of which Weston's was one. The shallop from Monhegan was also short of provisions. Instead of a boat-load of stores from Weston, they got a letter from him by which they were informed that he had sold his "adventure and debts" and was "quit" of them.

Bradford writes in his *Journal:* "Amids these streighths, and ye desertion of those from whom they had hoped for supply, and when famine begane now to pinch them sore, they knowing not what to doe, the Lord, (who never fails his,) presents them with an occasion, beyond all expectation. This boat which came from ye eastward brought them a letter from a stranger, of whose name they had never heard before, being a captaine of a ship come ther a fishing."[1]

---

[1] This letter is here given for its quaint kindliness and suggestion:

"'To all his good freinds at Plimoth, these, &c.

"Freinds, cuntrimen, & neighbors: I salute you, and wish you all health & hapines in ye Lord. I make bould with these few lines to trouble you, because unless I were unhumane, I can doe no less. Bad news doth spread it selfe too farr; yet I will so farr informe you that my selfe, with many good freinds in ye south-collonie of Virginia, have received such a blow, that 400. persons large will not make good our losses. [The writer evidently refers to the massacre of the Virginia settlers.] Therefor I doe intreat you (allthough not knowing you) that ye old rule which I learned when I went to schoole, may be sufficente. That is, Hapie is he whom other mens harmes doth make to beware. And now againe and againe,

INDIAN WARS OF NEW ENGLAND

Bradford continues: "By this boat ye Govr returned a thankfull answer, as was meete, and sent a boate of their owne with them, which was piloted by them, in which M^r· Winslow was sente to procure what provissions he could of ye ships, . . . by which means he gott some good quantitie and returned in saftie."[1]

---

wishing all those y^t willingly would serve ye Lord, all health and happines in this world, and everlasting peace in ye world to come. And so I rest, Yours,

JOHN HUDLSTON."

[1] This incident has given rise to more or less controversy, by which some, having suggested that there might have been a settlement at Pemaquid anterior to the coming of the Plymouth settlers which may have furnished some store of supplies to Winslow on this occasion, have got into a "battle of the chips." It is on a par with the strenuous efforts of those who have indulged in a contest of opinion over the Weymouth expedition to the Sagadahoc. Usually the controversialist who has no certain proof of his assertions is troubled with a cocksureness that invokes ridicule. No one *knows* what occurred on Weymouth's voyage, except that he was on the New England coast, some portion of which he actually explored. Whether there was or was not a settlement at New Harbor before 1620 no one can state. So what is the use to argue, when there is no evidence either way? Your historical dilettante, whose zeal swallows up his fairness, fairly snorts his disdain at the suggestion of even a fisher-hut being on the New England coast before Plymouth. New Harbor offers much more than a probability.

Bradford is far from being obscure. He went to Pemaquid. He met Hudleston, who gave him what he could and helped

THE EARLY SETTLER AND THE INDIAN

In addition to the short commons which at that time was the common lot of the entire colony, there were indications of trouble on the part of the Indians. Massasoit had cooled somewhat in his ardor for the English after the disinclination of the latter to part with Squanto, as he was justly entitled under the treaty. News had come from Virginia of the massacre of March 27 of the current year, in which three hundred and forty-seven of the Virginia settlers had been butchered by the savages of

---

him to others who also contributed. There is no statement of Bradford's that shuts out the one or confirms the other. Here was a fishing-station. Thirty vessels were here, had been here the whole season, and were to remain until they had made up their "fares." It is not to be supposed that the decks of their vessels were large enough to accommodate their flakes. They would naturally prefer the shore, with so superior a harbor as New Harbor afforded. After 1614 the English sent considerable fleets into these waters, as many as fifty fishermen being here at once. There must have been a fishing-station here, by the very force of circumstances; and that the community had no chronicler like Mourt to paint its daily living is more its misfortune than it is its repudiation. That was Samoset's country. He had some knowledge of the English language. He liked the English "beere," and he gave Bradford the names of many English captains who came to Monhegan. He spoke of them as of his friends and familiars — an acquaintance that could come only with a continuous friendly intercourse, and perhaps intimacy. History is the opposite of unelastic. It is like a human biography: something is told; much remains to be told; and a great deal is inferred.

INDIAN WARS OF NEW ENGLAND

that region; and, alarmed for their own safety, they began immediately the erection of a fort of ample dimensions.[1] The *Fortune* had come and gone; and while their numbers had been added to, they were not particularly strengthened, from a defensive point of view. They were, too, almost on the verge of starvation.

To increase their anxiety, the month previous (it was in February, 1622, O. S.), Canonicus, the Narragansett sachem, had sent into the Plymouth settlement by one of his men a bundle of arrows tied about with a rattlesnake skin. The meaning of this episode was a mystery to the Plymouth governor until Squanto informed Winslow that it was a declaration of war on the part of the Narragansett sachem. Governor Bradford at once returned the rattlesnake skin to Canonicus filled with powder and shot, sending word to the belligerent sachem that he defied him and invited him to begin

---

[1] Immediately following the hostile message of Canonicus, Baylie says: "They also enclosed a part of the hill and made four bulwarks, or jetties, without the pale. In three of these bulwarks there were gates which were kept locked at night, and watch and ward was kept through the day. The ground which they enclosed was enough to supply a garden for each family."

Baylie's *History of New Plymouth*, p. 87.

He continues, p. 93: "They completed the fort, building it strongly of timber, with a flat roof and battlements; on this roof they mounted the ordnance, and kept constant watch."

THE EARLY SETTLER AND THE INDIAN

the conflict as soon as he pleased. The confident daring and insolence of the Plymouth messenger had the intended effect, and Canonicus was so fearful of the occult powers ascribed to the English that he refused to receive the emblem of defiance he had sent to Bradford, which, with its contents, passed from hand to hand until it had been returned to the Plymouth people. From this, on to 1635, Canonicus maintained a peaceful attitude toward the English.[1]

The *Charity* and the *Swan*, two small vessels, dropped anchor in Plymouth Harbor late in June of 1623. They came over in the interest of Thomas Weston, bringing some sixty "rude fellows" who were to colonize Wessagusset, a solitary region that bordered upon the southerly shore of Boston

---

[1] "In a grave assembly, upon a certain occasion, Canonicus thus addressed Roger Williams: 'I have never suffered any wrong to be offered to the English since they landed, nor never will. If the Englishman speak true, if he mean truly, then shall I go to my grave in peace, and hope that the English and my posterity shall live in love and peace together.'

"When Mr. Williams said he had no cause to question the Englishmen's *wunnaumwauonck*, that is, faithfulness, having long been acquainted with it, Canonicus took a stick and, breaking it into ten pieces, related ten instances wherein they had proved false; laying down a piece at each instance. Mr. Williams satisfied him that he was mistaken in some of them, and as to others he agreed to intercede with the governor, who, he doubted not, would make satisfaction for them."

Drake, *Book of the Indians*, p. 50.

Harbor. These remained at Plymouth until into August, when the preliminaries for the occupation of the site of the new colony had been completed. Leaving Plymouth (much to the relief of the settlement, for they were a boisterous set), the Weston party made their way thither under the charge of one Saunders, who had assumed the direction of Weston's enterprise upon the death of Richard Green, a brother-in-law of Weston. Weston remained in England, where he was consummating his plans for the further development of Wessagusset, which he intended should rival the Plymouth adventure. Unfortunately for all concerned, the Weston party was made up of "profligate miscreants," altogether unfit for any employment, unless it might be piracy upon the high seas.

This same month the Plymouth settlement had another visitor, the *Discovery*, which was sailed by an old acquaintance, Captain Jones, who brought the *Mayflower* over in 1620. He brought along a lading of trinkets for the Indian trade. A few days later the *Sparrow* dropped anchor at Plymouth. She had been laying in a fare of fish about Monhegan, and was one of Weston's vessels. Later, the *Sparrow* sailed for Wessagusset.

Weston's company, from the start, was a flat failure. It was without organization, leadership, or definite purpose, apparently. A short time sufficed to accomplish its complete disintegration, but not until it had involved the Plymouth settle-

THE EARLY SETTLER AND THE INDIAN

ment in a war with the Massachusetts. Some were taken sick; not a few died; and the remainder were soon so debilitated by their improvidences that they were reduced to becoming servants for the savages, who repaid their dependence upon them by plotting to rid the country about Wessagusset of their obnoxious presence. They were a lot of unscrupulous thieves who stole from the Indians whenever opportunity offered — a most degenerate lot, gathered from the scum of London docks and other trading-ports.

It was at this place the incident occurred that gave a "merry gentleman," Mr. Butler, the inspiration for some portion of his "Hudibras," a fine poetical satire on the times.[1] The lines referred to were suggested by the hanging, for the theft of another, a poor "decrepit old man that was unserviceable to the company [an old bed-ridden weaver] and burdensome to keep alive."[2]

Thomas Morton, afterward of famous Merry Mount, who was of Weston's company but who was absent at this time, charges the troubles at Wessagusset to the instigation of the Plymouth people. Morton made some observations on affairs in New England which he entitled, *New English Canaan*, in which there is something of quaint and curious information, much acerbity, some malice,

---

[1] Drake, *Book of the Indians*, p. 32.
[2] *Coll. N. H. Hist. Soc.*, vol. iii., p. 148.

and not a little stretching of the truth at times. It is a rare production, and is seldom seen except in later reprints. Drake introduces a whole chapter from Morton's work into his story of the troubles at Wessagusset, which is here given. Morton's pen is dipped in caustic at times, especially when he refers to those who interfered with his "scandalous" revelries at Merry Mount a few years later.

Morton says: "Master *Weston's* plantation being settled at Wessaguscus, his servants, many of them lazy persons, that would use no endeavor to take the benefit of the country, some of them fell sick and died.

"One amongst the rest, an able-bodied man, that ranged the woods, to see what it would afford, lighted by accident on an Indian barne, and from thence did take a cap full of corne. The salvage owner of it, finding by the foot [track] some English had been there, came to the plantation and made complaint after this manner. The chief commander on this occasion, called a Parliament of all his people, but those that were sick and ill at ease. And wisely now they must consult, upon this huge complaint, that a privy [paltry] knife or string of beads would well enough have qualified: And Edward Johnson was a special judge of this business. The fact was there in repetition, construction made, that it was fellony, and by the laws of England punished with death, and this in execution must be put for an example, and likewise to appease the

THE EARLY SETTLER AND THE INDIAN

salvage; when straightways one arose, moved as it were with some compassion, and said he could not well gainsay the former sentence; yet he had conceived, within the compass of his brain, an embrio, that was of special consequence to be delivered, and cherished, he said; that it would most amply serve to pacify the salvage's complaint, and save the life of one that might (if need be) stand them in some good stead; being young and strong, fit for resistance against an enemy, which might come unexpectedly, for any thing they knew.

"The oration made was liked of every one, and he intreated to show the means how they may be performed. Says he, you all agree that one must die, and one shall die? This young man's clothes we will take off, and put upon one that is old and impotent, a sickly person that cannot escape death; such is the disease on him confirmed, that die he must? Put the young man's clothes on this man, and let the sick person be hanged in the other's stead. Amen, says one, and so says many more. And this had like to have proved their final sentence; and being there confirmed by act of Parliament to after ages for a precedent. But the one, with a ravenous voice, begun to croak and bellow for revenge, and put by that conclusive motion; alleging such deceits might be a means hereafter to exasperate the minds of the complaining salvages, and that, by his death, the salvages should see their zeal to justice, and therefore, he should die. This was concluded; yet, nevertheless, a scruple was made; now to countermand this act did represent itself unto their minds, which was how they should do to get the man's good will: this was indeed a special obstacle: for without that (they all agreed) it would be dangerous, for any man to attempt the execution of it, lest mischief should befall them every man. He was a person that, in his wrath, did seem to be a second *Sampson*, able to beat out their brains with the jaw-bone of an ass: therefore they called the man, and by persuasion got him fast bound in jest, and then hanged him up hard by in good earnest, who, with a weapon and at liberty, would have put all these wise judges of this Parliament to a pitiful *Non Plus*, (as it hath been credibly reported,) and made the chief judge of them all buckle to him."[1]

This is an entire chapter of the *New Canaan*, which, on account of its great rarity, we have given in full. In his next chapter Mr. Morton proceeds to narrate the circumstances of the "massacre" of Wittuwamet, Peksuot, and other Massachusetts Indians, and the consequences of it. But we shall

---

[1] *New English Canaan*, 4to, Amsterdam, 1637.
Hubbard contradicts this story of Morton's. Mr. Hubbard had the account from the Plymouth people conversant with the incident, who avouched the fact that the person hanged was as guilty of stealing as any of the others, and suffered justly, for that matter. Thacher leans toward the Morton tale.
Thacher, *History of Plymouth*, p. 49.

THE EARLY SETTLER AND THE INDIAN

draw from the Plymouth historian, and afterwards use Morton's chapter as we find occasion.

Mr. Winslow says that Mr. Weston's men "knew not of this conspiracy of the Indians before his [*John Saunders*, their 'overseer'] going; neither was it known to any of us until our return from Sowaams or Puckanokick: at which time also another sachim, called Wassapinewat, brother to *Obtakiest*, the sachim of the Massachusets, who had formerly smarted for partaking with Conbatant, and fearing the like again, to purge himself, revealed the same thing [as *Massasoit* had done]."

It was now the twenty-third of March, 1623, "a yearly court day" at Plymouth, on which war was proclaimed, "in public court," against the Massachusetts Indians. "We came to this conclusion," says Winslow, "that Captain *Standish* should take so many men, as he thought sufficient to make his party good against all the Indians in the Massachusetts Bay; and as because, as all men know that have to do with them in that kind, it is impossible to deal with them upon open defiance, but to take them in such traps as they lay for others; therefore he should pretend trade as at other times: but first go to the English, at *Wessagusicus* and acquaint them with the plot, and the end of their own coming, that, comparing it with their own carriages towards them, he might better judge of the certainty of it, and more fitly take opportunity to revenge the same: but should forbare, if it were

INDIAN WARS OF NEW ENGLAND

possible, till such time as he could make sure *Wittawamet*,[1] that bloody and bold villian before spoken of; whose head he had order to bring with him, that he might be a warning and terror to all that disposition."[2]

Morton, in his story of this transaction, says: "After the ending of Parliament, (which ended in

---

[1] Wittawamet was a sachem of the Massachusetts, also Pecksuot. As to both, the locality of their residence is uncertain, if not obscure. Wittawamet was a desperately bold savage and, as well, bloodthirsty. He delighted in pouring out the blood of his enemies. No doubt, like others of his race, his deep-seated hatred of the English was born of his knowledge of the abuses put upon the savage by the white man. He was one of those who attacked the crew of the French vessel which tradition reports as having been cast away on Cape Cod. That these two sachems were in a plot to destroy the English in 1623 is not to be doubted from what occurred subsequently. There was also a plot to kill Standish, but it fell through by reason of the extreme coldness of the February night, which kept Standish awake. Massasoit had been solicited to engage in this conspiracy; but, instead of yielding to their persuasions, he directed Hobomok to reveal the plot to the English. Massasoit designated Nauset, Paomet, Succonet, Mattachiest, Manomet, Agowaywam, and the Island of Capawick as involved in this conspiracy. Massasoit advised the English through Hobomok, "without delay, to take away the principals, and the plot would cease." Wessagusset was to be attacked and destroyed first; then the Plymouth Colony.

Drake, *Book of the Indians*, p. 31.

[2] Drake's *Book of the Indians*, p. 34.

THE EARLY SETTLER AND THE INDIAN

the hanging of one,) some of the plantation there, about three persons, went to live with *Checatawbeck* and his company, and had very good quarter, for all the former quarrel with the Plimouth planters. They are not like *Will Sommers*, to take one for another." Sommers was the man who proposed the hanging of a sick man instead of the real offender. These three who had attached themselves to the Indians proposed to remain with them until the coming of Weston; but Morton charges the Plymouth people as "intending no good" to Weston's interest.[1]

---

[1] While Baylie says that much obloquy has been thrown upon the Pilgrims by reason of the manner in which this attack on the Massachusetts was carried out, and while it has been charged up to Plymouth as one of their own fictions (this conspiracy of the savages to exterminate the English, created because they did not wish Weston's colony to prosper, the condition of things being ideal among the Massachusetts and the colony itself for the ridding themselves of unwelcome neighbors, both red and white), he asserts that "any one who examines the proofs with impartiality, will be convinced of its [the conspiracy's] existence, and that the colonists were actuated neither by interest nor revenge; but only endeavored to secure their own safety by attacking those who, when their projects were matured, would have destroyed them."

Baylie, *History of New Plymouth*, p. 106.

Baylie does not go back sufficiently far. The Indians had cause to conspire, unless they were to be regarded as a wholly spiritless people, without sense or courage. The intimidating disposition of Miles Standish was not calculated

INDIAN WARS OF NEW ENGLAND

When Standish had completed his preparations for the punishment of Wittawamet, and before he had set out from Plymouth, one of Weston's men arrived from Wessaguscus, half-starved, and related to the Plymouth folks the precarious condi-

---

to conciliate the savage. Standish himself did not intend that to be the effect; for from the first the measures of the English were openly coercive. The results of hatred, suspicion, and covert reprisal were the logical conclusion. They were the only qualities to be opposed to the English aggression and dominancy. These were not the factors which would make for comity between two strange peoples anywhere, or in any time. The savage had much to avenge, and that he rebelled finally affords one something in the Indian character to admire. Standish preferred the Indian as an enemy, rather than as a friend. War was his trade, his normal condition, and the Englishman throve upon it to the ultimate extinction of the aborigine.

The English were kindly disposed toward Massasoit. Winslow played Esculapius most successfully to the sick sachem. Massasoit never forgot Winslow. But the great sachem was very needful to the English at that time. It was upon this occasion that Winslow was accompanied by the afterwards famous John Hampden, who led the Roundheads into the first struggle for the overthrow of the British monarchy, and who paid the price all patriots pay. He had come over to Plymouth and, curious to see the country about Pokonoket, he went on this visit to the Wampanoag sachem. It was this kindly ministration of Winslow, however, that led Massasoit to reveal to him, through Hobomok, the plot to destroy the Weston colony, accompanied with the wise suggestion that the people of Plymouth had better strike the first blow, or, in other words, "scotch the snake."

THE EARLY SETTLER AND THE INDIAN

tion of those he had left at the Weston settlement. He complained that the least of their troubles was being insulted by the Indians, "whose boldness increased abundantly; insomuch as the victuals they got, they [the Indians] would take it out of their pots, and eat before their faces," and upon objection from the white men they would threaten them so far as to brandish their knives in their faces.

To satisfy the savages, they were compelled to hang one of the company. He related, further, that the Weston men "had sold their clothes for corn, and were ready to starve both with cold and hunger also, because they could not endure to get their victuals by reason of their nakedness." This is rather a rugged picture of the first colony at Boston Harbor. Winslow says, upon learning this, it "gave us good encouragement to proceed in our intendments." Standish, being prepared for this movement, as has already been noted, set out the next day for Wessaguscus with Hobomok and eight Englishmen. Drake says that his taking few men shows how "a few English guns were yet feared by the Indians;" but historians, however, who write of this particular matter, accord the reason that Standish thought possibly the Indians would mistrust that he came to fight them, which might frustrate his purpose. Some other historians have credited it to Standish's alleged valor. When Standish reached Wessaguscus, he found Weston's men considerably scattered and, apparently apprehending no danger, conducting their affairs as ordinarily. When he revealed to them the danger they were in from the Indians their reply was, "They feared not the Indians, but lived, and suffered them to lodge with them, not having sword or gun, or needing the same."

Standish then informed them of the plot. This was the first intimation they had of it. Standish directed them to call in all their men, and enjoined secrecy upon them as to the punishment he intended to mete out to the savages. It would seem, however, from Winslow's *Relation*, that the Indians, in some manner, were informed of this intention of Standish. They may have mistrusted his design. It is not improbable that some of Weston's men, by reason of their having been somewhat dependent upon the Indians for their sustenance, warned the latter; or that Weston's men, doubting the existence of the plot, betrayed Standish's confidence.

After Standish arrived at Wessaguscus the Indians sent one of their men into the settlement, apparently to trade with the men from Plymouth, but undoubtedly to discover, if possible, the purpose of Standish. Alert to the situation, equally sagacious as he related the incident afterwards, he said that he "saw treachery in his [visitor's] eye, and suspected his end in coming there was discovered." The situation was strained; each party was watching the other. The Indians, not long before, had committed an overt act of hostility by

THE EARLY SETTLER AND THE INDIAN

butchering three Englishmen of Weston's party. These had taken up their residence with the natives and had been killed as they slept, in their wigwams, at the instigation, no doubt, of Chikkataubut, by whose people this triple crime was consummated.

Shortly after the coming of the first Indian to Standish, Peksuot, "who was a paniese, being a man of notable spirit," came to Hobomok, saying he understood Standish was to kill him and all the Indians in the neighborhood of Wessaguscus. Peksuot gave this message to Hobomok to be reported to Standish: "Tell him, we know it, but fear him not, neither will we shun him; but let him begin when he dares, he will not take us unawares." As a natural result of this condition of affairs, the savages made immediate preparation to meet any hostile measures Standish might take against them; and, while it would seem natural, as well, that the savages would have avoided the English at that time, they came, many of them, and frequently, into the Wessagusset settlement, and while there "would whet and sharpen the point of their knives," which sinister acts were accompanied by insulting gestures and words. Wittuwamat, especially, boasted of the excellent qualities of his knife. Drake says that on the end of the handle was pictured a woman's face. When Wittuwamat's attention was called to the picture, he said, "I have another at home, wherewith I have killed both French and English, and that one hath a man's face on it; and by and by these two must marry."

He further expressed himself in his own language, which sounded to the English like, "*Hinniam namen, Hinnaim machen, Matta Cuts.*" Wittuwamat meant to say by this, "*By and by it should see, and by and by it should eat, but not speak.*" Historians have it that Standish was a man of diminutive stature. Peksuot was a stalwart savage. As if deriding Standish for being a little man, although a great captain, he said of himself, "Though he was no sachem, yet he was a man of great strength and courage." It is creditable to Standish's self-control that he and his men were able to bear with patience these open insults of the savages. Standish's design was not to fight the Indians in a body, but to accomplish his end by getting the ringleaders of the plot into his power, after which he would most summarily execute his purpose. After more or less manœuvering he succeeded in getting Peksuot and Wittuwamat, with another man, also a youth, who was a brother to Wittuwamat, into one of the Wessagusset cabins. Opposed to these four savages were Standish and three of his soldiers. Hobomok was in the party. The door being "fast shut," Standish gave the signal. He at once attacked Peksuot, "snatching his own knife from his neck, though with much struggling, and killed him therewith, with the point thereof made as sharp as a needle, and ground on the back also to

THE EARLY SETTLER AND THE INDIAN

an edge." Wittuwamat and his fellow-savage were killed by the other white men. The youth, taken alive, was then and there hanged by the order of Standish before they left Wessaguscus.

Winslow was evidently present. He writes: "But it is incredible how many wounds these two panieses received before they died, not making any fearful noise, but catching at their weapons, and striving to the last."[1] We have noted that Hobomok was in the room at the time, although he did not appear to take any part in this mêlée, but was the rather watchful for the outcome of the fight. After it was over, he told Standish that Peksuot, the day before, had boasted to him of his own strength and stature, and had said that although Standish was a great captain, he was only a little man. Hobomok, unable to conceal his admiration of Standish, added, "I see you are big enough to lay him on the ground." Standish ordered a portion of Weston's men to kill all the Indians among them. They succeeded in killing three. Another savage was killed by the Standish party. They intended to kill every

---

[1] *Vide New English Canaan*, vol. iii.

"The Panieses are men of great courage and wisdom, and to these the Devill appeareth more familiarly than to others, and, as wee concieve, maketh covenant with them to preserve them from death by wounds with arrows, knives, hatchets, &c."

Winslow's *Relation*.

The Pilgrims evidently believed the Indian to be super-

INDIAN WARS OF NEW ENGLAND

Indian upon whom they could lay hands; but by the escape of one savage, through the negligence of one of the Weston party, their scheme was balked. The Indian who got away disclosed the hostile intention of the English to his people. Standish, with Weston's men, kept up the pursuit of the fleeing savages, who were making for a near-by rise of ground. Standish directed his party to make the hill, which they did; and the Indians, after shooting a few arrows, ran away. Hobomok threw his coat on the ground, and gave chase to the savages, in the pursuit far outstripping the English. All the advantage the English got in this foray was a shot which broke the arm of one of the savages. The Indians gained the shelter of a swamp, which ended the enterprise on the part of the English. Standish assisted the Wessaguscus settlers to get away from the place. This accomplished, on the following day the entire party returned to Plymouth. The English took along with them the head of Wittuwamat, which they set up in their fort. A part of the Weston colony remained at Plymouth permanently, and a part went with Saunders, who sailed for the fishing-stations on the Maine coast.

---

naturally endowed and assisted in his malign subtleties by the Devil.

Charlevoix describes an Indian nation he calls "*Panis*." Some told him that the *calumet* was given by the *sun* to the Panis, a Missouri nation, who when engaged in important deliberation blew the smoke of their pipes toward the sun.

THE EARLY SETTLER AND THE INDIAN

Going back to the story of the man who found his way to Plymouth and advised the Plymouth people of the condition of affairs at Wessaguscus, the Indians, suspecting the object of his departure, having in some way become cognizant of the fact, had him pursued by one of their tribe, who had his instructions to waylay him and kill him. Pratt, for that was the name of the white man, by good fortune strayed from the direct path, by reason of which the Indian missed him. Pratt afterwards settled at Charlestown, and later petitioned the General Court of Massachusetts for assistance, setting out in his narrative, "the straights and hardships that the first planters of this Colony underwent in their endeavors to plant themselves in Plymouth, and since, whereof he was one, the Court judgeth it meet to grant him 300 acres of land where it was to be had without hindering the plantation."[1] His Christian name was Phineas. The savage who followed Pratt from Wessaguscus, as he returned from Manomet, stopped on his way at Plymouth; but for all his friendly manner, which evidently was assumed for the occasion as a precaution, he was arrested and put in irons.[2] After

---

[1] At a court, 3 May, 1665, land was ordered to be laid out for *Prat* "in the wilderness on the east of Merrimack River, near the upper end of Nacook Brook, on the southeast of it." *Court Files*, State House, Boston.

[2] Drake's *Book of the Indians*, p. 37.

INDIAN WARS OF NEW ENGLAND

Standish returned from Wessaguscus the savage was asked if he could recognize the head of Wittuwamat. When it was shown him he confessed the plot and said that his sachem, Obtakiest, had been drawn into the conspiracy by the clamor of the people. He, however, denied for himself having any hand in the plot, and begged that his life might be spared, alleging that he was a stranger to the Massachusetts tribe, and that he knew nothing of their plots, or practices. It is recorded that Hobomok interceded for him, and that he was bribed to do so. The savage was spared, mainly because the Plymouth Colony wished him to carry to Obtakiest its message, in which the Plymouth people assured him the colony had not intended to engage in any warfare with the Massachusetts; nor did they do so until they were compelled by treachery. He was further admonished that they might have themselves to thank for their own overthrow. Standish directed him further to say that if the savages proceeded in this course, having reference to Obtakiest and the savages under him, "his country should not hold him." He also particularly charged his messenger to demand that the three Englishmen that were held captive should not be killed, but sent at once to Plymouth.

It was a long time before an answer was obtained to this message. Finally Obtakiest sent a squaw to the English to say that he was sorry the three Englishmen were killed; but he urged in ex-

THE EARLY SETTLER AND THE INDIAN

tenuation that this event had taken place before he received the warning of the Plymouth people; that none of his men had dared to come to Plymouth to treat of the matter, for that reason.[1] This sachem was in great fear of the English. He abandoned his place of abode, and with his people moved daily from place to place, not doubting but the English would follow him up with a vindictive reprisal for the killing of the white men. The fear of the sachem was as well imparted to the members of his tribe. Not being able to stay in one place for any length of time, or to raise any crops by which life might be sustained, a large number of them died through want. One gleans this story from Winslow's narrative. Winslow says, having in mind this incident, "It is strange to hear how many of late have, and still daily die among them, neither is there any likelihood it will easily cease, because through fear they planted little or no corn, which is the staff of life, and without which they cannot long preserve health and strength." Some of the savages, driven by their sufferings to desperation, resolved to appeal to the English governor for

---

[1] Morton, in his *New Canaan*, vol. iii., says these men who were killed went to live with Chikkataubut's people. He suggests that if the Plymouth people were really sincere in their professed good intentions toward Weston's colony at Wessagusacus they would have made certain that all the Wessagusacus settlers were out of danger before punishing the conspirators.

pardon, endeavoring to appease his anger towards them by presents. Four of these set out by water in a boat for Plymouth. Their boat was overturned on the journey and three were drowned. The other went back to his people.

When Mr. Robinson, the father of the Plymouth church, was informed how the Plymouth people had carried this particular affair with the Massachusetts, he wrote them in relation to Captain Standish. From his letter one infers that he regarded the action of Captain Standish as premature and ill-judged, if not inhuman; but he hoped the Lord had sent him (Standish) among them for a good purpose, *if they used him as they ought.* "He doubted," he said, "whether there was not wanting that feeling of tenderness of the life of man, made after God's image," which is commendable in all men, and as well that "it would have been happy if they had converted some before they killed any."

In making up a summary of the relations of the English toward the Indians two things are made clear. The one is that while the English in their earlier conflicts with the Indians came in contact with them outside the limits of their own settlements, their purpose, apparently, was not only to kill as many of the savages as they could, but as well to intimidate them to that degree that they would hesitate, as they did, to become openly aggressive—a state of affairs which lasted until Philip had obtained an assured sway over the

THE EARLY SETTLER AND THE INDIAN

Wampanoags. The other is that the white settlers, constantly increasing in numbers, found themselves somewhat circumscribed in their occupation of the country adjacent to the original settlements, and found it necessary to occupy and improve larger areas, to the exclusion and ignoring of every right of the savage to the lands of his forefathers. There was never any inclination of the English to share with the Indians any part of the civilization for which the former stood. On the other hand, the English not only coolly and premeditatedly despoiled the savage of his patrimony, but deliberately set to work to compass his destruction. The English justified their action on the ground that their right was a God-given one to exterminate the heathen, which was early crystallized into a "pious belief" that they were the messengers of a Divine Providence, through whom was to be wrought out the redemption of the land to which they had come in the interests of that religion which was the fundamental of their every code of action.

It is noticeable in the history of the occupation of the New World, both by the Spaniards and the Puritans, who were diametrically opposed in their religious tenets, that their right of dominancy over the savage native was supreme and incontrovertible. Their plea was that conversion was the primary object of this dominancy. The Spaniard gave the savage the ultimatum: the church, or annihilation. The Puritan avowed his purpose to be a most charitable one, by which the glory of God was to be vindicated by the imposing of its propaganda upon the New World savage; and in all the letters of the promoters of the earlier projects for the establishment of settlements on the New England coast the plea is for the conversion of the Indian. One notes it in various relations of Gorges; it is the burden of the great patent of the English king. The Puritan failed of his avowed object, because, once acquainted with the Indian, he saw the futility of the performance; else he was too slothful in carrying out his design. He began by antagonizing the savage; and with the whistle of the first savage arrow he had marked the men who wielded this rude weapon for the slaughter. Instead of being a Gospel-bearer, seeking the fruits of peace and good-will, he clothed himself in the garb of subtlety, and, without a spark of mercy, set himself to the acquisition of the domains of the aboriginal dwellers, and their extermination. The Puritan was worse in this respect than the Pilgrim. While the latter was no less active in committing those overt acts which could have but one result, and that to arouse suspicion and even hatred in the hearts of these children of the woods, it remained for Puritan John Mason to exemplify the Puritan creed of extinction for the heathen, when, during the Pequod War, he wiped out an entire Indian settlement in a holocaust of flame. Between six and seven hundred savages were destroyed by fire

THE EARLY SETTLER AND THE INDIAN

and sword; and like some old prophet he glorifies the destruction of these New World Amalekites in these words: "Thus was God seen in the Mount, crushing his proud enemies."

The Indian was doomed from the first. His was an alien race whose mode of living, whose habits, and whose instincts were incompatible with every demand of civilization. The savage, to the English settler, was a wild, primeval thing, as untameable as the beasts that roamed the wilderness. In many things, the savage to the settler was a mere beast of prey, a creature to be avoided. The Indian was a lover of the sun-flecked woods; a roamer of its mysteries. He lived at haphazard; he had no use for highways, fences, and clearings that grew wider with every year. His living was rude and primitive; his conceptions were not less so. He was the white man's opposite, both by tradition and living. There could, in the Puritan mind, be no amalgamation of the red race and the white. The civilizing and Christianizing of the savage were forgotten by the white man once he had experienced the savagery of the Indian's method of warfare. One recalls the message of Governor Cradock to Endicott as early as 1629: "Be not unmindful of the main end of our Plantation, by endeavoring to bring the Indians to a knowledge of the Gospel." He also reminded Endicott to keep in mind to be just and courteous to the Indians; to win their affection and their good opinion; and as well to train their offspring in "learning and religion." In this, Cradock but follows the spirit of the charter under which the Massachusetts Colony were able to establish their settlements. The Puritans, as Mr. Ellis observes, were "expected to be missionaries of the Christian Religion, and the heralds of civilization to the heathen."

The early efforts of Eliot were crowned with partial success, but he was not whole-heartedly sustained, in that while he taught the gospel of peace, the colonists belied his teaching by their acts of aggression.

With the earliest voyagers the kindness and hospitality of the New World savage have been proverbial. It was only after the numerous kidnappings along the coast that savages concealed themselves in the recesses of the wilderness, as the dun sail of the white man broke through the haze of the ocean's horizon, or sent down a shower of arrows upon their supposed enemies from some overhanging cliff. The savage was right in his later suspicion of the integrity of these strangers from over the sea; and yet, the white man resented the treatment, and made it the excuse for his subsequent reprisal.

We have alluded to the paramount right of the Indians to the soil of New England, which was disposed of by the king by patents that not only covered the New England coast, but reached out across

THE EARLY SETTLER AND THE INDIAN

the continent into the interminable wilderness westward. The English idea of the territorial rights of the aborigines, having reference to their normal life, was extremely hazy. They were able to discover none of those boundaries or lines of demarcation by which in the country from which they came the right of the individual to the realty was established. An isolated opening in the woods, which the savage used as a corn-field, but irregularly perhaps; their scattered burial-places; or a straggling village of clustered wigwams were at most the evidences of their title. The English regarded them as transients, and so treated them. With the English, the two tests of title were occupancy by prescriptive right, or use and adverse possession, and established and visible monuments by which metes and bounds were able to be ascertained. These were the prerequisites to title, the muniments of ownership of which others were bound to take cognizance, the substitutes for a more specific conveyance under seal.

Of all these the Indian was ignorant. For such, he had no use. He maintained his right by the prowess of his tribe, and as for landmark, permanent structure, or improvement, they were at the mercy of mute Nature; therefore he had neither. He went where for the time being his living was easiest to be obtained. Nature had taught the savage only too well the lesson of improvidence. A few deeds from the aborigine have been preserved. Vast areas were conveyed for some implement of metal, a coat, an old kettle, a few trinkets that glittered in the sun, or a strip of gaudily colored cloth — a mere trifle for incalculable values. These titles were more for conscience' sake than for any special value the settler attached to them. The sachem assumed to sell the land of his tribes as he chose; but, if the Indians had any title that could be conveyed, all the members of the tribe must be taken as co-partners. There was little of honesty or fairness in any of these transactions, and no one knew it better than the grantee, to whom the savage intended to convey no more than the right to occupy the land in common with himself. When the fences began to go up, and the white man ordered him off the premises thus fenced in, he knew he had shut himself out from his old hunting and fishing grounds, and he hated alike the meager paper to which he had placed his sign-manual, and the white man to whom he had given it. Massasoit had been generous of his lands; so had Philip. The Plymouth people had profited much by their generosity; but when the palings began to go up the Indian accepted them as so many affronts, which he found small difficulty in resolving into deliberate injuries. It was these, along with many other unfriendly manifestations, that spurred the savage to vengeance. When the Indian began to shun the white man may be reckoned as the beginning of those plots and conspi-

THE EARLY SETTLER AND THE INDIAN

racies that egged on the feuds between neighboring tribes, which gave occasion for conflict between the savages themselves; that set the first torch to the desolate cabin of the white settler, which was all the excuse the English wished for. The policy of the white man was to keep the neighboring tribes at war. They made their alliances with them as best suited their purpose. They were first allied against the Narragansetts, and later, with the Narragansetts, against the Pequods; then, with the Mohegans, against the Narragansetts.

The English policy with the savages was tortuous. That could have but one result; and so far as the Puritans were concerned, once engaged in a war with the savages they were hardly less savage themselves, and their hatred of the Indian was no less implacable. The war spirit prevailed in the pulpits of the times. It controlled legislative action, and it furnished inspiration for those who left the events of those early days in numerous *Relations* wherein their own treacheries and inhumanities are justified and even lauded — the acts that had avowedly the complete extermination of the Indians stamped across their faces. To the white the savage was a creature of romance and curious habit, until, upon a nearer acquaintance, the glamour was dispelled, and the white discovered the Indian to be not so different from himself — more guileless, perhaps, but less civilized. The Indian balked when the Englishman endeavored to make him amenable to the law[1] of the colony. Then came the ominous signs of unrest, and finally open hostility. But they had waited too long. Then came the night attack, the ambush, the torch, and the scalping-knife, the ultimate solution of which was to be the ridding New England of the red man.

When the General Court offered a bounty for Indian scalps, irrespective of sex or age, the climax of the Puritan malignity was reached. A letter of the Rev. Solomon Stoddard, written to Governor Dudley shortly after the Deerfield massacre, desires that the English at Northampton "may be put into ye way to hunt Indians with dogs, *as they doe bears.*" He continues: "If ye Indians were as other people are, and did manage their war fairly after ye manner of other nations, it might be looked upon as inhumane to pursue them in such a manner. But they are to be looked upon as thieves and murderers; they doe acts of hostility without proclaiming war; they don't appear openly in ye feeld to bid us battle; they use those cruelly that fall into their hands; they act like wolves and are to be dealt withall as wolves."[2]

---

[1] In July, 1631, the Court ordered: "The Sagamore of *Agawam* is banished from coming into any Englishman's house for a year, under penalty of 10 beaver skins."
Prince, p. 357.
Manasconomo was sagamore of Agawam at this time.
[2] *Mass. Hist. Coll.*, vol. iii., pp. 235-237.

THE EARLY SETTLER AND THE INDIAN

It will be remembered that the savages of Virginia had practically exterminated the settlers of that country, and that the news came to the Pilgrims when they were in great distress, and possibly in greater danger. The name "savage" was a quick terror to women and children after that, and in the hearts of the men was a stern purpose to retaliate should the occasion offer. It was slow in coming, but it was nevertheless efficacious.

If the Rev. Mr. Stoddard may be taken as standing for the sentiment of the clergy of those days, what must have been the zeal of the layman!

The drastic termination of the Weston settlement at Wessaguscus, and the summary execution of the ringleaders in the conspiracy, of which Wittuwamat and Peksuot were the star actors, rounded out the final episode in the relation of the Indian troubles with the settlers of Massachusetts Bay.

From this time to the open disaffection among the Pequods, who had their habitat to the southward, peace prevailed, with the exception of a few isolate instances of punishments inflicted by the English upon their own people, as well as upon the savages, for serious infractions of the laws of the colonies. With this survey, the situation during the first decade of the English occupancy of New England is closed.

After 1626 the number of the English was constantly increasing about Massachusetts Bay. The settlements were reaching out towards Cape Ann, while along the Connecticut and Rhode Island shores were the beginnings of other white settlements.

In 1630 the population of Plymouth was about three hundred; Salem had about the same number. Morton had his May-pole up, at Merry Mount; Endicott was at Salem; between that place and Plymouth wreathings of isolate cabin-smokes at greater or lesser intervals broke the solitude of the seashore.

The settlers were taking up the land under King James I.'s patent, often fortifying their titles by releases from the local sachems. The savages about Massachusetts Bay were apparently in a fair way of complete subjugation; and if any trouble was to be apprehended it was most likely to come from those tribes to the eastward, of which the Tarratines, a belligerent tribe along the Penobscot River, both numerous and powerful, were the most to be dreaded. The Penobscots made their excursions at the most unexpected times and seasons. Before the death of Nanepashemet they were wont to come in the fall, when the corn was ripe, to reap the harvests of the Massachusetts for them. After that the Indians about the Piscataquay River became the object of their predatory forays.[1] They

---

[1] In the year 1632, or "about that time," the Tarratines swooped down upon the Agawams with a great force of

THE EARLY SETTLER AND THE INDIAN

ravaged their corn-fields, burned their villages, and harried their women and children to seek the inmost recesses of the wilderness for safety. These borderlands were in a state of aboriginal feud; nor

---

warriors. They made an attack upon Manasconomo, the sagamore of that tribe, having for an excuse for their foray that he had treacherously killed "some of those Tarratine families."

Hubbard's *New England*, p. 145.

From another account it appears that they came against the English, who would possibly have been utterly cut off, but for one *Robin*, a friendly savage of Ipswich. The English at Ipswich numbered about thirty, and this day upon which the attack was to be made most of the men were away from home. By some means *Robin* discovered their hostile intention and went to John Perkins, to whom he revealed the danger impending over the little settlement, telling him that four Tarratines would come into the settlement on the pretense of trade. Their real purpose would be to "draw them down the hill to the water-side," when forty canoes filled with armed Tarratines would make an attack on them. It turned out as *Robin* had said; but the Indians were frightened off by an exaggerated show of numbers on the part of the English, the beating of a drum, and the noise of a few muskets.

Cobbett's *MS. Narrative*.

John Perkins was quartermaster of the settlement, "living in a little hut upon his father's island on this side of Jeofry's Neck."

MS. Narrative.

As for Manasconomo, nothing more is heard of this sagamore until 1643, when he, with Cutshamekin and squawsachem, Nashacowam and Wassamaquin [Massasoit], two

INDIAN WARS OF NEW ENGLAND

were the Tarratines averse to preying upon the unwary English settlers as late as 1631.

The year 1632 marked the wider dissemination of the settlers. Cammock was building his manor at Black Point. "Cleve driven from his Spurwink lands was sulking where the waters of Casco shimmered in the autumn sunshine; Brown and Shurts were at Pemaquid; Purchas, at Merry Meeting Bay; Vines and Bonighton were laying the foundation of Biddeford and Saco along the Saco tide waters." Hilton was planting corn on the upper waters of the Piscataquay; Mason and Gorges were planning to open up the country around Accomintas and Newichawannock; Godfrey was spying out York River for his domicile. Ancient Shawmut had become prosaic Boston, while Winthrop was directing the affairs of the Massachusetts Bay

---

sachems near the great hill to Wachusett, desired to profit by protection of the English, upon the same terms as had other neighboring sachems. "So we, causing them to understand the articles, and all the ten Commandments of God, and they freely assenting to all, they were solemnly received and presented the Court with twenty-six fathoms of wampum, and the Court gave each of them a coat of two yards of cloth, and their dinner, and to them and each of their men, a cup of *sac* at their departure; so they took leave and went away joyful."

Gookin, *MS. History of Praying Indians.*

Winthrop has a different account of this episode. *Vide* Winslow's *Journal.*

[174]

THE EARLY SETTLER AND THE INDIAN

Company at Salem. Farther to the eastward, at Pentagoët, Allerton had established a trading-house in the interest of the Plymouth people; so that a little more than a decade had sufficed to give the English the apparent dominancy of the New England coast.

The initial labors of the Plymouth settlers accomplished, it must be admitted that, in much they did, the end justified the means. Thrown upon their own resources, without friends at court, the sport of circumstances of their own creation, they were swayed by an asceticism as virile as it was ænemic. Their first thought was ever of themselves. Nor were they over-selfish, but, rather, a hardheaded, matter-of-fact people, whose strenuous practices were but faintly colored by those humanities which are the token of a great purpose. Nor were they unlike others; for they were kind to their own and considerate of the stranger within the gate, if he were not a red man, as far as their means would allow.

If there was any defect in their common polity it was this disposition to withhold from the aborigine any of the benefits which might accrue to him from closer contact with the civilization for which they themselves stood. It was an attitude at once ungenerous, reprehensible, and unchristian, for which they were to make an involuntary recompense. They had borrowed the seed from the corn-fields of the red man as the soldier of the

INDIAN WARS OF NEW ENGLAND

Low Country would have helped himself to the plunder of a vanquished enemy. They had placed their loans with the New England savage at usurious rates. The corn and the lands were to be paid for; and while the Indian kept no books of account, his memory was unimpaired and his collections would be made in defiance of the statute of limitations, which in his court was no plea in bar.

The character and habits of the Indian suggest his environment. A product of the rugged wilderness, the woods and streams — the only schooling he ever knew — were inadequate associations for a successful contention with the duplicities of the white man. Whatever of kindly virtues he possessed were the simple gifts of Nature. Whatever of haughty stoicism and ineptitude of speech, by which he was able to most successfully conceal his emotions, were the natural expression of a nature which had been moulded in difficulties and amid privations,— a nature whose traits were those of a stern, yet simple and enduring purpose.

The aborigine has been thought incapable of a kindly sympathy and affection. No one, however, will deny the savage something of kindly virtue, once one recalls the sachem of the Sagadahoc country, and that other of Pokonoket. The Indian has been the sport of the civilized annalist. He was a creature to be wantonly provoked into a futile rebellion; to become the prey of mercenary strangers;

THE EARLY SETTLER AND THE INDIAN

to be hunted like a beast of the wilderness by greedy colonists; to invite indiscriminate calumny at the hands of religious bigotry, once he had been exterminated by those whose apologists would justify the outrages of a frontier civilization. The Indian's ignorance was his weakness; his inexperience, his undoing; for, to the Puritan, he was not only a heathen, but an animate challenge to a rapacious hostility. To the Englishman, the Indian had no rights. When he was not being duped by the former he was become an object of persecution,— a creature toward whom no shred of mercy was to be extended. To the white man he was a degenerate, viciously corrupt, once he had sounded the depths of the white man's hospitality. Once an undisputed lord of the lands of his ancestors, he became an exile, or an object of sordid traffic. He saw the graves of his people robbed and defaced, and, later on, himself debauched and unscrupulously plundered. He has been called cowardly, treacherous, and cruel. Obloquy has been heaped upon his memory by the early New England historians, which has overshadowed the true character of the red man. The red man and the prejudiced annalist have long since disappeared, but the story of the red man's wrongs and wretchedness, which were the unsavory heritage of his acquaintance with the Anglo-Saxon, is writ in ruddy stains across the sun-lit glades of old Fort Mystic, as it is across the night-mists of Fairfield Swamp, the atrocities

INDIAN WARS OF NEW ENGLAND

of which the savage, in his later raids of butchery and reprisal, was never able to surpass.

It is Irving who says: "How different is virtue, clothed in purple and enthroned in state, from virtue, naked and destitute, and perishing obscurely in a wilderness!"

But the haunts of the savage have disappeared. The areas of the mighty woods that afforded him both subsistence and seclusion have given way to the spell of a new race. The streams that swept seaward, whose palpitant bosoms knew only the rough caress of the storm or the lightsome keel of the birchen canoe, have been waylaid by an alien spirit and harnessed to the ignoble tasks of men. Like the Indian whose highways they were, they have been ruthlessly shorn of their rugged virginity. Only their romance and tradition remain to the forgetfulness of a sordid utilitarianism.[1]

---

[1] The contemporary authorities on the Indians of New England are Smith, *New England* and *Generall Historie;* Bradford, *Plimouth Plantation* (Deane); Mourt, *Relation* (H. M. Dexter); Winslow, *Good Newes;* Gorges, *Briefe Narration;* Winthrop, *New England;* Higginson, *New England Plantation;* Dudley's *Letter;* Young's *Chronicles;* Johnson, *Wonderworking Providence* (*2 Mass. Hist. Coll.*, vol. ii.); Wood, *New England Prospect;* Morton, *New English Canaan;* Lechford, *Plaine Dealing* (*3 Mass. Hist. Coll.*, vol. iii.); Drake, *Book of the Indians;* Barry, *History of Massachusetts;* Eliot, *Brief Narrative;* Trumbull, *History of Connecticut.*

THE EARLY SETTLER AND THE INDIAN

The account of the Indian was to be crossed out with the knife, the torch, and the tomahawk.

In June, 1634, came the first liquidation,— the country about Hartford, Conn., was the scene of the first butchery by the Pequods. The storm was soon over, and when it cleared away the Pequods as a race had paid the penalty which all their red brethren of the wilderness were eventually to pay as the price of having been an *aborigine*.

So the Pilgrim and the Puritan wrought, side by side, in their state-building; and so they died, having reached the end of their earthly labors, in blissful ignorance of the bloody legacy they had imposed upon their posterity, to whom the scroll of the future was to be unrolled.

THE PEQUOD WAR

THE PEQUOD WAR

IN our consideration of the Pequod War it is necessary to recur to the earlier settlements of Connecticut and the first coming of the English into this part of the country. Six years before the settlement at Plymouth (1614), Block, Corstiaensen, and Mey, Dutch navigators, came into these parts upon an exploring expedition. They found themselves at the mouth of the Hudson River, where a Dutch settlement, consisting of four houses, had already been commenced on Manhattan Island. At Manhattan these navigators separated, each to sail in a different direction. Mey cruised about the southern shore of Long Island, extending his investigation as far southward as Delaware Bay, while Corstiaensen sailed in the direction of the eastern New England coast.

Block, shortly after coming to the Hudson, lost his vessel by fire; but, undiscouraged, he laid the keel of a sloop, and when he had completed it, got on board ship, to pass out through East River,[1] and

---

[1] This little vessel was the first built on the New England coast after the pinnace *Virginia* at Pemaquid. It was forty-four feet, six inches long, and had a width of beam of eleven feet, six inches. Block named his craft the *Restless*. It is presumed that he returned to Holland in it. To the passage

[183]

thence into Long Island Sound. One can imagine the low reaches of shore on either side, brilliantly green, above stretches of yellow sand, while beyond the outer edge was a vast and unexplored wilderness of woods. Keeping his course along the Sound, he came to the Connecticut coast, which hitherto had not been explored. He located the Norwalk River as that of the Archipelagoes; further on, as he came to the Hoostanic, he called it "The River of the Red Mountain." Still further eastward he found another stream, which he named Fresh River. This was the great Connecticut. Block explored this river almost to the present site of Hartford. Here he found an Indian fort surrounded by an Indian village of the tribe of the Nawaas. Retracing his voyage down the stream, he reëntered the Sound to discover and explore Narragansett Bay, which he named Nassau Bay. Here he met the Nehantics.[1] Block had discovered

---

in East River known in these days as Hell-gate, Block gave the appellation of *Hellegat*.

Hudson was here (1609), and the four houses at Manhattan were the beginnings of the Dutch at what was to be the capital of the New Netherlands.

O'Callaghan, vol. i., pp. 72, 73.

[1] The natives which Block has designated as the Nawaas in his relation of his exploration of the region about the Connecticut River cannot be located. He calls the Nehantics the "Nahicans." He describes them as of a retiring shyness; of a shy disposition.

THE PEQUOD WAR

Connecticut and Rhode Island.[1] After this the Dutch traders came here yearly. A large trade, which amounted often to 10,000 beaver-skins in a single season, besides other commodities of the country, was soon established with the natives.[2]

On the Hudson, the Dutch settlements had been superseded by the West India Company in 1621. Eleven years later (1632), Hans Eencluys, of Manhattan, purchased land from the savages at the mouth of the Connecticut and proceeded to erect the Arms of the States Governor of the Netherlands. It was known as Kievet's Hook.[3] His purpose,

---

[1] Rhode Island was called by the Indians "Acquidneck." According to Dr. Arnold, that is the spelling in the Indian deed of a portion of its territory. Block discovered this island in 1614. It was in the autumn days he sailed over these waters, and "the Leaves of the Trees and Shrubs had, as in These Days, assumed a reddish hue." He called it "der Rood Eylandt — the Red Island."

Moulton, *History of New York*, in Arnold's *Rhode Island*, vol. i., p. 70.

Hubbard, *Indian Wars*, vol. i., p. 37, note.

Rider says the origin of the name is uncertain. It was known as Acquidy.

Lands of Rhode Island, pp. 117-121.

[2] Winthrop, vol. i., p. 113.

[3] Kievet's Hook was so named from the cry of the peweets, or pewees, which were numerous in that country at that time. The Dutch call the pewee "kieveet."

DeForest, *Indians of Connecticut*, p. 71.

evidently, was to secure the trade of the Connecticut River, which was more fully carried out by Van Twiller, Governor of New Netherlands, the next year. He sent Jacob Van Curler and a party of men into the valley of the Connecticut with directions to purchase land which had been plotted previously by Van Twiller, upon which a trading-post was to be erected and fortified. The place chosen was on the Connecticut west bank at that point now covered by the city of Hartford. The Dutch recognized the title in the Indian tribes, which, however, was complicated from the fact that the Pequods claimed the country by right of conquest, its former sachem having been driven into exile.[1] Van Curler made his purchase of Wopigwooit, the Grand Sachem of the Pequods. Land by savage

---

[1] This part of the country, before its conquest by the Pequods, was ruled by a sachem who was known as Sequeen, or Sequassen. This sachem was driven into exile by the ferocious Pequods, whose sachem was Wopigwooit. Sequeen, about 1633, sold a vast tract of country about Hartford to the English, probably through William Holmes, who set up a trade near the mouth of the Farmington River, in October of that year, in the interests of the Plymouth people. For a bit of barter with the savages no adventure was too perilous.

Wopigwooit is described in the treaty with the Dutch as the chief of the Sickenames (Mystic) River, and owner of Connecticut. The Dutch were wholly for trade, hence their effort to establish their trading-post as *neutral ground.*

DeForest, *Indians of Connecticut,* p. 71.

THE PEQUOD WAR

conquest ever had an uncertain tenure; but on June 18, 1633, an agreement was entered into between the parties, and a tract of land, a Dutch mile in length along the river, that extended back into the country less than half a mile was transferred to the Dutch by the Pequods. The price was "27 ells of a kind of coarse cloth called duffals, six axes, six kettles, 18 knives, one sword-blade, one pair of shears and a few toys or trinkets." The Dutch afterwards made a way for the exiled sachem to return into the country, and he took up his residence near the Dutch trading-house. This sachem was Sequassen.[1] Sequassen afterwards disposed of a large tract of land about Hartford to the English. He afterwards became a close ally to the Narragansetts. The conveyance of this land about Hartford carried with it the right of protection to trade with all the Indians of the surrounding country. This particular territory was to be peaceful; in it the hatchet was to be forever buried; it was agreed that within its borders no savage was to molest his enemy. A small trading-fort which Van Curler erected here was armed with two pieces of cannon, and was called by him "The House of the Good Hope."

The Pequod Indians, afterwards known as the most ferocious of the local tribes, very soon established their character for treachery by breaking this

---

[1] DeForest, *Indians of Connecticut*, p. 71.

INDIAN WARS OF NEW ENGLAND

compact, which so angered the Dutch that, by way of punishment, the Pequod sachem from whom they had their conveyance, along with several of his men, were punished by death. This sachem was succeeded by Sassacus, who was fated to be the last great man of his tribe.[1] He was known as a noble and high-spirited Indian. The death of Wopigwooit was succeeded by a desultory conflict

---

[1] Hubbard says of the Pequods (gray foxes) that they were "a more cruel and warlike people than the rest of the Indians," and "a terror to all their neighbors." Though fewer in number than the Narragansetts, who bordered next upon them, they held the latter tribe in awe of their unconquerable prowess.

They held sway over all the Connecticut River savages. They had their seat of government in the immediate vicinity of New London. Drake says the first great chief of this nation was Sassacus. At the apex of his power he had many sachems under him, of whom Uncas was formerly one, and his domain extended from the Hudson River to Narragansett Bay. Long Island was also in his bailiwick. It was the manifest desire of the English in some way to circumscribe the power of this tribe, if not to annihilate it. The Pequods were a constant menace to the extending of the English colonization to the Connecticut Valley.

Roger Williams wrote Winthrop minutely how the English should proceed to accomplish this, and he accompanied his communication with a chart of the Pequod country, with its rivers, its strongholds, and villages. He recommended two Pequods (he had urged in his letter that the English "employ faithful guides") who had for three or four years lived with the "Nanhiggonticks" (Narragansetts), who knew every

THE PEQUOD WAR

between the Dutch and the Pequods, which lasted for perhaps a year or more, and by which the trading of these newcomers was somewhat interrupted. These events have been referred to as having no inconsiderable bearing upon the future relations of the Pequods to the white settler. The massacre of Stone and his crew came later, and resulted in the loss of the Dutch trade and in the Pequods inducing the English of Massachusetts Bay to settle in Connecticut—"*Quonehtacut.*"

At this time the English had been located along the Massachusetts coast some thirteen years, and their numbers, estimated at two thousand, commanded the respect of the Indians of that section, and impelled many of the smaller tribes to seek their assistance as a means of protection from the attacks of those more powerful. In 1631 Wahgin-

---

pass and forest trail through, or across, the Pequod country. The massacre of Captain Stone and his crew, and the subsequent butchery of John Oldham, gave a sufficient provocation. Nothing, however, was done at that time.

Hubbard's *Narrative*, vol. i., p. 16.
Drake, *Book of the Indians*, p. 104.
Gookin, *Coll. Mass. Hist. Soc.*, vol. i., p. 147.
Hubbard, *History of New England*, p. 33.

Dr. Increase Mather says Wequash was a Pequod sachem, but in some way dissatisfied with his people. He went to live with the Narragansetts, where he became a leading warrior under Miantonomoh.

Relation, p. 74.

INDIAN WARS OF NEW ENGLAND

acut,[1] a Podunk sachem, requested the English to send a colony into his part of the country. He appealed to Winthrop, then Governor of Massachusetts Bay, offering to provide with corn, along with eighty skins of beaver, such settlers as he might send. He suggested to Winthrop that he send two men to verify his statement as to fertility and natural resources of the country. It does not appear that Winthrop was particularly interested. Concerning this, Winthrop records in his journal that he afterwards learned that this sachem was a

---

[1] Drake says very little is known of the sachem Wahginacut, except that he lived somewhere on the Connecticut River. He came to Boston to see Winthrop; but for some reason his offer of eighty beaver-skins, yearly, and corn to meet the necessities of the English settlers he hoped to induce to colonize the Connecticut Valley did not interest the Governor of Massachusetts. From a later correspondence with the Dutch on the Connecticut, it is evident that Winthrop had taken a more than ordinary interest in the Connecticut prospect. Jack Straw came along with Wahginacut as his interpreter. "Straw," says Drake, "had lived sometime in England with Sir Walter Raleigh." How Sir Walter came by him does not satisfactorily appear. It is as obscure as many other things the Indian story-tellers state as actual happenings.

Drake, *Book of the Indians*, pp. 54, 55.
DeForest, *Indians of Connecticut*, p. 73.
Winthrop, p. 62.

Wahginacut was probably a Podunk, one of the river tribes.
DeForest, *Indians of Connecticut*, pp. 46–73.

[190]

THE PEQUOD WAR

treacherous savage, and at that time was at war with the more powerful sachem Pekoath.[1]

Wahginacut, unsuccessful with Winthrop, betook himself to the Plymouth people, with no better result, although their inclination was towards undertaking the settlement. To inspire them with the proper degree of interest in this offer, it remained for the English to learn of the immense trade in furs which the Dutch were carrying on amongst the Indians of the Connecticut Valley. Winthrop wrote to Van Twiller, making a formal protest against the Dutch settling upon the Connecticut River, for the reason that it conflicted with the New England charter. The result of this was that the Massachusetts Bay people began to send vessels to the Connecticut River, for the purpose of trading, as early as 1633. The overland trip of

---

[1] Drake, *Book of the Indians*, p. 54, note.

"He [Governor Winthrop] discovered after (*Wahginnicut* was gone,) that the said sagamore is a very treacherous man, and at war with the *Pekoath*, (a far greater sagamore.)"

Drake comments on Winthrop's ignorance, and cites another instance. Drake confesses himself unable to locate the name.

DeForest notes that at the time Connecticut had not been settled, and supposes Winthrop mistook the name of the tribe for that of a sachem. It is a suspiciously near cry to Pequot, a tribe mentioned in early colonial annals as the *Pequin*, or *Pequetan*.

Indians of Connecticut, p. 67, note.

INDIAN WARS OF NEW ENGLAND

John Oldham to the Connecticut River is a matter of history,[1] where he was entertained most hospitably and was presented with some fine beaver-skins. Oldham carried back to Boston specimens of hemp which grew wild in that section of the

---

[1] *Vide* Barry, *History of Massachusetts*, p. 220.

John Oldham was killed in the neighborhood of Block Island. The crime fell at the doors of six Narragansett sachems. Neither Canonicus nor Miantonomoh was connected with the affair.

Drake, *Book of the Indians*, p. 48.

Canonicus gave Oldham an island in Narragansett Bay on condition that he (Oldham) should dwell there. His death prevented his acceptance of the gift. This island was afterward offered to Roger Williams on the same condition, but the Pequot War prevented further consideration of the matter. The Bay colonies, not being able to get satisfaction in the matter of Oldham, made it a pretense for sending a force of ninety men into the Pequot country to punish them for Oldham's murder. This was in 1636.

Drake, *Book of the Indians*, pp. 48, 50, 58.

Oldham had been expelled from Plymouth in 1624. He then settled at Nantasket (Hull), where he was joined by Roger Conant and some others. Oldham's offence was "plotting and writing against the Colony and attempting to excite a sedition." Although banished from Plymouth, where his wife and children were allowed to remain, he came back, and the company ordered him to be punished with blows from a musket. Described as a "turbulent man, and a spy," he remained at Nantasket until 1630, when he went to Watertown, and Conant to Cape Ann.

Baylie, *History of New Plymouth*, pp. 130, 197.

THE PEQUOD WAR

country, and also the information that there were many desirable places of settlement upon which many people might be supported. Oldham reported his discoveries to the Plymouth people, and in July, 1633, Winslow and Bradford proposed to the Winthrop interests the establishment of a trading-place somewhere on the Connecticut, for the obtaining of hemp and furs. The proposition was not favorably received by Winthrop. Unfavorable reports, to which he gave a greater credence, had reached him respecting the country. Winthrop declared the Connecticut River to be controlled by tribes of warlike savages, to the number of three or four thousand; and he also objected that at the mouth of the river was a bar of such shallowness that it was navigable only at high water, and even then navigation was possible only to smaller vessels; and that, by reason of the inclemency of the winter season the ice and the unusually strong current of the stream seaward were reasons which to him were sufficient to deter any enterprise on their part in that direction.

This representation of Winthrop, instead of dismaying the Plymouth people, rather reënforced their purpose to effect a settlement in their own behalf;[1] and, the following October, a vessel was sent into the Connecticut River, with William Holmes,

---

[1] The Plymouth people were much exercised over the Dutch occupation of the Connecticut River. It had been commended

master, and a small company of men; and on the deck of the vessel was the frame of a house. Holmes entered the Connecticut without difficulty, pushed his vessel up the river past the Dutch fort at Hartford, indifferent to remonstrances or threats on the part of the Dutch garrison,[1] and proceeded to erect his trading-house in what is now Windsor, a little below the junction of the Farmington stream with

to the former as a "fine place for habitation and trade." Overtures had been made to them "by a company of Indians who had been driven out by the Pequots;" and, "being in some better situation as to their affairs, they began to send that way." These savages had been to Winthrop, but for them it had proved a bootless errand. Two years later, June, 1633, Bradford and Winslow went to Boston to interest Winthrop in preventing the Dutch from building a fort "twenty leagues" up the Connecticut. Winthrop, over-politic, declined interfering. Winthrop's policy was always to wait. He drove a better bargain with a man who had wearied under his load. Notwithstanding Winthrop's declination, the Plymouth people, in October of that same year, despatched William Holmes in a small vessel to take possession of the Connecticut country.

Barry, *History of Massachusetts, First Period*, p. 216.
Winthrop, vol. i., p. 125.
Hutchinson, vol. i., p. 148.
Hubbard, p. 170.
Trumbull, vol. i., p. 29.
Broadhead, *New York*, pp. 237, 240.

[1] Bradford says: "But y\ue Dutch begane now to repente, and hearing of their purpose & preparation, indevoured to prevente them, and gott in a little before them, and made a

THE PEQUOD WAR

the Connecticut. When Holmes returned to Plymouth he brought with him one of the sachems of

slight forte, and planted 2. peeces of ordnance, thretening to stopp their passage. But they having made a smale frame of a house ready, and haveing a great new barke, they stowed their frame in her bed [hold] & bords to cover & finish it, haveing nayles & all other provisions fitting for their use. . . . When they came up ye River to trade ye Dutch demanded what they intended & whither they would goe; . . . they bid them strike & stay, or els they would shoote them; & stood by their ordnance ready fitted. . . . So they passed along & though the Dutch sent word home to ye Monhalas what was done: & in process of time, they sent a band of aboute 70. men in warlike maner, with collors displayed, to assaulte them; but seeing them strengthened, & that it would cost blood, they came to parley & returned in peace."

Bradford, *Journal*, p. 373.

When the party under Holmes had sailed up the river as far as the Dutch fort, a slight entrenchment, the Dutch ordered them to sail down the river the way they came; but Holmes kept on up-stream, landing at the mouth of Little River, where he set up the house brought from Plymouth and fortified it with a "strong palisade." The Dutch gathered a force with the determination to dislodge Holmes; but the English showed a disposition to fight, so the Dutch, after sailing up the river and displaying the usual amount of Dutch courage, simply betook themselves down-stream, and the first English colony on the Connecticut was established.

Baylie, *History of Plymouth*, pp. 218, 219.
Winthrop, vol. i., pp. 113, 134.
Bradford, Prince's edition.
Hubbard, p. 172.
Trumbull, pp. 33, 36, 111.
Hazard, vol. ii., p. 262.

the country, who had been exiled by the Pequods.[1] By so doing a distinct affront was offered the Pequods, who held this portion of the Connecticut Valley by conquest, and who had subjugated the

---

[1] On his return voyage to Plymouth Holmes took along with him one of the sachems who had been dispossessed by the Pequots. It was of this same sachem that Holmes purchased the country about the Farmington River, thus ignoring the title of the Pequots which had before been recognized by the Dutch. Possibly he was able to drive a better trade. It was, however, a mistake on the part of Holmes. This country belonged to the Pequots by right of conquest. The validity of their title had been acknowledged by the Dutch, as it was as well confirmed by ancient custom. The savages were very punctilious in all matters of ownership, especially of boundary-lines. Between the Narragansetts and the Pequots these were most faithfully observed.

DeForest, p. 76.

It was about this time a conflict broke out between the Narragansetts and the Pequots over the right to lands between the Paucatuck River and Wecapaug Brook. This was a tract of country some ten miles wide and twice as long. Canonicus attracted to himself a number of Massachusetts sachems and, altogether, they kept up the savage broil until 1635, when the Pequots were compelled to give in their pretensions. Canonicus afterward gave this land to Sochoso, a Pequot who had espoused the cause of the former, who as well made this Pequot a chief among the Narragansetts.

Drake, *Book of the Indians*, p. 51.

Roger Williams says the Indians are "very exact and punctual in the bounds of their lands," . . . "even to a river or a brook."

THE PEQUOD WAR

savages who held the country before them.[1] The Pequods were incensed against the English because they had taken their title to this part of the country from those whom the former had vanquished in war, which, though a praiseworthy performance, could hardly be regarded as a stroke of diplomacy; but the English had preferred to recognize the original owners of the soil, and for some reason had seen fit to ignore the claims of the Pequods. Possibly the English may have regarded the Pequods as trespassers, and it may have been, by refusing to accept the rights of the Pequods to convey, they thought they might be better able to dispute the claims of the Dutch, who held their title under the Pequods. It, however, planted a germ of hostility which was later to develop into the overt act.

About this time the Connecticut coast was proving very attractive to traders, and it was in the summer of 1633 that a small vessel sailed up from Virginia to trade along the New England coast. The master of this vessel was one Captain Stone, and, like many adventurers of the times, he was of dissolute habit. He was in Massachusetts Bay for a short time, where his disorderly behavior made some trouble for the magistrates.[2] From Massa-

---

[1] Prince, *Chronicles*, pt. ii., sec. 2
New England Memorial, 1633.
DeForest, p. 76.

[2] When Stone was at Boston he was served with a process

chusetts Bay he set sail for the Connecticut River with a Captain Norton and a crew of seven. Once at the Connecticut River, Stone began his trade with the natives, who, apparently friendly, came and went, or loitered about the vessel, as their fancy happened to be. One day three of the crew were on shore after wild fowl. Stone was on his vessel, asleep in his cabin. There were some Indians on the deck, among whom was their sachem. The crew, unsuspicious of danger, were engaged in the galley. The three men on shore were attacked and killed. On the vessel the sachem brained the sleeping captain, and, at the same time, the savages who kept him company had seized the muskets of the English. One of the crew aimed a musket in his own defence. So fearful were the savages of these weapons in the hands of a white man that they dropped over the rail into the water and swam for shore. In some way a store of powder was ignited, and, exploding, destroyed the vessel

---

which he avoided by sailing for Plymouth to effect a compromise. In his dispute with the governor he lost his temper and made an effort to stab Winthrop; but was prevented by the latter's attendants. After this he went to Connecticut, accompanied by Captain Norton. Before the attack by the savages Norton had set out some powder on a table, and in the mêlée with the Pequots it became ignited. The explosion blinded Norton, so that he was easily taken advantage of and killed.

Baylie, *History of Plymouth*, p. 215.

THE PEQUOD WAR

and most of the crew. A few moments later the Indians had returned, gained the deck, and had killed those who had remained alive, after which they plundered the ship.[1] The perpetration of this attack upon Stone was charged to the Pequods, and, while it merited a swift punishment, the English passed it over with an appearance of indifference. The time was not far distant when they would have the opportunity of demanding ample satisfaction.

It is to be noted that the Pequods at this time had possibly reached the climax of their power and influence. Whether or not they were guilty in the inception, or in the actual carrying out, of this attack upon Captain Stone and his crew does not particularly matter. Their career of success on the war-path, and in the subjugation of the surrounding tribes, from this time on, seems to have been reversed. They were unable to control the Narragansetts as formerly, or even to keep them within their bounds. The sovereignty of Block Island had passed from them to the Nehantics.[2] The tribes along the upper waters of the Connecticut, encouraged by the advent of the Dutch and English

---

[1] Winthrop, vol. i., p. 123.
Stone was a West Indian of St. Christopher.

[2] Ninigret was the sachem of the Niantics, a tribe of the Narragansetts. Their habitat was Wekapaug (Westerly, R. I.). He was a cousin to Miantonomoh. He was also known

INDIAN WARS OF NEW ENGLAND

traders into the region, and perhaps instigated in some degree by the Dutch, had thrown off their allegiance to the Pequods. Wopigwooit[1] was dead — a fact which the Mohegan sachem, Uncas, undoubtedly discounted to his own advantage by engaging in rebellion. The result of the difficulties which arose between the Pequods and the Dutch resulted in a loss of a number of warriors to the former; and it as well, in a degree, broke up their intercourse with the Dutch, which was not only a loss to them in the way of trade, but also a loss of some considerable influence. This conflict between the Dutch and the Pequods continued for some time, when Sassacus made overtures to the English for their friendship and their trade.

---

as Janemo. The Niantics were supposed to have been implicated with the Pequots in the massacre of Stone and his crew.

Drake, *Book of the Indians*, pp. 60, 67.

Roger Williams, *Letters*.

[1] Wopigwooit was the father of the famous Sassacus. The Pequots did not observe the conditions of their treaty with the Dutch,— that the fort of the latter, and the lands appurtenant to it under their jurisdiction, were to be absolutely neutral; for they killed some of their savage enemies within the Dutch territory, which so incensed the latter that they killed Wopigwooit and several of his warriors. This act on the part of the Dutch was possibly the cause of the attack on Stone. It was the loss of the Dutch trade that led the Pequots to offer inducements to settle in the Connecticut Valley.

DeForest, *History of the Indians of Connecticut*, pp. 67, 73.

THE PEQUOD WAR

In October, 1634, a Pequod came into the Bay settlement. He brought the usual gifts, which he presented to Ludlow, at that time deputy-governor. He supplemented these by indicating, with two bundles of sticks, the number of beaver and other furs which the Pequods would give the English, and also proffered a considerable amount of wampum, to be delivered later. Following this, he demanded an alliance with his people on the part of the English. Ludlow accepted the message and the gifts. In return, he presented the Pequod with a coat made of moose-skin. Ludlow was not disposed to treat with this messenger, and by him sent word back to Sassacus that his respect for the English would be better shown if he sent deputies of higher rank than the one he had chosen; and he must also send a number, if he was really serious in his desire to make a treaty with the English. That would be necessary before he could treat of the matter with the authorities of the colonies.

This was in accordance with the usages of the Indians; for in sending their embassies to other tribes or nations of any importance, these honors were given to individuals who were entitled to that distinction by reason of their rank and consideration in their own tribe.

Two weeks later Ludlow was visited by two Pequod sachems, bearing another present. They were received by the deputy, and by him taken to Boston. Negotiations were opened, although in the absence of Dudley. Ludlow told the Pequods that the English desired peace with their tribe; but that it was useless to talk about a treaty or alliance with their people until the Pequods had given up the murderers of Stone and had recompensed the colony for the destruction of Stone's vessel and the plunder which they had taken from it. Neither of the sachems denied the responsibility of their nation for the crime, but based their defence upon the statement that Stone had brought the trouble upon himself and his crew by his own meddlesome conduct. They charged Stone with having taken two Indians captive, whom he conveyed to his vessel for the purpose of compelling them to show him the way up the river. They admitted killing the men ashore, who were after wild fowl, but they denied having anything to do with the destruction of the vessel or the killing of Stone. They intimated also that Sassacus might be induced to deliver up to the English two of the alleged perpetrators of this crime, provided they could be proven guilty.

This story was told by these two ambassadors with so much semblance of truth that the English, who had no evidence otherwise, were of a disposition to accept it. In the end, a treaty was agreed upon, and, being put into proper shape, was signed by both parties.[1] As usual, the English were

---

[1] This treaty hardly had been entered upon before Boston

THE PEQUOD WAR

to profit by the connection, materially; for they were to have whatever land in the valley of the Connecticut they needed, provided they would make a settlement upon the same. The Pequods were to render them all possible aid in effecting this settlement, also to surrender the perpetrators of Stone's murder whenever the English should see fit to demand them; and in addition, to pay the English forty beaver-skins, thirty otter, and four

---

was thrown into a complication of sensations by the report that a considerable force of Narragansetts, some two or three hundred in number, were at Neponset for the purpose of waylaying the Pequot messengers who had left Boston upon their return journey into their own country. The Boston citizens were armed and marched promptly to Neponset with a message from Governor Winthrop that he wished them to come to Boston for a "talk."

When the English reached Neponset they found there two sachems, accompanied by some twenty warriors, who explained their presence by saying they had been hunting, and had come to Neponset on a friendly visit to some of their acquaintances among the Neponset tribe. It matters not whether the story was true or false; they allowed the Pequots to go their way unmolested.

DeForest, p. 81

The Boston Colony undertook to establish a peace between these two tribes. They even offered to divide with the Narragansetts the wampum which the Pequots were to pay under the treaty. This was as had been agreed with the Pequots. Some authorities have offered this incident to show the eminent fairness which actuated the English.

hundred fathoms of wampum.[1] They agreed, further, to bring to the English all their furs, in consideration for which the English were to send a vessel into the Connecticut for the sole purpose of trade. They were not to be called into any conflict in which the Pequods might see fit to engage. Such was the purport of the agreement between the Pequods and the Massachusetts Bay Colony consummated in November, 1634.

---

[1] Winthrop, vol. i., pp. 147, 149.

The Plymouth settlers obtained their knowledge of wampum from the Dutch, in 1627. De Razier, a Dutch factor from New Amsterdam, came over to make the Plymouth people a visit. He was received and treated with great ceremony. Before he sailed away for Manhattan he sold them fifty pounds', sterling, worth of wampum, commercial value. For two years it remained on their hands; but afterward, from being an unsaleable commodity, it became an important medium of trade, especially with the Indians inland, who did not understand its manufacture. "*Wompompague*," says Gookin, "is made artificially of a part of the wilk's shell: the black is double the value of the white. It is made principally by the Narragansett and Long Island Indians. Upon the sandy flats and shores of those coasts, the wilk shells are found."

Roger Williams classes wampum as the Indian's money. He describes it in one of his tracts, — "One fathom of this, their stringed money, is worth five shillings. Their white money they call wampum; their black *suckawhock, suki* signifying black."

The wilk is undoubtedly the quahaug. It is a deep-sea bivalve, and not infrequently is washed in shore by the heavy storms. This description is taken from a contemporary ob-

THE PEQUOD WAR

The people of New Plymouth may be considered the first English settlers of this part of the country, although the name of Sir Richard Saltonstall and as well that of John Hampden are connected with the earliest relations of Connecticut.[1] Both Dutch and Pilgrims claimed to be the legal owners of the soil — a state of affairs that led to a commission being issued to the eldest son of Governor Winthrop, as one of the grantees under the Earl of Warwick, to enter and occupy the territory. It seemed inevitable that there should be controversy, and, as a result, the Massachusetts Colony was led later to

---

server of 1760: "In my way I had an opportunity of seeing the method of making wampum. It is made of a clam-shell; a shell consisting within of two colors, purple and white, and in form not unlike a thick oyster-shell. The process of manufacturing it is very simple. It is first clipped to a proper size which is that of a small oblong parallelopiped, then drilled, and afterwards ground to a round smooth surface and polished. The purple wampum is much more valuable than the white; a very small part of the shell being that color."

Thacher, *History of Plymouth*, p. 69.

[1] Not long after the massacre of Captain Stone a vessel belonging to Sir Richard Saltonstall came into Boston Harbor. It was on the way to Connecticut, where it was intended to plant a colony. This was furthered by Lord Say and Seal and Lord Brook under the direction of Mr. Lion Gardener, who built the fort at Saybrook.

Barry, *History of Massachusetts*, vol. i., p. 218.

Winthrop writes, 1631: "Mar. 29th, Sir Richard Saltonstall and two daughters, and one of his younger sons, (his two eldest

[205]

take definite measures in consequence of the removal of certain of its inhabitants, notably around Newtowne and Dorchester, into Connecticut. These people made their way to Mitteneag (Windsor), where Holmes had built a trading-house.

The people from Massachusetts, from time to time, had complained to Winthrop of lack of room. They had petitioned for the colony's permission to go into Connecticut, but Winthrop refused. A little later a ship of Sir Richard Saltonstall's came into Boston, which afterwards was sent up the

---

sons remained in the country,) came down to Boston, and stayed that night at the Governour's, and the next morning, by seven of the clock, accompanied by Mr. Pierce and others in two shallops, they departed to go in the ship riding to Salem."

Life and Letters of John Winthrop, p. 62.

In the latter part of May following, Saltonstall sailed for England. Palfrey says (*History of New England*, vol. i., p. 366) that he was expected to return in 1633, as he was elected an assistant at the May election.

Though Saltonstall never returned to New England, he had always the welfare of the colony at heart. He was actively engaged with Lords Brook and Say and Seal and "other Puritans" in promoting the first settlement in Connecticut. A portrait of Sir Richard Saltonstall by Rembrandt is still cherished by his descendants; but even more famous than that is the letter by him against intolerance, about the year 1650, which had in some degree the effect it was intended to have by its author.

Mass. Hist. Coll., 4th Series, vol. iii., pp. 171, 172.

Vide note to Winthrop's *Life and Letters*, p. 61.

THE PEQUOD WAR

Connecticut River "to plant at Connecticut." The Dorchester people went overland, and they had found their way to Windsor and were settled when Saltonstall's ship arrived. This was early in the year 1635.[1] In the fall they were followed by another contingent from Newtowne, of about sixty. These people in Connecticut suffered even greater privations than the Plymouth people. In the spring another reënforcement was sent out from Newtowne, and in the autumn of that year the Dorchester church was removed to Windsor. That same summer a commission was sent to John Winthrop, Jr., to treat with the Pequods who had murdered Captain Stone and his companion Captain Norton. Reference has been made to the presents which were brought to Winthrop, and the Pequods were to be informed that if they refused to make reparation for this crime their presents would be returned, accompanied with a declaration of war.

The Pequod warriors at that time were estimated at about seven hundred, and when this message from the English was received, if they ever had any friendly feelings towards the latter, it is not to be doubted that they were at once changed to those of

---

[1] Trumbull says that in August, 1635, the Indians "inhumanly murdered a Mr. Weeks and his whole family, consisting of a wife and six children, and soon after murdered the wife and children of a Mr. Williams residing near Hartford." *Indian Wars*, p. 47.

INDIAN WARS OF NEW ENGLAND

hatred and revenge. Perhaps the most tragic incident of the time was the murder of John Oldham (1636) by some of the Block Island savages. His vessel was robbed, and his two boys were taken captives.[1] Roger Williams made some inquiry into this affair, and Canonicus sent three messengers to Governor Vane with a letter in which Mr. Williams set out the particulars of this tragedy. One of these

---

[1] John Oldham was of Dorchester. This massacre was a source of much trouble between the English and the savages. The crime was discovered and punished by a trader along shore, one John Gallop. He was on his way from Connecticut to Long Island. Sailing near Mannisses, he saw Oldham's pinnace manned by sixteen savages. Alongside was a canoe with other Indians in it. It was loaded with plunder from the pinnace, and was just pushing off for the shore. Gallop knew it for Oldham's craft at once, and, changing his course, he came up with her and hailed the savages, who made no reply. His suspicions were further aroused when he discovered them armed with guns. The savages hoisted a sail on the pinnace; but, the wind and tide being off-shore, the vessel took a northward course toward the Narragansett shore. Gallop delayed no longer. He cut across the bow of the pinnace and began a discharge of duck-shot, which drove the savages under the hatches. Standing off somewhat, he put his rudder hard up and headed direct for the pinnace to ram her quarter, so she was almost overturned. Six of the savages, terrified at this strange mode of attack, went over the rail into the sea. Gallop rammed the pinnace again; but, not being able to dislodge the remaining savages, he began to pour the shot into her shell-like woodwork, so the other savages in hiding plunged into the sea, where they were drowned. Im-

THE PEQUOD WAR

savages, who was subjected to a rigid examination, confessed that "all the sachems of the Narragansetts except Canonicus and Miantonomo" were in conspiracy to accomplish Oldham's death, because he traded with the Pequods. As these two sachems were making every effort to ferret out and capture the assassins, Miantonomoh having gone to Block Island with two hundred of his warriors, further action on the part of the English was deferred, except to write to Mr. Williams for the return of the two lads who sailed with Oldham; and to Canonicus, asking him for his assistance in the arrest of the murderers. The English sent a deputation to Canonicus shortly after, to whom he denied all connection with the crime and offered his

---

mediately, Gallop and his crew of three men and two boys boarded the pinnace. The savages were captured and bound as they came on deck. Gallop, afraid that they might release themselves, threw one overboard. There were two other savages in the hold, but, being armed, and Gallop unable to reach them, he made search for Oldham, whom he found under an old sail with his head split with an axe and his legs mutilated, as if the savages had tried to cut them off. *Rigor mortis* had not set in, so recently had the murder been committed. The body was solemnly committed to the sea. Gallop carried to his own vessel the sails and such of Oldham's cargo as was left. This done, he took the pinnace in tow; but a shifty wind and a nasty sea compelled him to set her adrift with the savages still aboard. Left to her fate, the pinnace drifted upon the Narragansett shore.

Winthrop, vol. i., pp. 189, 190.

services upon "safe and wary conditions" to accomplish their arrest. The boys were reclaimed and sent to Boston.

This murder of John Oldham, in its results, was decisive. The incident had startled the English into activity; they had discovered that the Pequods were uncertain, treacherous, and not to be relied upon, and that it was unsafe for the English to settle in or adjacent to their territory. The correspondence between Governor Bradford and Winthrop is quoted from the Pilgrim governor's *Journal,* commonly known as Bradford's *History of Plimoth Plantation:*

"In ye year 1634, the Pequents (a stoute and warlike people), who had made warrs with sundry of their neigbours, and puft up with many victories, grue now at varience with ye Narigansets, a great people bordering upon them. These Narigansets held correspondance and termes of freindship with ye English of ye Massachusetts. Now ye Pequents, being conscious of ye guilte of Captain-Stones death, whom they knew to be an-English man, as also those y^t were with him, and being fallen out with ye Dutch, least they should have over many enemies at once, sought to make freindship with ye English of ye Massachusetts; and for y^t end sent both messengers & gifts unto them, as appears by some letters sent from ye Govr hither.

"'Dear & worthy S^r: &c. To let you know somwhat of our affairs, you may understand that y^e

THE PEQUOD WAR

Pequents have sent some of theirs to us, to desire our freindship, and offered much wampam & beaver, &c. The first messengers were dismissed without answer; with ye next we had diverce dayes conferance, and taking ye advice of some of our ministers, and seeking the Lord in it, we concluded a peace & freindship with them, upon these conditions: that they should deliver up to us those men who were guilty of Stones death, &c. And if we desired to plant in Conightecute, they should give up their right to us, and so we would send to trade with them as our freinds (which was ye cheefe thing we aimed at, being now in warr with ye Dutch and ye rest of their neigbours). To this they readily agreed; and that we should meadiate a peace betweene them and the Narigansets; for which end they were contente we should give the Narigansets parte of y^t presente, they would bestow on us (for they stood so much on their honour, as they would not be seen to give any thing of them selves). As for Captein Stone, they tould us ther were but 2. left of those who had any hand in his death; and that they killed him in a just quarell, for (say they) he surprised 2. of our men, and bound them, to make them by force to shew him ye way up ye river; and he with 2. other coming on shore, 9. Indeans watched him, and when they were a sleepe in ye night, they killed them, to deliver their owne men; and some of them going afterwards to ye pinass, it was suddainly blowne up.

INDIAN WARS OF NEW ENGLAND

We are now preparing to send a pinass unto them, &c.'

"In another of his, dated ye 12. of ye first month, he hath this.

"'Our pinass is latly returned from ye Pequents; they put of but litle comoditie, and found them a very false people, so as they mean to have no more to doe with them. I have diverce other things to write unto you, &c.

Yours ever assured,
Jo: Winthrop.

Boston, 12. of ye 1. month, 1634.'

"After these things, and, as I take, this year, John Oldom, (of whom much is spoken before,) being now an inhabitant of ye Massachusetts, went wth a small vessell, & slenderly mand, a trading into these south parts, and upon a quarell betweene him & ye Indeans was cutt of by them (as hath been before noted) at an iland called by ye Indeans Munisses, but since by ye English Block Iland. This, with ye former about the death of Stone, and the baffoyling of ye Pequents with ye English of ye Massachusetts, moved them to set out some to take revenge, and require satisfaction for these wrongs; but it was done so superfitially, and without their acquainting of those of Conightecute & other neigbours with ye same, as they did litle good. But their neigbours had more hurt done, for some of ye murderers of Oldome fled to ye Pequents, and though the English went to ye Pequents, and had

THE PEQUOD WAR

some parley with them, yet they did but delude them, & ye English returned without doing any thing to purpose, being frustrate of their oppertunitie by ye others deceite. After ye English were returned, the Pequents tooke their time and oppertunitie to cut of some of ye English as they passed in boats, and went on fouling, and assaulted them the next spring at their habytations, as will appear in its place. I doe but touch these things, because I make no question they will be more fully & distinctly handled by them selves, who had more exacte knowledg of them, and whom they did more properly concerne.

"This year M^r. Smith layed downe his place of ministrie, partly by his owne willingnes, as thinking it too heavie a burthen, and partly at the desire, and by ye perswasion, of others; and the church sought out for some other, having often been disappointed in their hops and desires heretofore. And it pleased the Lord to send them an able and a godly man, and of a meeke and humble spirite, sound in ye truth, and every way unreproveable in his life & conversation; whom, after some time of triall, they chose for their teacher, the fruits of whose labours they injoyed many years with much comforte, in peace, & good agreemente.

"Anno Dom: 1637.

"In ye fore parte of this year, the Pequents fell openly upon ye English at Conightecute, in ye lower parts of ye river, and slew sundry of them,

INDIAN WARS OF NEW ENGLAND

(as they were at work in ye feilds,) both men & women, to ye great terrour of ye rest; and wente away in great prid & triumph, with many high threats. They allso assalted a fort at ye rivers mouth, though strong and well defended; and though they did not there prevaile, yet it struk them with much fear & astonishmente to see their bould attempts in the face of danger; which made them in all places to stand upon their gard, and to prepare for resistance, and ernestly to solissite their freinds and confederats in ye Bay of Massachusetts to send them speedy aide, for they looked for more forcible assaults. M^r. Vane, being then Govr, write them from their Generall Courte to them hear, to joyne with them in this warr; to which they were cordially willing, but tooke opportunitie to write to them aboute some former things, as well as presente, considerable hereaboute. The which will best appear in ye Govr answer which he returned to ye same, which I shall here inserte.

"'S^r: The Lord having so disposed, as that your letters to our late Govr is fallen to my lott to make answer unto, I could have wished I might have been at freedome of time & thoughts also, that I might have done it more to your & my owne satisfaction. But what shall be wanting now you may be supplyed hereafter. For ye matters which from your selfe & counsell were propounded & objected to us, we thought not fitte to make them so publicke as ye cognizance of our Generall Courte. But as

THE PEQUOD WAR

they have been considered by those of our counsell, this answer we think fitt to returne unto you. (1) Wereas you signifie your willingnes to joyne with us in this warr against ye Pequents, though you cannot ingage your selves without ye consente of your Generall Courte, we acknowledg your good affection toward us, (which we never had cause to doubt of,) and are willing to attend your full resolution, when it may most seasonably be ripened. (2ly.) Wheras you make this warr to be our peopls, and not to conceirne your selves, otherwise then by consequence, we do in parte consente to you therin; yet we suppose, that, in case of perill, you will not stand upon such terms, as we hope we should not doe towards you; and withall we conceive that you looke at ye Pequents, and all other Indeans, as a comone enimie, who, though he may take occasion of ye begining of his rage, for some one parte of ye English, yet if he prevaile, will surly pursue his advantage, to ye rooting out of ye whole nation. Therfore when we desired your help, we did it not without respecte to your owne saftie, as ours.

"'(3ly.) Wheras you desire we should be ingaged to aide you, upon all like occasions; we are perswaded you doe not doubte of it; yet as we now deale with you as a free people, and at libertie, so as we cannot draw you into this war with us, otherwise then as reason may guid & provock you; so we desire we may be at ye like freedome, when any occasion may call for help from us. And wheras it is objected to us, that we refused to aide you against ye French; we conceive ye case was not alicke; yet we cannot wholy excuse our failing in that matter.

"'(4^ly.) Weras you objecte that we began ye warr without your privitie, & managed it contrary to your advise; the truth is, that our first intentions being only against Block Iland, and ye interprice seeming of small difficultie, we did not so much as consider of taking advice, or looking out for aide abroad. And when we had resolved upon ye Pequents, we sent presently, or not long after, to you aboute it; but ye answer received, it was not seasonable for us to chaing our counsells, excepte we had seen and waighed your grounds, which might have out wayed our owne.

"'(5^ly.) For our peoples trading at Kenebeck, we assure you (to our knowledg) it hath not been by any allowance from us; and what we have provided in this and like cases, at our laste Courte, M^r. E. W. can certifie you.

"'And (6^ly.) wheras you objecte to us y^t we should hold trade & correspondancie with ye French, your enemise; we answer, you are misinformed, for, besids some letters which hath passed betweene our late Govr and them, to which we were privie, we have neither sente nor incouraged our to trade with them; only one vessell or tow, for ye better conveace of our letters, had licens from our Govr to sayle thither.

THE PEQUOD WAR

"'Diverce other things have been privatly objected to us, by our worthy freind, wherunto he received some answer; but most of them concerning ye apprehention of peticuler discurtesis, or injueries from some perticuler persons amongst us. It concerns us not to give any other answer to them then this; that, if ye offenders shall be brought forth in a right way, we shall be ready to doe justice as ye case shall require. In the meane time, we desire you to rest assured, that such things are without our privity, and not a litle greeveous to us.

"'Now for ye joyning with us in this warr, which indeed concerns us no other wise then it may your selves, viz.: the releeving of our freinds & Christian breethren, who are now first in ye danger; though you may thinke us able to make it good without you, (as, if ye Lord please to be with us, we may,) yet 3. things we offer to your consideration, which (we conceive) may have some waight with you. (First) y^t if we should sinck under this burden, your opportunitie of seasonable help would be lost in 3 respects. 1. You cannot recover us, or secure your selves ther, with 3 times ye charge & hazard which now ye may. 2^{ly}. The sorrowes which we should lye under (if through your neglect) would much abate of ye acceptablenes of your help afterwards. 3^{ly}. Those of yours, who are now full of courage and forwardnes, would be much damped, and so less able to undergoe so great a burden. The (2.) thing is this, that it concerns us much to hasten this warr to an end before ye end of this somer, otherwise ye newes of it will discourage both your & our freinds from coming to us next year; with what further hazard & losse it may expose us unto, your selves may judge.

"'The (3.) thing is this, that if ye Lord shall please to blesse our endeavours, so as we end ye warr, or put it in a hopefull way without you, it may breed such ill thoughts in our people towards yours, as will be hard to entertaine such opinione of your good will towards us, as were fitt to be nurished among such neigbours & brethren as we are. And what ill consequences may follow, on both sids, wise men may fear, & would rather prevente then hope to redress. So with my harty salutations to your selfe, and all your counsell, and other our good freinds with you, I rest

Yours most assured in ye Lord,

Jo: Winthrop.

Boston, ye 20. of ye 3. month, 1637.'

"In ye mean time, the Pequents, espetially in ye winter before, sought to make peace with ye Narigansets, and used very pernicious arguments to move them therunto: as that ye English were stranegers and begane to everspred their countrie, and would deprive them therof in time, if they were suffered to grow & increse; and if ye Narigansets did assist ye English to subdue them, they did but make way for their owne overthrow, for if they were rooted out, the English would soone take

THE PEQUOD WAR

occasion to subjugate them; and if they would harken to them, they should not neede to fear ye strength of ye English; for they would not come to open battle with them, but fire their houses, kill their katle, and lye in ambush for them as they went abroad upon their occasions; and all this they might easily doe without any or litle danger to them selves. The which course being held, they well saw the English could not long subsiste, but they would either be starved with hunger, or be forced to forsake the countrie; with many ye like things; insomuch that ye Narigansets were once wavering, and were halfe minded to have made peace with them, and joyned against ye English. But againe when they considered, how much wrong they had received from the Pequents, and what an oppertunitie they now had by ye help of ye English to right them selves, revenge was so sweete unto them, as it prevailed above all ye rest; so they resolved to joyne with ye English against them, & did. The Courte here agreed forwith to send 50. men at their owne charg; and with as much speed as posible they could, gott them armed, and had made them ready under sufficiente leaders, and provided a barke to carrie them provisions & tend upon them for all occasions; but when they were ready to march (with a supply from ye Bay) they had word to stay, for ye enimy was as good as vanquished, and their would be no neede.

"I shall not take upon me exactly to describe

their proceedings in these things, because I expecte it all to be fully done by them selves, who best know the carrage & circumstances of things; I shall therfore but touch them in generall. From Conninghtecute (who were most sencible of ye hurt sustained, & ye present danger), they sett out a partie of men, and an other partie mett them from ye Bay, at ye Narigansets, who were to joyne with them. Y^e Narigansets were ernest to be gone before ye English were well rested and refreshte, espetially some of them which came last. It should seeme their desire was to come upon ye enemie sudenly, & undiscovered. Ther was a barke of this place, newly put in ther, which was come from Conightecutte, who did incourage them to lay hold of ye Indeans forwardnes, and to shew as great forwardnes as they, for it would incorage them, and the expedition might prove to their great advantage. And so they went on, and so ordered their march, as the Indeans brought them to a forte of ye enimies (in which most of their cheefe men were) before day. They approched ye same with great silence, and surrounded in both with English & Indeans, that they might not breake out; and so assaulted them with great courage, shooting amongst them, and entered ye forte with all speed; and those y^t first entered found sharp resistance from the enimie, who both shott at & grapled with them; others rane into their howses, & brought out fire, and sett them on fire, which soone took in their matts, &, standing

THE PEQUOD WAR

close togeather, with ye wind, all was quickly on a flame, and therby more were burnte to death then was otherwise slaine; it burnte their bow-strings, and made then unservisable. Those y^t escaped ye fire were slaine with ye sword; some hewed to peeces, others rune throw with their rapiers, so as they were quickly dispatchte, and very few escaped. It was conceived they thus destroyed about 400. at this time. It was a fearfull sight to see them thus frying in ye fyer, and ye streams of blood quenching ye same, and horrible was ye stinck & sente ther of; but ye victory seemed a sweete sacrifice, and they gave the prays therof to God, who had wrought so wonderfuly for them, thus to inclose their enimies in their hands, and give them so speedy a victory over so proud & insulting an enimie. The Narigansett Indeans, all this while, stood around aboute, but aloofe from all danger, and left ye whole execution to ye English, exept it were ye stopping of any y^t broke away, insulting over their enimies in this their ruine & miserie, when they saw them dancing in ye flames, calling them by a word in their owne language, signifing, O, brave Pequents! which they used familierly among them selves in their owne prayes, in songs of triumph after their victories. After this servis was thus happily accomplished, they marcht to the water side, wher they mett with some of their vessells, by which they had refreshing with victualls & other necessaries. But in their march ye rest of ye Pequents drew into a body, and acoasted them thinking to have some advantage against them by reason of a neck of land; but when they saw the English prepare for them, they kept a loofe, so as they neither did hurt, nor could receive any. After their refreishing & repair to geather for further counsell & directions, they resolved to pursue their victory, and follow ye warr against ye rest, but ye Narigansett Indeans most of them forsooke them, and such of them as they had with them for guids, or otherwise, they found them very could and backward in ye bussines, ether out of envie, or y^t they saw ye English would make more profite of ye victorie then they were willing they should, or els deprive them of such advantage as them selves desired by having them become tributaries unto them, or ye like. For ye rest of this bussines, I shall only relate ye same as it is in a letter which came from M^r. Winthrop to ye Govr hear, as followeth.

"'Worthy S^r: I received your loving letter, and am much provocked to express my affections towards you, but straitnes of time forbids me; for my desire is to acquainte you with the Lords great mercies towards us, in our prevailing against his & our enimies; that you may rejoyce and praise his name with us. About 80. of our men, haveing costed along towards ye Dutch plantation, (some times by water, but most by land) mett hear & ther with some Pequents, whom they slew or tooke prisoners. 2. sachems they tooke, & beheaded; and

THE PEQUOD WAR

not hearing of Sassacous, (the cheefe sachem,) they gave a prisoner his life, to go and find him out. He wente and brought them word where he was, but Sassacous, suspecting him to be a spie, after he was gone, fled away with some 20. more to ye Mowakes, so our men missed of him. Yet, deviding them selves, and ranging up & downe, as ye providence of God guided them (for ye Indeans were all gone, save 3. or 4. and they knew not whither to guid them, or els would not), upon ye 13. of this month, they light upon a great company of them, viz. 80. strong men, & 200. women & children, in a small Indean towne, fast by a hideous swamp, which they all slipped into before our men could gett to them. Our captains were not then come togeither, but ther was M^r. Ludlow and Captaine Masson, with some 10. of their men, & Captaine Patrick with some 20. or more of his, who, shooting at ye Indeans, Captaine Trask with 50. more came soone in at ye noyse. Then they gave order to surround ye swamp, it being aboute a mile aboute; but Levetenante Davenporte & some 12. more, not hearing that comand, fell into ye swamp among ye Indeans. The swamp was so thicke with shrub-woode, & so boggie with all, that some of them stuck fast, and received many shott. Levetenant Davenporte was dangerously wounded aboute his armehole, and another shott in ye head, so as, fainting, they were in great danger to have been taken by ye Indeans. But Sargante Rigges, & Jeffery, and 2. or 3. more, rescued them, and slew diverse Indeans with their swords. After they were drawne out, the Indeans desired parley, & were offered (by Thomas Stanton, our interpretour) that, if they would come out, and yeeld them selves, they should have their lives, all that had not their hands in ye English blood. Wherupon ye sachem of ye place came forth, and an old man or 2. & their wives and children, and after that some other women & children, and so they spake 2. howers, till it was night. Then Thomas Stanton was sente into them againe, to call them forth; but they said they would selle their lives their, and so shott at him so thicke as, if he had not cried out, and been presently rescued, they had slaine him. Then our men cutt of a place of ye swamp with their swords, and cooped the Indeans into so narrow a compass, as they could easier kill them throw ye thickets. So they continued all ye night, standing about 12. foote one from an other, and ye Indeans, coming close up to our men, shot their arrows so thicke, as they pierced their hatte brims, & their sleeves, & stockins, & other parts of their cloaths, yet so miraculously did the Lord preserve them as not one of them was wounded, save those 3. who rashly wente into ye swampe. When it was nere day, it grue very darke, so as those of them which were left dropt away betweene our men though they stood but 12. or 14. foote assunder; but were presently discovered, & some killed in ye pursute. Upon searching of y^e

THE PEQUOD WAR

swampe, ye next morning, they found 9. slaine, & some they pulled up, whom ye Indeans had buried in ye mire, so as they doe think that, of all this company, not 20. did escape, for they after found some who dyed in their flight of their wounds received. The prisoners were devided, some of those of ye river, and the rest to us. Of these we send ye male children to Bermuda, by M^r. William Pierce, & ye women and maid children are disposed aboute in ye townes. Ther have been now slaine & taken, in all, aboute 700. The rest are dispersed, and the Indeans in all quarters so terrified as all their freinds are afraid to receive them. 2. of ye sachems of Long Iland came to M^r. Stoughton and tendered them selves to be tributaries under our protection. And 2. of ye Nepenett sachems have been with me to seeke our freindship. Among ye prisoners we have ye wife and Children of Mononotto, a woman of a very modest countenance and behaviour. It was by her mediation that the 2. English maids were spared from death, and were kindly used by her; so that I have taken charge of her. One of her first requests was, that the English would not abuse her body, and that her children might not be taken from her. Those which were wounded were fetched of soone by John Gallop, who came with his shallop in a happie houre, to bring them victuals, and to carrie their wounded men to ye pinass, wher our cheefe surgeon was, with M^r. Willson, being aboute 8. leagues off. Our people are all in health, (ye Lord be praised,) and allthough they had marched in their armes all ye day, and had been in fight all ye night, yet the professed they found them selves so fresh as they could willingly have gone to such another bussiness.

"'"This is ye substance of that which I received, though I am forced to omite many considerable circomstances. So, being in much straitnes of time, (the ships being to departe within this 4. days, and in them the Lord Lee and M^r. Vane,) I hear breake of, and with harty saluts to, &c., I rest

Yours assured,

Jo: Winthrop.

The 28. of ye 5. month, 1637.

The capatins reporte we have slaine 13. sachems; but Sassacous & Monotto are yet living.'

"That I may make an end of this matter; this Sassacouse (ye Pequents cheefe sachem) being fled to ye Mowhakes, they cutt of his head, with some other of ye cheefe of them, whether to satisfie ye English, or rather ye Narigansets, (who, as I have since heard, hired them to doe it,) or for their owne advantage, I well know not; but thus this warr tooke end. The rest of ye Pequents were wholy driven from their place, and some of them submitted them selves to ye Narigansets, & lived under them; others of them betooke them selves to ye Monhiggs, under Uncass, their sachem, with the approbation of ye English of Conightecutt, under whose protection Uncass lived, and he and his men

THE PEQUOD WAR

had been faithful to them in this warr, & done them very good service. But this did so vexe the Narigansets, that they had not ye whole sweay over them, as they have never ceased plotting and contriving how to bring them under, and because of ye English who have protected them, they have sought to raise a generall conspiracie against ye English, as will appear in an other place."[1]

This correspondence is somewhat anticipatory. The Plymouth people and those of the Bay Colony were able to agree upon immediate action. It was as necessary that the savages in the neighborhood of the Massachusetts colonies should be checked in any aggressive design they might be willing to entertain in support of a general uprising of the savages against the English as that the Pequods about the Connecticut should be suppressed and punished. An expedition to Block Island was planned, and the volunteers to undertake the same coming in in sufficient number, they were formed into a company and fitted out for the campaign. Less than one hundred of the most resolute were placed under the direction of John Endicott, Esq., as general, by whom they were divided up into four companies under Captains Underhill and Turner. This little troop embarked in three small vessels, taking two Indians along with them as guides and

---

[1] Bradford's *History of Plimoth Plantation*, pp. 415-431. Winthrop, *Life and Letters*, p. 194.

INDIAN WARS OF NEW ENGLAND

interpreters. They were instructed to "put to death the men of Block Island, but to spare the women and children; and from thence to go to the Pequods to demand the murderers of Captain Stone and other English, and one thousand fathoms of wampum, for damages, and some of their children for hostages, which if they should refuse, they were to obtain it by force."[1] These were extraordinary powers, but the little fleet set sail, and reached Block Island about dusk a few days after, when a slight skirmish was had with the natives, and a few arrows cut the air; but under a discharge of their muskets the English landed upon the island, where they spent the next two days destroying wigwams, canoes, corn, and other property. The casualties in this unimportant conflict were all on one side. Some fourteen savages were killed, and a number of others wounded.[2] From Block Island they went to Saybrook, at the mouth of the Connecticut.

---

[1] Winthrop, vol. i., pp. 192, 193.

[2] It was almost night when Endicott made Block Island. A single savage was in sight. The shore was apparently deserted. John Underhill, "a brave soldier, though a bad man," with a dozen soldiers, pushed in shore in a shallop, to discover some sixty savages arrayed against him. They were sheltered behind a low dune, and as Underhill came within bow-shot they let fly a shower of arrows; but no one was harmed. The surf was so heavy they could not get a steady aim with their muskets, so they sprang into the water, which was hardly hip-deep. With a volley of bullets, they scrambled

THE PEQUOD WAR

They were not made particularly welcome here. Neither the English in Connecticut nor the Plymouth people regarded this movement of Winthrop's as wise. Johnson[1] declares it to have been a bootless voyage. Deaf to remonstrances of the Connecticut settlers, General Endicott was determined to carry out the instructions of his superiors at Boston. Gardener,[2] commander of the fort at

---

up the sands of the shore. Endicott had made a landing at the same moment. The savages, intimidated by the fire-arms and the appearance of so many soldiers, ran away and hid themselves in the woods.

It was now night. Posting their sentinels, they slept undisturbed. With the break of day they were exploring the island, which was of some considerable area (ten miles in length by half that in width). The woods were broken and seamed with paths or trails running in all directions, but so narrow the English were obliged to follow them in single file. After a little, they discovered two villages, altogether containing some sixty wigwams, some of which were quite large and commodious; but which were deserted.

They burned the wigwams, destroyed all the canoes, and two hundred acres of corn. They were two days on the island. The savages were so closely hidden they found but few of them. Underhill says this foray resulted in the killing of some fourteen of the savages; but Hubbard had it from the Narragansetts that but one was killed.

Underhill, *Mass. Hist. Coll.*, vol. xxxvi., p. 192.
Underhill, *Pequot War.*
Winthrop's *Journal*, vol. i., pp. 192, 194.

[1] *Wonder-working Providence.*
[2] Gardener, who was in command at Saybrook, criticized

INDIAN WARS OF NEW ENGLAND

Saybrook, fitted him out with boats and men,[1] and with five vessels they entered the Pequod River (now the Thames), where they held a conference with the savages.[2] The explanations of the savages not being satisfactory, the troops landed and began their work of devastation, which was similar to that committed at Block Island.[3] Gardener makes note that after this was accomplished the Boston party left his [Gardener's] men "to shift for themselves,"

---

this Block Island incursion severely. He told Endicott, "You have come to raise a nest of wasps about our ears, and then you will flee away." He says in his *Pequod Warres*, "As they [Endicott and his men] came without our knowledge, so went they away against our will."

Mass. Hist. Coll., vol. xxxiii., p. 140.

Gardener's *Pequod Warres*, p. 12.

It was Gardener who said, "War is like a three-legged stool,— want one foot, and down comes all."

Gardener's *Pequod Warres*, p. 10.

[1] *Ibid*, p. 16.

[2] This conference ended in a fight. Gardener says: "The Bay-men killed not a man, save that one, *Kichomiquim* [Cutshamequin], an Indian Sachem of the Bay, killed a Pequit; and thus began the war between the Indians and us in these parts."

Ibid, p. 18.

Cutshamequin came along with Endicott from Massachusetts.

Gardener, *Mass. Hist. Coll.*, vol. xxxiii., p. 144.

[3] For particular accounts of this expedition, *vide*, Gardener and Underhill in the *Mass. Hist. Coll.;* also Winthrop, vol. i., pp. 194, 197.

THE PEQUOD WAR

and he remarks that it was "a marvellous providence of God, that not a hair fell from the head of any of them, nor any sick or feeble person among them."[1]

The Pequods and the Narragansetts had always been at feud, but reports began to reach the Boston Colony that the Pequods had made a truce with the Narragansetts, and were trying to induce them, through the argument of self-preservation, to join in a movement to exterminate the English. The Massachusetts colonists were aroused to a keen sense of their danger, and realized that their only hope in the way of preserving peace was through the intercession of Roger Williams, whose influence with the Narragansetts was possibly greater than that of any other Englishman. They were in a dilemma here. Roger Williams, on account of his religious belief, had been expelled from the Massachusetts Colony. His sentence was practically one of banishment, and the question arose whether or not, under this ignominious procedure on the part of those who should have been his friends, they would be entitled to any consideration at his hands.[2] Williams was greater than his

---

[1] Winthrop, vol. i., pp. 232, 235.
Gardener, *Mass. Hist. Coll.*, vol. iii., p. 141.
Underhill, *3 Mass. Hist. Coll.*, vol. vi., p. 11.
Massachusetts Records, vol. i., p. 88.

[2] "Mr. Wiliams did lay his axe at the very root of the Magistratical power in matters of the first table, which he

persecutors; for he at once, upon understanding the situation, at an extreme hazard, hardly informing his wife of his intention, embarked in a frail canoe and alone made his way through "stormy wind, with great seas," to the house of Canonicus; but the Pequods had anticipated his coming, possibly, and were there before him. For a succession of

---

drove on at such a rate, so as many agitations were occasioned thereby that pulled down ruin upon himself, friends, and his poor family."

Hubbard, *History of New England*, p. 166.

John Cotton remarks of Roger Williams that he "Looked upon himself as had he received a clearer illumination and apprehension of the State of Christ's Kingdom, and of the purity of Church Communion, than all Christendom besides."

Ibid, p. 203.

Cotton goes on to relate that one of the causes of Williams's banishment was the latter's protesting against the king's being credited, in the patent under which the Puritans occupied Massachusetts Bay, as being the first Christian prince who had discovered these parts, and his injustice in giving this country to his English subjects, which belonged to the native Indians. He urged the Puritans to humble themselves "to return the patent back again to the King."

Ibid, p. 210.

Evidently Roger Williams was a misfit for the Puritan conscience.

It was in October, 1635, that Roger Williams was sentenced by the General Court of Massachusetts to depart out of their jurisdiction within six weeks. Such was the spirit of intolerance in the Bay Colony at that time that in the January following Winthrop was convicted by the Puritan leaders for

THE PEQUOD WAR

three days and three nights Williams was compelled to remain in their company, in momentary danger of sharing the fate of Oldham. He was able, however, through his kindliness of attitude, and more directly through the friendship of Canonicus, to frustrate the designs of the Pequods.[1] As a result of his commission, Miantonomoh and two sons of Canonicus went to Boston, where they joined the

---

having shown "too much leniety in this matter," and Captain Underhill was despatched to apprehend Williams for continuing to preach the doctrine for which he had been banished. Vane was governor at this time.

John Winthrop, *Life and Letters*, p. 137.

Roger Williams has been called the founder of Rhode Island. He escaped Underhill to find an asylum among the Narragansetts. He was noted for his uprightness and kindliness of manner; and by the exercise of these qualities he obtained a very considerable influence over the Narragansett sachem.

Winthrop, vol. i., pp. 236, 238.
Vide William's *Letters*, *Mass. Hist. Coll.*, vol. i., p. 237.
3 Mass. Hist. Coll., vol. i., p. 159.
Trumbull, vol. i., pp. 74, 76.

[1] Upon his expulsion from the Bay Colony by Winthrop's court Williams found himself shelterless. He went first to Massasoit, and then to Canonicus. The latter received him at first with distrust, so fearful was he of the "sorcery of the whites;" but, taken by Williams's kindly behavior, he afterward received him into full companionship. Williams attempted a settlement at Seekonk. Upon finding it to be in the Plymouth jurisdiction he crossed the water to Rhode Island. He was the first white man here, where no prior title could

INDIAN WARS OF NEW ENGLAND

magistrates and ministers in a treaty of peaceful alliance.[1]

The expedition to Block Island could have but one result. That was to exasperate the savages, whet their thirst for revenge, and to stir them to greater insolence and warlike spirit, so that no

---

interfere with his rights. He was given this land by the Indian sachem.

Frost, *Book of the Colonies*, p. 176.

Not long before, the Narragansetts had made some pretense of enmity against the English. Baylie says: "In the spring of 1630 John Sagamore, a friendly Indian, betrayed a plot of the Narragansetts to the English, a conspiracy of many of the tribes of whom the Narragansetts were the leaders, to destroy the English. They requested the governor of Plymouth that they might have some sport there; but the governor would not permit it. The savages retorted if they might not come 'with leave,' they 'would without.' The English, apprehending their purpose, made preparations for defence, and the Indians decided to put off their purpose, friendly or otherwise, until better opportunity should offer."

Baylie's *History of Plymouth*, p. 154.

[1] There was at that time a move on foot for the confederation of the Connecticut tribes; the Pequots had become the active movers in this matter, and, as their first step toward the consummation of their purpose against the English, they buried the hatchet so long reddened in the Narragansett feud. These overtures to the latter were in the way of being accepted when Roger Williams made his advent into the village of Canonicus. The Narragansetts would be a powerful ally, and they would also be in no danger from them; otherwise, Sassacus, having fully considered the benefits to be had with

THE PEQUOD WAR

Englishmen were safe in their company.¹ They gathered at the garrison at Saybrook, and chal-

---

the accession of the Narragansetts to his machinations against the English, sent two sachems to Canonicus to gain him over to their purpose. Canonicus called a general council of his warriors, and before the assembled Narragansetts the Pequots urged the confederation for the extermination of the English. They did not overlook the superior training and armament of the English, but explained that it would not be necessary to face the latter's muskets or expose themselves in the open; but they could waylay them by ambuscade as they tilled their crops; fire their cabins by night when they slept; kill their cattle; harass them by day and night in the most unexpected places, until, in their fear, and beset by the perils of starvation, they would quit the country voluntarily. The Pequots argued, and with a show of reason, once the Pequots are destroyed the Narragansetts will fall a still easier prey to the English rapacity; and they dilated upon the unprovoked attacks of the English in reprisal for the murder of Oldham, of which they were not guilty, in attempting to extort from them large quantities of wampum and demanding their children as hostages, whom the English would undoubtedly condemn to slavery. The Narragansetts were moved by this plausible speech, and were on the point of forming an alliance with the Pequots; but they remembered their former enmity, and they feared the Pequots no less than the English. The appearance of Williams at the moment when the decision of the Narragansetts hung in the balance was most opportune, for his influence prevailed, and the Pequot sachems had failed in their embassy.

DeForest, *Indians of Connecticut*, p. 101.

Roger Williams's *Letters*, R. I. Hist. Coll., vol. iii., p. 160.

¹Gardener was in command of the fort at Saybrook. It

INDIAN WARS OF NEW ENGLAND

lenged it to come out and fight. The chief episode of this foray by the Pequods, it appears, was the capture of Samuel Butterfield, who was out with some others getting hay. Butterfield was tied to a stake and roasted alive by the Pequods.[1] Another attack followed two weeks later. Five or six of the Englishmen were wounded. After the winter came on, Gardener went out, one March day, with nine or ten men, to burn weeds. He was drawn into an

---

was harvesting-time. The Saybrook garrison went to gather their corn. They had cut and stored a portion of it. Leaving five men to guard it until a shallop could be manned and sent to bring it to the fort, he ordered the men to be on their guard. Having muskets, they were over-confident, and three of them started to hunt sea-fowl, which were abundant. They followed their sport until they were a mile from the fort. The wooded marshes echoed with the noise of their muskets. Having obtained all the fowl they wished, they started on their return to the corn-field. The Pequots, watching them, planned an ambuscade. Once the English were fallen into it, the savages surrounded them and let fly a volley of arrows. Two of the English were so terrified they allowed the savages to take their guns from them without resistance. The other, drawing his sword, escaped. The two captured were afterward put to the torture.

The following day the men came in the shallop, but were afraid to finish the harvesting. Loading their boat, they sailed back to the fort, the smoke of their burning storehouse trailing after them over the water.

Gardener, *Mass. Hist. Coll.*, vol. xxxiii., p. 142.
DeForest, *Indians of Connecticut*, p. 107.
[1]Gardener, *Mass. Hist. Coll.*, vol. xxxiii., p. 142.

THE PEQUOD WAR

ambuscade, and lost two of his men.[1] The Pequods supposed Gardener was killed, and at once invested

---

[1] It was right after this that "old Mr. Michell, against the protest of Gardener, went to cut some hay on Six-Mile Island, with four men to assist him, only to find the Pequots lurking around the tall grass." Michell, with three others, made a run for the boat, and got away safely. The other, "a godly young man named Butterfield," the savages captured and roasted alive.

Gardener, *Mass. Hist. Coll.*, vol. xxxiii., pp. 142, 143.
Winthrop, vol. i., p. 198.
Drake's *Boston*, p. 203.
Hubbard, p. 252.

"In the 22d of February, I went out with ten men, and three dogs, half a mile from the house, to burn the weeds, leaves and reeds, upon the neck of land, because we had felled twenty timber-trees, which we were to roll to the water-side to bring home, every man carrying a length of match with brimstone-matches with him to kindle the fire withal. But when we came to the small of the Neck, the woods burning, I having before this set two sentinels on the small of the Neck, I called to the men that were burning the reeds to come away, but they would not until they had burnt up the rest of their matches. Presently there starts up four Indians out of the fiery reeds, but ran away, I calling to the rest of our men to come away out of the marsh. Then Robert Chapman and Thomas Hurlbut, being sentinels called to me, saying there came a number of other Indians out of the other side of the marsh. Then I went to stop them, that they should not get the wood-land; but Thomas Hurlbut cried out to me that some of the men did not follow me, for Thomas Rumble and Arthur Branch, threw down their two guns and ran away; then the Indians shot two of them that were in the reeds, and

the fort, crying out, "Come fetch your Englishmen's clothes! Come out and fight, if you dare! You dare not fight! You are all like women!"

sought to get between us and home, but durst not come before us, but kept us in a half-moon, we retreating and exchanging many a shot, so that Thomas Hurlbut was shot almost through the thigh, John Spencer in the back, into his kidneys, myself into the thigh, two more were shot dead. But in our retreat I kept Hurlbut and Spencer still before us, we defending ourselves with our naked swords, or else they had taken us all alive, so that the two sore wounded men, by our slow retreat, got home with their guns, when our two sound men ran away and left their guns behind them. But when I saw the cowards that left us, I resolved to let them draw lots which of them should be hanged, for the articles did hang up in the hall for them to read, and they knew they had been published long before. But at the intercession of old Mr. Michell, Mr. Higgisson [Higginson], and Mr. Pell, I did forbear. Within a few days after, when I had cured myself of my wound, I went out with eight men to get some fowl for our relief, and found the guns that were thrown away, and the body of one man shot through, the arrow going in at the right side, the head sticking fast, half through a rib on the left side, which I took out and cleansed it, and presumed to send to the Bay, because they had said that the arrows of the Indians were of no force.

"Anthony Dike, master of a bark, having his bark at Rhode Island in the winter, was sent by Mr. Vane, then Governor. Anthony came to Rhode Island by land, and from thence he came with his bark to me with a letter, wherein was desired that I should consider and prescribe the best way I could to quell these Pequits, which I also did, and with my letter sent the man's rib as a token. A few days

THE PEQUOD WAR

The news reaching the Bay Colony resulted in the sending of Captain Mason to their relief, and

after, came Thomas Stanton down the River, and staying for a wind, while he was there came a troop of Indians within musket shot, laying themselves and their arms down behind a little rising hill and two great trees; which I perceiving, called the carpenter whom I had shewed how to charge and level a gun, and that he should put two cartridges of musket bullets into two sakers guns that lay about; and we levelled them against the place, and I told him that he must look towards me, and when he saw me wave my hat above my head he should give fire to both the guns; then presently came three Indians, creeping out and calling to us to speak with us: and I was glad that Thomas Stanton was there, and I sent six men down to the Garden Pales to look that none should come under the hill behind us; and having placed the rest in places convenient closely, Thomas and I with my sword, pistol and carbine, went ten or twelve poles without the gate to parley with them. And when the six men came to the Garden Pales, at the corner, they found a great number of Indians creeping behind the fort, or betwixt us and home, but they ran away. Now I had said to Thomas Stanton, Whatsoever they say to you, tell me first, for we will not answer them directly to anything, for I knew not the mind of the rest of the English. So they came forth, calling us nearer to them, and we them nearer to us. But I would not let Thomas go any further than the great stump of a tree, and I stood by him; then they asked who we were, and he answered Thomas and Lieutenant. But they said he lied, for I was shot with many arrows; and so I was, but my buff coat preserved me, only one hurt me. But when I spake to them they knew my voice, for one of them had dwelt three months with us, but ran away when the Bay-men came first. Then

the Pequods were expelled. Reënforced by the arrival of Captain Underhill and some of his men,

they asked us if we would fight with Niantecut Indians, for they were our friends and came to trade with us. We said we knew not the Indians one from another, and therefore would trade with none. Then they said, Have you fought enough? We said we knew not yet. Then they asked if we did use to kill women and children? We said that they should see that hereafter. So they were silent a small space, and then they said, We are Pequits, and have killed Englishmen, and can kill them as mosquetoss, and we will go to Conectecott and kill men, women, and children, and we will take away the horses, cows and hogs. When Thomas Stanton had told me this, he prayed me to shoot that rogue, for, said he, he hath an Englishman's coat on, and saith that he hath killed three, and these other four have their cloathes on their backs. I said, No, it is not the manner of a parley, but have patience and I shall fit them ere they go. Nay, now or never, said he; so when he could get no other answer but this last, I bid him tell them that they should not go to Conectecott, for if they did kill all the men, and take all the rest as they said, it would do them no good, but hurt, for English women are lazy, and can't do their work; horses and cows will spoil your corn-fields, and the hogs their clam-banks, and so undo them: then I pointed to our great house, and bid him tell them there lay twenty pieces of trucking-cloth, of Mr. Pincheon's, with hoes, hatchets, and all manner of trade, they were better [to] fight still with us, and so get all that, and then go up the river after they had killed all us. Having heard this, they were mad as dogs, and ran away; then when they came to the place from whence they came, I waved my hat about my head, and the two great guns went off, so that there was a great hubbub amongst them. Then two days after, came down Capt.

THE PEQUOD WAR

the Indians disappeared in the direction of Wethersfield, where two hundred of them swooped down upon the town.[1] Nine of the settlers were killed,

---

Mason, and Sergeant Seely, with five men more, to see how it was with us; and whilst they were there, came down a Dutch boat, telling us the Indians had killed fourteen English, for by that boat I had sent up letters to Conectecott, what I heard, and what I thought, and how to prevent that threatened danger, and received back again rather a scoff, than any thanks, for my care and pains. But as I wrote, so it fell out to my great grief and theirs, for the next, or second day after, (as Major Mason well knows,) came down a great many canoes, going down the creek beyond the marsh, before the fort, many of them having white shirts; then I commanded the carpenter whom I had shewed to level great guns, to put in two round shot into the two sackers, and we levelled them at a certain place, and I stood to bid him give fire, when I thought the canoe wherein the two maids were, that were taken by the Indians, whom I redeemed and clothed, for the Dutchmen, whom I sent to fetch them, brought them away almost naked from Pequit, they putting on their own linen jackets to cover their nakedness; and though the redemption cost me ten pounds, I am yet to have thanks for my care and charge about them; these things are known to Major Mason."
 Gardener's *Pequot Warres*, p. 15.

[1] The Wethersfield Colony had its land from Sequin, or Sowheag, and was situated on the Connecticut River. One of the conditions of this sale was that the *grantor might reside in the near vicinity*, and under the *protection* of the English. The settlers built their cabins, and not far away Sowheag set up the poles for his wigwam. For some reason or other, not long after, the English picked a quarrel with this sachem and drove him out of the settlement. Unable to redress his

men, women, and children, and two young women were taken captives. These were afterwards redeemed by the Dutch. It was shortly before Gardener went out to burn the grass that John Tilly was captured, tied to a stake, flayed alive; burning coals were thrust into his flesh, and his hands and

---

own wrongs, he turned to the Pequots, who acceded to his desire for revenge.

It was in April, 1637. A man riding his horse near this settlement discovered a considerable body of savages stealing upon the town. Retracing his journey, he put spurs to his horse and galloped into the settlement to give the alarm.

He met some women who doubted his tale of the Pequots, so he spurred his horse anew to find more credulous listeners. He was too late. The elder woman, a few minutes later, was brained on the spot. The two girls who accompanied her were captured. Wethersfield was *surprised*. The men were taken at their work in the fields. Two other women and six men were butchered, and twenty head of cattle were killed. It does not seem that the Pequots thought of burning Wethersfield. The two girls were later redeemed by the Dutch.

Johnson's *Wonder-working Providence.*
Mass. Hist. Coll., vol. xxiv., p. 30.
Winthrop, vol. i., p. 218
DeForest, *Indians of Connecticut*, p. 113.

Trumbull mentions two girls, "daughters of Mr. Gibbons," who "were in the most brutal manner put to death. After gashing their flesh with their knives, the Indians filled their wounds with hot embers, in the meantime mimicking their dying groans."

Indian Wars, p. 48.

The writer does not find this incident mentioned elsewhere.

THE PEQUOD WAR

feet cut off, in which condition he lived three days.[1] This was a succession of tragic incidents which carried alarm to all the colonists, and thoroughly aroused the English to a realization that an effectual blow against the Pequods must be struck without further delay.

Reference has been made to the General Court which sat at Hartford. On this occasion it con-

---

[1] "There came from the Bay, Mr. Tille, with a permit to go up to Harford [Hartford], and coming ashore he saw a paper nailed up over the fort gate, whereon was written, that no boat or bark should pass the fort, but they come to an anchor first, that I might see whether they were armed and manned sufficiently, and they were not to land anywhere after they passed the fort till they came to Wethersfield: and I did this because Mr. Michell had lost a shallop before coming down from Wethersfield with three men, well armed."

Gardener's *Pequot Warres*, p. 19.

Tilly was incensed at what seemed to him an interference with his prerogative, and Gardener records that the gentleman from Boston used "ill language" toward him. When Tilly had vented his anger, Gardener told him to go to his warehouse, which the former had put up when here before. Tilly discovered that his house and storehouse had been destroyed; but Gardener, anticipating the savages, had stored Tilly's property in a safer place.

Gardener gave Tilly his goods, after which Tilly went up the river. Returning, he landed at what is now Tilly's Point, to which Gardener gave the name of "Tilly's Folly." "Having a fair wind, he came to anchor, and with one man went ashore, discharged his gun. The Indians fell upon him, killed the others, and carried him alive over the river in our

sisted of two magistrates and three committeemen from each of the three towns of Windsor, Hartford, and Wethersfield. This trio of towns comprised the Connecticut Colony. It was held on the eleventh day of May, and was one of the most important meetings, having reference to its results, in the history of Connecticut. While the court were of the opinion that the prospect was doubtful of maintaining their footing against the Indians, on account of the great numbers of the latter, and were somewhat disturbed over the apparent defection of the Narragansetts, whom they looked upon as their allies, they were no less determined to take the chances. While the Indians were scantily armed, their knowledge of the country, their subtlety and audacity, in a large degree balanced the chances of war. A defensive war would be of little use; and so far as an offensive position on their part was possible, it would seem to be of small efficacy, as the

---

sight before my shallop could come to them; for, immediately I sent seven men to fetch the Paik (small vessel) down, or else it had been taken, and three more."
Gardener's *Pequot Warres*, p. 20.
Tilly was put to the torture. His hands and feet were cut off. Hot coals were thrust into his flesh. He died like the savage stoic, without a moan. The Pequots could not conceal their admiration of his courage and endurance.
Gardener's *Mass. Hist. Coll.*, vol. xxxiii., p. 147.
Winthrop, vol. i., p. 200.
Underhill, *Mass. Hist. Coll.*, vol. xxxvi., p. 15.

THE PEQUOD WAR

three towns contained hardly more than two hundred and fifty men. No help had been offered by the Bay Colony, yet it was as evident that some decision must be made; and the court finally decided that war should be carried into the enemy's country. For the first company, a levy of ninety men was made on the three towns. Hartford was to furnish forty-two; Windsor, thirty; and Wethersfield, eighteen. The needed supplies and munitions were voted. John Mason was made commander-in-chief.[1]

These settlers were poor; they lacked most of the comforts of civilization; and, as has been noticed, the first winter they suffered from lack of food. The Bay Colony had been singularly indifferent. No help had been received from it, except the expedition of Endicott, which, as Gardener prophesied, could bring only misfortune. In various letters the Connecticut Court had described to the government

---

[1] John Mason had served under Sir Thomas Fairfax in the Netherlands, where his abilities and courage attracted his general's attention. He was a very tall man, of large physique; energetic, of a stern, but not headlong disposition; moral, yet not religious; for the work in hand, he was of the same relentless fiber as Miles Standish. It was a crisis in the affairs of the Connecticut Colony, and Mason was "the man for the hour."

Allen, *Biographical Dictionary of New England.*
DeForest, *Indians of Connecticut*, p. 119.
Trumbull's *History of the Indians*, p. 52.

of Massachusetts their situation. They disapproved of Endicott's expedition, and had enumerated the troubles which had befallen the colonists of Connecticut in consequence of it. They charged the provocation of the war upon the people of Massachusetts; and they urged upon the latter that, so long as they had begun it, it was most desirable that the procedure of the same should go on under their direction. They finally notified Governor Vane that they had decided to push the war against the Pequods into their own country. Uncas was a Pequod[1] who had rebelled against Sassacus; and, joined by a number of Indians, he made his appearance in Hartford and offered himself as an ally to the Connecticut Colony. His warriors numbered about seventy. Massachusetts and Plymouth, be-

---

[1] The Pequot country extended from Niantic on the west to the Rhode Island line on the east, taking in Waterford, New London, and Montville west of the Thames River and Groton, Stonington, and North Stonington on the east, including the country to north of this, with the county of Windham, and a portion of Tolland.

A difference has been made between the Mohegans and the Pequots. Uncas, the great Mohegan sachem, was of royal Pequot blood. His ancestors were Pequots. His wife was the daughter of the sachem Tatobam. Uncas had been a sachem under Sassacus, the royal head of the Pequot nation. When the English came to Connecticut Uncas was carrying on a rebellion, and to save himself from the vengeance of Sassacus he lent his allegiance to the English.

Uncas is described as a savage of huge stature, and of great

THE PEQUOD WAR

ing fully convinced that the Connecticut Colony had determined to proceed forthwith against the Pequods, came to a realizing sense of the situation.

---

bravery and strength. He was a past-master in stratagem, and cared more for plunder than for glory. He was careful of his own men, and, therefore, popular. An apt politician, he was selfish, jealous, and inclined to play the tyrant. Possessed of many bad traits, he had no great ones. He served the English as the means to an end, which was the consummation of his own personal animosities. In these days he would have been a political ward-boss.

Uncas was buried in the royal burying-ground of his race, just by the falls in the Yantic River, "a beautiful and romantic spot."

Gardener's *Pequot Warres*, p. 7.

Drake's *History of the Indians*, p. 89.

James Fitch, who was sent among the Mohegans as a missionary, calls Uncas "an old and wicked, wilful man, a drunkard, and very vicious."

There was a feud between Uncas and Miantonomoh. The former came near being killed by an arrow from a Pequot bow-string, at the instigation of the latter. For this, Miantonomoh was sent for by Winthrop. Miantonomoh took the would-be assassin along with him. The Pequot was proven guilty, "out of his own mouth." Winthrop would have sent him to Uncas. Miantonomoh protested that he would send the Pequot to Uncas himself, to be examined and punished. Contrary to his promise, he killed his accomplice ("cut off the Peacott's head that he might tell no tales"). Subsequent attempts were made on the life of Uncas, once by poison.

After this one of Sequassen's company, a sachem whose intimacies with Miantonomoh had engaged them as confederates in many obscure matters, shot an arrow at Uncas

INDIAN WARS OF NEW ENGLAND

Both voted to furnish men in behalf of the Connecticut people. The Massachusetts Colony were to raise two hundred men; the Plymouth Colony,

---

as he was going down the Connecticut River. Uncas complained to the English of these assaults upon his safety, whereupon the English endeavored to unite Sequassen and Uncas in overtures of peace. Sequassen referred the Narragansetts to Miantonomoh as his superior sachem. This was followed by Miantonomoh's marching against Uncas with one thousand warriors. They found Uncas unprepared, having but four hundred men to oppose to this considerable force. After a stout battle, the Narragansetts were routed and Miantonomoh was taken prisoner. He was given up by two of his own men, who expected to save their lives by their treachery. When Miantonomoh was captured he was discovered to be encased in a *coat of mail*.

When his captive, who showed his indifference by his silence, was brought to him, Uncas said, "If you had taken me, I should have besought you for my life." Uncas then took Miantonomoh to Hartford, where he delivered him into the hands of the English until it should be decided what should be done with his inveterate enemy. The government at Boston was of the opinion it would not be safe to give him his liberty, and there seemed no sufficient ground to put him to death. With the aid of the council, "five of the most judicious elders," they came to a decision. Enjoining secrecy upon all, they made known their ruling to Uncas privately, instructing him to attend to the execution of Miantonomoh within his own jurisdiction, and without witnesses. Pilate-like, the Puritans washed their hands of responsibility, willing that the Mohegans should have the odium of the matter.

Uncas was promised the protection of the English; and

THE PEQUOD WAR

forty.[1] Captain Daniel Patrick was despatched with forty men overland, by the Bay Colony, to connect with the Narragansetts. The Pequods had sent their women and children to Block Island, which was also Patrick's destination.[2] When they

---

the former being willing to conform to the desire of the English, once within his own domain, "Uncas' brother, following after Miantonomoh, clave his head with a hatchet." Mather has it, "They very fairly cut off his head."

[1] Winthrop, vol. i., p. 222.
Mass. Hist. Coll., vol. xxxiii., p. 133.

[2] "The march of those from Massachusetts was retarded by a most singular Cause that ever influenced the Operation of a Military Force. When they were mustered previous to their Departure, it was found that some of the Officers, as well as the private Soldiers, were still under the Covenant of Works; and that the Blessing of God could not be implored or expected to crown the Arms of such unhallowed Men with Success. The Alarm was general, and many Arrangements necessary in order to call out the Unclean, and to render this little Band sufficiently pure to fight the Battles of a People who entertained high Ideas of their own Sanctity."
Robertson's *America*, bk. x.
Neal's *History of New England*, vol. i., p. 184.

Winthrop does not give the date of Patrick's march from Boston. Hubbard says Winthrop was so busy "engineering at Elections" that he did not date this and other happenings of that time, so it is not known how much Patrick was delayed by the "Covenant of Good Works."
Indian Wars, p. 20, note.

In this election Governor Harry Vane was defeated by Winthrop. Vane was thought to be tainted with the so-called

INDIAN WARS OF NEW ENGLAND

had subdued Block Island, the plan was for them to return to the mainland, where they were to join the Connecticut soldiers for immediate proceedings against the Pequods.

May 20, 1637, Captain Mason, with ninety Englishmen and seventy Indians, dropped down the river in three small vessels. After repeated delays by grounding, on account of the shallowness of the water, the Indian allies were set ashore, with instructions to make Saybrook by land. On their way through the woods they met a party of Pequods, numbering thirty or forty. They killed seven of them, with one man wounded on their own side. Mason proceeded by water in the three small craft

---

heresy of antinomianism. Wheelwright, a leader of the cult, preached to crowded audiences. Vane, who is described as a young man of great talents and heir to a princely fortune, the son of the chief secretary of Charles i., took to the Puritan tenets with a singular zeal. He came over to Boston and took up his residence with Mr. Cotton. He was most warmly welcomed, and at the gubernatorial election following his arrival he was made governor, at the age of twenty-four. At the succeeding election he was defeated by the country outside Boston, which followed the influence of its old ministers. This election was held at Cambridge, lest the electors should be influenced by the Boston interests, which supported Vane by a considerable majority. After his defeat he returned to England, where, after the restoration of Charles ii., he was tried for alleged political offences, and judicially murdered.

Pierce, *Book of the Colonies*, p. 182.
Pictorial History of the United States.

THE PEQUOD WAR

which De Forest describes as a pink, a pinnace, and a shallop. After lightening these small vessels the English got on very well down stream, joining Uncas and his party at Saybrook. On hearing the relation by Uncas of his exploit in the woods, they felt assured of his fidelity. Lieutenant Lion Gardener, whose knowledge of the savages made him less credulous, asked Mason how he could trust the Mohegans, who had been so short a time away from their own people, who had become open enemies of the English. Mason replied to him that he was "forced to trust them, for we want them to guide us." Gardener, still doubtful, suggested to Uncas, "You say that you will help Captain Mason, but I will first see it; therefore send twenty men to Bass River, for there went six Indians there in a canoe, fetch them dead or alive and you shall go with Mason, or else you shall not."[1] Uncas started off on his errand, discovered the enemy, killed four of them, and made prisoner of another. This captive was called Kiswas. He had lived much of the time in the neighborhood,

---

[1] Lion Gardener was sent over by Lords Say and Seal and Brook to construct a fort at the mouth of the Connecticut River, to command it, etc. He was said to be a skilful engineer, and on that account was selected. He had seen some service in the Low Countries under General Fairfax. He came to this country about the year 1633, or 1634, and erected a fort at Saybrook in Connecticut, which was so named in honor of Lord Say and Seal and Lord Brook. . . . He was

a portion of which he spent at the fort, and could speak English. Since the Pequod outbreak he had been around the fort much of the time, where he had acted as a spy upon the garrison; and he had as well been present at those massacres which had taken place in the immediate neighborhood. Uncas claimed him as a captive, and demanded that he be turned over to his people for disposition.[1]

It may be noted here that a Dutch vessel arrived

---

in command of this fort when Capt. John Mason conquered the Pequots.

Gardener was in command of the fort for some time, and once came near being captured by the Pequots. He later removed to Gardener Island, in Gardener Bay, where he died. The area of this island is about twenty-five hundred acres, and it is a most beautiful spot. It was an entailed estate, whose proprietors were known as Lords. There is a tradition that the island was conveyed to Lion Gardener by the sachem Waiandance out of the latter's gratitude for Gardener's efforts to ransom this sachem's daughter, who had been captured and carried off by Ninigret during the war between the Nehantics and the Indians of Long Island.

Gardener's Island has a history under the Lords of the Gardener Manor, by itself.

Gardener, *Pequot Warres.*
Vincent, *Mass. Hist. Coll.*, vol. xxxvi., p. 36.
DeForest, *Indians of Connecticut*, p. 121.

[1] Among the prisoners was one who was recognized as "a perfidious villain." In this designation of the savage, Trumbull refers to Kiswas. This savage had lived much at the fort and understood English fairly. Upon the commencement of hostilities on the part of the Pequots he was apparently at-

THE PEQUOD WAR

in the river to drop anchor under the guns of Saybrook a little before the arrival of Mason. Gardener, ascertaining that the Dutch were on their way to trade with the Pequods, forbade them doing so, fearful that out of the supplies which the Dutch might carry to the Indians some might be converted into arrow-heads or other weapons of offence. A dispute arose, which the Dutch finally ended by proposing that, if they were allowed to go to the

---

tached to the English. Once the first overt act was committed, he left the fort to become a guide to the Pequots. Through his instigation, many of the English were captured and killed. Kiswas was captured by some of Uncas's party, and Uncas insisted that he be put to the torture in accordance with the ancient customs of the Narragansetts. The English yielded to this request out of policy; so the savages kindled a fire near which was a stake, to which Kiswas was securely bound. They kept him there until his skin was flayed with the heat. The Mohegans then violently tore him limb from limb, and barbarously cutting his flesh in pieces, handed it around from one to another, eating it, while they sung and danced around the fire in a manner peculiar to savages; the bones and such parts of the unfortunate captive as were not consumed in this dreadful repast were committed to the flames and consumed to ashes.

Trumbull, *Indian Wars*, p. 54.
DeForest, *Indians of Connecticut*, p. 121.
Gardener's *Warres*, p. 21.
Drake doubts Trumbull's relation of the cannibalism of the Mohegans at the torturing of Kiswas.
Drake, *Book of the Indians*, pp. 86, 103.
Trumbull, *History of the Indians*, p. 59.

Pequods, they would ransom the two English girls who had been captured a short time before by the Indians, in their raid on Wethersfield. This offer was accepted by Gardener, and the Dutch kept on up the river until they came to Pequod Harbor, where they anchored. They sent their men on shore, as was their wont, offering to trade. They would sell the Indians whatever they had in their store; but in return for the same, instead of the usual articles of furs and wampum, they would take the two English girls. The sachem Sassacus, who happened there, refused to give up his captives, while the Dutch, with something of a spirit of reprisal and without exerting their conscience in the matter, succeeded in getting seven of the Pequods on board their vessel. Some of these were sachems, whom they immediately made prisoners. After that was accomplished the Dutch called to the Pequods on the river-bank, "We have seven of your people on board our vessel; if ye desire them again ye must give us the two English girls; tell us quickly whether ye will do so; for if not, we will hoist sail and drop all your men overboard in the main ocean." The Pequods shouted back in derision, regarding this as an empty threat, still refusing to deliver the captives, upon which the Dutch got up their anchor. By the time they reached the mouth of the stream the Pequods became convinced that the Dutch meant what they said, and followed them in several canoes, taking

THE PEQUOD WAR

along with them the two English girls. When they had overtaken the Dutch another parley was had. The ruse was successful. The Indians were released and the two girls were in the way of being restored to their friends. The Dutch, true to their word, kept on to Saybrook, where they met another Dutch vessel which the New Netherlands governor had despatched for the express purpose of obtaining these girls upon any conditions, and to engage in a war with the Pequods, if it were necessary, to get them.[1]

As before mentioned, Mason had reached Saybrook. It was here the Dutch found him. Mason had thus an opportunity of acquiring through these girls the latest intelligence concerning the Pequods, which was that the latter had sixteen guns, with a small quantity of powder and shot. They reported also that the Indians were very curious as to whether they could make powder, and were much disappointed when they found they could not. As a result of their ignorance, the savages set less value on the fire-arms. They said they had been kindly treated, which was due to one of the squaws of Mononotto, who ranked next to Sassacus as a

---

[1] DeForest, *Indians of Connecticut*, p. 123.

These two girls were carried from Saybrook to New Amsterdam at the Dutch governor's special request, so curious was he to see them "with his own eyes."

Ibid, supra.

sachem. They thought it was through that squaw they had been saved from torture. The Pequods had taken them from place to place, and had exhibited to them their wigwams and such things as they held in high value, and had endeavored in many ways to please them, and to make their captivity less irksome. From Saybrook the girls were taken to New Amsterdam, as the governor wished to see them; after which they were returned in safety to Wethersfield, forty-six miles up the river.[1]

Mason's instructions were that he should attack the enemy by making an immediate landing at Pequod Harbor. He was so instructed in a letter which the magistrates caused to be conveyed to him while he was at Saybrook. His knowledge of military affairs led him to disprove of this plan, and he expressed his desire to sail first to the country of the Narragansetts. He said of the Pequods: "They keep a continual guard upon their river, night and day, they were armed as the maids said they were, with sixteen pieces, also powder and shot. Their numbers being greatly superior to ours would make it difficult for us to land in their faces, also, if we affect the landing they will fly away and hide in their swamps and thickets, whereas if we go first to Narragansett, we shall come upon them at

---

[1] Underhill, *Mass. Hist. Coll.*, vol. xxxvi., pp. 17, 18, 19, says, "Gardener says he paid the Dutch ten pounds for ransoming the girls."

THE PEQUOD WAR

their backs and so may take them by a surprise, where they least expect it."[1] His officers and men were not agreeable to this proposition; they were not in favor of a long march through the wilderness. They did not conceal their anxiety to get back to their families, and were in favor of taking the shorter way to Pequod Harbor, and there make a decisive battle with the savages. When the court issued the commission to Mason giving him the direction of the Connecticut forces they appointed a chaplain by the name of Stone. It was at this point of the argument they all agreed in desiring the chaplain to make invocation that they might be given the wisdom and guidance of God, that whatever they did might be done in accordance with the Divine Providence. It is reported that the chaplain devoted the larger part of the night to prayer. In the morning he told Captain Mason and the rest of the party that he was convinced they should go to Narragansett. Without further hesitation Mason's plan was accepted. Mason despatched twenty men up the river, that they might assist in the defence of the settlers if necessary. This diminution of Mason's forces was supplemented by an addition to it by Capt. John Underhill[2] and nineteen others from the fort.

---

[1] Mason, *Mass. Hist. Coll.*, vol. xviii., p. 134.

[2] Captain John Underhill was an original member of the Ancient and Honorable Artillery Company of Boston. An

INDIAN WARS OF NEW ENGLAND

They set sail from Saybrook May 29, Friday. On Saturday, by dusk, they had dropped anchor off the shores of Narragansett. Time was precious, yet they realized the futility of making land that night.

---

eccentric man, he went to excess in whatever he undertook. In religion he was an enthusiast; in practice, a debauché. He was a member of the Puritan Church of that time, before which he was once arraigned for offences. One of the curious charges brought against him was that he dated his conversion from an occasion when he was smoking tobacco. When "the spirit set home upon me an absolute promise of free grace, with such assurance and joy that he had never since doubted his good estate, neither should he, whatever since he might fall into." In a trial before the court, he was found guilty of abusing them with a "pretended retraction," for which on the following day he was banished. Allowed the opportunity, however, of attending public worship, his zeal found expression in this, "that as the Lord was pleased to convert Saul while he was persecuting, so he might manifest himself to him while making a moderate use of the good creature tobacco; professing withal that he knew not wherin he had deserved the censure of the court." Reproved by the elders for making this inconsiderate speech, the Rev. Mr. Cotton told him "that though God often laid a man under a spirit of bondage while walking in sin, as was the case with Paul, yet he never sent a spirit of comfort, but in an ordinance, as he did to Paul by the ministry of Ananias; and therefore exhorted him to examine carefully the revelation and joy to which he pretended." That same week he was privately dealt with on suspicion of adultery, which he disregarded; and being questioned before the church the following Sabbath, he was only admonished, as the evidence was not considered sufficient to warrant a conviction. Underhill, after

THE PEQUOD WAR

The next day, Sunday, was conscientiously observed by their remaining on their vessel. On Monday, by reason of a stiff northwest gale which continued through the entire day, they were unable to

---

this, betook himself from under Winthrop's jurisdiction, going to Dover, where he assumed the governorship of New Hampshire in place of the disreputable George Burdett, who, on Sept. 8, 1640, was indicted by the General Court of Agamenticus for some acts of incontinency with one Mary Puddington, and as well for "Deflowering Ruth, wife of John Gouch of Agamenticus," for which he was fined twenty pounds (Sylvester, *Old York*, pp. 98, 99). After a varied career in New Hampshire, Underhill obtained permission to return to Boston, where, during a session of the court, he made a full confession of his shortcomings, declaring "that his pretended assurance had failed him and that the terror of his mind had at some times been so great, that he had drawn his sword to put an end to his life." He was sentenced to sit on the stool of repentance in the church, a white cap on his head, and in his predicament make a public confession of his sins. After this he was placed upon a probation of six months, and finally restored to full communion. He was released and his punishment for confessed adultery was remitted by the court, for the reason that the law which made such a capital crime, having been enacted after the crime was committed, did not apply to him. After this he entered the employ of the Dutch governor of Manhattan, who gave him command of a company of one hundred twenty men. He made himself very useful in the wars between the Dutch and the Indians, continuing in their service during the remainder of his life. Wood says that Underhill settled at Stamford, Conn., and was a delegate from that town to the New Haven Court in 1643; when he was appointed Assistant Justice for that colony. From 1643

INDIAN WARS OF NEW ENGLAND

embark. On Tuesday it was the same until just before sundown, when they succeeded in making a landing and took up their march towards the headquarters of Canonicus. Here they held an interview with the sachem, in which they informed him of their purpose, which was to attack the Pequods in their fastnesses. Mason requested a passage through the Narragansett country. He was answered by Miantonomoh, who expressed himself as

---

to 1646 he had command of the Dutch forces against the Indians. After the battle of Strickland's Plain, in which he obtained rather a difficult victory, he settled at Flushing, Long Island. He was also, in 1665, a delegate from Oyster-Bay to the Assembly convened at Hempstead by Governor Nicolls, by whom he was appointed under-sheriff to the North Riding, of Yorkshire or Queen's County. He is supposed to have died at Oyster-Bay in 1672. He was a singular man and a natural product of the times in which he lived, and not altogether unlike many of his contemporaries of the early settlements.

History of Ancient and Honorable Artillery Company.

Pierce, *Indian History*, p. 32, note.

Belknap's *History of New Hampshire*, pp. 23-27.

Hubbard, in his *History of New England*, p. 365, says that "in Sept., 1641, Captain Underhill not able longer to subsist at Pascataqua upon the occasions fore-mentioned, and being recalled to the court of Massachusetts, and Church of Boston, returned thither with his family to seek some way of subsistence, where, having no employment that would maintain him, and having good offers by the Dutch governor, he speaking the Dutch tongue freely, (and his wife a Dutch woman,) he removed thither."

THE PEQUOD WAR

being very much pleased at the coming of the English. He acknowledged that their purpose was a good one, and had his approval; but it must be realized that the Pequods were very skilful in war, that they had many great sachems; and as he looked over Mason's little army he was doubtful of their success, because the Pequods were so many and the white soldiers were so few. He allowed the English to pass through the country of the Narragansetts, but seemed somewhat coldly inclined, as neither he nor his people made any proffer of assistance. While encamped here, a letter from Captain Patrick was brought him by an Indian runner. Patrick had come as far as Providence, which was the settlement of Roger Williams.[1] In the letter he desired Mason to halt where he was until he should come up with him; and while Mason was anxious to

---

[1] Roger Williams resided at Plymouth some three years, where he preached the Gospel, going there in 1631. From Plymouth he went to Rhode Island, where he began a settlement of that colony. He had been liberally educated, and was for a time a pupil of Sir Edward Coke. He was a man of brilliant talent and great acquirements. In matters of religion he was at first considered eccentric. Later, he was charged with promulgating unsound doctrine, by reason of which he became especially odious to the Puritans, when he was dismissed from his office of religious teacher. He was a man of broad gauge for his time, and of larger intellectual gifts than either of the Mathers, though not gifted with their credulous verbosities. He possessed the courage of his convictions; and likewise that rare diplomacy of kindness and gentleness

have under his command as large a force as could be obtained, appreciating the advantage of the addition of Patrick's forces to his own, he called a council of war, which decided that it was not profitable to them to delay longer. The soldiers were anxious to go on, as they had been away from home two weeks, and the planting season was coming on; for which reason they were anxious to make quick

---

toward others that appealed even to the hearts of the savage Narragansetts.

He openly avowed and strenuously maintained "that an universal liberty of conscience ought to be allowed in all religious matters." The integrity of this proposition was recognized by being made a part of the Constitution of the thirteen colonies when they became a confederacy. He was the prophet of his time, possessing a spiritual outlook which was as incomprehensible to the Puritans as the wonders of witchcraft, which left an indelible stain upon their little commonwealth sixty years later, and offers not a single extenuating circumstance.

Thacher, *History of Plymouth*, p. 266.

Williams was forbidden the jurisdiction of Massachusetts, and what was apparently a grievous misfortune proved otherwise. Rhode Island became a home, a place of refuge, "for all sorts of consciences." Winthrop always fell back on his charter as a vindication of all his civil and religious restrictions. The son of a lawyer, and bred as a lawyer himself, as the master-spirit of the Bay Company his interpretations of his authority were doubtless sound.

Barry says: "Dignified, yet unassuming; learned, yet no pedant; sagacious, yet not crafty; benevolent in his impulses; ardent in his affections; attractive in his manners; mildly

THE PEQUOD WAR

work of this business. They also urged that further delay might make their designs known to the enemy, inasmuch as they realized that the Pequods had many friends among the Narragansetts, by whom the information might be transmitted. His allies, as well, were getting uneasy. Those savages who had deserted, as well as some of the others who were desirous to desert, sneered at Mason and his little company, saying that while the English did a great deal of talking and less fighting, it was apparent their courage was not sufficient to take them into the country of Sassacus. Appreciating the seriousness of the situation, Mason made answer by immediate preparations for an advance into the Pequod country.

The following morning a sloop sailed away for the mouth of the Pequod River, carrying thirteen whites and a small party of Indians. The party to go overland was made up of seventy-seven English, and about sixty savages, under Uncas. They started westward through the wilderness. They

---

conservative, and moderately ambitious — he was the man for the colony, every way elaborated and perfected for its purposes."
Barry, *History of Massachusetts*, p. 184.
Vide Belknap, *American Biography;* Moore's *Governors of Massachusetts.*
Winthrop's *History (Journal);* Eliot's and Allen's *Biographical Dictionary.*
Ellis, *Memorial History of Boston*, vol. i., pp. 174, 176.

came into a road[1] which seemed to be one of the highways of the Pequods. It was rough and arduous; but, making their way over the stones and fallen trees, they finally came to Nehantic. They had traversed some eighteen or twenty miles. Here at Nehantic was a fort and palisadoes, which had been erected as a barrier against the Pequods. This was occupied by one of the Narragansett sachems, who was called a noted character among the savages, and who was best known to the English as Ninigret.[2] As they continued their march, the Narragansett savages joined them, from time to time, until upon their arrival at Nehantic there

---

[1] The savages had their cross-country thoroughfares, or trails, which were well marked and distinct, and which extended from Florida to New Brunswick. It was by following these that Ingram made his way north to the St. John River, where he found a French vessel by which he was able to reach England. This was in the latter part of the sixteenth century. Ingram had been marooned by the buccaneer Hawkins at Pamlico, on the Florida coast, along with a hundred other unfortunates. Ingram found considerable villages along these trails. It was over the Algonquin trails the earliest Jesuits found their way into the villages of the Abenake. Some of the old Indian trails are marked by the more ancient highways among the shore counties in Maine, and notably in that part of the country watered by the tributaries of the Sagadahoc. See Ingram's curious *Relation* of his travels to the city of the Bashaba on the Penobscot.

Sylvester, *Maine Pioneer Settlements*, vol. v., pp. 73, 78.

[2] Ninigret was the chief of the Nehantics, whose habitat was

THE PEQUOD WAR

were fully two hundred Narragansetts in the party. Mason noted that the Nehantics were suspicious, and refused to allow the English to enter the fort, which aroused Mason's anger. Doubting their integrity, and regarding their attitude as hostile, he was suspicious of them, and to prevent them from sending any notice to the Pequods of his approach he sent a message to the sachem, "Since none of us may come in, none of you shall go out," upon which he posted sentinels by which they were kept securely within the fort until the following morning.[1] While they were there at Nehantic their number was being continuously increased by the arrival of other Narragansetts, by reason of which many of the Nehantics were induced to join them. On this

---

at Wekapaug, now Westerly, R. I. He was of the Narragansetts. Janemo was the first name by which he was known to the English. He was a cousin to Miantonomoh. The story of Ninigret begins with the death of Miantonomoh. In his dealings with the English he was always on the delinquent list. He never kept his agreements with them, unless he was actually forced to do so. He was proud, self-seeking, and always went about with a chip on his shoulder.

Prince, *Chronology*, vol. ii., pp. 7, 10.

Drake, *Book of the Indians*, p. 67.

On the division of the captive Pequots, 1637, Ninigret was to have twenty, "when he should satisfy for a mare of Eltweed [Eltwood] Pomroye's killed by his [Ninigret's] men."

Drake, *Book of the Indians*, p. 83.

[1] Hubbard, *Indian Wars*, p. 23.

Mason's *Account*.

occasion they engaged in a war-dance, making a great noise, shouting their courage, and protesting how they alone, without the assistance of the English, would destroy the Pequods.[1]

The following morning the English again took up their march, estimating the number of their savage allies at five hundred. It was one of those spring days to which the sun brings an excessive warmth, and as they toiled over the country and through the woods, want of food, the heat of the day, and the fatigue of the march so affected several of the English that they found it difficult to keep up with the main body. A march of some twelve miles brought the English to the Paucatuck River. Here they came upon a fording-place where, as the Narragansetts said, was a favorite fishing-place of the Pequods. The savages discovered signs of the Pequods having been here a little before, and from the remains of fish which had been recently dressed they informed Mason that undoubtedly the Pequods were holding a great festival at their fortress.[2]

Mason halted his little army by the stream, where the men refreshed themselves with what food they had and a short interregnum of restfulness. It was here the savage allies betrayed their fear of the Pequods. This little stream was the Rubicon,

---

[1] *Mass. Hist. Coll.*, vol. xviii., p. 136.
[2] Johnson, *Wonder-working Providence.*
Mass. Hist. Coll., vol. xxiv., p. 47.

THE PEQUOD WAR

upon the other side of which were the savages who had always held them in the bondage of fear. Here their boasts of courage of the night before were forgotten; and it was here the disintegration process began among the allies. Mason, disturbed by the attitude of these children of the woods, had a conference with Uncas, of whom he asked what he thought the Indians were likely to do. It may be recalled here that Uncas was a Pequod, and was regarded by the Pequods as a renegade; he had been practically outlawed by them. Uncas replied to Mason, "The Narragansetts will all leave you, but as for myself, I will never leave you;" and in Mason's account of this war one finds this: "For which expression and some other speeches of his [Uncas], I shall never forget him, indeed he was a great friend and did us great service."[1] Fording the Paucatuck, Mason pushed on with his little force for some three miles, until he came to an open ground which the Pequods had lately planted with Indian corn. He was so near the enemy that he ordered a halt and called a council, into which some of the Indians were brought, who stated that the Pequods had two large forts in the neighborhood. One was in the immediate neighborhood; but the other might be several hours distant. It was at the latter that Sassacus had his residence.

---

[1] Mason's *Account.*
Mass. Hist. Coll., vol. xviii., pp. 136, 137.

INDIAN WARS OF NEW ENGLAND

The original design was to make a simultaneous attack on both these places; but the idea had to be abandoned. Taking up their march again, they made toward the nearest fort. Up to this time the savage allies had been in the lead; but now it became incumbent upon the English to take the van of the movement. The Indians dropped back to the rear, where they took occasion to desert by scores, and to put the Paucatuck between them and the Pequods. It was about an hour after night-fall. The English found themselves upon the edge of a swamp between two hills, and it was here they camped for the night, with the knowledge that the fort was close by. The place of this encampment is still pointed out, and is marked by two curiously-shaped boulders which are known as "Porter's Rocks." Their location is about two miles northeast of the site of the old Pequod fort. It is also a half-mile north of what is locally known as "the Head of the Mystic."[1] The night was star-lit and cool, and the landscape was made luminous by the moon. While the English and their savage allies slept on the ground without covering, their sentinels paced to and fro, their feet keeping time to the shouts and songs of the Pequods in their revelry, which were carried far over the rough woods through the silence of the night. The Pequods were holding a festival of gladness. They had seen the

---

[1] DeForest, *History of the Indians of Connecticut*, p. 128.

THE PEQUOD WAR

English vessels pass, apparently without purpose of making a landing in the Pequod country, which convinced the latter that the white men were afraid of them. This fort near-by had been reënforced by Sassacus; so the Pequods, elated by their escape from what to them might prove a serious conflict, were recounting their successes in war, filling the time with feasting and rejoicing, for on the next day they were to go out against the English. This revelry was kept up until late into the night, but at last, sunk in sleep, the fort of the Pequods was as silent as was the camp of the English.

At daybreak[1] — it was Friday, the fifth of June, 1637 — the English were up and making their preparations to proceed against the Pequods. Through the chaplain they commended themselves to the care of their Creator, and invoked his blessing upon their enterprise. They followed an Indian path for some two miles without discovering the fort or anything which might suggest it. Mason halted his troop at the foot of a hill, and whispered word was sent back to the savages for some of them to come forward. This request was answered by two savages,

---

[1] Mason's account has it: "About two Hours before Day we marched toward the Fort . . . about Break of Day we came Fair in view of the Fort standing on the Top of an Hill."
Indian Wars, p. 25.

Barry makes the date May 26, 1637, which is probably correct reckoning, O. S.
History of Massachusetts, p. 225.

Uncas and Wequash.[1] Mason made a sign with his hand, a mute inquiry, "Where is the fort?" The two savages replied, "On the top of the hill." Mason's next inquiry was, "Where are the rest of the Narragansetts?" to which Uncas replied, "In the rear, very much afraid." Mason sent Uncas back to them to assure them, telling them not to flee, but to stand behind at what distance they pleased, and "see now whether Englishmen will fight." At this time the English were on the western side of the hill. Mason sent Underhill with a few men around to the southern slope. Underhill was to take the fort on that side. Mason, when Underhill was well away, with the remainder of his force, started directly toward the main entrance.

Wearied with their dance of the previous evening, the Pequods were steeped in a profound slumber. Sunrise was reddening the east. It was that time in the day when one sleeps soundest; and, if one recalls the tragedies which occurred at Schenectady, Hadley, Deerfield, and Dover, it will be remembered that this, with the Indian, was the favorite moment of attack upon his unsuspecting

---

[1] Wequash, who acted as a guide for Mason on the expedition against Fort Mystic, was a "renegade Pequod." In that quaint work, *New England's First Fruits*, p. 5-7, he was made a "saint of." Hubbard says Roger Williams does not give him a favorable character.

Hubbard, *Indian Wars*, p. 20.

THE PEQUOD WAR

enemy. Mason and his party made the advance with great care and in absolute silence. They were undiscovered until they were able almost to put their hands upon the palisades. The silence was broken by the sharp bark of a dog. The aroused Pequods cried, "Owanux! Owanux!" ["English! English!"]. At that, Mason pushed his men forward, and, after pouring a volley through the palisades, they made a rush for the entrance. It was obstructed with bushes and boughs of trees. While some went over them, others pulled them out of the way in their haste to follow.[1] This musket-volley was answered by the Pequods with loud cries of fear and astonishment; and, taken by surprise, most of them remained in their wigwams, uncertain as to the cause of this attack. It was the moment of hesitation which was fatal to the Pequods.

Mason and his party within the palisade made their way into the main passage through the village, where they were unable to discover a single Indian. Forcing his way into one of the wigwams, he was attacked by several warriors, who attempted to capture him; but Mason defended himself so well that he killed some of his assailants with a sword. A soldier by the name of William Heydon followed his captain, which so inspired the Indians with fear that they sought every possible place of

---

[1] Mason's *Account*.
Hubbard, *Indian Wars*, p. 26.

concealment.[1] A few minutes later the English were scattered over the fort and a desultory battle on a small scale was begun, in which a large number of the Pequods were slain and some few of the English were wounded. Mason says it was not a part of the original plan to destroy the fort, his desire being to consummate the destruction of the Pequods and yet save their property. Mason was convinced that this was an impossibility. The Pequods thronged the wigwams, from which they were continuously discharging arrows, and some of them, English muskets. Some of his men were stricken with wounds; others, acting without orders, became confused in the mêlée, and were uncertain what to do. Finding himself wearied with his own exertions, he gave the order to fire the fort. In one wigwam he discovered a fire, and, catching up a brand, he held it to the mats with which the wigwam was covered.[2] In a moment, as it were, the northeast wind was sweeping the flames from wig-

---

[1] "Then we suddenly fell upon the Wigwams, The *Indians* cryed out in a most hideous Manner, some issuing from their Wigwams, shooting at us desperately, and so creeping under beds they had."
Mason's *Account*.
Hubbard, *Indian Wars*, p. 26.

[2] "We had resolved a while not to have burned it [the fort]: but being we could not come at them, I then resolved to set it on fire. After Divers of them were slain, and some of our Men sore wounded: So entering one of their wigwams, I took

THE PEQUOD WAR

wam to wigwam and the entire area of the interior, which covered some one or two acres, thickly studded with lodges, was obscured in a holocaust of fire and smoke.

Underhill, on the southern side, had just made his entrance. The Pequods had rallied there for a stout resistance. One of the English had been killed, and Uncas had an arrow in his hip. Realizing that the village was to be destroyed by fire, he kindled it still further by using powder, falling back from the heat. Mason had followed the same tactics, and the English, under the common leadership of Mason, formed a circle about the blazing lodges with their allies behind them. Within the circle, the Pequods, men, women, and children, were being mowed down by the musketry of the English, and at the same time were being roasted in the fire of their own wigwams.[1] The war-whoop of the Pequods and the cries of the women and children were mingled with the exultations of the Mohegans

---

a Fire-brand *at which Time an Indian drawing an arrow had killed him* [Mason] *but one* Davis *his sargeant cut the Bowstring with his Courtlace* [cutlass], *and suddenly kindled a Fire in the Mats wherewith they were covered, and fell to a Retreat, and surrounded the Fort."*

Mason's *Account*.

Hubbard, *Indian Wars*, p. 27.

[1] "Of those who escaped the fire, some were slain by the sword and hewn to pieces, or run through by rapiers. It was a fearful sight to see them frying in the fire, streams of blood

INDIAN WARS OF NEW ENGLAND

and Narragansetts. The Pequods fought until their bow-strings were rendered useless by the heat of the fire. Some made no attempt to escape, while others rushed headlong into the flames in their terror. A small body of Pequods without the fortress, on the northward, shot their arrows at the English, until they, too, were vanquished by the muskets. A little party of forty of the boldest Pequods made a sally and forced their way through the English, hoping to make the neighboring woods. A few were successful; the others mostly were killed by the English or by their allies. The larger part of the Pequods lost their lives in the fort; and so rapidly had the fire swept over this little area that hardly an hour had elapsed before the destruction of this settlement had been completed.[1]

In this brief fight one realizes the terrible ven-

---

quenching the same; and horrible was the stench thereof. But the victory seemed a *sweet* sacrifice, and the people gave the praise to God."

Vide note, Morton.

Freeman, *Civilization and Barbarism*, p. 61.

Also, *ibid*, a quotation from the "learned and pious Rev. Cotton Mather:" "Many of them were broiled unto death in the avenging flames; many climbing to the tops of the palisades, were a fair mark for *mortiferous* bullets; and many who had the resolution to issue forth were slain by the English who stood ready to bid them welcome."

[1] DeForest, *History of Connecticut*, p. 133.

According to Mason, there were killed of the Pequods

THE PEQUOD WAR

geance the English had taken upon the Pequods, when only seven were made captive, while perhaps as many more made their escape to the woods. Mason lost two of his party, killed outright; twenty were wounded. Mason was saved by his helmet; Lieutenant Bull, by a hard piece of cheese which he carried in his pocket, by which the fatal arrow was stopped; while two other men were saved by the hard knot in their neckcloths.

While Mason had been victorious in his assault, he was yet in a dangerous situation. His soldiers were worn out by fatigue, loss of sleep, and the exertion of fighting; while four or five, by reason of their wounds, had to be carried by their companions.[1] Not over forty men were fit for active service. Some of the Indians were wounded. The Narragansetts, upon discovering that the English were going to the west, turned their faces towards their own country. Mason scanned the waters of the Sound for his vessels, which were nowhere

---

"about four hundred." Seven were made prisoners. "Seven, at the utmost, escaped."

Vide the narratives of Mason, Underhill, Vincent, and Gardiner in the *Mass. Hist. Coll.*, and compare accounts of Winthrop, Hutchinson, and Trumbull.

The campaign had consumed less than three weeks, once the English left Saybrook, and the English loss was less than twenty-five killed and wounded.

Trumbull, *Indian Wars*, p. 56.

[1] "Four or five of our men were so wounded that they must

to be seen, and for that reason he was uncertain whither to direct his march. Within an hour or so they discovered their little fleet sweeping into the Pequod River under a spanking breeze; but this satisfaction was not to last, for almost at the moment of his discovery of the wished-for assistance a considerable body of Pequods were approaching them from the west. Mason estimated their number to be about three hundred. These were the Pequods from the fort where Sassacus had his residence, being attracted hither by the noise of the guns. Furious at this invasion of their territory, there was no limit to their rage or desire for vengeance, and, filling the air with war-whoops, they swept down upon the English—only to be abruptly checked by two files of soldiers, numbering not more than fourteen men. These latter were able to cover the retreat of Mason and his party, who took up their march towards the mouth of the Thames. They were followed by the savages until

---

be carried, with the Arms of twenty more. We also being faint, were constrained to put four to one Man, with the Arms of the rest that were wounded to others: So that we had not above forty Men free. At length we hired several Indians, who eased us of that Burthen in carrying our wounded Men."

Mason, *Account*.

Vide Captain Stoughton's *Letter* in the Appendix to Mather's *Relation*, p. 286.

THE PEQUOD WAR

they came to the site of the fort which Mason had just destroyed, where they discovered, in the place of seventy wigwams surrounded by a stout palisade, only the smoking ruins and the dead bodies of their relatives and friends. The Indian had been called the stoic of the wilderness; but the Pequods, stunned by the blow for a little time, indulged in all the agony of grief and rage;[1] and then, with a sharp cry of vengeance, they came down the hill as if they would overwhelm the English, only to be stopped again by the muskets. At the foot of this hill was a brook, where Mason halted his party for a short rest, the Pequods keeping at a safe distance, their purpose evidently more to watch their enemy than to attack them. It was at this point that the Mohegans and the Narragansetts got their courage up to the pitch so that they began to engage with the Pequods. Underhill describes their manner of

---

[1] Mather says of the Indians who came up from Sassacus's fort: "They were like bears bereft of their whelps, and continued a bloody fight. When they came to see the ashes of their friends at the fort, and the bodies of their men horribly barbecued, *where the English had been doing a good morning's work* [the annotator has taken the liberty to italicize the original text], they howled, they roared, they stamped, they tore their hair, and (though they did not swear, for they knew not how yet,) they cursed and were pictures of so many devils in desperation."

Freeman, *Civilization and Barbarism*, p. 62, note.

fighting, in which he comes to the conclusion that in seven years they would not kill seven men.[1]

Mason, in describing this fight between the Pequods and the Narragansetts, said they stood at a distance from each other and aimed their arrows at an elevation. After letting the arrow fly, they watched its course deliberately; and it was their habit never to shoot a second until they saw the effect of the first.[2] Mason was still on the retreat, all the time getting nearer that point of the shore which was likely to be most adjacent to the vessels which were coming to his assistance. He had accomplished his errand, and for the present was satisfied with the result. The fighting on the part of the savages was of the most desultory description. At this time some fifty of the Narragansetts, taking advantage of what they thought was a most excellent opportunity to return to their own country, detached themselves from their allies. They were discovered by the Pequods, by whom they were pursued and surrounded. It was apparently the turn of the Pequod to satisfy his vengeance, being about to take a bloody revenge for the destruction of the Mystic fort. When those Narragansetts who remained with Mason discovered the dilemma in which their comrades were, they begged Mason and his officers to go to their assistance. Mason

---

[1] Underhill, *Mass. Hist. Coll.*, vol. xxxvi., pp. 25, 26.
[2] Mason, *Mass. Hist. Coll.*, vol. xviii., pp. 141, 142.

THE PEQUOD WAR

upbraided them for what he called a desertion; yet, being unwilling to have the Pequods triumph over any portion of his forces, he sent Underhill with thirty men to their rescue. The chroniclers of these events set Underhill down as a braggart of considerable dimensions.

Underhill's story is that the conflict with these Pequods lasted an hour, with the final result that the Pequods were driven off with a loss of one hundred or more killed or wounded.[1] Vincent records this episode, and DeForest intimates the former seemed to have a spite against Underhill. Vincent describes Underhill as a poltroon, and goes on to say that "after the discharge of five muskets, the Pequods took to their heels." Underhill says — and his statement seems perfectly reasonable — that the Indians were very much astonished at the English manner of fighting. They called it "matchit," or evil. As a method of fighting, for the Pequods, it was altogether too fast and furious, and, as well, too destructible. The fashion of fighting among the savages was to obtain the advantage of an enemy by strategy, skulking, or surprise. The savage never fought in the open, unless he was possessed

---

[1] Hubbard notes, in his *Indian Wars*, p. 15, that Capt. John Underhill "published a most interesting History of the Expedition of General Endicot, which like Gardener's has been reprinted. It carries evidence of Truthfulness with it, as well as the Quaintness of an Old Soldier of that Day."

of overpowering numbers. His preference was the ambush. In the early years of the settlements this method of attack on the part of the savages was not taken with the degree of seriousness that it deserved; and after the English discovered the practice of his assailant he began to adopt the same tactics, and the savage then saw the white man was no less wily and wary than himself. Once the English settler had learned the lesson, he was the superior of the Indian in the Indian's method of fighting.

Mason kept to his retreat, but slowly, sending out skirmishers in advance, prodding every thicket and swamp, and firing bullets into their mystery for the purpose of dislodging their secret enemy should any happen to be lurking in ambush. The Pequods clung to the rear of this retreating body, and from behind rocks and trees, and such other shelter as lay in their path, they shot showers of ineffectual arrows. This pursuit was kept up by the Pequods until the English had come within perhaps two miles of the ships, when the former congregated in a body, and, after an apparent consultation, were lost to sight in the woods. The English kept to their march shoreward, where they found their ships awaiting them, with Captain Patrick and forty men on board. Patrick did not reach Narragansett until after Mason's departure overland. He found the ships and decided to take passage on them around to Pequod Harbor. Mason says his men

THE PEQUOD WAR

would have joined Patrick on the vessels at once, had it not been for the objection of the Narragansetts to being left alone in the country of the Pequods. For that reason, only the wounded and thirty-five or forty others took ship, while Mason, with twenty men, and Patrick, with his forty, along with their Indian allies, set out through the woods for Saybrook. On the line of their march was a little village belonging to the western Nehantics, the dwellers of which, suspicious of the purpose of the English, abandoned their village to hide in an adjacent swamp. The English followed them, pushed through the swamp, and drove them out on the opposite side, to lose them among the rolling ground or hillocks which lay beyond. The savages were so scattered that the pursuit was difficult; so the English, coming together again, took up their march, and in the edge of dusk they made the mouth of the Connecticut. Their coming being made known, they were welcomed with a cannon salute from the fortress on the opposite shore.[1]

Thus ended a long and arduous day for Mason and his men. A famous expedition, as well, in which the Connecticut settlers had been pitted against their natural enemy, was brought to a victorious close. It was an expedition, from many points of view, conducted with great courage, with

---

[1] Mason, *Mass. Hist. Coll.*, vol. xviii., pp. 143, 144.

perhaps more good luck than skill, but crowned with a most satisfactory success to the Connecticut settlers. It was hardly more than a massacre and indiscriminate killing of everything animate that had resemblance to a Pequod, from which escape seemed almost impossible, and in which an entire aboriginal community was condemned to a most horrible method of destruction.[1] It was nothing more than retaliation, one wild beast flying at the throat of another; and however atrocious the circumstances may seem at this present time, there is no question but what there were extenuating circumstances.

Mason has been severely criticized for the barbarous manner by which the Pequods were wiped

---

[1] To Endicott and Mason, the punishment meted out to the Pequods was that merited by an incorrigible malefactor who defied all human law and restraint; whose bloodthirsty cruelty, subtlety, and treachery had as well placed him in the category of beasts of prey. Of all the New England savages of which history has made record, the Pequod was the acme of devilish ingenuity and Satanic perfection. That the intolerant Puritan found in the extinction of this race a vent for his vindictiveness, natural or accumulate, is evidenced by the thoroughness with which he followed up these homeless fugitives, putting them to the slaughter with as slight compunction as he would have shot the wildcat that preyed upon his sheepfold; or selling their helpless women and children into a slavery worse than death. Assuredly the Puritan should be handled tenderly, unless one is content to stir up more ghosts than ever walked Bosworth Field.

THE PEQUOD WAR

out of existence in this particular place; but Mason was a soldier, with a soldier's conscience, and, once he had put his hand to the plow, with him there was no turning back. It was, without question, an act of great cruelty, especially in the putting of the women and children to the slaughter; yet the provocation was great, and, to Mason, the necessity was imperative. The Pequods had no right to ask for quarter. They had no argument to make as to the violation of any particular rule of humanity. They had set the pace with Oldham and at Wethersfield, and openly boasted that whenever the opportunity came they would repeat their ferocities. They had roasted Butterfield at the stake, as well as Tilly. They had slain men and women at Wethersfield; they had carried their children away into captivity; and much of this had been a matter of visual experience on the part of the colonists. It is no wonder that the cup of vengeance, once at the white man's lips, should be drained to the very dregs. Mason's firing the wigwams was undoubtedly the only means of his salvation; he and his men were targets for unseen foes lurking among the shadows of the wigwams; all of them might have been shot down without discovering the source of the attack. He had run his quarry into this hole, and he purposed to smoke it out. The English were no doubt actuated by the spirit of desperation; for they were in a strange country, short of food, and exhausted by weariness. Some had been killed, others wounded; and theirs was to conquer, or submit to certain annihilation. With them, any means justified the end. It will be noticed in this consideration that the savage allies had not, up to the point of firing the fort, taken any active part in the assault. They were as likely to fly as they were to defend; and, as DeForest says: "Had Mason continued to fight on as he began, so many of his soldiers would have been killed and disabled that the rest might have been overwhelmed by their wounds, and, at best, obliged to abandon their wounded, making a clamorous retreat." When, the moment before, Mason seized the brand that set the matted roofs of the wigwams aflame his position was critical. He came near being killed himself. His men were scattered about a hostile enclosure, a disintegrate force acting without orders, each fighting apparently on his own account, and altogether beyond direction amid a bedlam of tumult which would have smothered any order he might have given. Had he sounded a retreat, the first backward step would have started the Narragansetts homeward. The savages they came to attack would have become the attacking party, and his expedition would have been a failure.

Mason was rough, but of good mettle; a man of stern policies and unyielding in his determination. This firing of the Pequod fort was bound to become efficacious, from the fact that the threatening and bloodthirsty Pequod was taught the lesson that

THE PEQUOD WAR

while the English settler, upon the surface, was apparently a pacific individual, yet upon emergency he could be as cruel and revengeful as himself.

It was a terrible lesson, roughly administered, and, to such tribes as had been uninfluenced by the Pequods, a suggestion of the punishment which would be meted out to them in case they committed any overt act against the English. This evidently was the phase which struck the Pequods most forcibly; for, on the following day, a council of the nation was called and held, which resolved itself into a discussion as to the course which they had better pursue for the future. Heretofore victorious in their forays upon their savage neighbors, they had received a sudden and unexpected defeat, which was an intimation to them of other defeats should they continue to array themselves against the English in a hostile manner. DeForest says that three plans of action were considered. The first was to flee the country; the second, to follow up the English with an attack; the third was to declare war against the Narragansetts and to visit upon them the devastation wrought by the English.[1] Their chief sachem, Sassacus, was in favor of carrying the war into the country of the Narragansetts, and even to the strongholds of the English. Perhaps, with the vision of a seer, he foresaw the ultimate ex-

---

[1] DeForest, *History of the Indians*, p. 141.
Underhill, *Mass. Hist. Coll.*, vol. xxxvi., p. 28.

tinction of his people and preferred to die in battle rather than to become a wanderer among strange tribes. The traditions of the Pequod were not such as would entitle him to any generosity at the hands of the neighboring nations. His people were to become strangers in their own land; they were without friends, or allies. The majority of his people were not inclined to accept his proposition. Unaccustomed to defeat, they were discouraged at the extent of their calamity and were in favor of quitting the domains of their forefathers and of going, at that moment, they knew not where. One thing they were determined upon, and that was to abandon their country. The ties of home were to be severed; and their wigwams, their corn-fields, their hunting and fishing grounds, and even the graves of their progenitors to be abandoned. Mason's attack had fallen upon them like lightning out of a clear sky. Heretofore, they had always seen the blow before it reached them, and had been able to ward it off. In this instance the hand of destruction smote them before they had seen it. This was their final decision in solemn conclave, and one can imagine the sorrow and heaviness of heart with which they seized the torch which they unhesitatingly thrust against the wigwams that had crowned the hill-top where Sassacus and his fathers had held royal sway.[1] Such of their belongings as

---

[1] Underhill, *Mass. Hist. Coll.*, vol. xxxvi., p. 28.

Before the Pequots destroyed their fortress they revenged

THE PEQUOD WAR

could not be carried with them they destroyed, with possibly one last, lingering look upon the wide country spread out at their feet, painted with the early blush of summer. Separated into little knots of savage humanity which were possibly made up of such as were nearest of kin, they hastily made their way to their canoes, and then they swept out over the mirroring waters of the stream to Quinepauge.

This seat of Sassacus has been located at New London. In the height of his power he is said to have been the lord of twenty-six sachems. Thus, the once conquerors of this Pequod country, themselves conquered, had abandoned it to the English settler. It is recorded that thirty or forty of the Pequod warriors with their families took their way

---

themselves upon Uncas, formerly of the ruling house of that nation, and his followers, as well, by killing all of Uncas's relatives then living among them.

DeForest, p. 140.

The site of Sassacus's royal residence was on a commanding eminence a little easterly of what has been known as Fort Griswold.

The fort destroyed by Mason was on Pequot Hill, near the Mystic River. Freeman says this latter was the royal seat, "the seat of the Pequot power."

Freeman, *Civilization and Barbarism*, p. 62.

But, *contra*, Hubbard says: "Wesquash . . . proved a good Guide, by whose Direction they were led to a Fort near *Mystic River, some miles nearer than Sassacus his Fort, which they first intended to assault.*"

Hubbard, *Indian Wars*, p. 20.

into the country to the westward. Longing for the sight of a familiar horizon, possibly disheartened by the strange situation in which they found themselves, they returned into their native country, secreting themselves in the recesses of a swamp.[1] The main body of several hundred, comprising other warriors, squaws, and children of the nation at whose head were Sassacus, Mononotto, and some other sagamores, carried out their purpose with a greater resignation. They kept on; whither, they knew not. To escape the hated English was their sole desire. On reaching the Connecticut River they had opportunity to wreak some slight vengeance upon the English. Three colonists were going down the river in a shallop. They were immediately attacked by the Pequods. The English fought for their lives, wounding many of the enemy with their muskets; but, overwhelmed by the Pequods, one was killed, and the other two were taken captive. Upon these the savages wrought a most ferocious vengeance. They split the bodies of their captives open from breast to back, and hung the mutilated remains on the trees by the side of the river, that whoever of the hated English sailed up or down might see what was in store for them should they have the misfortune to fall into the hands of these people.[2]

---

[1] Winthrop, vol. i., p. 232.

[2] Underhill, *Mass. Hist. Coll.*, vol. xxxvi., p. 28.

Trumbull says: "They ripped them from the bottom of

THE PEQUOD WAR

After this they crossed the Connecticut, where they shifted their course toward the coast. It was in the late spring-time, in the planting-season. Their provisions left over from the preceding year depleted or destroyed, their condition was precarious. The seashore would afford clams and oysters, with which life might be sustained until such time as their fortunes might change for the better. Scouring the forest for succulent roots; without shelter, exposed to the elements; sleeping on the ground in the open air, wet and drenched in the rain, their cup of misery must have been full. This retreat was slow, by reason of the accompanying children and squaws. Their journeys were short, and their halts frequent. Passing through a country which was without provisions, or means of supply; crossing the domains of the Quinnipiacs and the Wepawaugs, they finally found shelter in a considerable swamp in what is now Fairfield. For many of them it was to be a burial-place; for here was to take place the final conflict between the English and the Pequods.

The Bay colonists had been slow in assisting their neighbors, a trait which became proverbial in later years, when the savages began their incursions upon the settlements bordering along the Maine

---

their bellies to their throats, and in a like manner split them down their backs, and thus mangled, hung them upon the trees by the river-side."
Indian Wars, p. 51.

coast. It was only when the savages had broken over the New Hampshire border and the towns along the North Shore were likely to be attacked that Massachusetts Bay awoke to the necessity of undertaking a general defence against the Indians; and it so happened that the force which was raised in the Bay Colonies to be despatched to Connecticut did not get away until the latter end of June, when the main stroke against the Pequods had already been delivered; and even then Stoughton's force had been reduced to one hundred twenty men, for the reason that the Bay people had concluded that the power of the Pequods had been so much broken that it would require fewer men to complete their extermination.[1]

The overthrow of the Pequods by Mason at Fort

---

[1] "A rumor having reached Boston that all the English and the Indians had been cut off in the retreat from Fort Mystic, which rumor was confirmed by a post from Plymouth, the movement of the troops was delayed until word arrived from Roger Williams that the army was safe and that 'all the Pequots were fled, and had forsaken their forts.'"

Barry, *History of Massachusetts*, vol. i., p. 228.
Winthrop, vol. i., p. 169.
Mason, *2 Mass. Hist. Coll.*, vol. viii., p. 143.
Trumbull, vol. i., pp. 81, 82.

Barry says this delay on the part of Massachusetts in sending troops to the aid of the Connecticut settlers was on account of differences which existed between the Plymouth Colony and its more ambitious rival up the bay.

Barry, *History of Massachusetts*, vol. i., p. 227.

THE PEQUOD WAR

Mystic, and the utter destruction of that place, was a matter of great rejoicing among the colonists, who began to breathe more freely as their anxieties were relieved. The news was received in Massachusetts with great satisfaction, and the authorities, now that the savages were on the run, determined to give them no time to recover from the blow so thoroughly administered by Mason. It has been noted that Stoughton sailed with his contingent in June, almost at the last of the month, and, having good success, he landed at the mouth of the Pequod River, hoping there to make some connection with the Connecticut soldiery. Not finding any of the Connecticut people there, he took up his march to the westward, with some anticipation of meeting the Pequods; but, unsuccessful in his search for the enemy, — which was not at all surprising, from their well-known habit of skulking, — he retraced his steps, coming back to the mouth of the stream, where he was joined by a few of the Narragansett tribe, who brought him the welcome information that some of their people had discovered the hiding-place of the Pequods and were watching to see that they did not escape before the English could come up with them. This was the little band of savages first mentioned, which had started out upon a journey to the westward, but who had turned back into their own country.

The Narragansetts offered to guide Stoughton to the hiding-place of the Pequods. He at once

INDIAN WARS OF NEW ENGLAND

placed himself under their direction, and, making a quick march of about twelve miles, he came upon this unfortunate remnant. They were too few to make any successful defence, and they were unable to escape, as the Narragansetts had hemmed them about completely, with the result that they were every one captured. This little body of Pequods made no resistance. Two of their sachems were given their lives on the condition that they would lead Stoughton and his men to the place of hiding of the larger body, under the command of Sassacus. The other warriors captured at this time they slaughtered in cold blood.[1] In this raid they took

---

[1] Winthrop, vol. i., p. 232.
Hubbard, *Indian Wars*, p. 42.

Hubbard says of the fight with Sassacus and his savages: "The Men among them to the Number of thirty were turned presently into Charon's Ferry-boat, under the Command of Skipper Gallop, who dispatched them a little without the Harbor. The Females and Children were disposed of according to the Will of the Conquerors; some being given to the Narhagansets and other *Indians* that assisted in the Service."
Hubbard, *Indian Wars*, p. 30.

It was this sort of "service" that inspired Mather to prayers of thankfulness and praise.

This was the same John Gallop who recaptured Oldham's pinnace from the savages off the Manisees in 1636. Gallop was prominent among the settlers of Connecticut. He had a son John, a captain in King Philip's War, who was killed at the Narragansett Fort battle, December 19, 1675.
Miss Caulkin's *History of New London*.

THE PEQUOD WAR

captive some eighty squaws, with their children. Thirty of these were turned over to the Narragansetts, three to the Massachusetts Indians, and the remainder were sent to the Massachusetts colonists as slaves.[1]

No comment which the annalists of later times might attempt could possibly compass the vindictiveness of the English upon this occasion. The

---

[1] Winthrop, who had this year, 1636–37, been reëlected Governor of Massachusetts, defeating Vane after a tumultuous campaign in which the General Court nearly came to blows, had this letter from Captain Stoughton. The latter wrote: "By this pinnace, you shall receive 48 or 50 women and children, unless there stay any here to be helpful, concerning which there is one, I formerly mentioned, that is the *fairest* and *largest* amongst them to whom I have given a coate to cloathe her. It is my desire to have her for a servant, if it may stand to your good liking, else not. There is a little squaw that steward Culacut desireth, to whom he hath given a coate. Lieut. Davenport also desireth one, to wit, a small one, that hath three strokes upon her stomach thus; — | | | +. He desireth her, if it will stand with your good liking. Sosomon, the Indian, desireth a young little squaw, which I know not."

MS. Letter of Captain Stoughton, *State Papers.*

Drake, *Book of the Indians*, p. 106.

One hardly fails to note the truckling of these man-hunters to Winthrop. It is suggestive of the more modern Tammany, and as a side-light upon the political domination of the period it is fairly luminous.

Captain Israel Stoughton, who commanded the Massachusetts forces, was commissioned a colonel by Parliament and fought under Cromwell. Stoughton was not in the attack

INDIAN WARS OF NEW ENGLAND

only palliation available to the historian recording these transactions is to imagine himself surrounded with the perils which menaced the meager population of the English at that time. If one could imagine himself in a wilderness of woods beset by a pack of hungry wolves he might better appreciate the situation. The colonists in the aggregate as compared with these aboriginal people were but a handful; and had the savages been equipped with weapons and ammunition as were the English, and had they understood their manipulation as they did a century later, the story of the English occupation of New England would have afforded a

---

on Fort Mystic which Mason describes as, "the breaking of the Nest, and unkennelling those savage wolves."

Drake suggests that Stoughton, in writing this letter, had an eye to the profit he might derive from the sale of his captive; that he was less interested in fighting the savages. He refers to Mason as not giving Stoughton much credit. Stoughton stood for the avowed Puritan thrift in this transaction, to say nothing of the Puritan conscience. There was little difference between the Puritan slave-catcher and the government that profited by the transaction. Winthrop in the saddle, the course of affairs in the main responded to his touch upon the bridle-rein. Stoughton relied upon Winthrop to lend a willing acquiescence to his scheme of personal aggrandizement, and there is no evidence of any disagreement between them. The suggestion is a rather malodorous one; but in the early relations of the English with the Indian it is not to be passed over in silence by the historian.

Drake, *Book of the Indians*, p. 106.

THE PEQUOD WAR

much different narrative. The advantage which the English had over the savage was that the latter did not appreciate the numerical weakness of the former; and, as has been before noted, had it not been for the antagonisms which existed among these Indians prior to the coming of the English, a confederacy might have been established among them against which the English would have been unable to contest. With Endicott, Mason, and Stoughton, the punishment meted out to the Pequods was the same as would have been deserved by any incorrigible malefactor who had broken all the laws of humanity, and whose bloodthirstiness, subtlety, and treachery had placed him without the pale of humanity and human protection.

To the English, these aborigines were so many wild beasts; and they were to be shot with as slender consideration as one would annihilate a pack of wolves at his heels. To the English colonists the cruelties practised by the Pequods with every opportunity offered could not but strike terror to the heart of the bravest man or woman. These experiences of the English at the hands of the savages, which were acutely illustrated in the cases of Oldham, Butterfield, and Tilly, and latterly of the two Englishmen who had been split open and hung upon the trees above the banks of the Connecticut, afforded an illustration from which the English imbibed their spirit of retaliation.

Of all the New England savages of which history

INDIAN WARS OF NEW ENGLAND

has made any record, the Pequod was of a race for which one has but slender sympathy and compassion. He was the acme of devilish ingenuity and satanic savagery. His chief delight was in watching the slow agony of his captive under the torture, as the strands of human endurance broke one by one, and finally ended in the death of the victim. No wonder the retaliatory disposition of the English was aroused deeply, or that for a time they forgot themselves, to become, like the savages they had doomed to destruction, another parcel of wild beasts. It is barely possible that in the consummation of these killings of the Pequods the intolerancy of the Puritan found a natural vent, and that he carried on this work with a grim satisfaction. *En masse*, the Puritans were a rude sort, and it is, perhaps, not too much to say that these savage carnivals, carried on without much risk or danger to themselves, were tinged with fanaticism, as was the Jesuit whose hand consummated the massacre of St. Bartholomew.

As against the English bullet, the arrow of the Indian was an unavailing weapon; and one can imagine the exultant mood which contracted the muscles of the finger that pulled the trigger of the English musket. These men were of an adventurous spirit, as were most of their fellows at home, and not too much is to be expected of them. In every man is the latent disposition of retaliation, and it is only as the process of civilization is per-

THE PEQUOD WAR

fected that men overcome this disposition to revenge themselves upon others for injuries received at their hands; so it is not strange that these people, originally of the commoner stock of England, which, at that time, was more or less acquainted with the atrocities of warfare, should have entered into the hunting of their own kind, though of a different color, with the murderous zeal which apparently actuated them in their conflict with the Indians.

These colonists, by their long English training, were accustomed to the lording of others over them. Their traditions extended back to the days of feudalism, and they had imbibed from their ancestors the same rude characteristics which were the original foundation of the people from whom they had emanated. Many of them had left the Old Country for the New with the anticipation that, once among the wilds of New England, their personal liberties would be more ample, and that, once there, they might follow out their own personal inclinations. It is not to be disputed that the rulers of the Bay Colony understood the material out of which they were to mould the new State. This material, under the guiding hand of Winthrop and his assistants, who were largely made up of a court of his own choosing, was directed and controlled by an inflexible purpose; and yet, with the breath of the New World in their nostrils, they had assumed the rôle of master — but clumsily, and without the refinements common to a greater intelligence; and this perhaps may be their apology. We do the same thing in these later days, only in a different way; the result is the same. The weaker goes to the wall unnoticed and unnoted; and if the barbarities of the earlier years of the colonial settlements in their manner of expression have become obsolete, it is nevertheless true, in these days, that the strong succeed only at the expense of the weak.

Leaving the Puritans to their fortunes and to such commendation as they can win from their posterity, we return to Stoughton. After this massacre of the Pequods, which evidently was Stoughton's first experience, he was joined by Mason, whose forces consisted of forty Connecticut men. Together, they made up a considerable force, and a campaign of offence was planned. The fact that the Pequods had practically become a race of wanderers might have suggested the withdrawing of these forces, and their return to a more peaceful occupation; but it is evident that the forlorn condition of the Pequods had no appealing force with them. The Pequods had lost their courage, were starving, and in flight. Nevertheless, a pursuit of sixty miles through the wilderness into a country unfamiliar to the English settler, and perhaps where no English explorer had as yet been, was inaugurated. The action of the English is self-evident. Their determination was the annihilation of the Pequods. That these unfortunate people were to be reduced to a condition which should render them so

THE PEQUOD WAR

insignificant as a race, should make them so helpless in their contention against others, that they would have neither the desire nor the ability to resume the rude life which had made their original country habitable to their ancestors was the avowed purpose of the white settler, once the savage was in his power.

The English were apparently actuated by fanatic sternness, which in many other instances afterward marked the people in and about Massachusetts Bay with a singular inhumanity to their own kind. In their homes, possibly, they possessed the usual attributes of gentleness and consideration for those who were dependent upon them; but to such as dared to raise the voice of dissent against what they chose to regard as their peculiar and established principle along religious lines they were as inflexible and unyielding, as inconsiderate and ungenerous, as the stones upon which the sills of their habitations were laid.[1]

---

[1] Dr. Mather says in one of his remarkable perturbations of spirit: "By the year 1636, it was Time for the *Devil* to take the *Alarm*, and make some *Attempt* in Opposition to the *Possession* which the Lord Jesus Christ was going to have of *these utmost parts of the Earth.* These *Parts* were then covered with Nations of barbarous *Indians* and Infidels, in which the *Prince of the Power of the Air* did *Work as a Spirit:* nor could it be expected that Nations of Wretches, whose whole Religion was the most explicit Sort of *Devil-Worship,* should not be acted by the Devil to engage in some early and bloody

INDIAN WARS OF NEW ENGLAND

From this consideration of the motives which actuated the leaders, as well as the men who made up the colonial forces in this campaign, one notes they embarked at Saybrook to follow the Pequods in their vessels. Uncas, with the Narragansetts, took up the trail of the Pequods overland. They could follow them easily, and, taking note of their halting-places, and the frequency of them, and how they

---

Action for the extinction of a Plantation so Contrary to his Interests, as that of *New England* was."

Magnalia Christi Americana, bk. vii., p. 41.

Purchas, *His Pilgrimage*, p. 717.

Increase Mather, in his Election Sermon, 1677, p. 76 (1685 edition) says: "Our Fathers did not in their coming hither propound any great Matter to themselves respecting this world;" but they believed, according to Drake, that "here was the Place where Christ was to take up his Abode while on Earth, at his second Appearing."

With this accepted and regularly ordained minister's preaching such dogma, what expectation could one entertain of fair treatment of the aborigine at the hands of the Puritan?

Here is another excerpt from Mather: "The Natives of the Countrey now possessed by the *New Englanders*, had been forlorn and wretched Heathen ever since their first herding here; and tho we know not *when* or *how* those *Indians* first became Inhabitants of this mighty Continent, yet we may guess that probably, the Divil decoyed those miserable Salvages hither, in Hopes that the Gospel of the Lord Jesus would never come here to destroy or disturb his *Absolute Empire* over them."

Mather, *Life of the Renowned John Eliot* p. 64 (Boston edition, 1691).

THE PEQUOD WAR

had been compelled to dig up the scurf of the woods for edible roots, and alongshore where they had turned up the mud for shell-fish, they were able to estimate very accurately the time required for overtaking the fugitives. From time to time they captured a savage straggler from the main body under Sassacus, and from such they obtained the required information as to the number and condition of the Pequods. It will be remembered, two sachems were reprieved by Stoughton on the condition that they would guide the English into the near neighborhood of the main body of the Pequods. These two sachems became conscience-stricken, or, possibly, to save their lives had consented to an act of duplicity. It may have been an act of subtlety on their part, in which their purpose was reserved; for their loyalty to Sassacus now became manifest in that they declined to show the English where Sassacus had gone into hiding. As a reward for their loyalty to their own race, as soon as they reached Menunketuc (Guilford) they paid the penalty of what the English were pleased to call treachery,[1] for it was here they were killed out of hand. Winthrop has it that it was this episode by which the point of land stretching out into the stream came to be called Sachem's Head. Ruggles, in his history of Guilford, puts it differently. He records that during the march of Uncas and his

---

[1] Winthrop, vol. i., p. 233.

men overland they came upon a Pequod sachem and a few others, whom they at once pursued. These latter fled along the shore of the eastern point of Guilford Harbor, evidently with the idea, or the hope, that the Narragansetts would keep to the trail on the main land, and pass by them unwittingly. They turned the corner of this little cape to conceal themselves near its extremity. Uncas had been too long a hunter of his own kind to be put off by any such artifice, and he directed his men to scour the point for the fugitives, while he with some others would keep on their way, that they might gain the opposite shore. The Pequods, discovering themselves pursued and seeing no other way of escape, took to the water, swimming across the mouth of the harbor to the opposite shore, where, as they landed, they were easily captured by this stratagem of Uncas. Uncas shot an arrow at the sachem, and then, cutting off his head, he fixed it securely in the crotch of an oak-tree, where the grinning skull withered and bleached in the sun for many years.[1]

While Uncas had been making his way along the trail of the Pequods the vessels which carried the English hugged the coast to the westward, and three days later entered the harbor of New Haven. Their first discovery after their arrival was a considerable column of smoke, which rose above the

---

[1] *Mass. Hist. Coll.*, vol. x., p. 100.

THE PEQUOD WAR

tops of the woods. In a spirit of elation, believing that they had come upon the Pequods, there was a hasty landing of the troops, and a forced march through the forest. They followed the smoke to the fire which made it, and one can appreciate their disappointment when they found about it, instead of the Pequods, a little band of timid and friendly Indians who lived in the vicinity.

An instance which illustrates the depression under which the Pequods were laboring by reason of their many misfortunes, misfortunes which had so suddenly fallen to their lot, is afforded by the adventure of a Mohegan. At Quinnipiac, a Mohegan by the name of Jack Etow met three Pequods. Two of them he captured and carried to the English vessels.[1] Under ordinary circumstances the Mohegan would have been the captive; but these Pequods without doubt gave themselves up with the hope that the English might provide that food for them to which they had been a stranger for weeks, and possibly some shelter in the place of their life of exposure. One of these was granted his life upon condition. The English were in search of Sassacus; their object was to take his life or discover his place of retreat. To accomplish either of these two things the English would forbear their glut for vengeance. So the Pequod was let loose on the promise that he would either bring

---

[1] Mason, *Mass. Hist. Coll.*, vol. xviii., p. 146.

back the news of Sassacus's death, or such information as would enable them to find him. The Pequod had no difficulty in finding Sassacus, whose company he joined and with whom he remained for some days, during which he had no opportunity to carry out the wishes of the English. The Pequods at last became suspicious of this savage, and to avoid their watchful jealousy he was compelled to make his escape, which he did under the darkness of night. He kept his word with the English, returning to their camp, where he gave them the information which they required as to the number of the Pequods, and the place where they were to be found.

The English again took up their march, June 3, 1637, starting off to the westward toward a place called Sasco. Here was an extensive swamp, which lay not far from the seashore.

Johnson, an early New England writer whose quaintness is most interesting, relates an incident which in his telling of it takes on a laughable aspect. The English were pushing on through the forest. They had broken through a jungle of brush, where, unknown to them, two Pequod savages were hiding. These Pequods were not only watching the progress of the English, but, after their fashion, were lying in wait for an opportunity to perform some exploit by which the English might be injured. They watched patiently while the English filed by, and when, as they supposed, the last man

THE PEQUOD WAR

was passing, they broke cover, and, in this moment of surprise, they had thrown him across their shoulders and started with their captive for the depths of the swamp. The Englishman made an outcry, and it was a matter of good fortune for him that the lieutenant of his company closed up the rear, who, coming to his assistance, began a swift attack upon the Pequods with his sword. The Pequods turned their captive into a shield, who was tumbled and tossed about in a most marvelous way, and with such infinite swiftness that for a considerable time Davenport was unable to touch them with his sword. He finally succeeded in reaching the Pequods with his weapon, and as soon as the blood began to run out of their copper-colored skins they dropped their prize, to escape into the mysteries of the thicket.[1] This was the only incident in their march of some twenty or twenty-five miles which is worth notice.

The men in the van of the English force finally came into a corn-field, and upon a rise of ground just beyond they discovered a number of Indians. They were discovered by the Indians at the same time, who dropped behind the hill in their flight. These were pursued by the white men, and when they reached the hill-top they found themselves upon the verge of a swamp. On its farther side

---

[1] *Mass. Hist. Coll.*, vol. xiv., p. 50.
DeForest, *History of the Indians*, p. 147.

they counted about twenty wigwams. This swamp was divided by a ridge of firm ground. A dozen or more men were deployed to surround the narrower end of the swamp, while Lieutenant Davenport, with another small force, followed the ridge of dry land which broke the swamp apart. Before Davenport had pushed his way through to the wigwams the Pequods had been warned of the approach of the English and had at once fled to the swamp. Their sachem went with them, The English were made aware that hidden among the thickets of this low ground was the quarry of which they were in search. Here were some three hundred savages of both sexes, of which perhaps a third were warriors. Davenport and his men had not gone far before they were met with a storm of arrows, by which the English were wounded, some of them, who when they fell found themselves bogged in the mire. At that moment the Pequods closed in upon them to engage in a hand-to-hand fight. The result of this savage sortie was that the English under Davenport were repulsed. It was with difficulty that the wounded were pulled out of the mud and carried back to a place of safety on the solid ground.[1] From

---

[1]Mason, *Mass. Hist. Coll.*, vol. xviii., pp. 146, 147.
Winthrop, vol. i., p. 231.

The order was given to surround the swamp, but Lieutenant Davenport failed to get it in season. "With a dozen more of his Company in an over-eager Pursuit of the Enemy,

THE PEQUOD WAR

this moment on, the movements of the English were of a rapid character. They threw a cordon of men around the outside of the swamp and a leisurely musket-fire upon the savages was begun. No attempt was made to force the swamp.

The English, realizing after a time that this method of attack was resulting only in the killing of women and children, decided upon a parley, which was undertaken by Thomas Stanton, who offered himself as interpreter. He approached the swamp, and, penetrating its thickets for a short distance, hailed the Indians, telling them that an amnesty would be given to all those who were innocent of killing the English. Much to the surprise of the latter, the savage sachem at once accepted the offer, and at the head of his people led them to the outer edge of the swamp. Within the next two hours, in little groups, the savages emerged from the thickets, until about two hundred of the Indians had given themselves up to the English.

[he] rushed immediately into the Swamp where they were very rudely entertained by those Evening Wolves that were being newly kennelled therein; for Lieut. *Davenport* was sorely wounded in the Body, *John Wedgewood* of *Ipswich* in the Belly, and was laid hold on by some of the *Indians.*"

Hubbard, *Indian Wars*, p. 34 (S. G. Drake Edition).

Vide Hubbard's note. This was Richard Davenport, of the Castle in Boston Harbor, where he was struck by lightning and killed, July 15, 1665. Captain Nathaniel Davenport, killed at the Fort Fight at Narragansett, was his son.

But not all had left the swamp. Sassacus and his warriors had turned over to the English those of their company who during the last few weeks had been a burden upon their movements. These were the old men of the tribe, whose years of usefulness had been left behind, and as well the women and the children. It was evident, with these helpless people removed from the swamp, that the Pequods had decided upon a fight to the finish; and when a messenger of peace had conveyed to them the last message, they shrilled at him, "We will fight it out to the last"! and they followed their defiance with a flight of arrows; and, not satisfied with that, they assailed him with such vigor that he would have been killed had the English not gone to his rescue.

For the remainder of the afternoon the English were passive, but after nightfall they so disposed of their men that the savages were completely surrounded; the line of the English about the swamp was circumscribed, so that the distance between the soldiers was not more than twelve feet. After the guards were set, the Pequods occupied their time by creeping stealthily upon them, and, as occasion offered, discharging their arrows; so that while quite a number of the soldiers had their clothes pierced, none were wounded. The English kept up a broken fire of musketry through the night, by which means, Hubbard says, "many of them were killed and buried in the mire as they found the next day." This is not to be wondered at, for the

THE PEQUOD WAR

reason that the English, in placing their sentinels, had cut a lane through the narrows of the swamp, using their swords as hatchets, whereby the savages were practically impounded at close quarters.[1]

As the night waned a heavy fog drifted in from the river, which suggested to the Pequods some opportunity to escape from the English. They made a ruse by throwing themselves suddenly with loud cries against the line of sentinels guarding the swamp. The attack was made upon that portion of the guard made up of Patrick's men, who repelled them without much difficulty; but as fast as the Pequods were driven back they renewed their assault upon the line. After a little, what began as a savage sortie became a battle; and as others of the English came to the relief of Patrick the savages were broken and driven back into the swamp. The ruse was fairly successful; for while Mason was making the round of the swamp he found a considerable body of the savages pushing their way outside the line of the guards. The mist concealed the movements of the savages to a great degree, but Mason, trusting to his instinct, ordered his

---

[1] Hubbard says: "By this Time, Night drawing on, our Commanders perceiving on which Side of the Swamp the Enemies were lodged, gave orders to cut through the Swamp, with their Swords, that they might better hem them round in one Corner, which was presently done, and so they were begirt in the Night."

Indian Wars (S. G. Drake Edition), vol. ii., p. 35.

men to discharge their muskets toward the swamp, with the result that the Indians were repulsed; but, desperate in their determination to escape the fate that awaited them at daybreak, they renewed their attack on Patrick's line, which was broken, and through it some sixty or seventy Pequods made their escape. After the battle of the swamp, which resulted in the slaughter of the remaining Pequods, a pursuit was made after those who had escaped through the morning fog, some of whom were found dead by the pursuing party. A considerable quantity of wampum and other property prized by the Indians was captured, along with one hundred eighty prisoners, mostly women and children.[1]

The Pequod sachem, Sassacus, had no part in this battle. Uncertain as to the loyalty of some of the Pequods, two or three of whom had been engaged in an effort to betray him, and realizing that he was to be relentlessly pursued by the English, he determined to leave the larger portion of his people to their fate. Revealing his purpose to Mononotto,[2] the secret of his proposed flight was imparted to some twenty, or, as some authors say, forty, of his most redoubtable warriors, and he quietly gathered together some five hundred pounds'

---

[1] Mason, *Mass. Hist. Coll.*, vol. xviii., p. 148.
Winthrop, vol. i., pp. 32, 279.

[2] Mononotto among the Pequots was placed next to Sassacus by Drake. Hubbard also calls him "a noted Indian." In the

THE PEQUOD WAR

worth of wampum, and fled like a thief in the night, into the country of the Mohawks. Sassacus has come down through the historians as a warrior famous for his leadership and his bravery. For all that, he was apparently not above deserting those dependent upon him for counsel and protection. Whatever view may be taken of this action, it is evident that he was controlled by the instinct which has always marked his race as a subtle and treach-

---

troubles with the Pequots it was among his tribe that the English began their murders. The writer agrees with Drake: "There is no more to excuse the murder of a Pequot than an Englishman."

After the foray of the English at Block Island they sailed up the Connecticut River to continue their errand of destruction. As they sailed, they were hailed by many of the Pequots on either side of the river to know their errand. Their reply was that they wished to speak with Sassacus. He had gone to Long Island. Then they demanded Mononotto. He was away as well. Then the English went ashore to demand the perpetrators of the Stone massacre. They were told if they would wait they would have them sent for, and that Mononotto would shortly come to them. In the meantime, while the savages were holding the English in this interview, "others transported their goods, women and children to another place." Finally the English were informed that Mononotto would not come. Upon that a skirmish ensued. One Indian was killed, and an Englishman wounded.

Drake's *Book of the Indians*, pp. 108, 109.

Gardener's account varies: "They went and demanded the Pequit Sachem to come to a parley, but it was returned for answer that he was from home, but within three hours he

INDIAN WARS OF NEW ENGLAND

erous people. One writer has excused his apparent cowardice by alleging that he was accused by his people of being the author of their misfortunes; that they would undoubtedly have killed him in their distemper, had not some of his own sachems interposed. It is suggested that these animosities followed him closely after the destruction of Fort

---

would come; and so from three to six, and thence to nine, there came none. But the Indians came without arms to our men, in great numbers, and they talked with my men, whom they knew; but in the end, at a word given, they all on a sudden ran away from our men, as they stood in rank and file, and not an Indian more was to be seen; and all this while before, they carried all their stuff away, and thus was that great parley ended. Then they [the English] displayed their colours, and beat their drums, burnt some wigwams and some heaps of corn, and my men carried as much aboard as they could, but the army went aboard, leaving my men ashore, which ought to have marched aboard first. But they all set sail, and my men were pursued by the Indians, and they hurt some of the Indians, two of them come home wounded. The Bay-men killed not a man, save that one Kichomiquim [Cutshamequin], an Indian Sachem of the Bay, killed a Pequit; and thus began the war between the Indians and us in these parts."

Gardener's *Pequot Warres*, p. 13.

This sachem seems to be the only one who escaped the Mohawks. Drake is of the opinion that he was killed by the English.

One finds this in a manuscript letter of Captain Stoughton: "Captain Mason and 30 men are with us in Pequot River, and we shall the next week joine in seeing what we can do

THE PEQUOD WAR

Mystic by Mason, and the destruction of his own village by himself.[1] This state of affairs, it is claimed, in some degree forced him to abandon his people, against his real inclination. The argument is a specious one, and does not seem to be founded upon a real condition. Sassacus had been the inveterate enemy of the English; and following the settlement along the Connecticut River, the outrageous attacks upon the English by his people, manifestly at his instigation, and oftentimes by his actual participation, had so incensed the English that to him remained but two courses of action. The one was to place himself beyond the reach of

---

against Sassacus and another great sagamore, Monowattuck [Mononotto]."

Massachusetts State Papers.

[1]Johnson, 2 *Mass. Hist. Coll.*, vol. iv., pp. 49-51.

Mason, 2 *Mass. Hist. Coll.*, vol. viii., pp. 146-148.

Gardener, 3 *Mass. Hist. Coll.*, vol. iii., pp. 150, 151.

Morton's *Mem.*

Trumbull, vol. i., pp. 83-85.

Barry says: "On the return of the Massachusetts troops, a day of Thanksgiving was ordered to be observed, and the soldiers were to be feasted by their several towns."

Barry, *History of Massachusetts*, vol. i., p. 229.

Massachusetts Records, vol. i., p. 204.

Morton's *Mem.*, pp. 99-106.

Increase Mather *piously* observed, "It was supposed that no less than 500 to 600 Pequot souls were brought down to hell that day."

Mather's *Relation*, p. 47.

the hated English; and the other was to meet them at the head of his warriors, to share with them the disasters which were so surely bound to overtake them.

As a race, the Pequods were feared by all tribes adjacent to their domain, and at some time or another all had suffered more or less by reason of the ferocious dispositions of this people. They were really the buccaneers of that part of the country — spoiling wherever spoil was to be had, and annihilating wherever power was to be obtained. Once the power of the Pequods was broken, they were a race of wanderers, without friends, and the sport of every barbarous circumstance. No one knew this better than Sassacus; and no one knew better than he, by reason of the neighboring tribes joining themselves to the English as allies, the purpose of that confederate movement.

Some authors, in writing of him, have argued that, seeing there was no salvation for him or his people except in an abrupt flight, he took occasion to urge upon his people that it was the best course to be pursued, and applied himself to the following out of his own advice only when he discovered that it was not acceptable to his people. He was a fugitive from justice; by an unwritten law he was doomed. When he made his asylum with the Mohawks, from whom he had no particular reason to expect other than treachery, it is evident that his action was based, not upon sound consideration,

THE PEQUOD WAR

but upon the spur of the moment. Shortly after, he found himself, much to his satisfaction, in the midst of the Mohawk tribe, who — possibly with the desire to gratify the English, and perhaps to pay off some old scores which until then they had no opportunity of settling — surprised him and his warriors, all of whom were killed by the Mohawks, with the exception of Mononotto, who, although wounded, made his escape. In the following August the Mohawks sent to the English on the Connecticut River the scalps of Sassacus and one of his brothers; also the scalps of five of his sachems.[1] The captive Pequods taken by the English were made servants. Common parlance would denominate them slaves. The restless disposition, however, of these wild people of the woods was productive of so much discomfort to their taskmasters that but few of them were held for any length of time in a condition of servitude.[2] Such as were not retained by the English in their service were shipped away to the West Indies by the Massachusetts government, where they were sold as slaves.

---

[1] Winthrop, vol. i., p. 35.

"The few that fled with Sasacus to the westward were totally destroyed by the Mohawks. The scalp of Sasacus was in the fall of 1638 presented to the govornor and council of Massachusetts."

Trumbull, *Indian Wars*, p. 59.

[2] Mason, *Mass. Hist. Coll.*, vol. xviii., p. 148.

INDIAN WARS OF NEW ENGLAND

Among these prisoners who were captured in the Fairfield Swamp were Mononotto's wife and daughters. As has been recorded in a note to one of the preceding pages, it was credited to her that her influence had saved the lives of the two girls who were captured and taken away in the attack upon Wethersfield. Her modesty and intelligence attracted to her the interest of the English, and her humanity won something of their gratitude.[1] Unobtrusive in her gentleness and patient in her uncomplaining, she commended herself to her captors, preferring to them but two requests. The one

---

[1] Mononotto's wife was known among her people as Wincumbone. She seems to have been noted for her pity and humanity for those who were in trouble or in danger. Besides the incident of the two English maids, Gardener relates an incident of some men who went up the Connecticut River to trade, and, landing in the neighborhood of the tribe over which Mononotto held sway, one "Thomas Hurlbut stepping into the Sachem's wigwam, not far from the shore, enquiring for the horses, (these horses had been stolen from a man whose name was Eltow,) the Indians went out of the wigwam, and Wincumbone, his mother's sister, was then the great Pequit Sachem's wife, who made signs to him that he should be gone, for they would cut off his head; which, when he perceived, he drew his sword and ran to the others, and got aboard, and immediately came abundance of Indians to the water-side and called to them to come ashore, but they immediately set sail and came home, and this caused me to keep watch and ward, for I saw they plotted our destruction."

Gardener's *Pequot Warres*, p. 12.
Stoughton *Letter, State Papers*.

THE PEQUOD WAR

was that the sanctity of her person might be regarded; the other, that her children might not be separated from her. Her final disposition is unknown, but like many of the most tractable of her race, she probably became a servitor to some English family; and it is with a very considerable satisfaction that one finds it recorded that Governor Winthrop enjoined upon those having her in service to treat her with the utmost kindness.[1]

This battle of the Fairfield Swamp was the end of the Pequod race, it being estimated that in that fight fully seven hundred Pequods had been taken captive or killed. It was given out by those who were captured that out of the twenty-six sachems of the Pequod nation, only thirteen were known to

---

[1] Hubbard relates: "Amongst the rest of the prisoners special notice was taken of the wife of a noted Indian called Mononotto, who with her children submitted herself, or by the chance of war fell into the hands of the English: it was known to be by her mediation that two English maids (that were taken away from Wethersfield upon Connecticut River) were saved from death, in requital of whose pity and humanity, the life of herself and her children was not only granted her, but she was in special recommended to the care of that honourable gentleman, Mr. John Winthrop, for that time being the worthy Governour of the Massachusetts; who taking notice of her modest countenance and behaviour, as well as of her only request (not to suffer wrong either as to the honour of her body, or fruit of her womb) gave special charge concerning her according to his noble and Christian disposition."

Hubbard's *Indian Wars*, pp. 37, 38.

have survived; and it is probable that these survivors were among those who fled with Sassacus to the Mohawks, only to perish in the massacre which took place shortly after their arrival in that country.[1] From this on, the few wandering Pequods scattered here and there through their old domain from time to time became the easy prey of the Mohegans and the Narragansetts, who for some time after were bringing the heads and hands of their Pequod victims into the settlements of the English, as the gory relics of their man-hunting expeditions. It is recorded that among these was the hand of the sachem who directed the massacre of Stone and his crew off the Manisses.

Of the Pequods who escaped this slaughter, some found asylum among those from whom they had formerly exacted tribute,— the western Nehantics, some of the tribes on Long Island, and some on the Hudson River. It is possible that some found their way as far south as Virginia and the Carolinas. Many gave themselves up to Uncas, and, possibly, to the eastern Nehantics and the Narragansetts; although by treaty the latter had covenanted not to receive them, and it is recorded that they kept their agreement with varying fidelity. It was the habit

---

[1] Drake says that Sassacus destroyed his habitations, and, with some eighty of his warriors, "fled to the Mohawks who treacherously beheaded him."
Drake's *Book of the Indians*, p. 106.

THE PEQUOD WAR

of the latter to deliver all Pequods who came to them into the custody of the English at Boston, for disposition at the hands of the Puritan magistrates — upon one occasion as many as eighty of these unfortunate people, among whom were one considerable sachem and twenty warriors.

Outside of the Narragansetts, the other tribes were under no obligation to the English, and, as was the custom with such people, the refugees were taken into these tribes by adoption. This fact led to a controversy between the Nehantics and the Massachusetts people, which developed into an open quarrel. This occurred in July of 1637. Ninigret, the sachem of the Nehantics, made no pretension of secrecy in his harboring of the Pequods.[1]

---

[1] Drake makes note that there was a manifest disposition on the part of the sachems of the Narragansetts and Mohegans (it will be remembered here that the Nehantics were of the Narragansett race) to afford an asylum for the homeless Pequots. One finds in the *Mass. Hist. Coll.* some of the correspondence between Roger Williams and the Governor of Massachusetts, wherein it is apparent that Williams was employed to explain to the sachems of these tribes what they might depend upon if they did not adhere strictly to the terms of their agreement concerning the Pequots, which was, evidently, that all Pequots happening within their domain should be brought to Boston, to be dealt with by the magistrates. It is apparent that Massachusetts Bay was not averse to the slave traffic. Williams received a letter from the Massachusetts governor upon this subject at the hands of an Indian,

INDIAN WARS OF NEW ENGLAND

With every accession of Pequods, the numerical strength of these tribes, or clans, was increased; and so it came about that the clan of Uncas, which was notably weak upon the breaking out of the

whose name was Otash. It is to be noted here as one of the inconsistencies of the Bay government that they should solicit the assistance of Williams, who had been exiled by them. While they objected to his presence, they were still willing to take advantage of his offices with a people to whom the presence of Williams was more grateful, evidently, than their own. Williams, obliging as he apparently always was, went to the Narragansetts; and he says in his report to the Massachusetts authorities: "Having got Canounicus and Miantunnomuh, with their council together, I acquainted them faithfully with the contents of your letter, both greivances and threatenings; and to demonstrate I produced the copy of the league (which Mr. [Sir Henry] Vane sent me,) and with breaking of a straw in two or three places, I showed them what they had done."

The reply of the sachem to Williams was that when the Governor of Massachusetts understood what they had to explain, their conduct would be satisfactory to him; they had not wished to make trouble, but they "could relate many particulars when the English had broken their promises."

Since the ending of the Pequot War, Canonicus admitted that he had heard of some squaws escaping from the English, and had ordered them to be returned, but knew nothing more of them; he would have the country searched for them. Miantunnomoh had heard of six. He had seen four of them. When they were brought to him he had showed anger and demanded why they had not carried them to Mr. Williams, that they might be delivered up to the English. They told him the squaws were lame and unable to go; upon which the sachem

THE PEQUOD WAR

war of the earlier spring, the first real conflict of which took place at Fort Mystic, began to be as formidable, by reason of the number of refugees being absorbed into it, as it had been hitherto

had sent to Mr. Williams to come and take them. Williams evidently did not care for the office and in turn ordered the sachem to attend particularly to that matter, whose reply was that he was busy and could not. "The sachem was," says Williams, "in a strange kind of solemnity, wherein the sachem eats nothing but at night. While these festivities were being carried on, the squaws made their escape." This sachem said that he was sorry that the governor should charge him with wanting these squaws, for he did not. When Williams told him that he knew of his sending for one at least, Miantunnomoh said that the squaw was not for himself, but for Saussamun, who at that time had been at his house, who on some occasion had lamed himself, and that the latter "fell in there on his way to Pequt, whither he had been sent by the governor." The squaw he desired was the daughter of a sachem who during his lifetime had been a great friend of Miantunnomoh, and it was in a spirit of kindness that he wished to ransom her.

He assured Williams that himself and his people were true "to the English in life or death," whereupon he charged Uncas and his Mohegans had long since played false, and he was afraid they would continue to be so. He said that the Mohegans had never yet found a Pequot; to which he added, "*Chenock, ejuse, wetompatimucks!*" ("Had ever friends dealt so with friends!") Williams wished for a more lucid explanation, and the sachem replied: "My brother, Yotaash, had seized upon Puttaquppuunck, Quame, and 20 Pequots, and 60 squaws; they killed three and bound the rest, whom they watched all night. Then they sent for the English, and de-

feeble. To the English, once the Pequods had become amalgamated with the Mohegans or Nehantics, it was a matter of difficulty to distinguish them as individuals from those of the tribes upon

livered them in the morning to them. I came by land, according to promise, with 200 men, killing 10 Pequots by the way. I desired to see the great sachem, Puttaquppuunck, whom my brother had taken, who was now in the English houses, but the English thrust at me with a pike many times, that I durst not come near the door."

"Mr. Williams told him that they did not know him, else they would not; but Miantunnomoh answered, 'All my company were disheartened, and they all, and Cutshamoquene, desired to be gone.' Besides, he said, 'two of my men, Wagonckwhut and Maunamoh (Meihamoh) were their guides to Sesquankit, from the river's mouth.' Upon which, Mr. Williams adds to the governor: 'Sir, I dare not stir coals, but I saw them too much disregarded by many.'

"Mr. Williams told the sachems they received Pequts and wampom without Mr. Governor's consent. Cannounicus replied, that although he and Miantunnomu had paid many hundred fathom of wampom to their soldiers, as Mr. Governor did, yet he had not received one yard of beads nor a Pequt. Nor, saith Miantunnomu, did I, but one small present from four women of Long Island, which were no Pequts, but of that isle, being afraid, desired to put themselves under my protection."

Drake, *Book of the Indians*, p. 107.

In 1637 Miantunnomoh went to Boston, where he met the officials of the colony, who treated with him, and with whom he parted upon "fair terms." He evidently carried with him a complaint against the Nehantics; and in Winthrop's *Journal*, vol. i., p. 243, it is noted: "We gave him leave to

THE PEQUOD WAR

whose mercy they had thrown themselves. They were practically the same people; and, once their interest became common, they were identical. It was only through the Narragansetts, who were

---

right himself for the wrongs Janemoh [Ninigret], and Wequash Cook had done him, and for the wrongs they had done us, we would right ours in our own time."

The following year the Long Island Indians who paid tribute to the English complained that this same Ninigret had robbed them of some of their property, whereupon Captain Mason was despatched from Connecticut to the Nehantics to obtain satisfaction. Ninigret responded by going to the English without delay; and so the matter was disposed of in a friendly fashion. When, afterward, the English were advised that Miantunnomoh was conspiring against them, and making some endeavor with some other tribes that they assist him in his enterprise, the English sent to learn the truth of the report. This sachem satisfied the English as to his own fidelity; but Winthrop says in his *Journal*, "Janemoh, the Niantick sachem carried himself proudly and refused to come to us, or to yield to anything, only he said he would not harm us except we harmed him." Drake finds in this attitude of the Nehantic sachem the occasion of unqualified approval.

On this occasion Winthrop says: "So the governor gave him a fair red coat and defrayed his and his men's diet, and gave them corn to relieve them homeward, and a letter of protection, &c., and he departed very joyful."

It is apparent, in the dealings of the English with the Indians to the westward, that they had very little consideration for those of the Narragansett race, except in so far as they might be able by their adroit use of them to carry out their purpose, which was evidently the annihilation of the aborigines. The people nearest the English were the Wam-

bitterly hostile to the Mohegans, that this condition of affairs was revealed; and so it came about that just a year after the quarrel of the Massachusetts government with the Nehantics had transpired,

---

panoags, of which tribe Massasoit was the ruling sachem. It was for the interest of the English that they should maintain the most amicable relations with these latter people, who acted as a buffer between them and the more aggressive tribes of Rhode Island and Connecticut. The English were aware of the animosities existing between the Pequots, the Mohegans, and the Narragansetts, and were not averse to fomenting their alleged differences into causes which might lead to their engaging each other in war. In such case, the English inclined toward one side or the other, but always to the disadvantage of the savages. Winthrop's attitude in dealing with these sons of the forest was that of an astute diplomat. He looked upon the extinction of the red man as inevitable. He exacted tribute from them; gave them in return very little of value, and much questionable advice. His captains slaughtered them in their distant fastnesses; and, not content with having reduced them to a state of defencelessness, he traded upon the freedom of their women and children, by which they were condemned to a future worse than had overtaken the warriors of their tribe. This traffic in Pequot women and children for money on the part of the Massachusetts Colony has left a stain upon its integrity that neither time nor the most friendly historian can efface.

Winthrop's *Journal*, under his own hand, is the indubitable evidence upon which this criticism is based. The carefulness which he exhibits in recording this evidence is indicative of the conscience of the times.

Winthrop's *Journal*, vol. i., pp. 265, 266.

However punctiliously devout the Puritans might have

THE PEQUOD WAR

and while the scattered Pequods were being hounded by their enemies to destruction, Uncas with thirty-seven of his most notable warriors found their way to Boston. They made it a cere-

---

been in matters of religious observance and consolation, the "Covenant of Works," and such like cleansings of the "outside of the platter," they were experts in twisting their consciences when it came to matters of business with the Indians.

Referring again to Miantunnomoh, it will be noted that early in 1637, to show the English at Boston how well he was keeping his promise of making war against the Pequots, he sent them a Pequot's hand by one of his men. This war, as the current chapter indicates, was of short duration, to the accomplishment of which the Narragansetts lent one hundred warriors. For their services they received a portion of the prisoners as slaves. Miantunnomoh received eighty, according to Mather's *Relation*, p. 39. After the Pequot War was over, this sachem still maintained his allegiance to the English by seizing upon such Pequots as made their escape from their masters, who were promptly returned to the English. They also relinquished their right of conquest in Block Island and such other territory as they had taken from the Pequots.

It was in March, 1637, that Miantunnomoh, with four other sachems, sold to William Coddington and others the island of Rhode Island, also other islands in Narragansett Bay, "for the full payment of 40 fathom of white peag, to be divided" between the five sachems. In addition to "eight fathom of peag," Miantunnomoh was to "have 10 coats and 20 hoes to give to the present inhabitants, that they shall remove themselves from the Island before next winter." Specific description of the lands include, "the great Island of Aquidneck lying from hence [Providence] eastward . . . ,

monial visit; and when admitted to the presence of the Colonial Council Uncas presented to it twenty fathoms of wampum as a gift for the governor. His gift was refused, upon the ground, as the council informed him, that until he had discovered to them fully his transactions with the Pequods in receiving and harboring them they could not receive him with friendly consideration.

Uncas was in a quandary. It was plain to him that he was to be tried by the council upon the question of his sincerity. A man of quick resource, he at once decided that to bring upon himself the anger of the English people was to invite the fate of Sassacus. Likewise, determined not to allow himself to be separated from any of his followers there present, he protested with great earnestness that all the warriors with him were of the Mohegan race.

---

also the marshes, grass upon Qunnonigat and the rest of the islands in the bay excepting Chabatewece, formerly sold unto Mr. Winthrop, the Gov. of Mass., and Mr. Williams of Providence, also the grass upon the rivers and capes of Citackamuckqut, and there thence to Paupasquat."

It appears that the aged Massasoit joined in this conveyance, by reason of the following memoranda in the deed: "I, Osemequon freely consent that they may make use of any grass or trees on the mainland of Pacausit, having received 5 fathom of wampum also." To this memoranda is attached the sign-manual of Osemequon.

Drake's *Book of the Indians*, pp. 60-70.
Winthrop's *Journal*, vol. i., p. 267; vol. ii., p. 8.
State Papers, Boston.

THE PEQUOD WAR

His grief was as evident as were his protestations, which the magistrates accepted, as they did his gift, a few moments later. Acquiring a new courage, he covered his heart with his hand and said to the governor: "This heart is not mine; it is yours. I have no men; they are all yours. Command me any hard thing and I will do it. I will never believe an Indian's words against the English. If any Indian shall kill an Englishman, I will put him to death, be he never so dear to me."[1]

In accordance with his usual habit when dealing with others, Uncas maintained his protestations to the extent of his own interest, which he found was furthered by yielding to the demands of the English. Uncas was far-seeing in this respect, in that he recognized the power of the English. It is evident that he adhered to them for the reason that that adherence would be to his own advantage. As DeForest says, "He was faithful to them just as the jackal is faithful to the lion; not because he loves the lion, but because it gains something by remaining in his company."

The letters of Roger Williams throw some light upon Uncas's sincerity; for, as the sachem was returning into his country from Boston, his journey homeward took him into the near neighborhood of where Williams lived. One of his company, falling lame, found his way to the latter's house. The

---

[1] Winthrop's *Journal*, vol. i., pp. 265, 266.

name of this savage was Wequaumugs, being by birth of mixed blood. His father was a Narragansett and his mother a Mohegan, which fact accorded him a friendly reception as he happened to be with either tribe. He informed Williams, having reference to Miantunnumoh, that there were only two Pequods in the company of the latter, both of whom had been captured by the Narragansett sachem's men. He also said that among the Nehantics there were about sixty Pequods under Wequash Cook, the same alluded to by Drake as "the renegade Pequot who betrayed his people at Fort Mystic into the hands of Mason, and as well those who had taken refuge in the Fairfield, or New Haven swamp."[1] Being asked if Uncas had taken along with him to Boston any Pequods, he told Williams there were six in the company, two of whom, Pematesick and Weaugomhick, had killed some of the English. Williams made a note of these, also an account of the conversation, which he despatched to Winthrop, evidently with the in-

---

[1] In a letter to Winthrop, Roger Williams alludes to "Wequash (whose name signified a swan,) and Wuttackquiackommin, valient man, especially the latter, who have lived these three or four years with the Nanhiggonticks, and know every pass and passage amongst them, who desire armor to enter their houses."

Drake's *Book of the Indians*, p. 105.

Drake says in a note to his extract, "the same elsewhere called Wequash Cook, 'which Wequash' (says Dr. I. Mather)

THE PEQUOD WAR

tention of verifying the statement of the Mohegan sachem before the magistrates.[1] Williams felt that this was due to Uncas by reason of the gifts and hospitable treatment which had been extended to him and his warriors by Winthrop.

A portion of the Pequod tribe, notwithstanding the disasters which had befallen them at the hands of Mason and Stoughton, had endeavored to maintain a precarious independence; but, finding themselves a continual prey to the Mohegans and Narragansetts, who harried them from one hiding-place to another, they came to the inevitable conclusion that their only safety lay in establishing some sort

---

was by birth a sachem of that place, (where Sassacus lived,) but upon some disgust received he went from the Pequots to the Narragansetts, and became chief captain under Miantonomoh."

Mather's *Relation*, p. 74.

Hubbard's *Indian Wars*, vol. ii., p. 20.

He became a noted praying Indian after the Pequot War, and was supposed to have died from poison.

Vide note to Drake, *Book of the Indians*, p. 94.

In *New England's First Fruits*, pp. 5-7, "he is made a Saint of."

Gardener refers to him, in his relation of the foray of Stoughton upon the Pequots at the Fairfield Swamp: "I sent Wequash after them, who went by night to spy them out, and the army followed him and found them at the Great Swamp."

Gardener's *Pequod Warres*, p. 22.

[1] *R. I. Hist. Coll.*, vol. iii., pp. 140, 141.

of friendship with the English.[1] To that end, some of their chief men went to Hartford, where they proposed to the English to become their servants, upon the condition that their lives might be preserved to them. To the great credit of the English this offer of surrender was accepted, whereupon Uncas and Miantunnumoh were called to a conference with the magistrates as to the final disposition of these Pequods.

This concession to Uncas indicates in a degree the importance of the Mohegan sachem at that time. His star was in the ascendent; otherwise a request to attend the English in their deliberations would not have been extended to him. DeForest suggests that the English had come to regard him as an ally upon whom they could safely depend as against such other of the New England aborigines as might entertain hostile designs against them.

---

[1] "Mather says, in his boastful account of 'troubles with Pequots:' 'By such methods as these was a period put to the war; the few Pequots that survived submitted themselves to English mercy, and the rest of the Indians who saw a little handful of Englishmen massacre and capture seven hundred adversaries and kill no less than thirteen Sachems in one short expedition; such a terror from God fell upon them that after, for near forty years together, the land rested from war, even unto the time when the sins of the land called for a new scourge, and Indians, being taught the use of guns, were capable of being made instruments of inflicting it.'"
Freeman's *Civilization and Barbarism*, p. 66, note.

THE PEQUOD WAR

He was to be the savage watch-dog; to sound the alarm of possible savage invasion. This writer suggests, as well, that as the Pequods and Mohegans had already ceased their wars against each other, and had placed themselves under the authority and protection of Uncas, they were not averse to using this circumstance as a means to future tranquillity. It was also apparent that new quarrels were upon the point of breaking out between the Mohegans and the Narragansetts. The differences between these two savage races resulted in their chief sachem's being called to Hartford with a view to adjusting them, their controversies having degenerated into a series of personal injuries and insults by reason of which the situation was most acute, and which threatened to break out into open warfare. In addition to this, the distribution of the Pequods was no less important.

The Narragansett sachem attended upon the Hartford Commission, accompanied by his entire family, several sachems, and a retinue of some one hundred fifty fighting-men. He had three Englishmen in his company, Roger Williams being one of them. The taking along of this considerable number of warriors is an indication of his apprehension in regard to Uncas. On his way to Hartford he was met by numerous Narragansetts, who told him that they had been robbed by the Pequods and Mohegans. At one of his camping-places a party of Wunnashowatuckoogs, probably of the Nipmucks, who were subject to Canonicus, came to him with the tale that they "had been robbed two days before by a band of six or seven hundred Indians composed of Pequots and Mohegans, and others who were their confederates. This great band had spoiled twenty-three fields of their corn and had rifled several Narragansetts who were staying among them. Now they were lying in wait to stop Miantinōmo on his journey; and some of them had threatened to boil him in a kettle."

As they continued their way these stories were augmented, to the degree that Williams and the other two Englishmen recommended a discontinuance of their journey and a return, with a view to avoiding a possible encounter with Uncas and his people. The suggestion of Williams and his friends was disregarded by the Narragansett sachem, for the reason that he had accomplished a large part of his journey and was determined to continue the same, indifferent to any hostile action on the part of Uncas. They renewed their journey, the Narragansett sachem occupying the center of the march, with Roger Williams and the two Englishmen in the van. As they proceeded, forty or fifty scouts were sent in advance; and in this way they pursued their journey without obstacle, to finally reach the Connecticut, which they crossed, to find themselves at the end of their present perplexities.

Once at Hartford, Miantunnumoh sought out the English magistrates, and, without hesitation,

THE PEQUOD WAR

entered his complaints to them against Uncas, going over in detail, not only acts of actual violence and injustice, but as well those which had been reported to him. Uncas was not present at this hearing. He had avoided the contentions of the Narragansett sachem by sending a messenger to say that he was disabled by a lameness and could not come. This excuse was not acceptable to the council, especially to Mr. Haynes, who afterward became governor of the Connecticut Colony. A request, which was equivalent to a command, was despatched to Uncas that he should attend upon the council. The result was, the recovery of Uncas from his lameness was accelerated, so that shortly after he was able to reach Hartford. Upon his appearance, the charges preferred against him by the Narragansetts were taken up, and the examination of their integrity begun. One of the Mohegans was produced by Uncas in his defence, who, going over the story of the Wunnashowatuckoogs, declared there were but a hundred men; and as for the destruction of the corn-fields, they took a few ears to roast; and as for anything else that they might have done, it was of a harmless character. The Narragansetts asserted this story of the Mohegan to be untrue, the consequence of which was that the hearing became almost immediately a scene of violent recrimination.

Awearied by this war of words, the council finally dismissed the charges, after which an attempt was made to reconcile the two sachems. It is recorded that they shook hands, after which the Narragansetts cordially twice asked Uncas to a venison feast. One is compelled to observe, in passing, that the instincts of a gentleman were more apparent in the Narragansett than in the Mohegan.[1] Whatever of hostile design the latter may have had against the Narragansett sachem, it is evident, in this refusal to accept of the proffered hospitality, that he reserved the right to undertake whatever design he had in mind, unfettered by the restraint which this breaking of bread with Miantunnumoh might impose upon him. In a private conference with the council the latter revealed the names of the six Pequod sachems remaining, as well as the surviving Pequods who had been mixed up in the killing of the English. This list, afterward written out, was read to Uncas, who acknowledged its correctness. The sachems were Nausibouck, of Long Island; Puppompogs, a brother of Sassacus; Kithansh; Nanasquionwut at Mohegan; and Mausaumpous at Nehantic.

The result of this was an investigation to discover the number and whereabouts of the remaining Pequods. The Narragansetts said Canonicus

---

[1] Hubbard says of Miantonomoh, he "was a very good personage, of tall stature, subtil and cunning in his contrivements, as well as haughty in his designs."
History of New England, p. 446.

THE PEQUOD WAR

had no Pequods; Miantunnumoh, ten or eleven, who were those left of the seventy who had made submission to him at one time and another, but who had never actually come into his country, else they had left him of their own accord. With the exception of these above enumerated, the Narragansetts asserted that the remainder of the Pequods held their ancient territory in occupancy, or were to be found among the Mohegans. When Uncas was questioned as to his knowledge of this, he avoided it after his characteristic fashion. As an adept in duplicity Uncas was a savage Talleyrand. He did not know the names of his Pequods; he could not state them. He had but a few, anyway. He said Ninigret and three other Nehantic sachems had Pequods. As for himself, he had "only twenty."

He was bluntly charged by Thomas Stanton with lying about the matter. Others present charged Uncas with bringing over thirty to forty Pequods from Long Island at one time; whereupon he then acknowledged that he had thirty, but still asserted that he did not know their names. Such was the uncertainty involved in this examination that the council directed him to appear before them again at the end of ten days, at which time he was expected to be able to inform it as to the names and exact numbers of the Pequods in his country.

A special messenger was sent to the Nehantics to obtain a census of the Pequods who were with that tribe.[1] Whether or not these conditions were afterward fulfilled is somewhat obscure, as there is no existing record of any further transactions in this direction by the Hartford Council. A subsequent meeting, however, was held, at which the remaining number of the Pequods was agreed upon, which number was finally estimated at two hundred, not including the women and children.

On October 31, 1638, what was at that time regarded as the final act in the consummation of the purpose of the English with the Indians was entered into by John Haynes, Roger Ludlow, and Edward Hopkins, as the English representatives of Connecticut; by the sachem of the Narragansetts, in behalf of his people; and by Uncas, for himself and his sagamores. This was a tripartite agreement, by which was to be preserved a lasting peace between all parties, by means of which all past provocations, controversies, and quarrels were to be forever forgotten.

The English, undoubtedly realizing that this latter was an impossible condition, so modified the treaty that in case differences should arise between the Narragansetts and the Mohegans the complaining party was to appeal to them as the court of last resort, whose findings in any matters brought before them, affecting the interest of either of these

---

[1] Roger Williams's *Letters.*
R. I. Hist. Coll., vol. iii., pp. 145-148.

THE PEQUOD WAR

tribes, should be accepted as final. A proviso was inserted as well,— that should either the Narragansetts or the Mohegans refuse to be guided by the judgment of the English, the latter would be justified in employing force to compel submission. It also provided that the Mohegans and Narragansetts were to engage in the common cause against such of the Pequods as had killed any of the English; and they agreed to cut off their heads and bring them to the magistrates at Hartford. The two hundred male Pequods mentioned as at that time being distributed among the Mohegans, Narragansetts, and Nehantics were to be divided. Ninigret was to have twenty; Miantunnumoh, eighty; the remainder were given to Uncas.[1] An annual tribute was exacted of a fathom of wampum for each male, a half-fathom for each youth, and a hand for each male child. The Pequods were prohibited from occupying any portion of their former country, and stripped of their name. They were thereafter to be known only as Narragansetts and Mohegans.

With their usual disposition to drive a good, stiff bargain upon every favorable opportunity, the English prevailed upon the Narragansetts and the Mohegans to relinquish any rights of conquest they might have to the Pequod territory, which, by that treaty, was to pass into the hands of the English of Connecticut.[2] When this treaty was concluded,

---

[1] Mason, *2 Mass. Hist. Coll.*, vol. viii., pp. 148, 149.
[2] *R. I. Hist. Coll.*, vol. iii., p. 177.

INDIAN WARS OF NEW ENGLAND

and the sachems of the Narragansetts and the Mohegans had bidden the council farewell, and had betaken themselves upon their journey to their several domains, the curtain had for the last time fallen over the fortunes of the Pequods. It is safe to assume that a peace obtained in such manner, the foundations of which were almost wholly made up of acts of injustice, hatred, and bloodshed, could not be otherwise than of short duration. Within a year and a half the national existence of a courageous, yet savage race had been obliterated; and while the wars of the English and the Pequods were forever at an end, the rival jealousies of Uncas and Miantunnumoh were to afford a no less disreputable chapter of history for the English than that which records their dealings with the Pequods.

From that moment when Holmes passed the Dutch fort at Hartford, as he sailed up the Connecticut with his handful of colonists, the English had sown to the wind. The harvest was inevitable. Blinded by self-interest, indifferent to the red man, taking refuge behind pretense, adepts in dissimulation, and not above the degrading meanness involved in the trafficking in their own kind,[1] it was fortunate for the English, at this time, that to them

---

[1] "Although Governor Winthrop tells us how 'the male children were disposed of,' and also what disposition was made of 'the women and maid children,' he is silent in regard to the disposal of a great body of the adult males. Hutchinson says,

THE PEQUOD WAR

the future was an unknown quantity; for across the wall of every English cabin was already written in invisible letters the prophecy that the sins of the fathers should be visited upon the children.

'Many of the captives were sent to Bermuda and sold as slaves.' Enslaving Indians had become a mania with speculators. Felt, in his annals of Salem and Ipswich, informs us that it was a common occurrence for voyages to be made to sell captured Indians, and bring back cotton, tobacco, salt, negroes, etc. Mather enlightens us by the fervor with which he relates, under the caption '*Arma virosque cane*,' troubles which the churches have undergone in the wars with the Indians. He says, 'The dispersed became as so many unkenneled wolves. However, Heaven so smiled upon the English hunting after them that here and there whole companies were trepanned into the hunter's hands. Particularly at one time some hundreds of them were seized by Captain Stoughton, with little opposition, who, sending away the females and children as captives, put the men on board a vessel of one Skipper Gallup, which proved a Charon's ferry-boat unto them, for it was found the quickest was to feed the fishes with 'em. Our forces had frequently the satisfaction of cutting them off by companies.'"

Freeman's *Civilization and Barbarism*, p. 64, note.

WARS OF THE MOHEGANS

WARS OF THE MOHEGANS

TO fully comprehend the policy of the English toward the aborigine it is necessary to follow somewhat further the fortunes of the Indians of Connecticut, who, like so many dogs, were to be set at the throats each of the other, as occasion offered, which the English were not slow to encourage.[1] From the close of the Pequod War, in 1637, to the outbreak of King Philip, 1675, the English settlements along the Connecticut River westward, and those extending east of the Piscataquis River as far as Pemaquid, are to be regarded as forming the frontier of the English occupation in New England. East, and north of Narragansett Bay, the attitude of the Indians toward the English was pacific. South and west, jealousies of long standing between

---

[1] "Only because the Indians were set against the Indians, giving opportunity to the whites to find most effective allies in their forest warfare, could the early colonists from Spain, France or England have been so uniformly the conquerors. . . . The policy of the whites was to aggravate the dissension of the tribes, and to make alliance with one or more of them."

Ellis, *Memorial History of Boston*, vol. i., p. 252.

It is evident from the dealings of the English with the Narragansetts that, as to this particular tribe, from the first their policy was to leave it to its fate so far as any interference on their part might be called for.

INDIAN WARS OF NEW ENGLAND

the Narragansetts, Mohegans, and latterly the Mohawks had shifted to Western Connecticut those savage activities which became not infrequently a source of much anxiety and uneasiness to the Rhode Island and Connecticut colonies. Immediately after the subjection of the Pequods the Narragansetts largely outnumbered the other Connecticut tribes. Either by reason of their discontent; or realizing, perhaps, that the English had not taken them into their full confidence, as seemed to be the fact with the Mohegans; or possibly because their importance in numbers had not procured for them sovereignty over the smaller tribes; or possibly out of a spirit of envy against Uncas, a Mohegan sachem, who had been able to ingratiate himself with the English,[1] and who seemed always to be

---

[1] "The alliance into which the whites had entered in order to divide their savage foes were the occasions of future entanglements in a tortuous policy, and of later bloody struggles of an appalling character."
Ellis, *Memorial History of Boston*, p. 254.

The religious belief that their possession of New England was fortified by "Divine Rights" was the Puritan excuse for a duplicity and inhumanity which proved but steps to a savagery to which that of the untutored aborigine was incomparable; for while they read their way to the complacent heights of faith taught by the Nazarene, they besmeared their Bibles with the blood of helpless women and children. Even clergymen like Mather, Hubbard, and some others were no less malignant in their exultant comment over the destruction of a "subtle Brood and Generation of Vipers."

WARS OF THE MOHEGANS

engaged in some mischievous machinations against them; or incapable, as well, of forgetting the ancient traditions of their people; or dissatisfied with the distribution of the spoils of the Pequot enterprise; — for some one, or perhaps all, of these reasons, it was inevitable that the inveterate hatred of the savage for his enemy should terminate in an open and disastrous quarrel.[1]

Between the advent of Massasoit and the later assumption of power by Philip of Mount Hope, the Mohegan sachem Uncas may be regarded as the most prominent and influential of the New England savages; for it was about 1638 this sachem was nearing the zenith of his power. His career may be regarded as having begun the previous year, upon the extinction of the Pequods by the English, before which time he was overshadowed by the prestige of Sassacus and his fear of that belligerent sachem. After the massacre of Sassacus and his warriors by the Mohawks — a tragic incident which no doubt had its inspiration in the desire of the Mohawks to obtain some friendly footing

---

[1] "Impartial history has entirely and fully decreed that the Narragansetts were the aggrieved and wronged party."
Hubbard's *Indian Wars*, vol. ii., p. 39, note.
Mather's *Relation*.
Governor Hopkins, in *Mass. Hist. Coll.*
Arnold, *Rhode Island*.
Drake, *Book of the Indians*.
Hubbard, *History of New England*, p. 446.

INDIAN WARS OF NEW ENGLAND

with the English — Uncas, relieved from the perils of the war-path, cherishing the traditional enmity of his people for the Narragansetts, and anxious to maintain his prerogative with the English, began to plot the downfall of his rival, Miantunnumoh.

For reasons that are somewhat obscure as attaching to the policy of the English toward the Narragansetts, the course of which was so uneven that it might well have aroused suspicion on the part of that people,— as it inevitably did at a later day,— it may be regarded as the cause of much of the ill-feeling which finally deprived the Narragansetts of their leader.[1] Drake has remarked that "the continual broils which prevailed between them" (having reference to the Narragansetts and the Mohegans), of which the English were generally the instigators and not infrequently the aggressors, may

---

[1] "The English seem to always have been more favorably inclined toward other tribes than the Narragansetts, as appears from the stand they took in the wars between them and their enemies, and so long as other tribes succeeded against them, the English were idle spectators; but whenever the scale turned in their favor, they were not slow to intercede."
Drake, *Book of the Indians*, p. 60.

To accomplish the death of Miantunnumoh the English were actively allied to the Mohegan sachem Uncas. Miantunnumoh disposed of, afterward, when the Narragansetts and Nehantics had Uncas penned in his fort, to finally achieve a considerable victory over the Mohegans, the English left Uncas to get out of his difficulty as he might.
Ibid, p. 68.

WARS OF THE MOHEGANS

be regarded as among the causes which led King Philip ultimately to question the integrity of his English neighbors. The old Narragansett sachem Canonicus,[1] like Massasoit, had shown toward the English a most friendly disposition. The Narra-

---

[1] After the incident of 1622, when Canonicus sent to Bradford a bundle of arrows tied with the skin of a rattlesnake, which might have been a ruse to try the temper of the Plymouth Colony, the Narragansett sachem became an avowed friend of the English. The act may have been occasioned by a feeling of jealousy against Massasoit, who had been taken into open favor by the Plymouth government. His sending the Narragansetts to Neponset may have been actuated by a more honest purpose than was credited by Winthrop, recalling the killing of Oldham by the Pequots, and the commission of other outrages by them upon the Connecticut River settlers, following so closely upon the departure of this savage embassy.

"While the murder of Oldham was the work of the Nehantics, Cannonicus and Miantunnumoh were fully exonerated from any connection with the crime."

Hubbard, *History of New England*, p. 250.

"Lieut. Gibbons and Mr. Higginson were sent soon after, with Cushammakin, the sachem of the Massachusetts, to Cannonicus, to treat with him about the murder of J. Oldham. They returned with acceptance and good success of their business; observing in the sachem much state, great command of his men, and marvellous wisdom in his answers; and in the carriage of the whole treaty clearing himself and his neighbors of the murder, and offering revenge of it, yet upon very safe and wary conditions."

Ibid, p. 251.

INDIAN WARS OF NEW ENGLAND

gansetts had not been known as a warlike people, yet there were not lacking those who set all sorts of rumors afoot, alleging their hostility toward the early settlers. An instance of this is afforded, in 1631, when Boston was thrown into a sudden ferment over a report that three hundred Narragansetts were concealed in the neighborhood of the Watertown marshes, whose errand was hostile, and who were biding the favorable moment when they might descend upon Charlestown, which was just across the Mystic.[1]

As early as 1632, Miantunnumoh, who at this time had assumed the leadership of the Narragansetts, paid the English a visit in Boston, where he remained two nights. He was known at that time as Mecumeh. While here he attended church with the English, and it was during this absence from his warriors, twelve of whom had kept him company on his journey thither, that some of them broke into a

---

[1] Hutchinson says, "The colonists were frequently alarmed this year (1631), but happily for them in their feeble, infant state, only alarmed." The Tarratines made a descent on Agawam (near Ipswich), and there was some trouble between the English traders and some of the Narragansetts at Sowam (near Bristol). These disturbances impelled the settlers to be constantly watchful.

Ellis says, "There was never any serious collision on the spot between the natives and the occupants of Boston and its immediate neighborhood."

Winsor's *Memorial History of Boston*, p. 250.

WARS OF THE MOHEGANS

house and committed some depredations which were complained of to the English governor, "who told the sachem of it and with some difficulty caused him to make one of his sannaps [attendants], beat them." Those who had been engaged in this mischief were immediately sent out of the town, after which Miantunnumoh and those warriors who had remained behind were entertained by the governor at his house, "who made much of them."[1]

That the English had nothing to complain of on the part of the Narragansett sachem is evidenced by the alacrity of the latter in assisting the English in the carrying out of their purpose against the Pequods. Miantunnumoh was not only generous toward them as to his service, but likewise as to his lands — a generosity of spirit which certainly was

---

[1] "Amongst the rest, August 5, 1632, one of the great sachems of the Narragansetts, (that most populous company of all the Indians in those parts,) called Mecumeh, but afterward Miantunnumoh, came down to Boston to make peace or a league with the English, either of fear or love. While himself and his followers were at the sermon, three of them withdrew from the assembly; and being pinched with hunger, (for 'venter non habet aures,') broke into an English house in sermon time to get victuals. The sagamore, (an honest spirited fellow as his after actions declared,) was hardly persuaded to order them any bodily punishment; but to prevent the shame of his attendants, forthwith sent them out of town, and followed himself not long after."
Hubbard, *History of New England*, p. 144.

[349]

INDIAN WARS OF NEW ENGLAND

ill requited at the hands of the English.[1] Miantunnumoh's errand to Boston was to obtain the assistance of the English in the settlement of some claims for grievous wrongs inflicted upon him and

---

[1] The Narragansetts were generously disposed toward the English settler. In the disposition of their lands, Roger Williams had fared well; also Samuel Gorton and some of his friends, who purchased Shawomet (afterward Warwick) of Miantunnumoh and Canonicus. The Puritans did not approve of Gorton and his settlement, and they put Pumham, sachem of Shawomet, forward to claim the territory conveyed to Gorton. Supported and advised by the English, Pumham claimed the chief sachemship of the Narragansetts. The government at Massachusetts Bay, to lend to their contention the appearance of disinterestedness, which, from their subsequent effort at self-vindication, they "thought there was a chance to doubt," made entry of the transaction. "Send for the foresaid sachems [who had complained of Mr. Gorton and others through the instigation of the English] and upon examination find, both by English and Indian testimony, that Miantunnumoh was only a usurper, and had no title to the foresaid lands." Drake says this is "against the testimony of every record and the annulment of the powers fully vested in Cannonicus." Miantunnumoh was the son of the sachem Mascus, nephew of Canonicus. Pumham was sachem of Shawomet, and had received somewhat of the consideration paid by Gorton. To complicate matters, the Plymouth Colony laid claim to Shawomet through Massasoit. In the controversy Pumham was stabbed by the Wampanoag Nawwashawenck, while the commissioners of the United Colonies, after several years of delayed consideration, decided "that though said tract of land fell within Plimouth bounds, it should henceforth belong to Massachusetts." Drake remarks

WARS OF THE MOHEGANS

his people by Wequash Cook, the Pequod spy, and the Nehantic sachem Ninigret. In this instance the Narragansett sachem was sent home with the assurance that he might right his own wrongs as he pleased;[1] and it is to be noted here that in the following year, when Ninigret was complained of to the English by the Long Island Indians,— that the former had committed some robberies upon them,— Captain Mason was at once despatched from Connecticut with seven men to require satisfaction from the Nehantic sachem forthwith, with the result that the matter was amicably settled.[2] This is the last we hear of the Nehantic sachem until after the death of Miantunnumoh.

The following three years passed without incident. The overthrow of the Pequods had opened up large areas of land to the English occupation; considerable numbers of immigrants were arriving from England; and the natives, grateful for their delivery from the robberies of the Pequods, and as well impressed with the power of the English, were

---

that "by reason of this conveyance the Puritan government soon made evident its resentment toward Miantunnumoh, and here we cannot but discover the germ of all the subsequent disasters of that sachem."

Drake, *Book of the Indians*, vol. iii., pp. 71, 72.
Massachusetts *State Papers*.
Hutchinson, and Hazard *Papers*.

[1] Drake, *Book of the Indians*, vol. iii., p. 68.
[2] *Ibid.*

INDIAN WARS OF NEW ENGLAND

silent while this absorption of their lands was being consummated. With their usual improvidence, they failed to forecast the results of this establishment of so many of the English in their country; nor did it occur to them, as a further result of this occupation, that their hunting-grounds would be depleted of game, while their extinction as a race was no less inevitable. They valued their lands lightly, but looked with childish admiration upon the gauds and ornaments and some common utensils which the English offered them; and without thought or regret they accepted the latter for vast areas of lands; nor had they come to a realizing sense of their condition, by reason of this impoverishment of natural resources, until the situation was beyond their recall.

In the treaty mentioned in the preceding chapter, the English were to retain the country of the Pequods as by right of conquest; and being situated between the Niantic and Paucatuck streams, which was comprised in the once considerable townships of New London, Groton, and Stonington, it is not made clear by the English that they otherwise ever obtained any of these lands by legitimate title; and while no one disputed their title under these pretenses, it was not until some time thereafter that any settlement of importance was erected within these boundaries.

It was a fine country, with which the English became better and better acquainted as they carried

WARS OF THE MOHEGANS

on their hunts for the refugee Pequods. Its climate was mild, and its soil fertile and well disposed toward the seacoast west of the Connecticut River. Reports of the excellence of the territory reached Boston, from which place there came, in the spring of 1638, a colony of planters. They preëmpted the lands about the little Bay of New Haven, which was the habitation of the Quinnipiacks, who raised no objection. As a matter of fact, the Indians welcomed these white strangers; for the reason, doubtless, that their coming would lend them greater security against the incursion of marauding savages to the westward, especially the Mohawks.

At the close of this year, December 4, the Quinnipiacks entered into a treaty with these planters. Monauguin, the Quinnipiack sachem, under this treaty gave to the English all the lands of Quinnipiack, their rivers, ponds, and trees; and, for this, stipulated that they were to hunt and fish throughout the domain as had been their custom; and, in addition, a reservation was made of a small tract on the east side of the harbor, which was to be used by them as their planting-grounds. The English were to use the meadows, and cut down trees; nor were the savages to set traps and other snares which would cause injury to the cattle of the English; along with numerous other conditions too unimportant to be considered here. They agreed that each should not molest the other; and in case any personal injury or damage was committed, suitable reparation should be made. As a singular part of this treaty, a census of these people is mentioned, by which one learns that the men and youths of the Quinnipiacks were forty-seven, which is followed by a curious condition,— that the Quinnipiacks would allow no other Indians among them without first obtaining leave of the English. To this treaty are attached the totems of the sachem, his four councillors, and his sister. The sachem's totem was a bow; the others were comprised of a fish-hook, a crooked line, a war-club, and a curious hieroglyphic which as much resembles a tobacco-pipe as anything else.[1]

The consideration for this large tract of land was made up of twelve coats of English trading-cloth, twelve alchemy-spoons, twelve hatchets, twelve hoes, two dozen knives, twelve porringers, and four cases of French knives and scissors. From the English point of view, these considerations represented the value received. It is probable that this savage people were practically ignorant of the English ways of living; and it is evident that it did not occur to them that the English would endeavor to obtain a living by any other means than trading, fishing, and hunting. Had they for a moment been gifted, like the Cobbler Keezar, with a lap-stone to have given them the vision of a seer, they would

---

[1] DeForest, p. 164, and *Appendix*, pp. 231–236; also art. iv. *Records of New Haven Colony.*
Bacon's *Historical Discourses.*

WARS OF THE MOHEGANS

have looked in vain for the wigwam of their own race; the graves of their forefathers would have been obliterate; and whatever vestige of themselves remained would have become charges upon the State. Their immense forests would have disappeared; the wild animals that haunted their recesses would have vanished with them; the rivers would have been barren of their fish; while for every rude cabin of the white settler would have arisen a populous city from which stretched away toward the hills the spacious open places of cultivated lands. Only the far horizon of the hills would have remained to them as familiars, upon which the flying clouds painted their pictures of mystery, from which they had many of their tribal traditions. Had they thus been able to have broken the veil of the future apart, to have discounted the vast ambitions of this alien race with its unscrupulous greed of aggrandizement, its indifference to the commonest claims to humanity wherever the savage was concerned, and its hypocritical pretenses, they possibly would have preferred the Pequod as their tax-collector and the scalping-knife of the Mohawk as a lesser peril; for wherever the white man set his foot the trail of the savage was forever blotted out. In the white man's cup they were to discover the poison for which their knowledge supplied no antidote.[1]

---

[1] It was the story of Sinbad and the Old Man of the Sea in

INDIAN WARS OF NEW ENGLAND

The Puritans of the New Haven Colony, in their peaceful and friendly disposition toward the savages, have been likened to the Quakers of Philadelphia, between whom and the Indians with whom they transacted business was an invariable peace and quietness. It is recorded that between the settlers at Quinnipiack and their savage grantors no difficulty or dispute arose, so long as the Indians remained in their immediate neighborhood. These people occupied their little reservation before mentioned, on the east side of the Bay, and here they made habitat for a long time in unnoticed seclusion, making their living mostly upon the shell-fish which were abundant in the harbor. With a fort to lend them a sense of security, they felt themselves immune from invasion. A few days after the Quinnipiack treaty, or, to be more exact, December 21, the land northeast and northwest of the tribe was conceded to the New Haven settlers. It comprised an area of possibly one hundred thirty square miles. In return for it the usual consideration of coats and small tools was given; and in this case, as with the Quinnipiacks, a small reservation

---

a more modern version. "A few years back an Indian was recognized as a brother, and a friend and ally of King James; now he is liable to charge of sedition if he does not tamely submit to injury. Mather confesses 'There were near approaches to war between the English and several nations of Indians, but war was happily avoided by an *obsta principiis*.'"

Freeman, *Civilization and Barbarism*, p. 66.

was retained, which was to afford a living-place for the savages.[1]

In the following year, in February, for some coats, blankets, a kettle, some hoes, knives, hatchets, and a looking-glass, the Paugessets conveyed to the English what is now a large part of Milford. The ancient custom of delivery by twig and turf was observed in this case. The sachem Ansantawae stuck the twig into the turf and gave both into the hands of the English. By this he had passed to the English the land and all that it sustained.[2] This tribe at this time was so numerous that the colonists, after laying out their village, which compassed a mile square, surrounded it with a palisade — evidently that they might be better protected by requiring the Indians to enter the town at certain designated places.

This same year a small tribe had their habitat in what is now Fairfield, which compassed a large tract; but as the records of Fairfield were destroyed,

---

[1] This treaty was made on the part of the Indians by Montowese, a son of Sowheag, the sachem who was the cause of the foray on the Wethersfield settlement. His totem was a bow with an arrow fitted to its string. In this treaty he says that he obtained his land from his deceased mother, which allows the inference that the savages observed certain rights in heredity.
Records of New Haven Colony.
DeForest, p. 166.

[2] Lambart's *History of New Haven Colony*, p. 86.

the particulars are unknown. One other settlement was made during this year, at what is now Guilford, the date of its purchase being October 9. It probably included some part of the present East Haven. The usual consideration was varied in this case by the addition of some wampum, some shoes, stockings, hats, and spoons. As a part of the consideration, the savages agreed to abandon the property to the English, which they did, joining their kindred further to the west.[1]

In the previous pages, the differences between Sowheag and the planters of Wethersfield have been referred to in the relation of an incident which preceded, by a short interval of time, the breaking out of the Pequod War. While the Pequod War was going on this matter was brought before the General Court of Connecticut, which adjudicated finally that the settlers of Wethersfield had been the aggressors. An offer of friendship was sent to the Waugunk sachem (whose warriors had been implicated in the raid on Wethersfield), providing he would surrender those concerned in the attack. The issue between the English and the Pequods being at that time somewhat uncertain, Sowheag, relying upon the former prowess of the Pequods, and as well in the fighting-men of his own tribe, declined to listen to the English; but in August, 1639, the Pequods having been thoroughly vanquished, this matter was again renewed, by the resolve upon the

---

[1] *Vide Guilford Records.*

WARS OF THE MOHEGANS

part of the Connecticut magistrates to mete out to Sowheag the same punishment which had been visited upon the Pequods. The General Court ordered a levy of one hundred men; and the different settlements were notified so they might provide for their own defence.

It is evident that the mantle of peace set lightly upon the English shoulders. This course of action on the part of the Connecticut magistrates was not agreeable to Governor Eaton and his friends, who hitherto had been inclined in a friendly way to the Indians, nor had their experience taught them either to hate or fear the savages. They protested with great earnestness against this design, summing up with the relation of the great expense and suffering which had been the natural outcome of the war with the Pequods, urging upon the settlers the fact that to prosecute the development of the country successfully, they not only needed all the means at their command, but their men as well. The argument was so convincing that all preparations for war were laid aside, to be followed by an amicable adjustment of the differences between the Wethersfield settlers and Sowheag, who, having removed to Mattabesett (Middletown), was left to his own devices.[1]

---

[1] The treaty with Montowese — *Records of New Haven Colony.*
Colonial Records, vol. i., pp. 19, 31.
Trumbull, vol. i., p. 108.

INDIAN WARS OF NEW ENGLAND

Following this, it was reported to the court that the Pequods were violating the treaty of 1638, by reason of their having united themselves into a considerable body, after which they established themselves anew in their ancient country. They had set up their wigwams adjacent to the Nehantics along the shore of the Paucatuck, with the consent of this latter tribe, to which they had become tributary. They had not only broken the treaty, but had become trespassers on that part of the Pequod territory claimed by the English; and it was ordered by the court that they should not only be punished, but should be ejected from these lands. John Mason, with forty men, who was at once joined by Uncas, with twenty canoes and one hundred Mohegans, was despatched to the mouth of the Paucatuck, where he encountered a party of three Pequods. To these he committed a message which they were to carry to the Pequod settlement, which was that they "must leave the country immediately or he would drive them away by force, carry off their corn, and burn their wigwams." These involuntary messengers pledged themselves to return with the answer; but, once free of the English, they forgot their promise to Mason. Mason, waiting somewhat, landed his men to make a sudden attack upon the village, where he captured a few old men who through their infirmities were unable to escape. They found in the wigwams an abundance of corn, which was given over to Uncas and his people; and, while engaged in securing this plunder, sixty of the Pequods broke over the crest of a neighboring hill, to charge into their midst. The Mohegans awaited this onslaught until the Pequods were some thirty yards from them, when the silence was broken by a tumult of war-whoops. Swinging their weapons above their heads, they met the Mohegans, to engage in the confusion of noise and conflict, while Mason and his men remained passive spectators.

It was an almost bloodless conflict, in which no lives were lost. A movement on the part of Mason and his men caused the Pequods to take instant flight. In this mêlée seven Pequods were captured. None were killed by the English, Mason's anxiety being, evidently, not to arouse the Pequods to a spirit of revenge; but those captured were so insulting that Mason was about to "make them a head shorter" when Yotaash, a brother of Miantunnumoh, interceded, saying, "They are my brother's men. He is a friend to the English. You shall have the heads of seven murderers in their stead." Mason gave the Pequods into the hands of Uncas; but as to their final fate, history is silent.

Nightfall found Mason and his men here on the bank of the river, where they spent the night; and early in the morning, as they looked across the stream, they were surprised by the appearance of a considerable body of Indians, whose number they estimated at three hundred. They at once caught up their muskets, but the Indians had disappeared. In response to the hail of the English, who expressed a desire to hold a parley with them, some few of the savages emerged from their hiding places and came to the edge of the stream; and to these, Mason, through his interpreter, related the reason for his apparently hostile expedition among them, which was that the Pequods, having broken the Hartford treaty by organizing themselves as a separate community, and as well by making their ancient country their habitat, had compelled the English to this action. The reply which came across the waters was, "The Pequots who live here are good men, and we will certainly fight for them and protect them." Mason challenged them at once by saying, "Very well; it is not far to the head of the creek; I will meet you there, and you may do what you can at fighting!" To which the savages returned, "We will not fight with the English, for they are spirits; but we will fight with Uncas."

As it turned out, the savages with whom Mason was holding his conference were of the Nehantics and Narragansetts, who had interfered in behalf of their tributaries in this effort to drive them from their country. They were loth, however, to engage in the fight with the English, whom they regarded as *Manittos* (supernatural beings). In reply to this, Mason announced that he should occupy himself that day in the destruction of the Pequod village, and the carrying away of the Pequod harvest;

WARS OF THE MOHEGANS

moreover, that if they wished to attack him they could do so at their leisure. The roll of the English drums filled the woods with their vibrant echo, while the English took up their work of devastation, which they accomplished without further interference. When he had destroyed the Pequod village and loaded his vessel with the product of their harvest, Mason sailed away up the river, followed by his allies, who had accumulated for themselves a considerable store of mats, kettles, and other property of the Pequods, which they had loaded into their own canoes and, as well, into thirty others which the Pequods had left behind them in their flight.[1] This, evidently, was the last foray against the Pequods, of whom little or nothing is recorded for almost a decade after; unless one may attach something of importance to the isolate instances wherein perhaps punishment was meted out to those who were regarded by the English (and not always justly) as worthy of peremptory disposition.[2]

---

[1] Mason's *History*.
Mass. Hist. Coll., vol. xviii., pp. 149–151.
DeForest, p. 172, note: "The band thus broken up was probably under Wequash, or Wequash Cook, who, as we learn from Roger Williams' Letters [*R. I. Hist. Coll.*, vol. iii., p. 141] had collected, even during the previous year, about sixty Pequots in the Nehantic country. After this disaster, Wequash removed to near Saybrook on the Connecticut, where he died in 1642."

[2] A Connecticut historian notes that the New Haven settle-

INDIAN WARS OF NEW ENGLAND

As the years grew, the population along the Connecticut River increased. Purchases of lands from the Indians were being consummated, and the purchase of 1636 from Sequassen was followed by another purchase of the same territory in 1640 — evidently with the intention of putting the Indians into better humor. During this and the following year other convenient and fertile lands were bought by the English; and it has been noted by one historian that while private sales and gifts at

---

ment never had any quarrels with the Indians in its vicinity, but it was not without its instance of manifest injustice.

A Pequot sachem, Nepaupuck, was apprehended as a criminal, and summarily executed. He fought the English with his people, and was noted as among the bravest of their warriors. He had killed a Wethersfield settler, one Abraham Finch, and as well other white men, whose hands he had cut off and carried to Sassacus. His tribe disrupted, he wandered about for some time homeless and probably without friends. On one of these occasions he happened into the New Haven settlement, accompanied by another Indian. He was no sooner recognized than he was deprived of his liberty. The English bound him, as they thought, securely; but by the assistance of his companion he had nearly gained his freedom when he was fastened in the stocks, and his savage acquaintance was dismissed with a flogging. The authorities summoned the Quinnipiacks to tell what they knew of the prisoner. The evidence was conclusive; but one of his kinsmen interceded, only to be compelled to confess that the charges against the Pequot accused were true. Nepaupuck was put upon his explanation, but declared that he was not Nepaupuck. He was confronted with his kinsman, Mewhebato,

WARS OF THE MOHEGANS

one time were not infrequent, they were less so during these early years than afterward. To obviate any possibility of fraud being perpetrated upon the Indians, the General Court of Connecticut, in 1638, passed an order that no one was to take a conveyance of land from the Indians without the authority of the court.[1] These laws were not always observed, and it is no doubt true that wherever the

---

and Wattone, a Quinnipiack, which latter asserted that he saw the Pequot kill Abraham Finch. The Pequot's identity was so thoroughly established that he confessed: "He knew he must die; he was not afraid of death; the English might cut his head off, or kill him in any other way; only fire was God, and God was angry with him; wherefore he desired not to fall into his hands." The Pequot was returned to the stocks, to be brought before the General Court the next day to be tried for his life. He was found guilty of murder and sentenced, and his head was cut off and fastened upon a pole in the market-place.

New Haven Records.

The crime for which this savage was tried and executed, as a matter of fact, was committed not only outside the jurisdiction of the New Haven Colony, but even before there was any such colony. This is a fair specimen of the English justice. His head was set up on a pole as a barbarous token because he had been loyal to his own nation, and had openly helped to fight its battles. He was in no particular amenable to the English law. By this farcical trial the English but carried out a policy which was as unmerciful and relentless as it was unjustifiable. The English demanded absolute submission, or extermination.

[1] Dr. Johnson mentions this law. He was at one time the

INDIAN WARS OF NEW ENGLAND

Indians had reason to make complaint that they had been unfairly used, or cheated of their lands, the private individual might be regarded as the source of the same. Having in view the disposition of the English to increase their territorial holdings at whatever cost, the question may arise, to the unprejudiced observer, as to whether the General Court, in promulgating this order, had the welfare of the Indians so much in view as the desire to control the unoccupied lands of the colony.

In 1640 the Norwalk tribe disposed of the land from the Norwalk to the Saugatuck River, which extended back into the country a day's walk from the sea. The consideration for the same was of the usual kind, except that it varied in that ten jew's-harps and ten fathoms of tobacco might be regarded as an innovation. In the same year Captain Daniel Patrick, who had a hand in the adventures of the English against the Pequods, secured by purchase two islands at the Norwalk River mouth; also a

---

Connecticut agent in England in the trial of the so-called Mohegan Case.
Indian Papers, vol. i., doc. 277.
While it is distinctly referred to in at least one place of the *Colonial Records*, it does not appear to have been recorded.
Colonial Records, vol. i., p. 214.
Trumbull mentions the restriction as having been adopted both by New Haven and Connecticut.
Trumbull, *History of Connecticut*, vol. i., p. 117.

WARS OF THE MOHEGANS

tract of land on its west shore.[1] The following year, that part of the country now Stamford was sold for a lot of merchandise of the usual description, the value of which Trumbull estimates to be about thirty pounds.[2]

While to the observer these various commodities are seemingly of slight value as compared with the large areas of territory which in these later years have become of enormous value, it will be remembered that at the time of the conveyance these lands were undeveloped, and that whatever of value has attached to them since has been the result of well-directed labor and investment. Outside of the sequestration of the Pequod lands, the hands of the Connecticut settlers seem in these transactions to be comparatively clean,— these lands were not obtained by coercion, neither by that process of debauchery which was practised by the English upon the Indians to the eastward,— and as for the commodities themselves, they were brought from over the water at some expense in those days, when a very considerable value was attached to what in times of greater abundance was an apparently insignificant article. There appears as a part of each individual consideration, in all these transactions with the savages, a certain number of hoes and hatchets (probably axes). By the use of the latter

---

[1] Hall's *History of Norwalk*, pp. 30, 41.
[2] President Stiles's *Itinerary*, vol. ii.

the lands were to be cleared of their forests, and by the use of the former the clearings were to be wrought into productive fields. We do not find it a matter of record that at this time the plow was sufficiently common to have become a matter of notice. If there were any in Connecticut they were so few in number as to hardly take their place among the tools common to cultivation. It is a matter worthy of curious remark just here that in 1637, as Trumbull notes, there were but five or ten plows in use in Connecticut; and in Massachusetts, with its considerable population for the time, there were only thirty plows in use among its inhabitants.[1]

No one knows how long the Indians had occupied this country, which at the coming of the English was but a vast and unimproved wilderness, whose history was comprised in the unwritten traditions of its savage dwellers; nor is it less uncertain as to the span of the centuries to come, through which the same wild, untutored conditions might prevail. But the English came, and with their advent began the rude and strenuous civilization before which the Indian was to disappear ultimately. Whatever of humane observation may arise out of these considerations as to whether the English are to be regarded as trespassers without right upon these wild domains of the aborigine, or as to

---

[1] Trumbull, *History of Connecticut*, p. 69, note.

WARS OF THE MOHEGANS

whether they should have taken a milder course with the latter, is generally discarded as an idle discussion; for wherever civilization has obtained a foothold upon the shores of barbarism the conflict between the two has been no less unequal than that which resulted in the annihilation of the red men and the redemption of the wilderness, which afforded him at best but a precarious livelihood. Whatever may be said as to the influence of the Christian faith among the Indians, the results as anticipated by Eliot and those who wrought with him cannot be regarded as other than meager. The Indians were a superstitious race, without religious traditions, and absolutely devoid of those traits of character without which soundness of religious principles cannot exist.[1]

---

[1] "It so happens, that in attempting to substitute one faith for another, in the minds of the Indians, that the one proposed admits of no better demonstration than the one already possessed by them; for their manner of transmitting things to be remembered, is the most impressive and sacred, as will be elsewhere observed in our work. . . . That anything false should be handed down from their aged matrons and sires, could not be for a moment believed; and hence, that the stories of a strange people should be credited, instead of what they had heard from day to day from their youth up, from those who could have no possible motive to deceive them, could not be expected; and therefore no one will wonder for a moment that the gospel has met with so few believers among the Indians. All this aside from their dealers in mysteries, the powwows, conjurers or priests, as they are variously denominated,

INDIAN WARS OF NEW ENGLAND

It may be noted in this place, in reference to this assumption, that at the time of the breaking out of King Philip's War, some forty years later than the period of which we are writing, there were some thirteen thousand of what were known as the "praying Indians" in Massachusetts, Rhode Island, and Connecticut. Notwithstanding their religious intercourse with the English, and the teaching of the Word which had been so conscientiously carried on by Eliot and Mayhew; notwithstanding the softening influences, and the refinements of sensibility and feeling, by which one is made his brother's keeper, to become the possessor of the "peace that passeth all understanding," it is unfortunate as an illustration of the futility of these most commendable efforts toward the Christianizing of a savage people — which perhaps is the only redeeming spot in the fabric of events in the shaping of which the English were almost the sole arbiters

---

whose office is healing the sick, appeasing the wrath of the invisible spirits by charms and unintelligible mummery. These characters took upon themselves, also, the important affair of determining the happiness each was to enjoy after death; assuring the brave and the virtuous that they should go to a place of perpetual spring, where game in the greatest plenty abounded, and everything that the most perfect happiness required. Now, as a belief in any other religion promised no more, is it strange that a new one should be slow in gaining credence?"

Drake's *Book of the Indians*, pp. 110, 111.

WARS OF THE MOHEGANS

— that after the breaking out of hostilities in Swanzey the larger portion of these "praying Indians" at once attached themselves to the cause of King Philip. Whether the difficulty in this matter was primarily chargeable to the soil, or whether the seed sown by Eliot was lacking in spiritual efficacy, is not within human knowledge; but the fact remains, that, like the leopard's spots, the instinct of savagery in the Indian was ineradicable.[1]

---

[1] "Notwithstanding one of the ostensible objects of nearly all the royal charters and patents issued for British North America was the Christianizing of the Indians, few could be found equal to the task on arriving here; where wants of every kind required nearly all their labors, few could be found willing to forego every comfort to engage in a work which presented so many difficulties. Adventurers were those, generally, who emigrated with a view to bettering their own condition, instead of that of others.

"At length Mr. John Eliot, seeing that little or nothing could be effected through the medium of his own language, resolved to make himself master of the Indian [tongue], and then to devote himself to their service. Accordingly he hired [Neal, *History of New England*, vol. i., p. 222] an old [*New England Biographical Dictionary*, art. Eliot] Indian, named Job Nesutan, to live in his family and teach him his language."

Drake's *Book of the Indians*, p. 111.

"It was in 1685 that the second edition of the famous Indian Bible was completed. From the following testimony of Mr. Eliot will be seen how much the success of that undertaking was considered to depend on James-the-printer. In 1683, in writing to the Hon. Robert Boyle at London, Mr. Eliot says, 'I desire to see it done before I die, and I am so

INDIAN WARS OF NEW ENGLAND

It was through the train of events enumerated in this chapter that one is led to a consideration of the influence of the Mohegan sachem Uncas. After the spoiling of the Pequods, Uncas claimed the leader-

---

deep in years, that I cannot expect to live very long; besides, we have but one man, viz. the Indian Printer, that is able to compose the sheets, and correct the press with understanding.' In another, from the same to the same, dated a year after, he says, 'Our slow progress needeth an apology. We have been much hindered by the sickness the last year. Our workmen have been all sick, and we have but few hands, (at printing,) one Englishman and a boy, and one Indian,' &c.

"This Indian was undoubtedly James-the-printer. And Mr. Thomas adds, 'Some of James's descendants were not long since living in Grafton; they bore the surname of Printer' [*History of Printing*, pp. 292, 293].

"There was an Indian named Job Nesutan, who was also concerned in the first edition of the Indian Bible. He was a valient soldier, and went with the English of Massachusetts, in the first expedition to Mount Hope, where he was slain in battle. 'He was a very good linguist in the English tongue, and was Mr. Eliot's assistant and interpreter in his translation of the Bible and other books in the Indian language' [Gookin, *History of Praying Indians*]."

Drake's *Book of the Indians*, p. 57.

Eliot's first attempt at Christianizing the Indians was made October 28, 1646. Near what was once Watertown Mill, upon the south side of Charles River, in Roxbury, was the habitat of the Nonatum Indians, of whom Waban was one of the leading men. It was in Waban's wigwam that Eliot conducted his first service, which was attended by a considerable number of natives, to hear what Neal calls "the daybreak of the Gospel in New England" (Neal, vol. i., p. 223). After

ship of their country by reason of his connection with the royal Pequod family. He relinquished his right to that portion along the sea-coast which had been appropriated by the English, but that lying in-

---

prayers, Eliot read the ten commandments and explained them. This was followed by some pertinent questions on the part of the Indians, one of which was, if "*Jesus Christ could understand prayers in Indian? Whether Englishmen were ever so ignorant of him as the Indians?*"

November 11, of the same year, Eliot held a second service, at which the Indian children were catechised, and which was followed by a sermon of an hour's length, after which the Indians put this question to him,—"*How the English came to differ so much from the Indians in their knowledge of God and Jesus Christ, since they had all at first but one father?*" Another wanted to know, "*How it came to pass that sea-water was salt and river-water was fresh?*"

On the 26th of this month fell the third meeting, which Drake notes was not so well attended; which fact was due undoubtedly to the influence of the powwows and the sachems, by whom threats and persuasions were used. Eliot had won the friendship of the savages, to whom came Wampas and two others, bringing their children, whom they desired to be instructed in the Christian faith.

At the next meeting, those Indians who were present "offered their children to be catechised and instructed by the English." Eliot upon this motion resolved to set up a school among them. One of Eliot's remarks at the inception of this work was that the Indian must be civilized as well as be, if not in order to being, Christianized. This allows one to infer that he was aware that something other than preaching was necessary to accomplish the reformation of this savage people.

The first Indian mission was established at Natick. The

INDIAN WARS OF NEW ENGLAND

land he regarded as absolutely his own. He thus acquired the control of much of northern New London County, and as well the southern portions of Tolland and Windham Counties. While the

---

following curious code of conduct by which the Indians, becoming residents at the mission, were to be guided in their pursuit after the civilization of the English is as here quoted: "I.— If any man be idle a week, or at most a fortnight, he shall pay five shillings. II.— If any unmarried man shall lie with a young woman unmarried, he shall pay twenty shillings. III.— If any man shall beat his wife, his hands shall be tied behind him, and he shall be carried to a place of justice to be severely punished. IV.— Every young man, if not another's servant, and if unmarried, shall be compelled to set up a wigwam, and plant for himself, and not shift up and down in other wigwams. V.— If any woman shall not have her hair tied up, but hang loose, or be cut as men's hair, she shall pay five shillings. VI.— If any woman shall go with naked breasts, she shall pay two shillings. VII.— All men that wear long locks shall pay five shillings. VIII.— If any shall kill their lice between their teeth, they shall pay five shillings."

In the following January another mission was established at Concord. After that, several other meeting-places were established from Cape Cod to Narragansett [Neal, vol. i., pp. 226–230]. These formed a circuit which Eliot visited as he could. The arduous character of his work may be inferred from a letter which he wrote to Winslow: "I have not been dry night or day from the third day of the week to the sixth, but so travelled, and at night pull off my boots, wring my stockings, and on with them again, and so continue. But God steps in and helps" [*Magnalia*, vol. iii., p. 196].

His chief obstacles in the prosecution of his work were the powwows and the sachems, whose opposition would have

WARS OF THE MOHEGANS

Pequods were in power they had numerous tributaries, who, relieved of the dominancy of the former, were inclined to assume independence. Some, however, remained tributary to Uncas. Some were

---

been more marked had they not been afraid of the English. Neal accepts this as a condition, "for if it be very difficult to civilize barbarous nations, it is much more so to make them Christians: All men have naturally a veneration for the religion of their ancestors, and the prejudices of education (among the Indians this word is taken in an opposite sense to its common meaning. Instruction in superstition is the antithesis of education) are insuperable without the extraordinary grace of God."

Eliot's zeal had not only enabled him to translate the Bible wholly into the Indian vernacular, but, as well, Baxter's *Call*, Shepherd's *Sincere Convert* and his *Sound Believer*, a grammar, psalter, some primers and catechisms, also the *Practice of Piety* (Mather's *Magnalia*, bk. 3, p. 197). Mather, in speaking of the Bible, says, "It was printed here at our Cambridge, and is the only Bible that was printed in America from the foundation of the world." He goes on to observe that "the whole translation was written by one pen, which pen, had it not been lost, would certainly have deserved a richer case than was bestowed upon that with which Holland writ his translation of Plutarch." The vernacular alluded to was that of the Natick or Nipmucks.

Drake's *Book of the Indians*, p. 114.

Drake also notes that a census of these "praying Indians" was calculated the year before King Philip's War, and they were estimated to have been at that time about 1,150. At the close of King Philip's War, 1677, Gookin locates there were "seven places where they met to worship God and keep the Sabbath, viz. at Nomantum, Pakemit or Puncapag, Cowate,

forced to submit. Others yielded by reason of policy. The one hundred Pequods allotted to him by the treaty of 1638 considerably increased his tribe. Other Pequods, of whom the English had no account, came to the Mohegans; and, as one writer has said, "It was natural that the Pequots, rather than fly from their country or become servants to the English, or join their natural foes, the Narragansetts, should choose to identify themselves with

---

alias, Fall of Charles River, Natik, Medfield, Concord, at Namekeak, near Chelmsford."

At the breaking out of this war the "praying Indians" were removed for better supervision to one of the islands in Boston harbor; but upon the death of Philip they were allowed to return to their habitats; and Drake notes that their enfeebled condition from this enforced isolation made them unable to carry on religious worship at so many places. Drake further observes, "We have seen that 1150 'Praying Indians' were claimed before the war in the end of the year 1674, but not half of this number could be found when all such must come out of their towns and go by themselves to a place of safety." Mr. Gookin says that "at one time there were about five hundred upon the islands, but when some had been employed in the army, and other places, generally such as were indifferent to religion," there were but about three hundred remaining. Six years after that disastrous war Mr. Eliot could claim but four towns.

Drake's *Book of the Indians*, p. 115.

Ellis designates Eliot's work as a "fond experiment" (*Memorial History of Boston*, p. 271), "which movement was most seriously affected by King Philip's War."

Ibid, pp. 267-273.

WARS OF THE MOHEGANS

the fragment of their own tribe, even though that fragment had been rebellious and hostile. Wanderers from other nations, too, collected around Uncas, and increased the numbers and influence of the Mohegans. Among these warlike and unsettled communities, wherever a sachem distinguished himself by his abilities and success, he was sure to attract many adventurers from the neighboring tribes. Some came out of a desire for protection, some from a wish to distinguish themselves under so fortunate a leader, and some, doubtless, because they were forced to come by the sachem himself in his efforts to increase the number of his followers."

Uncas had married the daughter of Sebequanash, the Hammonassett sachem. By this action he came into possession of the lands bordering on the sea as far as East River, in Guilford; but in 1641 he had sold nearly all that entire tract, and the most of the tribe to which his wife belonged had become a portion of the Mohegans.[1] He had made himself so useful in the Pequod War that he had commended himself to the favor of the English colonies, and his services were repaid whenever opportunity happened, with or without justice, according to circumstance; for the colonies were not indifferent to the advantages arising from having so powerful a sachem under their direction. An ally in war, he was as useful in more peaceful times, when he acted

---

[1]*Guilford Records.*

as a spy upon his neighbors. So long as Uncas could gratify his desire for power and greed, he was willing to act as such for the English.

The treaty of 1638 has been mentioned. Another agreement was entered into October 8, 1640, which afterward became a source of litigation between the Mohegans and the Connecticut Colony. The English regarded it as a deed of conveyance; the Indians, as according the simple right of preëmption, by which Uncas was restrained from disposing of any portion of his realty to any but the Connecticut Colony, or its settlers. The English claimed that Uncas had given them title to the entire territory over which he exercised control, with the exception of that portion which the Mohegans were using as planting-lands. The consideration for this alleged conveyance was "five yards of cloth and a few pairs of stockings."[1]

It is a question as to the validity of the Mohegan title, as it had been in his hands less than three years. There was no doubt as to his subjection by Sassacus, which, according to the Indian custom, created a forfeiture in these lands. But these considerations had small effect upon Uncas; for during his lifetime the English were satisfied to leave the matter in a quiescent state, while his power and influence were augmented to the extent that among the surrounding chieftains he was not only looked

---

[1] DeForest, *Appendix*, art. v.

upon with feelings of jealousy, but the fear of his ultimate purposes with them was alike entertained, and not without reason. The old spirit of the feud actuated the Narragansetts, and for Uncas, who to them was a Pequod, they entertained nothing but an inveterate hatred. He was disliked bitterly by Sequassen, the Connecticut River sachem, who was a kinsman and ally of the Narragansetts. Whatever ambitions the Narragansett sachems may have entertained upon the overthrow of the Pequods, they were buried under the exaltation of Uncas. It was not unnatural that these sachems should be actuated by a common sentiment toward the Mohegan sachem, and that they should engage in a conspiracy for his destruction. As an offset to this disposition on the part of his enemies, he caused it to be reported to the English that the Narragansetts were entertaining hostile designs against the settlers; one of which was that Miantunnumoh was plotting to "make himself sachem of all the Indians in New England. Miantunnumoh is trying to bring all the Indians into a great conspiracy against the white men."[1]

As a result of these stories circulated by the Mohegans at the instigation of Uncas, in November, 1640, the Boston authorities ordered the Narra-

---

[1] "When it was reported, in 1640, that Miantunnumoh was plotting to cut off the English, as will be found mentioned in the account of Ninigret, and several Englishmen were sent to

gansett sachem to appear before them, forthwith. Miantunnumoh's obedience to this summons was immediate, and his prompt compliance was productive of a good impression in his favor. He was interrogated as to the reports which had reached them, his answers to which were well considered; nor would he reply when questioned, unless some of his councillors were present, that they might hear what he said. His observations were well chosen,

---

him to know the truth of the matter, he would not talk with them through a Pequot interpreter, because he was then at war with that nation. In other respects he complied with their wishes, and treated them respectfully, agreeing to come to Boston, for the gratification of the government, if they would allow Mr. Williams to accompany him. This they would not consent to, and yet he came, agreeable to their desires. We shall presently see who best acted the part of civilized men in this affair. He had refused to use a Pequot interpreter for good reasons, but when he was at Boston, and surrounded by armed men, he was obliged to submit. 'The governor being as resolute as he, refused to use any other interpreter, thinking it a dishonor to us to give so much way to them.' The great wisdom of the government now displayed itself in the person of Gov. Thomas Dudley. It is not to be expected but that Miantunnomoh should resent their proceedings; for to the above insult they added others; 'would show him no countenance nor admit him to dine at our table, as formerly he had done, till he had acknowledged his failing, &c., which he readily did.' By their own folly the English had made themselves jealous of a powerful chief, and they appear ever ready afterwards to credit evil reports of him."

Drake's *Book of the Indians*, p. 62.

and his perception of what was wise and equitable in policy was commendable. He protested that Uncas and the Mohegans were the authors of these damaging reports against him, and offered to prove the fact, demanding that his accusers should be brought before him that he might see them and hear what they had to say; and he further demanded that upon their inability to prove their charges, they should be put to death. "His dignity, his frankness, and the justness of his remarks silenced the complaints of the magistrates; they acquitted him of all suspicion of conspiracy, and he returned to his own country."[1]

His success in this affair could have no other influence upon Uncas than to add fuel to his hatred. Uncas had become to the Narragansetts a marked

---

[1] "In 1642, Connecticut became very suspicious of Miantunnomoh, and urged Massachusetts to join them in a war against him. Their fears no doubt grew out of the consideration of the probable issue of a war with Uncas in his favor, which was now on the point of breaking out. Even Massachusetts did not think their suspicions well founded; yet, according to their request, they sent to Miantunnomoh, who, as usual, gave them satisfactory answers, and, agreeably to their request, came again to Boston. Two days were employed by the court of Massachusetts in deliberating with him, and we are astonished at the wisdom of the great chief, even as reported by his enemies.

"That a simple man of nature, who never knew courts of law, should cause such acknowledgments as follow, from the civilized and wise, will always be contemplated with intense

man; for one evening, not long after the return of Miantunnumoh from Boston, as Uncas was making his way between the wigwams in his fort, an arrow whistled through the air, by which he was wounded in the arm. No further attempt was made upon his life at that time, and the wound was so slight that it soon healed. There was no clew to the would-be assassin. It fell out later that a young Pequod was discovered to be the possessor of a large quantity of wampum. Suspicion falling upon

---

admiration. 'When he came,' says Winthrop, 'the court was assembled, and before his admission, we considered how to treat with him, for we knew him to be a very subtle man.' When he was admitted, 'he was set down at the lower end of the table, over against the governor,' but would not at any time speak upon business unless some of his counsellors were present; saying, 'he would have them present, that they might bear witness with him, at his return home, of all his sayings.' The same author further says, 'In all his answers he was very deliberate, and showed good understanding in the principles of justice and equity, and ingenuity withal.'

"He now asked for his accusers, urging, that if they could not establish their allegations, they should suffer what he expected to, if they did; but the court said they knew of none, that is, they knew not whom they were, and therefore gave no credits to the reports until they had advised him of a former agreement. He then said, 'If you did not give credit to them, why then did you disarm the Indians?' Massachusetts having just then disarmed some of the Merrimacks under some pretence. 'He gave divers reasons,' says Gov. Winthrop, 'why we should hold him free of any such conspiracy, and why we should conceive it was a report raised by Uncas, &c., and

WARS OF THE MOHEGANS

him, he was asked how he came by the wampum, to which he could give no satisfactory reply. At the first opportunity he left the Pequods, to take refuge

---

therefore offered to meet Uncas, and would prove to his face his treachery against the English, &c., and told us he would come to us at anytime,' although he said some had tried to dissuade him, saying that the English would put him to death, yet he feared nothing, as he was innocent of the charges against him.

"The punishment due to those who had raised the accusations, bore heavily upon his breast, and 'he put it to our consideration what damage it had been to him, in that he was forced to keep his men at home, and not suffer them to go forth on hunting, &c., till he had given the English satisfaction.' After two days spent in talk, the council issued to the satisfaction of the English.

"During the council, a table was set by itself for the Indians, which Miantunnomoh appears not to have liked, and, 'would not eat, until some food had been sent him from that of the governor's.'"

Drake's *Book of the Indians*, pp. 62, 63.

"That wisdom seems to have dictated to Massachusetts in her answer to Connecticut, must be acknowledged; but as justice to Miantunnomoh abundantly demanded such decision, credit in this case is due only to them, as to him who does a good act because it is his interest so to do. They urged Connecticut not to commence war alone, 'alleging how dishonorable it would be to us all, that, while we were upon treaty with the Indians, they should make war upon them; for they would account their act as our own, seeing we had formerly professed to the Indians, that we were all as one; and in our last message to Miantunnomoh, had remembered him again of the same, and he had answered that he did so account

with Miantunnumoh, whereupon Uncas reported the matter to the Massachusetts authorities, who charged Miantunnumoh with the instigation of this attack. This being reported to the Narragansett sachem, he at once went to Boston, taking along with him the Pequod, who was examined by the magistrates in his presence. His story was that, having been at Uncas's fort, the latter engaged him to tell the English that he had been engaged by the

---

us. Upon receipt of this our answer, they forbare to enter into a war, but (it seemed) unwillingly, and not well pleased with us.' The main consideration which caused Massachusetts to decide against war was, 'That all those informations (furnished by Connecticut) might arise from a false ground, and out of the enmity which was between the Narraganset and the Mohigan sachems.' This was no doubt one of the real causes, and had Miantunnomoh overcome Uncas, the English would, from policy, as gladly have leagued with him as with the latter, for it was constantly pleaded in those days, that their safety must depend upon a union with some of the most powerful tribes.

"There can be no doubt, on fairly examining the case, that Uncas used many arts, to influence the English in his favor, and against his enemy. In the progress of the war between the two great chiefs, the English acted precisely as the Indians have been always said to do — stood aloof, and watched the scale of victory, determined to join the conquerors."

Drake's *Book of the Indians*, p. 63.

"Miantunnomoh had a wretched enemy in Waiandance, a Long Island sachem, who had assisted in the destruction of the Pequots, at their last retreat. He revealed the plots and plans of Miantunnomoh; and, says Lion Gardener, 'he told

WARS OF THE MOHEGANS

Narragansett sachem to kill Uncas; and that to make his arm appear as if it had been wounded by an arrow, he took the flint of his musket and cut the flesh of his arm on two sides. This story was regarded with distrust, and the Narragansetts fell under suspicion; and in a like degree the Mohegans were advanced in the esteem of the English. Miantunnumoh found himself under a deeper load of suspicion; for the story of the Pequod was regarded as a concoction of the moment, whereby it was hoped that the animus of the conspiracy might be removed from themselves. The magistrates were satisfied with the guilt of the Pequod, and decided that he should be delivered to Uncas.

---

me many years ago,' as all the plots of the Narragansetts had been discovered, they now concluded to let the English alone until they had destroyed Uncas and himself, then, with the assistance of the Mohawks, 'and Indians beyond the Dutch, and all the northern and eastern Indians, would destroy us, man and mother's son.'"

Drake's *Book of the Indians*, p. 64.

"Mr. Gardener relates that he met with Miantunnomoh at Meanticut, Waiandance's country, on the east end of Long Island. That Miantunnomoh was there, as Waiandance said, to break up the intercourse with those Indians. There were others with Miantunnomoh, and what they said to Waiandance was as follows: —

"'You must give no more wampum to the English, for they are no sachems, nor none of their children shall be in their place if they die. They have no tribute given them. There is but one king in England, who is over them all, and

INDIAN WARS OF NEW ENGLAND

Miantunnumoh protested against this, using the argument that as the man was under his protection he should be allowed to take him into his own country, where he would surrender him to Uncas.

---

if you should send him 100,000 fathom of wampum he would not give you a knife for it, nor thank you.' Then said Waiandance, 'They will come and kill us all, as they did the Pequits;' but replied the Narragansetts, 'No, the Pequots gave them wampum and beaver, which they loved so well, but they sent it back, and killed them because they had killed an Englishman; but you have killed none, therefore give them nothing.'

"Some time after Miantunnomoh went again 'with a troop of men' to the same place, and, instead of receiving presents as formerly, he gave presents to Waiandance and his people, and made the following speech:—

"'Brothers, we must be one as the English are, or we shall soon all be destroyed. You know our fathers had plenty of deer and skins, and our plains were full of deer and of turkeys, and our coves and rivers were full of fish. But, brothers, since these English have seized upon our country, they cut down the grass with scythes, and the trees with axes. Their cows and horses eat up the grass, and their hogs spoil our beds of clams; and finally we shall starve to death; therefore, stand not in your own light, I beseech you, but resolve with us to act like men. All the sachems both to the east and the west have joined with us, and we are all resolved to fall upon them, at a day appointed, and therefore I have come secretly to you, because you can persuade the Indians to do what you will. Brothers, I will send over 50 Indians to Manisses, and 30 to you from thence, and take an 100 of Southampton Indians with an 100 of your own here. And, when you see the three fires which will be made at the end of 40 days hence, in a clear night, then act as we act, and the next day fall on and

WARS OF THE MOHEGANS

He was allowed to depart with the Pequod, who was killed by Miantunnumoh on the way homeward.

Whatever motives may have prevailed in the accomplishment of this act of bad faith, it is safe to assume that Miantunnumoh was not unaware of the use to which Uncas might have put the treacherous Pequod in the way of involving himself irretrievably with the Massachusetts authorities. One is left to infer that the Pequod was killed for the reason that dead men tell no tales.[1] From this on,

---

kill men, women and children; but no cows; they must be killed as we need them for provisions, till the deer come again.'

"To this speech all the old men said, 'Wurregen,' i.e., 'It is well.' But this great plot, if the account given by Waiandance be true, was by him brought to the knowledge of the English, and so failed. 'And the plotter,' says Gardener, 'next spring after, did as Ahab did at Ramoth-Gilead.—So he to Mohegan, and there had his fall.'"

Drake's *Book of the Indians*, p. 64.

[1] *Ibid*, pp. 89, 90.

"When the commissioners of the United Colonies had met in 1643, complaint was made to them by Uncas, that Miantunnomoh had employed a Pequot to kill him, and that this Pequot was one of his own subjects. He shot Uncas with an arrow, and, not doubting but that he had accomplished his purpose, 'fled to the Nanohiggansets, or their confederates,' and proclaimed that he had killed him. 'But when it was known Uncas was not dead, though wounded, the traitor was taught to say that Uncas had cut through his own arm with a flint, and hired the Pequot to say he had shot and killed him. Myantinomo being sent for by the governor of the Massa-

the tide of animosity between these two savage nations rose higher with every day, until the overt act was committed by some of the warriors of Sequassen. A leading Mohegan warrior was killed. Uncas himself was waylaid with a shower of arrows as he was paddling down the Connecticut River in his canoe. He complained of these matters to the Hartford authorities, and Governor Haynes went so far as to require the two sachems to attend him at Hartford, where he attempted to reconcile them. Uncas demanded six Narragansetts for every Mohegan who had been killed, which he finally reduced, at the urgent solicitation of Governor Haynes, to the one who was acknowledged to have committed the crime; and it fell out, as well, that the murderer was a man of some consequence, and a relation and prime favorite of Miantunnumoh. Sequassen declined to deliver him up to Uncas, preferring to defend him even if he had to go to war. The two sachems were dismissed, and Uncas was

---

chusetts upon another occasion, brought the Pequot with him: but when this disguise would not serve, and that the English out of his [the Pequot's] own mouth found him guilty, and would have sent him to Uncas his sagamore to be proceeded against, Myantinomo desired he might be taken out of his hands, promising [that] he would send [him] himself to Uncas to be examined and punished; but, contrary to his promise, and fearing, as it appears, his own treachery might be discouerted, he within a day or two cut off the Pequot's head, that he might tell no tales.'"

WARS OF THE MOHEGANS

given the usual permission to right his own wrongs, in his own way. Uncas took advantage of this permission by making an immediate invasion of Sequassen's territory. He defeated Sequassen, killed seven or eight of his warriors, wounded more, then burned his wigwams, getting away with a quantity of plunder.[1]

This incident was not long in finding its way to the Narragansetts, and it fanned their animosity against the Mohegans into a hotter flame. Miantunnumoh, brooding over his real or fancied wrongs,

---

[1] "After this some attempts were made to poison Uncas, and, as is reported, to take away his life by sorcery. That being discovered, some of Sequasson's company, an Indian sagamore allied to, and an intimate confederate with Myantinomo, shot at Uncas, as he was going down Conectacutt River with an arrow or two. Uncas according to the foresaid agreement, which was, in case of difficulty between them, that the English should be applied to as umpires, complained to them. They endeavored to bring about a peace between Uncas and Sequasson; but Sequasson would hear to no overtures of that kind, and intimated that he should be borne out in his resolution by Myantinomo. The result was the war of which we have given an account in the life of Miantunnomoh (*post*, p. 393).

"These things being duly weighed and considered, the commissioners apparently see that Uncas cannot be safe while Miantunnomoh lives; but that, either by secret treachery or open force, his life will be still in danger. Wherefore they think he may justly put such a false and bloodthirsty enemy to death; but in his own jurisdiction, not in the English plantations. And advising that, in the manner of his death, all

was plotting how he might obtain his revenge. To him, war seemed the only resource. He complained to Governor Haynes that Uncas had committed serious acts of depredation upon Sequassen and his allies, to which the governor replied that the English had been in no way concerned in that affair, nor had they justified Uncas in such conduct as he had intimated. Miantunnumoh followed this complaint with another directed to Winthrop, the then governor of Massachusetts, to whom he put the question directly as to whether the Massachusetts Bay people would take umbrage should he make war upon the Mohegans. Winthrop's reply was what might have been expected from what has gone before, and was more to the point than the reply of Governor Haynes. Winthrop replied that if Uncas had done injury to himself and his friends, and persisted in refusing to make reparation for the same, he might take his own course to repair his injury.[1]

It is not to be questioned for a moment but what in these communications to the authorities of Con-

---

mercy and moderation be showed, contrary to the practice of the Indians who exercise tortures and cruelty. And Uncas having hitherto shown himself a friend to the English, and in this craving their advice; [therefore] if the Nanohiggansitts Indians or others shall unjustly assault Uncas for this execution, upon notice and request the English promise to assist and protect him, as far as they may, against such violence."

[1] Winthrop, vol. ii., p. 129.

necticut and Massachusetts Bay Miantunnumoh made the most of his opportunity. It is, as well, evident that the former did not regard the matter as of sufficient seriousness to make any special investigation as to the truth of the specifications set out by the Narragansett sachem, who had conformed in all respects to the treaty of 1638, one of the clauses of which was, that, before appealing to arms, he should submit his complaints to the English. Miantunnumoh at once set about perfecting his plans by which the punishment of Uncas and the Mohegans might be accomplished. With a notable promptness and energy he gathered together a considerable band of Narragansett warriors, with which he made a rapid and unexpected advance into the domains of the Mohegans. There is no question but what Uncas was anticipating this movement on the part of Miantunnumoh, for the reason that he had posted sentinels along the hills of Norwich, from which points of vantage the motions of the Narragansetts might be clearly discerned. They had not long to wait. As the Narragansetts broke the shadows of the woods along the banks of the Shetucket River, where it shallows a little way above its outlet into the Quinnibaug, they left the invaders to take their course, while they made their way hastily, some to the sachem, and some among the uncollected warriors of the tribe, to whom they communicated the news of the invasion.

WARS OF THE MOHEGANS

ticut and Massachusetts Bay Miantunnumoh
[ma]de the most of his opportunity. It is, as well,
[evi]dent that the former did not regard the matter
of sufficient seriousness to make any special
[inv]estigation as to the truth of the specifications
[set] out by the Narragansett sachem, who had con-
[form]ed in all respects to the treaty of 1638, one of
[the] clauses of which was, that, before appealing to
[arm]s, he should submit his complaints to the Eng-
[lish]. Miantunnumoh at once set about perfecting
[his] plans by which the punishment of Uncas and
[the] Mohegans might be accomplished. With a
[remark]able promptness and energy he gathered to-
[geth]er a considerable band of Narragansett war-
[rior]s, with which he made a rapid and unexpected
[adv]ance into the domains of the Mohegans. There
[is n]o question but what Uncas was anticipating this
[mo]vement on the part of Miantunnumoh, for the
[reas]on that he had posted sentinels along the hills
[of N]orwich, from which points of vantage the mo-
[tion]s of the Narragansetts might be clearly dis-
[cern]ed. They had not long to wait. As the Narra-
[gan]setts broke the shadows of the woods along the
[ban]ks of the Shetucket River, where it shallows a
[littl]e way above its outlet into the Quinnibaug, they
[left] the invaders to take their course, while they
[mad]e their way hastily, some to the sachem, and
[som]e among the uncollected warriors of the tribe,
[to w]hom they communicated the news of the in-
[vasi]on.

[391]

of their fighting-men. Hardly more than a bow-shot separated them. Unsuspicious of the treachery of Uncas, the Narragansetts awaited the result of the conference; while the Mohegans were as attentive upon the movements of Uncas, whose signal for action they were awaiting. After a protest upon the part of Uncas against engaging in a contest which must result in the death of many of their warriors, he suggested to Miantunnumoh: "Let us fight it out. If you kill me, my men shall be yours; if I kill you, your men shall be mine." This proposition was not favorably received by Miantunnumoh, who has been described by Hubbard as "a very good person of tall stature," whose courage was not to be questioned. He was so confident in the strength and prowess of his warriors that he was not inclined to disappoint them in making use of an opportunity which seemed so favorable to his cause. His attitude was one of certainty, and he replied abruptly to the Mohegan sachem, "My men came to fight, and they shall fight."

It was evident that Uncas knew his man; for he regarded the moment as having come when he should put into execution the plan for the defeat of the Narragansetts. No sooner had Miantunnumoh delivered this reply than the Mohegan sachem dropped to the ground, and his warriors, drawing their bow-strings to their shoulders, let fly a shower of arrows upon the Narragansetts. The latter were taken by surprise, especially when Uncas, leaping to his feet with a shrill war-whoop, led his men against the astonished Narragansetts, who at once took refuge in flight. Pursuing their enemy relentlessly, the Mohegans drove them across the fords of the Yantic into the depths of the woods beyond. Miantunnumoh's efforts to escape proved futile. An English corselet which he had put on for better protection against the weapons of the Mohegans so impeded his flight that the two Mohegans at his heels might have captured him; but that privilege was to be accorded only to Uncas. The first of the Mohegan sagamores to overtake Miantunnumoh was named Tantaquigeon. In Hazard's account, this sachem is designated as a Mohegan.[1] Drake has it that Miantunnumoh was

---

[1] "By way of preliminary to his communication, Mr. Hyde says, 'The following facts being communicated to me from some the ancient fathers of this town, who were contemporary with Uncas, &c.' That before the settlement of Norwich, the sachem of the Narragansett tribe (Miantunnomoh) had a personal quarrel with Uncas, and proclaimed war with the Mohegans: and marched with an army of 900 fighting men, equipped with bows and arrows and hatchets. Uncas being informed by spies of their march towards his seat, Uncas called his warriors together, about 600, stout, hard men, light of foot, and skilled in the use of the bow; and upon a conference, Uncas told his men that it would not do to let the Narragansetts come to their town, but they must go and meet them. Accordingly, they marched, and about three miles, on a large plain, the armies met, and both halted within bowshot. A parley was sounded, and gallant Uncas proposed a

WARS OF THE MOHEGANS

intercepted in his flight by two of his own men, who hoped by their treachery to save their own lives; that they were able to distinguish him from the others by reason of the coat of mail which he wore; and that Miantunnumoh was delivered up by these to Uncas. Drake goes still further into the matter by asserting that Uncas slew these Narragansetts instantly. However this may be, Uncas, being a man of robust and powerful physique, seized Mian-

---

conference with the Narragansett sachem, who agreed. And, being met, Uncas said to his enemy words to this effect: 'You have got a number of brave men with you, and so have I. A'nt it a pity that such brave men should be killed for a quarrel between you and I? Only come like a man, as you pretend to be, and we will fight it out. If you kill me, my men shall be yours; but if I kill you, your men shall be mine.' Upon which the Narragansett sachem replied: 'My men came to fight, and they shall fight.'

"Uncas having told his men, that 'if the enemy should refuse to fight him, he would fall down, and then they were to discharge their arrows on them, and fall right on them as fast as they could;' this was done, and the Mohegans rushed upon Miantunnomoh's army 'like lions,' put them to flight, and killed 'a number on the spot.' They 'pursued the rest, driving some down ledges of rocks.' The foremost of Uncas' men got ahead of Miantunnomoh, and impeded his flight, drawing him back as they passed him, 'to give Uncas opportunity to take him himself.'

"In the pursuit, at a place now called Sachem's Plain, Uncas took him by the shoulder. He then set down, knowing Uncas. Uncas then gave a whoop, and his men returned to him; and in a council then held, 'twas concluded by them,

tunnumoh by the shoulder, whereupon the latter, realizing his powerlessness in the presence of his enemy, showed his submission by sitting down upon the ground. His feelings at that moment can only be imagined. With the stoicism for which the Indian has always been noted, his lips were closed. The number of Narragansetts reported as slain in this fight was thirty; many more were wounded; and without any attempt to rescue Miantunnumoh, they continued their retreat into their own domain.

Miantunnumoh still maintained his silence, although some of his warriors were brought before him, where they were killed by the Mohegans.

---

that Uncas, with a guard, 'should carry said sachem to Hartford, to the governor and magistrates, (it being before the charter,) to advise what they should do with him.' 'Uncas was told by them, that as there was no war between the English and the Narragansetts, it was not proper for them to intermeddle, in the affair, and advised him to take his own way. Accordingly they brought said Narragansett sachem back to the same spot of ground where he was took: where Uncas killed him, and cut out a large piece of his shoulder, roasted, and eat it; and said, "it was the sweetest meat he ever eat; it made him have strong heart." There they bury him, and made a pillar, which I have seen but a few years since.'"

Drake's *Book of the Indians*, pp. 66, 67.

Drake says this MS. letter of March 1, 1833, of Mr. Hyde, as "a tradition is a valuable paper," but expresses his surprise "that Dr. Trumbull should have inserted it in his *History of Connecticut*" as "a matter of fact."

WARS OF THE MOHEGANS

Uncas could not contain his disappointment that his enemy should treat him with such silence and disdain. If he looked for any expression of wavering or fear, he certainly had reason to be disappointed. He finally broke the silence himself, by asking the Narragansett sachem, "Why do you not speak? If you had taken me, I would have besought you for my life." The Narragansett made no response to this, and shortly after Uncas conveyed his prisoner to his fort, after which he was taken to Hartford, where he was delivered[1] into the hands of the English, by whom he was held as a prisoner until his case should be disposed of by the authorities in Boston.

After the capture of Miantunnumoh a truce was agreed upon between the Narragansetts and the Mohegans, which was observed until the case of

---

[1] "The war brought on between Uncas and Miantunnomoh was not within the jurisdiction of the English, nor is it to be expected that they could with certainty determine the justness of its cause. The broil had long existed, but the open rupture was brought on by Uncas' making war upon Sequasson, one of the sachems under Miantunnomoh. The English accounts say (and we have no other) that about 1000 warriors were raised by Miantunnomoh, who came upon Uncas unprepared, having only about 400 men; yet, after an obstinate battle, in which many were killed on both sides, the Narragansetts were put to flight, and Miantunnomoh taken prisoner; that he endeavored to save himself by flight, but having on a coat of mail, was known from the rest, and seized by two of his own men, who hoped by the treachery to save their

the Narragansett sachem was finally disposed of. While the latter was in captivity, his people sent him several packages of wampum, which he gave away. One relation says that he gave some to Uncas, and some to the wife of Uncas, and some to the principal councillors. Whatever inference may be drawn, it is clear that his generosity was possibly for the purpose of repaying Uncas for his fair treatment of him; and as well, perhaps, as an inducement to the latter to refer his fate to the decision of the English. The people of his own tribe, according to Hazard, were strenuous in their assertion that the wampum was given to Uncas as a ransom; and as DeForest says, "They subsequently made it a strong ground of accusation against the Mohegan sachem."[1]

---

own lives. Whereupon they immediately delivered him up to the conqueror. Uncas slew them both instantly; probably with his own hand. This specimen of his bravery must have had a salutary effect on all such as afterwards chanced to think of acting the part of traitors in their wars; at least among the Narragansetts.

"Being brought before Uncas he remained without speaking one word, until Uncas spoke to him, and said, 'If you had taken me, I would have besought you for my life.' He then took his prisoner to Hartford, and at his request left him a prisoner with the English, until the mind of the United Colonies should be known as to what disposition should be made of him."

Drake's *Book of the Indians*, p. 65.

[1] "It does not appear from these records, that Uncas had

WARS OF THE MOHEGANS

Among the English of Rhode Island, Miantunnumoh's defeat and capture attracted to him a great deal of sympathy and interest. The Connecticut colonists, those especially who had come from Massachusetts, had found their way hither by reason of the religious intolerance of the Puritans, and it was within the domain of the Narragansetts

---

any idea of putting Miantunnomoh to death, but to extort a great price from his country-men for his ransom. That a large amount of wampum was collected for this purpose, appears certain, but before it was paid, Uncas received the decision of the English, and then pretended that he had made no such agreement, or that the quantity or quality was not as agreed upon, as will more at length be seen in the life of Uncas."

Drake's *Book of the Indians*, p. 67.

"The Narragansetts had, prior to the unfortunate decision against Miantunnumoh, paid a great sum, hoping to ransom their chief. They had also, besides what had been paid to Uncas, given to the Commissioners £40 sterling to insure his safety. They had not before the humiliating event of the Chief's murder, so much as dreamed that anyone could be faithless in the case. Faithful themselves, and trusting to the honor of their white allies, they continued in all simplicity, to attribute the act to Uncas. They did not for a long time suspect the Commissioners of having secretly corrupted the false Indian and employed him and [his] men to do the bloody deed."

Freeman, *Civilization and Barbarism*, p. 75.
Hazard, vol. ii., p. 9.
DeForest, pp. 192, 193, 212.

INDIAN WARS OF NEW ENGLAND

that they had set up their homes. This unfortunate sachem was a savage of generous characteristics, his manner was quiet and dignified, and his attitude towards the English in his immediate neighborhood had been that of the most friendly and inviting disposition, which had attracted to him much good-will on the part of these settlers; and no doubt, being best acquainted with the story of the Narragansetts' wrongs from their nearness to them, they were confirmed in the belief that the cause of Miantunnumoh was a righteous one, and that those who were trying to destroy his power and influence with the English authorities were entirely in the wrong.

One Samuel Gorton had settled at Warwick. He was a man of most generous instincts, enthusiastic, and, like many of similar characteristics, his actions were not always founded upon a due consideration of their results.[1] He is said to have written to Uncas commanding him to give the Narragansett sachem his freedom, which letter also

---

[1] Mr. Gorton's career is a part of the Indian history of the period. He came from London to Boston in the year 1636, where he was not long after adjudged a heretic and expelled from that Puritan community. He went to Plymouth, where the charge of heresy was renewed, and he was chastised publicly by judicial order, after which he sought asylum with Roger Williams, at Providence. The Massachusetts Bay people, not content with driving Gorton out of Plymouth, drove him out of Providence upon the pretense that that plan-

WARS OF THE MOHEGANS

contained the threat that upon his refusal he would be compelled to do so by the English. Uncas received this letter; and when it was explained to him by the messenger who had brought it, he was much troubled over the matter. Unwilling to give Miantunnumoh his freedom, for personal reasons no doubt, he had not the courage to carry out his desire upon him, which was to get him out of his way by killing him. The letter of Gorton as well aroused the apprehension in his mind as to whether he might be able to keep him safely in his custody, perhaps anticipating that an attempt at a rescue might be made under the wild-headed leadership of Gorton. In his dilemma, he conferred with the English authorities, taking the Narragansett sa-

---

tation was within the Massachusetts jurisdiction. Gorton and eleven others, "in order to be yet further removed," purchased the tract called Shawomet. It turned out the land purchased was already claimed by the Massachusetts government, who asserted it to be under its jurisdiction. Gorton's deed was from Miantonomoh, Chief Sachem of the Narragansetts, January 17, 1642; and purported to have been given in consideration of one hundred forty-four fathoms of wampum. A fathom of wampum was a string of beads two yards in length, the value of which was five shillings, eight pence, sterling. Gorton's purchase was subsequently known as Warwick, after the Earl of Warwick, by whose friendly influence the former had his Rhode Island home restored to him in 1648.

Freeman, *Civilization and Barbarism*, p. 69.
DeForest, p. 193.

chem along with him to Hartford, where he explained matters — to his own satisfaction — to the governor and council, with the request that they indicate to him the course he was to pursue with his prisoner. He was told by the magistrates that it was not for them to interfere in the matter, as there was no open rupture between the Connecticut authorities and the Narragansetts. They advised him, however, that the first meeting of the commissioners of the United Colonies of New England would take place in the September following, and they suggested to him that the case be referred to them for final disposition.[1] Miantunnumoh, well aware of the animosity of the Mohegan sachem, and distrusting his purpose with him, appealed to the Hartford authorities that the English would take him into custody. His reasons were fairly well founded that his life would be safe in their hands, and he felt equally as certain that, once returned with Uncas to the Mohegan country, the latter would not be satisfied until he had removed him from the path of his ambition. The magistrates sustained this plea of the Narragansett sachem, to which Uncas reluctantly consented, stipulating

---

[1] Hazard, vol. ii., pp. 7, 8.
Winthrop, vol. ii., p. 131.
As to Gorton's threatening Uncas in his letter, Winthrop at first stated that to be the fact; but he later erased the passage, as if in doubt over the matter.

WARS OF THE MOHEGANS

that Miantunnumoh should be regarded as a captive to the Mohegans.[1]

September 17, 1643, the Court of Commissioners opened the session at Boston. The commission was made up of John Winthrop and Thomas Dudley, of Massachusetts; Edward Winslow and William Collier, of Plymouth; Edward Hopkins and John Fenwick, from Connecticut; and Theophilus Eaton and Thomas Gregson, from New Haven. After deliberating upon the articles of confederation of the May previous, they took up the case of Miantunnumoh. Their judgment was not rapid in this matter. They were apprehensive of the power of the Narragansett sachem and, as well, aware of his independent disposition. Prejudiced in favor of the Mohegan sachem, they came readily enough to the decision that it was a matter of doubtful policy, and perhaps against the public safety, to give Miantunnumoh his freedom. They were, as well, convinced that the evidence was entirely lacking which would justify them in imposing upon him a death sentence. As was usual in cases of this kind, their disposition was to shift the responsibility to the shoulders of others, and they decided to call in the clergy, of which as many as fifty from all parts of New England were then assembled at Boston in a general convocation. Of these, a commission was chosen to adjudicate the matter in conjunction

---

[1] Winthrop, vol. ii., p. 131.

with the Court of Commissioners; and when they had been informed of such matters appertaining to the case as the court thought necessary, their opinion was desired. These pious gentlemen, evidently desirous to please the court and to carry out the policy so thoroughly inaugurated in the Puritan behalf against the Indians, decided offhand a matter at which not only laymen, but the magistrates, had balked. They "all agreed that he ought to be put to death."[1]

This decision of the ministers that Uncas might commit murder upon the Narragansett sachem shows how well trained they had been at the hands of Winthrop. Lacking the garb of judicial function, and contrary to the faith which should have been the foundation of their labors, they essayed to determine the question of life and death, assuming a responsibility which those appointed for that particular province declined to perform. It was another illustration that fools are prone to rush in where angels fear to tread. Their excuse was that the prisoner was at the head of a dangerous con-

---

[1] "The manner of the final sentence was base. Such decision respecting an ancient ally has been justly stigmatized as both ungenerous and iniquitous. No wonder if the indignation of Canonicus and Pessicus be stirred when they came to understand the circumstances; nor will it be strange if such proceedings foster in their breasts a contempt for Christianity."

Freeman, *Civilization and Barbarism*, p. 173, note.

WARS OF THE MOHEGANS

spiracy, in which the safety of the United Colonies was involved. Although this was a mere rumor, which could be readily traced to Uncas, yet they accepted it as a fact; and, over-credulous as ministers in this late day are apt to be as to the administration of public affairs, and the like uncertain course of public events, and possibly for the time only too willing to serve the magistrates, they advised the perpetration of this crime. It was urged against the Narragansett sachem that he was "proud, turbulent and restless; that he had betrayed the confidence of the English in killing the Pequot he had promised to deliver to Uncas." As one of the insignificant facts upon which they hinged their decision, it was alleged that he had made an assault upon one of Pumham's men, and taken his wampum from him, and challenged him to make complaint if he dared to the Massachusetts authorities.[1] Pumham was a sachem who had submitted to the English, and for that reason he was entitled to their protection, if he claimed it. They

---

[1] "Pumham lived on land adjoining those sold by Miantonomoh, but Mr. Winslow decided that 'Pumham had received no consideration.' It is not probable that either of the Indians conveyed to Boston understood the nature of the alleged transactions. They were both tributary to the sachem."

Freeman, *Civilization and Barbarism*, p. 70, note.

It was a matter of Indian comity that the sachem might dispose of the lands of his tribe as he saw fit.

also concluded, in summing up the case, that, by all Indian customs and those as well of other countries, he had forfeited his life; and it was upon such foundation of false, unjust, and frivolous pretense the commissioners of the Connecticut Colony sought a vindication of their action in this disposition of Miantunnumoh. It was false, for the reason that the general conspiracy among the Indians had not been discovered; nor could it be discovered, for the reason that it had no existence; and further, in Miantunnumoh's examination on that point, the Boston magistrates had acknowledged his innocence. It was unjust, because Miantunnumoh was possessed of an independent and dignified spirit. It was frivolous, because in order to bolster up the case against the Narragansett sachem,— an event of no importance, especially in a matter of a death sentence,— they were driven to consider a trifling matter of alleged personal dispute, which may have been true or untrue, between Miantunnumoh and a noted chief of his own tribe.[1]

Carrying out this decision of the clergy, the commissioners directed that Uncas should be called to Hartford, where the Narragansett sachem was to be surrendered to him, and where he was to be informed, as well, that the latter was to suffer the punishment of death outside the limits of the Eng-

---

[1] "The charges and accusation against the Narragansetts will be found at large in the *Records of the Commissioners of*

WARS OF THE MOHEGANS

lish settlements; that some of the English should go along with Uncas and his party, to see that he performed this despicable service, "for the more full satisfaction of the commissioners." This surrender to Uncas was conditional. If he refused to kill his prisoner, Miantunnumoh was not to be delivered to him, but was to be taken to Boston by ship, and there held in custody until a further decision of the court. Uncas was advised that if he

---

the United Colonies. There is no more detestable character in all our Indian history than that of Uncas. But affairs were so conditioned that it appeared all important to the English of Connecticut and Massachusetts to espouse the cause of that miscreant and thus was compassed the ruin of one of the noblest Indians of that or any other period."

Hubbard's *Indian Wars,* vol. i., p. 40, note.

"This is in accordance with the cold-blooded records of the time. The English had not, nor did they claim jurisdiction over those Indians then at war, and could not rightfully interfere in their quarrel. The battle which decided the fate of Miantonimo was fought in the end of the summer, 1643. The precise day and month does not appear. Being taken prisoner, Miantonimo was conducted to Hartford by Uncas, and there held until the English should direct how he should be disposed of. The meeting of the Commissioners of the United Colonies being near at hand, the matter was deferred to that body. It met at Boston on the 7th of September, 1643. Nearly the first business brought forward was that of the disposition of Miantonimo. Before coming to a decision the Commissioners went over all the array of testimony furnished during several years by Uncas and others of the most malignant of Miantonimo's enemies, in which was enumer-

would carry out the wishes of the magistrates in this matter Connecticut would undertake the burden of defending him against such enemies as might thus be aroused against him; and as a coincident condition, Plymouth agreed to restore to Massasoit all the lands to the westward which had been encroached upon by the Narragansetts; while Massachusetts was to take upon itself the onus of notifying the Narragansetts that the Mohegan sachem was acting under the direction of the English and would be protected by them. The tribunal to which the decision as to the fate of the Narragansett sachem was left, especially that part composed of the clergy, suggests a moot court from the point of view of sound judicial procedure, and is suggestive not only of the animus which prevailed against the Indians, indiscriminately, but as well

---

ated all the vague charges of plots, treasons, poisons and sorceries. The commissioners then continue: 'These things being duely weighed and considered, we apparently see that Uncas cannot be safe while Miantonimo lives, but that either by secret treachery or open force, his life will be still in danger. Whereupon they think he may justly put such a false and bloodthirsty enemy to death; but in his own jurisdiccon, not in the English plantacons; and adviseing that in the manner of his death all mercy and moderation be shewed, contrary to the practice of the Indians, who exercise tortures and cruelty.'"

Records of the Commissioners, United Colonies, vol. i., pp. 11, 12, 15.

Ibid, p. 43, note.

WARS OF THE MOHEGANS

of the timidity of the English wherever the savage was concerned.[1] To these colonies there was always impending, along the horizon of their living, the threat of savage invasion, which had a tendency to beget in their minds a host of baseless apprehensions, the dominant one of which was that a general conspiracy among the Indians against the English was continually existent. It is a trite saying that a guilty conscience needs no accuser, and

---

[1] "The sorrowful part of the tale is yet to be told. The commissioners of the United Colonies having convened at Boston, 'taking into consideration, they say, what was safest and best to be done, were all of the opinion that it would not be safe to set him at liberty, neither had we sufficient ground for us to put him to death.' The awful design of putting to death their friend they had not yet fixed upon, but calling to their aid in council, 'five of the most judicious elders,' 'they all agreed that he ought to be put to death.' This was the final decision, and to complete the deed of darkness, secrecy was enjoined upon all. And their determination was to be made known to Uncas privately, with direction that he should execute him within his own jurisdiction and without torture.

"We will now go to the record, which will enable us to judge of the justness of the matter. When the English had determined that Uncas should execute Miantunnomoh, Uncas was ordered to be sent for to Hartford, 'with some considerable number of his best and trustiest men,' to take him to a place for execution, 'carrying him into the next part of his own government, and there put him to death: provided that some discreet and faithful persons of the English government accompany them, and see the execution, for our

it is not to be questioned that there were many dissenters from the rigorous policy which the authorities had maintained against the savage from the beginning. So possessed were the English with the idea of a common danger from this source that any unusual noise at night was the occasion for instant alarm. An instance of this is recorded by Hubbard, who relates that, "September 19, 1642, a poor

---

more full satisfaction; and that the English meddle not with the head or the body at all.'

"The commissioners at the same time, ordered 'that Hartford furnish Uncas with a competent strength of English to defend him against any present fury or assault, of the Nanohiggunsetts or any other.' And 'that in case Uncas shall refuse to execute justice upon Myantenomo, that then Myantenomo be sent by sea to the Massachusetts, there to be kept in safe durance till the commissioners may consider further how to dispose of him.'

"Here then we see fully developed the real state of the case. The Mohegans had by accident captured Miantunnomoh, after which event they were more in fear of his nation than before; which proves beyond doubt, that they would never have dared to put him to death, had they not been promised the protection of the English.

"When the determination of the commissioners and elders was made known to Uncas, he 'readily undertook the execution, and taking Miantunnomoh along with him, in the way between Hartford and Windsor, (where Uncas hath some men dwell,) Uncas' brother, following after Miantunnomoh, clave his head with an hatchet.' Mather says they 'very fairly cut off his head.'"

Drake's *Book of the Indians*, pp. 65, 66.

WARS OF THE MOHEGANS

being, near the swamp at Watertown hearing the howling of a kennel of wolves, was so frightened that his calls for help occasioned alarm that extended remotely, even to towns near Boston."

Through all these years the Puritan community was a seething-pot of religious disputes and animosities; and as between the colonies themselves, there was much of variant policy, which, together with the continual reaching out after individual gain, could not but prejudice the Indians against the English and, as well, arouse the suspicions of the savages as to the ultimate purpose of the English with them. These conditions gave rise to enactments of courts and the inserting of provisional restraints in treaties between the English and the savages, which undertook the control of savage freedom, especially in matters of the disposal of lands occupied by the savages. With the English it was an epoch of greed and aggrandizement. With these influences prevailing in the relations between the English and the aborigine, it is not singular that these apprehensions should exist; and so it came about that this decision as to the final disposition of Miantunnumoh was not revealed by the members of the commission until it was made certain that those members who resided in Connecticut and New Haven had arrived safely at their respective homes. The reason for this was, it was feared that Miantunnumoh's people would make an effort to intercept them and to hold them as hostages for the safety of their sachem should they in any way obtain that information. That such a purpose had been entertained upon the part of the Narragansetts was doubtless a fact, and it was Miantunnumoh himself who with remarkable frankness and honesty notified Governor Haynes of the same.

As soon as the New Haven and Connecticut commissioners were safe from such interference, Uncas was summoned to Hartford, where he appeared shortly after with Wawequa and some of his favorite warriors. He was at once informed of the intended disposition of Miantunnumoh, which no doubt conformed to his own desire; and he, without objection, entered with them into immediate plans for the murder of the Narragansett sachem, who was delivered to him. Leaving Hartford, accompanied by the two Englishmen who were designated to be the official witnesses of the crime, they wound their way over the forest trail toward the Mohegan country, until they came to the locality where the capture of Miantunnumoh was consummated. Leaving the shadows of the woods, they came into an opening which has since widened into a stretch of country known as Sachem's Plain, where had taken place, as it turned out, the last battle of Miantunnumoh with his enemies. What may have been the thought that occupied the sachem's mind as he recalled his disaster,— which was no doubt colored by his momentary conjecture as to the meaning of this singular return,— it was punctuated by the stealthy

WARS OF THE MOHEGANS

tread of Wawequa at his heels. The eyes of the latter were upon his brother. He was awaiting the fatal signal. At a motion from Uncas, Wawequa swung his tomahawk with fatal swiftness, and in the twinkling of an eye the messenger of death claimed its victim.[1]

Such was the barbarous hatred entertained by Uncas. Sachem's Plain was not only the site of Miantunnumoh's assassination, but, as well, the place of his burial. The place where they laid him was marked by a heap of stones, and it was the custom of every Narragansett who passed that way to pay tribute to the memory of his sachem by adding one more stone to this rude cairn.[2] It was a custom, as well, through the subsequent years of the Narragansetts, to make a pilgrimage to this spot with every recurring September,—notwithstanding the hostility which still existed between them and the murderers

---

[1] See note *ante*, p. 396, as to the act of cannibalism alleged to have been committed by Uncas.

Drake notes (*Book of the Indians*, p. 66): "That this is a tradition may be inferred, from the circumstance of an *eminently* obscure writer's publishing nearly the same story, which he says, in his book, took place upon the death of Philip. Oneko, he says, cut out a pound of Philip's bleeding body and ate it." Referring to Henry Trumbull's book, Drake asserts, "There is barely a word of truth in it."

See, also, Freeman, *Civilization and Barbarism*, p. 74, note.

[2] Drake notes (Winthrop's *Journal*, vol. ii., p. 134): "As to the place of Miantonomoh's execution Winthrop seems to

of their leader,— where they indulged in lamentations and added new stones to the pile which they consecrated with cries of mourning and with gestures of grief. This mound remained for many years, to finally disappear at the hands of the owner of the land, by whom the stones were used as a foundation for one of his farm buildings.[1]

Such was the end of this Narragansett sachem, who had won the respect and affection of English and savage alike, except so far as they were apprehensive of his power. DeForest says, "There can be no doubt but that his death was perfectly in accordance with the Indian customs." He says further, "Had Uncas killed and scalped him on the field of battle, or had he tortured him to death in cold blood on his own responsibility, no one would have had occasion for surprise." Had Uncas fallen into the power of Miantunnumoh, it is doubtful if the latter would have appealed to the English, but the rather would have treated him in accordance with the customs of the Indians toward a captive

---

have made a mistake. It is not very likely that he was taken in an opposite direction from Uncas' own territory, as Windsor was from Hartford. It is also unlikely that Uncas had *near dwell* so far from his country upon the Thames."
Book of the Indians, p. 66, note.
Hazard, vol. ii., pp. 11-13.
Winthrop, vol. ii., p. 134.
DeForest, p. 198.
[1]*History of Norwich*, p. 20.

enemy. The attitude of the authorities in this particular matter was cowardly in the extreme; and as a single incident of their double dealing with the Indians, indiscriminately, is devoid of justification. It was an unjust and deliberately cruel action, and it is evident that it was from fear of him they were led into the error of receiving him into their hands; but, once committed by their unwarranted interference, they became accomplices of the savage Uncas, and by no stretch of law, reason, or imagination could these magistrates be regarded other than as *particeps criminis*. The excuse urged in palliation of this outrage upon justice was that Miantunnumoh was hostile to the colonies — a statement which is not borne out by fact; and it has, as well, been suggested that their action was likewise influenced by the fact that this sachem had been notably friendly to the settlements of Gorton and his community of Pautuxet.[1]

With Miantunnumoh disposed of and the specter of a powerful conspiracy stalking before them, Governor Winthrop, with the advice of the commissioners, sent messengers to the Narragansetts, who accused them of having betrayed their faith with the English and, as well, of having agreed with Miantunnumoh in his purpose to involve the Eng-

---

[1] The career of Samuel Gorton is very closely interwoven with the history of the Indians of Connecticut. In 1644 Gorton went to England with his deed from the Narragan-

lish colonies in destruction. They also served notice upon the Narragansetts that Uncas had the approval of the English in the execution of their sachem, and that it was their purpose to afford him complete protection. As has been noticed already, the English recognized Canonicus as having conducted the affairs of the tribe toward the colonies peaceably; and the Narragansetts were informed that, as to the late hostilities, they were due entirely to the turbulent disposition of their late sachem. They further conveyed to the Narragansetts an offer of peace, which should not only extend to the English, but comprise the Mohegans and

---

setts, by which the whole territory was transferred to the king of England. By order of Parliament, Gorton was given peaceable possession, and later he assumed the office of minister for the Warwick Plantation. *Vide* p. 400 *ante,* note 1.

For the story of Gorton and his supporters, *vide* Gorton's *Simplicitie's Defence.*

Winthrop, vol. ii., pp. 139, 140, 146–148, 318–320, 322, 323.

Winslow's *Hypocricie Unmasked.*

Palfrey, *History of New England,* vol. ii., pp. 133–140, note, 209–214.

Massachusetts Records, vol. ii., pp. 51, 52, 54.

Records in Hazard, vol. ii., pp. 10, 25–27.

Coddington's *Letter to Winthrop,* Aug. 5, 1644, in *Massachusetts Archives,* vol. ii., pp. 4, 5.

R. I. Hist. Coll., vol. ii., pp. 110, 204.

Johnson, *Wonder-working Providence of Zion's Saviour,* pp. 182, 188.

WARS OF THE MOHEGANS

Massasoit, as well as all other Indian tribes allied to the English.[1] While this was ostensibly a statement of conditions from the English point of view, it was no less a threat; and as they were at that time without organization and leadership, they accepted the dicta of the commissioners in apparently passive obedience. This nation at this time was panic-stricken with the blow which had fallen upon them. They were alike sorrowful and uncertain as to the future; yet the English entertained the idea that notwithstanding their defeat by the Mohegans, they would yet be victorious over them, from the fact that they were the more numerous people and still had Canonicus and other brave warriors to direct their movements. While Canonicus was alive, he had, as well, arrived at a great age, and it was inevitable the direction of his people should soon pass into the hands of younger and more active sachems.

With the tragedy of Sachem's Plain, the relation of the wars of Uncas is not wholly closed; therefore it seems necessary to continue this narrative somewhat further. Miantunnumoh was killed in 1643, and there is no doubt that, as time went on, the Narragansetts entertained more deeply their sense of injury toward the Mohegans and, as well, that their hatred of that sachem grew more implacable. Whatever may have been their design, they did not discover it to the Mohegans until 1644, when they

---

[1] Hazard, vol. ii., p. 12.

made an alliance with the Niantics against their ancient enemy; sometime prior to which event (wholly unsuspicious of the duplicity of the English in the death of their sachem), Pessicus, who had succeeded Miantunnumoh, sent to Governor Winthrop a valuable gift of furs and wampum, which he accompanied with the request that the colonies remain neutral "in an expiatory war" which he felt himself compelled to undertake against the Mohegans, which he regarded as a sacred duty.

Recalling the old saw, everything that came from the Indians to the Puritan mill was "grist;" and while the offering of the Narragansett sachem was at first accepted, it was very coolly suggested to him that "peace must be preserved." This was not satisfactory to the savage chieftain, and he again sent to the Puritans, urging upon them what to him seemed to be a reasonable request. While the conditions upon which the gift depended were refused by the governor, the latter, however, permitted it to be left; and the sachem's messengers were requested to wait, upon the plausibility that they wished "for time to advise with the sachems of the tribes involved in this controversy." The governor finally informed Pessicus, "If you or your people make war upon Uncas the English will fall upon you." The attitude of the English was so distasteful to the Narragansetts that they at once declared their intention to follow their own design in the matter. Their reply was, "We will not listen to peace so long as the head of Uncas remain upon his shoulders." These gifts and conferences of the Narragansetts with the English afford a sufficient proof that at that time they had ample confidence in the good faith of the latter; that their suspicions were unaroused. There is no question as to the fidelity of the Narragansetts in the main to the English, and, being themselves faithful, they did not look for treachery at the hands of their accepted friends. They were, however, in the way of being undeceived.

It is to be noticed that at this time the habits of the Indians were undergoing a change. Their intercourse with the whites so far had not been very beneficial. They had acquired the habit of spending much of their time loitering about the settlements, to the inhabitants of which they became a source of much annoyance. They entered the houses of the settlers with the same lack of formality that they would show in entering their own wigwams. Their barbarous aspect and their uncouth manners upon these occasions inspired among the women and children a sense of constant insecurity. They were apt to desire whatever they saw, and were not above getting deplorably into debt; but they had as well, in too many instances, a disposition to pilfer. They were not unlike the debtor of modern times. Once the savage became indebted to any considerable amount to the white men, he was sure to take his custom elsewhere, at the slightest suggestion of his indebtedness. The musket of the English settler possessed a great attraction for the savage, and if by chance one was left within his reach, he was not satisfied until he had the weapon in his hands, upon which occasion accidents were not only possible, but actual.

To prevent these annoyances, stringent laws were enacted by the colonial courts, and as well by some of the settlements; one of which was that the handling of a weapon by an Indian made him liable to a fine of a half-fathom of wampum. If his carelessness occasioned injury he was to pay the cost of the cure. If death was occasioned by the accident his life was forfeited.[1] In many of the towns watchmen were employed; and if an Indian happened within the town limits after dark, and was summoned by the watch to surrender, upon refusal he might be killed without hesitation.[2] In many instances these ordinances were given to the sachems of the neighboring tribes, that they might notify their people of the same.

In 1642, upon rumor of a conspiracy against the English among the savages, the head-center of which was located at Tunxis, the Connecticut court prohibited the ordinary citizen from admitting a savage into his house. Only magistrates were excepted from this restriction, who might receive a

---

[1] *Colonial Records*, vol. i., p. 52 (June, 1640).
[2] *Ibid*, pp. 46, 240.

WARS OF THE MOHEGANS

sachem if he were not accompanied by more than two men.[1] This law was somewhat amended in 1644, when it was permissible that traders, as well as magistrates, might entertain sachems when not accompanied by over four of their people. An exception was made, however, in the case of Uncas. He was permitted to come into the English houses with twenty; and his brother Wawequa, with ten.[2] Three years later the savages were prohibited from hiring lands of the English, it being alleged that by this freedom of intercourse they "corrupted the young men."[3] The moral example of the savage was more corrupting than otherwise. Within the jurisdiction of the colony, trade with the Dutch and French was prohibited.[4] These restrictions were undoubtedly with a view to preventing the savage from acquiring possession of, or becoming acquainted with the use of, fire-arms. In 1650 the boundary line of intercourse between the Indian and the whites was so closely drawn that the latter were prohibited by law from buying even wood from the Indians.[5] By this time the Indians had acquired an unnatural appetite for intoxicating liquors. Wherever they could obtain it they drank greedily, and

---

[1] *Colonial Records*, vol. i., p. 73.
[2] *Ibid*, p. 110.
[3] *Ibid*, p. 149.
[4] *Ibid*, pp. 197–218.
[5] *Ibid*, p. 402.

INDIAN WARS OF NEW ENGLAND

in 1654 the penalty for selling a pint of liquor to a savage was five pounds; for a sip, even, the penalty was forty shillings; and it has been noted that, notwithstanding all these restrictions, as liquor grew more abundant in the colonies the Indians were able to obtain it, and at a less expense.[1]

To go back somewhat: before the time when Pessicus was conferring with the English and making them rich gifts of furs and wampum, or, to be more exact, in 1642, some Dutch traders, after getting a savage drunk, robbed him of his garb, which consisted of some valuable beaver-skins. In return for this outrage the Indian killed two white men, after which he betook himself to a distant tribe for safety. The Dutch governor demanded the surrender of the murderer, which demand, not being promptly acceded to, finally resulted in his being able to take revenge into his own hands. The following winter some Hudson River Indians were surprised by the Mohawks. Many were killed; some were taken prisoners; while the remnant of several hundred sought protection of the Dutch at New Amsterdam. The Dutch governor at first afforded them a generous relief, but it was not long before it occurred to him that here was an opportunity to avenge the savage insult to the Dutch government. Broaching the matter to his councillors, they were agreeable to the project, which was that these dependents upon

---

[1] *Colonial Records*, vol. i., p. 263.

WARS OF THE MOHEGANS

his bounty should be annihilated. Surprised in their sleep by the Dutch soldiery, over one hundred of the savages were massacred in cold blood — a treachery which was not likely to go unpunished.

The Indians of the Hudson River Valley, joined by some of the Long Island tribes,— in all, a confederacy of fifteen hundred warriors,— began an attack upon the Dutch settlements which were scattered along the Sound from Manhattan down the Long Island and Connecticut shores, and as well up the Hudson. These ravages of the Indians extended as far east as Stamford, and in this foray to the eastward no discrimination was made between the Dutch and the English. It was in this raid that Ann Hutchinson, of Puritan fame, was killed.[1] This was followed by an expedition of the Dutch from New Amsterdam, the Dutch troops landing at Greenwich. They had received infor-

---

[1] In this raid on Stamford Village the savages appeared at the Hutchinson house after their customed manner, outwardly friendly; but a moment later, once they had gained the inner threshold, the tomahawk was bespattered with the blood of this unfortunate woman. After that the massacre became general, and seventeen of the Stamford people were killed. The live stock was impounded in the barns and outhouses, which were afterward set on fire.
DeForest, p. 205.

In Boston, Anne Hutchinson lived on the spot so long occupied by the Old Corner Book-store, at the corner of Wash-

INDIAN WARS OF NEW ENGLAND

mation of an Indian encampment in that vicinity, and marched all night in the hope of surprising it.

ington and School Streets. Governor Winthrop's home was nearly opposite, on the other side of Washington Street. She was among the most prominent of the Boston Antinomians. Antinomianism was to the Puritans the worst of heresies, and was dealt with most ruthlessly. In Boston Anne Hutchinson's name was to the Puritans the synonym of this detestable cult. She was a woman of great excellency and pure morals, to whose "person and conduct" no stain attaches. She had a strong following. The persecution which ended in the excommunication and banishment of this gifted woman was of the most bitter character. She was held in custody, pending her trial, in a house of the brother of the Rev. Thomas Welde, who was her most virulent accuser and the first pastor of Roxbury Church. While there, she was allowed to see neither her husband nor her children, unless by leave of court. Her most frequent visitor was the "holy inquisitor." Francis Drake notes that Welde's grandson married a granddaughter "of the woman he had stigmatized as an American Jezebel."

Memorial History of Boston, vol. i., pp. 173, 174, 413.

"The sequel to Mrs. Hutchinson's history is melancholy and tragical. Remaining at Aquidneck until the decease of her husband, she removed thence to the 'Dutch country' beyond New Haven; and the next year, with all her family save one daughter, was killed by the Indians. Her friends charged the guilt of her murder upon those who expelled her from Massachusetts; her enemies pronounced it a judgment of God. No one, it is presumed, will exonerate either party from blame in this affair. Encompassed with the privations of a wilderness life, and invested with the cares of a young and numerous family, the gentleness of her sex should have

WARS OF THE MOHEGANS

They had their labor for their pains. The Indians had escaped;[1] but this expedition was not entirely

---

moderated the enthusiasm of Mrs. Hutchinson's zeal, and have restrained it within those bounds which can never be exceeded without detriment to the character of woman, however extraordinary her genius or brilliant her accomplishments. On the part of her judges, too, there was inexcusable severity, and unnecessary virulence; and, had they profited by their own experience in the land of their nativity, they would have tempered their conduct with more charity and forbearance. The same spirit, doubtless, which, in 1646, adjudged Mrs. Oliver 'to be whipped for reproaching the magistrates,' and which actually inflicted the disgraceful punishment, and even added the indignity of placing 'a cleft stick upon her tongue for reproaching the elders,' might have hurried our fathers into similar excesses in their dealings with Mrs. Hutchinson, had it not been for the number and respectability of her friends."

Barry, *History of Massachusetts, First Period*, pp. 260, 261.

Winthrop, vol. i., pp. 338-340.

Morton's *Mem.*, pp. 106-108.

[1] On this account the Dutch believed that they had been intentionally misdirected by Captain Daniel Patrick, the same who led the Bay soldiers against Sassacus, who, with famous John Underhill, had removed from Massachusetts to Greenwich, a neighboring village. One of the Dutch soldiers, meeting Patrick, upbraided him with his supposed duplicity; whereat the Englishman retorted in kind, and, unable to control his anger, spit in the face of his accuser, who killed the former with a pistol-shot. This was the end of the Puritan Captain Patrick.

DeForest, p. 206.

INDIAN WARS OF NEW ENGLAND

unsuccessful, for before they returned to Manhattan they had surprised a small Indian village, which they destroyed.

The hostilities between the Dutch and the Indians assumed such importance that a new relay of troops was raised, and despatched to Connecticut, with the anticipation of surprising and destroying a large Indian encampment in that vicinity. This body of soldiers was under command of Captain Underhill and Ensign Van Dyck. They found the encampment, and Underhill, recalling Mason at Fort Mystic, wanted the village fired. It was a night surprise, and those savages who escaped the flame of their blazing wigwams were compelled to return to them by the guns and sabers of the Dutch. It was afterward asserted that in this foray five hundred savages were killed,— men, women, and children,— and that only eight escaped. The Dutch camped that night by the glowing embers of this carnage, and the following morning set out for Stamford, which they reached in the late forenoon. The gratitude of the Dutch for this victory led them to express themselves much as had the Puritans upon receiving the news of the Fort Mystic massacre. Public thanksgivings were ordered at New Amsterdam, where the event was celebrated as a special act of Providence. This incident closed the war between the Dutch and the Indians; the latter invoking the good offices of Underhill, whose hand had fallen thus heavy upon them, with the

WARS OF THE MOHEGANS

result that in April of this year a peace was agreed upon.[1]

This was followed by an outrage committed at Stamford in daylight. An Indian, entering one of the Stamford houses, found there a woman alone with her child. Leaving her for dead, he plundered the house and went away. This was followed by other minor offences upon the part of the savage, whereat the settlers were very much alarmed, and were finally led to request a conference by which they hoped to obtain some reparation. The savages paid no attention to their demands, and, leaving their fields untilled, they indicated their continued hostility by discharging muskets in proximity to the settlements, and by assuming, whenever they appeared among the whites, a turbulent and threatening aspect. They did not conceal their design to make a later attack upon the English, and the settlers at once called upon the Hartford and New Haven authorities for aid. In many places the English posted guards day and night. New Haven responded with alacrity, raising a small contingent of soldiers which was immediately despatched to the settlements most in danger, and another and more strenuous demand was made for the surrender of Ashquash, who had murdered an English servant near Fairfield. While the Stamford woman recov-

---

[1] O'Callaghan's *History of New Netherlands*, bk. iii., chaps. iii., iv., and v.

ered, her reason was destroyed. She was able after an incoherent fashion to describe the appearance of her assailant. The description was that of a savage named Busheag, whom the Indians were finally induced to deliver into the hands of the English. He was taken to New Haven, where he was convicted and sentenced to have his head cut off.[1] His execution was followed by a period of tranquillity.

While these somewhat tumultuous affairs were transpiring the Narragansetts were carrying on a guerilla warfare with the Mohegans. At the time of Miantunnumoh's death his brother Pessicus was about attaining his majority. We have noted his communication with the English at Boston, which was followed by a body-guard of some fourteen Englishmen being sent out of Hartford for the protection of Uncas — a proceeding which did not deter the Narragansetts from making frequent forays into the Mohegan country. Conditions became so serious, finally, that in September, 1644, the commissioners summoned Uncas and Pessicus to Hartford, and an investigation was begun into the rights in contention between these two sachems. These tribes were ordered to maintain a peace until their cause was decided, and were enjoined, fur-

---

[1] When Busheag was executed he sat erect, motionless. The executioner was so unused to his office that it was only after eight blows that he was able to sever the head of the savage from his body.

Hazard, vol. ii., p. 23.

WARS OF THE MOHEGANS

ther, not to interfere with the messengers of the court as they went to deliver the proper summonses. The Narragansetts, advising with Ninigret as to the course to be taken by them, sent Weetowisse and three councillors, who were to file their accusation against Uncas, who appeared before the magistrates for himself. The case opened before the commissioners, and the Narragansetts charged Uncas with breaking his bond to them in the matter of his killing Miantunnumoh;[1] also alleging that the latter's ransom had been agreed upon between themselves and the Mohegans, and that a considerable portion of this ransom had been paid. The reply of the Mohegan sachem was that no ransom had been agreed upon, and that the amount of wampum sent was totally inadequate, and that, having been left to Miantunnumoh for disposition, the latter had disposed of it for the purpose of obtaining future favor, or as a recompense for favors already received.

There is no doubt that the court was disposed to declare the innocence of Uncas, for they finally decided that the evidence of the complainants failed to maintain the charge. They told the Narragansetts, as well, that had Uncas been found guilty they would have compelled him to give satisfaction, and that whenever the Narragansetts were able to prove their contention the magistrates held them-

---

[1] Hazard, vol. ii., p. 25.

selves ready to compel Uncas to make ample reparation. They followed this up with the suggestion that the Narragansetts and the Nehantics were not to attack Uncas until they were able to satisfy them that he was guilty as alleged. Otherwise, they would incur the active hostility of the United Colonies. The Narragansett deputation after a brief consultation agreed not to attack the Mohegans until the next planting-time was over; nor would they then, until they had given thirty days' notice of their intention to the Massachusetts governor.[1]

---

[1] "Before the Narraganset deputies left the court, the English made them sign an agreement that they would not make war upon Uncas, 'Untill after the next planting of corn.' And even then, that they should give 30 days' notice to the English before commencing hostilities. Also that 'if any of the Nayantick Pecotts should make any assault upon Uncas or any of his, they would deliver them up to the English to be punished according to their demerits. And that they should not use any means to procure the Mawhakes to come against Uncas during this truce.' At the same time the English took due care to notify the Narraganset commissioners, by way of awing them into terms, that if they did molest the Mohegans, all the English would be upon them.

"The date of this agreement, if so we may call it, is, 'Hartford, the xviiith of September, 1644,' and was signed by four Indians; one besides those named above, called Chimough.

"That no passage might be left open for excuse, in case of war, it was also mentioned, that, 'proof of the ransom charged,' must be made satisfactory to the English before war was begun.

"The power of Pessacus and Ninigret at this time was

WARS OF THE MOHEGANS

They agreed, further, that they would not use any inducements with the Mohawks against the Mohegans, and that if the latter were attacked by the Nehantic Pequods they would deliver the transgressors to the English for punishment. This treaty bears the date of September 29, 1644. The commissioners signed it for the colonies. The sachems Weetowisse, Pawpiamet, Chimough, and Pummumshe, as councillors of the Narragansetts, signed for that tribe.[1]

Once the Narragansett deputation had returned to their own country, indifferent to their promises to the English, hostilities were again renewed and their warriors were once more scouring the domains of Uncas. Along in the spring following, without notice to the Massachusetts authorities, Pessicus led a large force of warriors against the Mohegans.

---

much feared by the English, and they were ready to believe any reports of the hostile doings of the Narragansets, who, since the subjection of the Pequots, had made themselves masters of all their neighbors, except the English, as the Pequots had done before them. The Mohegans were also in great fear of them, as well after as before the death of Miantunnomoh; but for whose misfortune in being made a prisoner by a stratagem of Uncas, or his captains, the English might have seen far greater troubles from them than they did, judging from the known abilities of that great chief."

Drake's *Book of the Indians*, vol. ii., p. 92.

[1] Hazard, vol. ii., pp. 25, 26.
Drake's *Book of the Indians*, vol. ii., p. 92.

Wherever they went destruction followed. Not a wigwam or village lay behind their path; all were obliterated. The Mohegans sought safety in flight, and their sachem was obliged to hasten to one of his forts for safety. The site of this fort is Shantok Point, a ragged headland on the western shore of the Thames, in the building of which the English had assisted. As against the armament of the Narragansetts, it was practically impregnable, and they had no way of reducing it except by starving its occupants. With that in view, they possessed themselves of the canoes of the Mohegans, to afterwards occupy the country adjacent with numerous bands of warriors. They had driven Uncas into one of his dens, where they proposed to keep him until starvation should deliver him into their hands. This proving futile, by reason of the Mohegans receiving substantial relief in the way of supplies from the English, they raised the siege to return to their own country.[1]

---

[1] "'At the time the Mohegan tribe of Indians were besieged by the Narraganset tribe, in a fort near the River Thames, between Norwich and New London, the provisions of the besieged being nearly exhausted, Uncas, their sachem, found means to inform the settlers at Saybrook of their distress, and the danger they would be in from the Narragansets, if the Mohegan tribe were cut off. Ensign Thomas Leffingwell, one of the first settlers there, loaded a canoe with beef, corn and peas, and in the night time paddled from Saybrook into the Thames, and had the address to get the whole into the

WARS OF THE MOHEGANS

This invasion was followed by another comprised of several hundred warriors, thirty of whom carried muskets. They came upon the Mohegans with great secrecy; and by a ruse of sending into Uncas's vicinity some forty of their warriors,— who, upon being pursued, took to their heels,— in this manner drew the Mohegans within their reach, the Narragansetts meeting them with a hail of bullets and arrows. It was the turn of the Mohegans to run, which they did to such purpose that they were able to regain their fort with a loss of four of their sagamores, two warriors killed, and some forty wounded. The Narragansetts continued the pursuit to the fort; but there happened to be a few Englishmen in the vicinity, upon the appearance of whom the Narragansetts at once retired. The wounded in the fort had their wounds dressed by John Winthrop, Jr., and Thomas Peeters, who were among the earliest of the New London settlers.[1] Uncas related to these the story of the fight, remarking that had it not been for the guns he would not have run for the Narragansetts.

---

fort of the besieged; — received a deed from Uncas of the town of Norwich, and made his escape that very night. In consequence of which, the besiegers, finding Uncas had procured relief, raised the siege, and the Mohegan tribe were saved, and have ever proved strict friends to the New England settlers.'"

Drake's *Book of the Indians*, vol. ii., p. 94.

[1] DeForest, p. 215.

INDIAN WARS OF NEW ENGLAND

For the remainder of this season the English kept a small force under arms in the Mohegan country. These incursions of the Narragansetts aroused the colonies to make some more strenuous exertion for the protection of Uncas, who had so many times lent himself to their purposes. At a meeting of the commissioners of the United Colonies at Boston in May, 1645, this matter was considered, and messengers were despatched to the Mohegans, Narragansetts, and Nehantics, with the invitation that they attend once more upon the magistrates for the purpose of settling the difficulties existing between these tribes. Benedict Arnold accompanied them as interpreter. When they arrived in the Narragansett country they were received with indifference by Pessicus.[1]

---

[1] "These messengers, Sergeant John Dames [Davis?], Benedict Arnold, and Francis Smyth, on their first arrival at Narraganset, were welcomed by the sachems, who offered them guides to conduct them to Uncas; but, either having understood their intentions, or judging from their appearance that the English messengers meant them no good, changed their deportment altogether, and in the meantime secretly despatched messengers to the Nianticks before them, giving them to understand what was going forward. After this, say the messengers, 'there was nothing but proud and insolent passages [from Ninigret]. The Indian guides which they had brought with them from Pumham and Sokakanoco were, by frowns and threatening speeches, discouraged, and returned; no other guides could be obtained.' The sachems said they knew, by what was done at Hartford last year, that the Eng-

WARS OF THE MOHEGANS

When the messengers had fully informed Pessicus as to their errand, he replied: "The reason I did not meet the English sachems at New Haven last year, is, they did not notify me. It is true I have broken my covenant these two years, and that now is constantly, and has been, the grief of my spirit. The reason I do not meet them now, at Boston is because I am sick. If I were but pretty well, I would go. I have sent my mind in full to Ninigret and what he does, I will abide by. I have sent Powpynamett and Pumumsks to go and hear, and testify that I have betrusted my full mind with Nenegratt. You know full well, however, that when I made that covenant two years ago, I did it in fear of the army that I did see; and though the

---

lish would urge peace, 'but they were resolved,' they said, 'to have no peace without Uncas his head.' As to who began the war, they cared not, but they were resolved to continue it; that if the English did not withdraw their soldiers from Uncas, they should consider it a breach of former covenants, and would procure as many Mohawks as the English had soldiers to bring against them. They reviled Uncas for having wounded himself, and then charging it upon them, and said he was no friend of the English, but would now, if he durst, kill the English messengers, and lay that to them. Therefore, not being able to proceed, the English messengers returned to the Narragansets and acquainted Pessacus of what had passed, desiring he would furnish them with guides; 'he, (in scorn, as they apprehended it,) offered them an old Peacott squaw.'"

Drake's *Book of the Indians*, vol. ii., pp. 92, 93.

English kept their covenant with me, yet they were ready to go to Narragansett and kill me and the commissioners said they would do it if I did not sign what they had written."

From Pessicus the messengers went to Ninigret, who received them with a contemptuous derision. It was evident, in the behavior of the Indians to this embassy, that they held the treaty but lightly; and it was no less apparent that their distrust of the English was about to take a definite shape. So impressed were the messengers with the attitude of these two sachems that they were afraid to continue their journey into the Mohegan country, and returned to Boston, where they related their experiences, not unmixed with indignation and some anger at the insult put upon their station.[1] On their way back they met Roger Williams, who gave

---

[1] "The messengers now thought themselves in danger of being massacred; 'three Indians with hatchets standing behind the interpreter in a suspicious manner, while he was speaking with Pessacus, and the rest frowning and expressing much distemper in their countenance and carriage.' So, without much loss of time, they began to retrace their steps. On leaving Pessacus, they told him they were to lodge at an English trading house not far off that night, and if he wanted to send any word to the English, he might send to them. In the morning, he invited them to return, and said he would furnish them with guides to visit Uncas, but he would not suspend hostilities. Not daring to risk the journey, the messengers returned home. Arnold, the interpreter, testified that this was a true relation of what had happened, which is necessary

WARS OF THE MOHEGANS

them a letter to the Massachusetts authorities, in which he declared that war with the Indians was about to ensue; and that the Narragansetts, in anticipation of its results, had entered into an amicable treaty with the Providence and the Rhode Island tribes. This aroused the commissioners to lay out an immediate campaign against the Narragansetts, the first step of which was to impress forty men, who were despatched three days later to take the place of the garrison at Mohegan, which was about to return to New Haven.[1] This little party was accompanied by two Massachusetts Indians as guides. They had along with them four horses. Forty men from Connecticut and thirty from New Haven were to join them at Mohegan,

---

to be borne in mind, as something may appear, as we proceed, impeaching the veracity of Arnold."

Drake's *Book of the Indians*, vol. ii., p. 93.

[1] "Meanwhile the commissioners set forth an armament to defend Uncas, at all hazards. To justify this movement they declare, that, 'considering the great provocations offered, and the necessity we should be put unto of making war upon the Narrohiggin, &c. and being also careful in a matter of so great weight and general concernment to see the way cleared and to give satisfaction to all the colonists, did think fit to advise with such of the magistrates and elders of the Massachusetts as were then at hand, and also with some of the chief military commanders there, who being assembled, it was then agreed: First, that our engagement bound us to aid and defend the Mohegan sachem. Secondly, that this aid could not be intended to only defend him and his, in his fort

INDIAN WARS OF NEW ENGLAND

and, under the command of John Mason, the company was to march at once against the Nehantics, who were designated as the instigators of the antici-

---

or habitation, but (according to the common acceptation of such covenants or engagements considered with the ground or occasion thereof,) so to aid him as hee might be preserved in his liberty and estate. Thirdly, that this aid must be speedy, lest he might be swallowed up in the meantime, and so come too late.'

"'According to the counsel and determination aforesaid, the commissioners, considering the present danger of Uncas the Mohegan sachem, (his fort having been divers times assaulted by a great army of the Narrohiggansets, &c.) agreed to have 40 soldiers sent with all expedition for his defence.' Lieut. Atherton and Sergeant John Davis led this company, conducted by two of 'Cutchamakin's' Indians as guides. Atherton was ordered not to make an 'attempt upon the town otherwise than in Uncas' defence.' Capt. Mason of Connecticut was to join them, and take the chief command. Forty men were ordered also from Connecticut, and 30 from New Haven under Lieut. Sealy. In their instructions to Mason, the commissioners say, 'We so now aim at the protection of the Mohegans, that we would have no opportunity neglected to weaken the Narragansets and their confederates, in their number of men, their cane canoes, wigwams, wampum and goods. We look upon the Nianticks as the chief incendiaries and causes of war, and should be glad they might first feel the smart of it.' The Nianticks, therefore, were particularly to be had in view by Mason, and he was informed at the same time that Massachusetts and Plimouth were forthwith to send, 'another army to invade the Narragansets.'"

Drake's *Book of the Indians*, vol. ii., p. 93.

WARS OF THE MOHEGANS

pated hostilities, and who were to be the first to experience the displeasure of the English. In addition to this enterprise, another was to be projected against the Narragansetts from the Massachusetts side, under the command of Major Edward Gibbons, with one hundred ninety men.[1]

It was thought fit to make a final effort with these people toward a possible adjustment. Two other messengers were sent to Pessicus, who informed him of the plans and preparations of the English. That sachem, upon being informed that the English force being despatched against him was four times as great as that which overthrew the Pequods, lost his courage. A brief cessation of hostilities was the

---

[1] Hazard, vol. ii., pp. 28-32.

"The commissioners now proceeded to make choice of a commander in chief of the two armies. Maj. Edward Gibbons was unanimously elected. In his instructions is this passage: 'Wheras the scope and cause of this expedition is not only to aid the Mohegans, but to offend the Narragansets, Nianticks, and other their confederates.' He was directed also to conclude a peace with them, if they desired it, provided it were made with special reference to damages, &c. And they say, 'But withal, according to our engagements, you are to provide for Uncas' future safety, that his plantations be not invaded, that his men and squaws may attend their planting and fishing and other occasions without fear or injury, and Vssamequine, Pomham, Sokakonoco, Cutchamakin, and other Indians, friends or subjects to the English, be not molested, &c.'"

Drake's *Book of the Indians*, vol. ii., p. 94.

result. Immediately, Pessicus, with several of his councillors, went to Boston, where before the commissioners their defence was resolved into their old complaint against Uncas.[1] Still holding to their animosity against the Mohegan sachem, they offered to refrain from making further attack upon the Mohegans until after next planting-season. Extending the time to a year, and then to a year and a quarter, all of which propositions were unfavorably received by the commissioners, one of them delivered to the commissioners a stick, the significance of which was that it was for the commissioners to tell them what they should do.[2] The com-

---

[1] "It was in the end agreed, that the chiefs, Pessacus, Mexam, and divers others, should proceed to Boston, agreeably to the desire of the English, which they did, in company with Harding and Welborne, who brought back the old present, and for which they also received the censure of the congress. They arrived at Boston just as the second levy of troops were marching out for their country, and thus the expedition was stayed until the result of a treaty should be made known."
Drake's *Book of the Indians*, vol. ii., p. 96.

[2] "It appeared, on a conference with the commissioners that the sachems did not fully understand the nature of all the charges against them before leaving their country, and in justice to them it should be observed, that, so far as the record goes, their case appears to us the easiest to be defended of the three parties concerned. They told the commissioners of sundry charges they had against the Uncas, but they said they could not hear them, for Uncas was not there to speak

WARS OF THE MOHEGANS

missioners replied to them that the price of peace with the English would be two thousand fathoms of wampum and a full indemnification of such expenses as had been incurred in the preparation for war; that they should restore all captive Mohegans and Mohegan canoes; and, as well, must not only put their contention with Uncas before the next session of the court, but they must abide by its ruling. The wampum was to be paid in quarterly

---

for himself; and that they had hindered his being notified of their coming. As to a breach of covenant, they maintained, for some time, that they had committed none, and that their treatment of the English had been misrepresented. 'But, (says our record) after a long debate and some priuate conferrence, they had with Serjeant Cullicutt, they acknowledged they had broken promise or couenant in the afore menconed warrs, and offerred to make another truce with Uncas, either till next planting tyme, as they had done last yeare at Hartford, or for a yeare, or a yeare and a quarter.'

"They had been induced to make this admission, no doubt, by the persuasion of Cullicut, who, probably, was instructed to inform them that the safety of their country depended upon their compliance with the wishes of the English at this time. An army of soldiers was at that moment parading the streets, in all the pomposity of a modern training, which must have reminded them of the horrible destruction of their kindred at Mystic eight years before.

"The proposition of a truce being objected to by the English, 'one of the sachems offered a stick or a wand to the commissioners, expressing himself, that therewith they put the power and disposition of the war into their hands, and desired to know what the English would require of them.' They

INDIAN WARS OF NEW ENGLAND

instalments, the last payment to be within twenty months. Four sons of Pessicus, Ninigret, and other chief sachems were to be delivered up as hostages within fourteen days; and until this last provision was complied with four sachems of the Narragansett party were to be retained as prisoners at Boston. This was followed up by the imposition of a tax in the nature of a poll, which was that for every Pequod man among the Narragansetts and the Nehantics they were to pay annually a fathom of white wampum, a half-fathom for every youth, and a hand-length for every child. The only point made in their favor was that the Mohegans should be obliged to restore to them whatever of plunder

---

were answered that the expenses and trouble they had caused the English was very great, 'besides the damage Uncas had sustained; yet to show their moderacon, they would require of them but twoo thousand fathome of white wampom for their owne satisfaccon,' but that they should restore to Uncas all the captives and canoes taken from him, and make restitution of all the corn they had spoiled. As for the last-mentioned offence, the sachems asserted there had been none such; for it was not the manner of the Indians to destroy corn.

"This most excellent and indirect reproof must have had no small effect on those who heard it, as no doubt some of the actors as well as the advisers of the destruction of the Indians' corn, previous to and during the Pequot war, were now present; Block Island, and the fertile fields upon the shores of the Connecticut, must have magnified before their imaginations."

Drake's *Book of the Indians*, vol. ii., pp. 96, 97.

WARS OF THE MOHEGANS

or captives they might have taken from these tribes. As to all other matters, the commissioners were unyielding, and on the fifth of September, 1645, a new treaty was signed — on the part of the Indians, with manifest reluctance.[1]

The following year Sequassen occupied the attention of the English in a minor way, being a rival of Uncas, whom he hated thoroughly, while he disliked the English because they were friendly to the Mohegans. He concocted a plot with a Potatuck savage, by which the latter was to accomplish the death of Uncas. This fell through, on account of the cowardice of the proposed perpetrator of the crime, who, instead of going into the Mohegan country, took his way to Hartford, where he disclosed the matter to the magistrates. Sequassen was summoned to Hartford. The court had been in session some time when two sagamores made their appearance, avowing that they were friends of Sequassen, and announcing that they had just returned from Massachusetts, where they had been with the former. They had carried a present to the governor, who, while he refused to accept it, "consented to give it house-room," which was in accordance with the traditions of the Bay authorities. Sequassen was afterward captured and brought to Hartford, where he was imprisoned; but, nothing

---

[1] For copy of this treaty see Drake, *Book of the Indians*, vol. ii., pp. 97, 98.

being proved against him, he was set at liberty.[1] While the incident is not important, it shows how credulous the English were in matters of accusation by one Indian against another, and how readily they clothed with the garb of veracity such as informed them of these so-called plots. The Potatuck "was unquestionably a liar and a villian."

In the same year the Milford people maintained a daily and nightly guard about their settlements, and when attending church Sundays took their muskets and side-arms along with them, fearful of an inroad by the Wepawaugs or Paugussets, who had grown uneasy, by reason of real or fancied wrongs imposed upon them by the English. The nearest approach to hostilities on the part of the savages was their setting fire to the woods about the town, which the settlers finally succeeded in extinguishing before it reached the palisades. The principal damage was the destruction of a large area of timber-lands and the burning of several meadows.[2]

With an occasional inroad from the Mohawks upon the settlements along the coast, nothing of any importance happened until about 1648, when a body of Mohawks hid themselves in a swamp in the neighborhood of Stratford Ferry. They were discovered by some of the settlers, who informed the

---

[1] Hazard, vol. ii., pp. 60, 61.
Winthrop, vol. ii., p. 333.
[2] Lambart's *History of New Haven Colony*, p. 128.

WARS OF THE MOHEGANS

Wepawaugs, who went out against them, by whom the Mohawks were defeated. As a curious incident of Indian torture, one captive Mohawk was stripped, tied hand and foot to a tree in one of the meadows, and left to the mercies of the mosquitoes, which at that season of the year were abundant. Thomas Hine, an English settler, came across the Mohawk, whom he relieved from his uncomfortable situation, afterward feeding him, and thereby enabled him to escape. For this kindness the Mohawks held the family of this settler in great esteem, and were wont to remark that the "Hines' did not die like the other pale-faces, but went to the west, where the Great Spirit took them into his big wigwam and made them great men."[1]

In 1649 a murder was committed by an Indian at Stamford. John Whitmore, a member of the General Court of New Haven, went to look over his cattle one day, and that was the last ever seen of him. The son of a neighboring sagamore was suspected of the crime; but he throwing the guilt upon another, who was absent, the matter was held in abeyance. Two or three months later Uncas came down to Stamford, accompanied by some of his fighting-men, and, being informed of this offence, began an investigation with the demand to know where the body was concealed. The saga-

---

[1] Trumbull, vol. i., pp. 162, 163.
Barber's *Hist. Coll. Conn., Milford.*

more's son and another savage who was suspected led the way directly to the place where the body was finally discovered. Nothing, however, was done in the matter.[1] By this time Uncas had become so confident of the English favor that his unrest and turbulency, his oppression of the Pequods subject to him, his abuse and despoiling of those who were not under his subjection, made him obnoxious to the colony. He deprived one man of his wife, another of his corn and beans; he failed to deliver to the English wampum which had been entrusted to him for that purpose; and, together with his brother Wawequa, he lost no opportunity of committing every possible depredation upon his neighbors. These acts on his part brought upon him the reprimands of the English, and, in one or two instances, punishment.[2]

---

[1] Hazard, vol. ii., pp. 127, 128.
Colonial Records, vol. i., p. 197.

[2] "At the same court Obechiquod complained that Uncas had forcibly taken away his wife, and criminally obliged her to live with him. 'Foxon being present, as Uncas' deputy, was questioned about this base and unsufferable outrage; he denied that Uncas either took or kept away Obechiquod's wife by force, and affirmed that [on] Obechiquod's withdrawing, with other Pequots, from Uncas, his wife refused to go with him; and that, among the Indians, it is usual when a wife so deserts her husband, another may take her. Obechiquod affirmed that Uncas had dealt criminally before, and still kept her against her will.'

"Though not satisfied in point of proof, the commissioners

WARS OF THE MOHEGANS

Uncas was inclined to carry things with a high hand, and from this time on gave the commissioners of Connecticut more or less trouble. In 1646 he made an inroad upon the country about New London with three hundred Mohegans, in reprisal because Cassasinamon had been driving the woods for game, that the people at New London might have something to eat, Thomas Peeters being ill and some of the other settlers being out of provisions. This was resented by Uncas on the ground that the Indian hunter was not an independent sachem and had assumed too much freedom in conducting this forage for game. Peeters complained to the commissioners, who had him before them at the next session, which resulted in very little other than the court's promising to take up his grievances.[1] Uncas had hardly been dismissed by the commissioners before a new complaint was made against him by William Morton, of New London, who brought along three Pequods to substantiate his complaint. The hearing resolved itself into a "labyrinth of lies," in which Uncas ap-

---

say, 'Yet abhoring that lustful adulterous carriage of Uncas, as it is acknowledged and mittigated by Foxon,' ordered that he should restore the wife, and that Obechiquod have liberty to settle under the protection of the English, where they should direct."

Drake's *Book of the Indians*, vol. ii., p. 100.

[1] Hazard, vol. ii., p. 65.

peared to his usual disadvantage, and the affair was dismissed.[1]

These incidents were followed by a series of petty tyrannies on the part of Uncas. He abducted the wife of Obechiquod; defiled the wife of Sanaps, one of his subjects; and to these injuries he added the robbery of the latter's harvest. The Indians were great gamblers, a pastime that was carried on quite generally between the Pequods and the Mohegans, and whenever the former won at play he (Uncas) justified the latter in not paying their debts. In his not infrequent excursions against the Long Island Indians he was wont to demand of the Pequods that they join him; when they refused to do so he cut up their fishing-nets, and committed other depredations upon their possessions. It was, however, of small importance to the English what happened to the Pequods, and these abuses were passed without reparation, so indifferent were the English to these tributaries.

The following year, 1647, a child of Uncas died, whereupon, after the custom of the tribes, the sachem carried gifts of consolation to the mother, and, threatening the Pequods, Uncas ordered them to do the same. Tassaquanot, a brother of Sassacus, who had survived the butcheries of the English and the Mohawks, refused to comply with this demand of Uncas, excusing himself with the ob-

---

[1] Hazard, vol. ii., p. 66.

servation that if he had any wampum it were better to give it to the English, as the obtaining of their favor would give them security against Uncas. Others of the Pequods, being fearful of Uncas, and knowing his retaliatory disposition, collected some one hundred fathoms and disposed of it as Uncas directed.

A few days later Wawequa came into the Pequod settlement with a message from Uncas that the latter and the Mohegan council had decided to put a number of them to death. Recalling the advice of Tassaquanot, they set about collecting a quantity of wampum to be given to the English, hoping thereby to purchase their safety from Uncas, who, being acquainted with their design, the following day appeared before their fort with his warriors. The Pequods succeeded in making their escape, to take up their residence under the protection of the New London settlers.

In July of this year, upon the meeting of the commissioners at Boston, Cassasinamon and Obechiquod, with forty-six Pequods and eighteen Nehantics, complained of the abuses of Uncas. Their relation comprised all the wrongs inflicted upon them by Uncas: his abduction of their wives; his robberies of their corn and beans; his destruction of their fishing-nets; his extortions of wampum; and his threats of personal injury. They alleged in their petition that they had refused to engage in the wars of Sassacus against the English settlers, and that they were not guilty of killing any of the English, and they claimed the English protection.[1] The chief councillor of Uncas, whose name was Foxon,[2] represented the Mohegan sachem at this hearing. Some of the charges he denied, and some he excused; of some he pretended ignorance; and with much plausible speech he defended the outrages of Uncas. He declared that Obechiquod, having fled the territory of Uncas, had forfeited his wife by Indian custom; that the Pequods had never sent wampum to the English, unless they had joined in so doing with the Mohegans; he was unaware of the destruction of the fishing-nets; it was a lie so far as Uncas favored the Mohegans against the Pequods in gaming. As for the statement of the Pequods regarding their attitude toward the English, it was false; for he alleged that some of them were in the fort destroyed by Mason, and under cover of the smoke they escaped to engage in other places against the Mohegans and the Narragansetts.[3]

The commissioners were not deceived by this defence; and though recognizing the shortcomings of

---

[1] Hazard, vol. ii., pp. 87-89.

[2] Foxon, Foxun, or Poxen was a crafty, plausible councillor, who is mentioned in one of the Apostle Eliot's letters as being considered among the Massachusetts tribes as "the wisest Indian in the country."
Mass. Hist. Coll., vol. xxiv., p. 57.

[3] Hazard, vol. ii., p. 90.

WARS OF THE MOHEGANS

their favorite, they were slow to deprive Uncas of the credit accorded him by the colonies. They directed the Pequods to return to the Mohegan country, and further directed Uncas not to interfere with them. They afterwards despatched a deputy to Uncas with a verbal reproof that the English would not support him "in such unlawful and outrageous courses."[1]

But this was not all; for John Winthrop, of New London, entered a new complaint against Uncas, and Foxon was again obliged to plead in extenuation of the Mohegan sachem. Winthrop's complaint was that Wawequa, with one hundred thirty Mohegans, had made a foray upon the Nipmucks,[2] from which tribe they had carried away thirty-five

---

[1] Hazard, vol. ii., p. 91.

[2] This tribe dwelt mainly in the eastern interior of Massachusetts, occupying many of the lakes and rivers. Their exact limits have not been defined; but they must have been very extensive, as there is proof that their boundaries reached as far as Boston on the east, as far south as the northern portion of Rhode Island, westward as far as Bennington in Vermont, and as far north as Concord, N. H.

Douglas-Lithgow, *Dictionary of American Indian Names*, p. 375.

The Nipmuck tribes of New Hampshire, occupying the southern part of this territory, constituted, with some of the Massachusetts tribes, what was known as the Pennacook Confederacy, of which the illustrious Passaconaway was the Bashaba. They lived along the intervales of the Pennacook, in the region of present Bow, Concord, and Boscawen, in

fathoms of wampum, ten copper kettles, ten large hempen baskets, and a considerable quantity of valuable furs. Foxon admitted the offence, but urged that Uncas with his chief men at that time were at New Haven and were ignorant of the affair; that he had no share in the plunder; and that some of the Mohegans had been robbed about the same time.[1] Winthrop complained, further, that this same brother of Uncas, with a band of men, some armed with guns, had at Fisher's Island frightened an Indian and broken a canoe. Another settler averred that Wawequa, upon his return from Fisher's Island, had halted his canoes off the settlement; that his movements had been such as to cause the Indians and some of the English settlers to immediately betake themselves and their goods into the houses of the colonists for safety. Winthrop was a man to whom the commissioners felt bound to listen, and Uncas was sentenced to pay a fine of one hundred fathoms of wampum. This

---

Merrimac County. Of the other confederated tribes were the Nashuas and the Sowhegans, on the Merrimac; the Namaoskeags, at Amoskeag Falls; and the Winnepesaukees, who lived about the lake of that name. Confederated with them were the Agawams (Ipswich), Wamesits or Pawtuckets (Lowell), and the Pentuckets (Haverhill). Passaconaway died about 1660.

Douglas-Lithgow, *Dictionary of American Indian Names*, Int., p. xii.

[1] Hazard, vol. ii., p. 91.

WARS OF THE MOHEGANS

fine was to be divided among those of the English and Indians who were injured in the foray of the Mohegans against the Nipmucks; and Foxon was dismissed with numerous reproofs and admonitions, which he was to convey to the avaricious and unscrupulous Uncas.[1]

The Pequods refused to return to the territory of the Mohegans, against whom Uncas made complaint at the next court, which, in October, 1648, authorized him to reduce the Pequods to obedience, a resolution being passed, as well, which forbade any one from offering the Pequods shelter. Uncas profited little by this order, as neither by force nor persuasion would the Pequods again live with the Mohegans. After this they distributed themselves indiscriminately among the Nehantics and Narragansetts, where they maintained a precarious existence, or herded in communities unrecognized by the English.

Soon after these incidents the commissioners were again called upon to defend Uncas. Uncas had abducted Sequassen[2] from the territory of the Pocomtucks of Deerfield. The latter, instigated by gifts of wampum from the Narragansetts and the Nehantics, in August, 1648, gathered a large body of warriors of that tribe. Gifts had been sent to the

---

[1] Hazard, vol. ii., p. 91.

[2] A sachem of the Tunxis tribe, who sold Hartford to the English. He was also known as Sequen, or Sequeen.

Mohawks, as well; and with the coming of this latter tribe the combined forces were to march against the Mohegans. Rumor placed the number of this hostile body at one thousand; that three hundred of these warriors were armed with muskets; that the Narragansetts were sending their old men, women, and children into the neighboring swamps for security, and had mustered a force of eight hundred men, who were to join the Pocomtucks and the Mohawks. A portion of the Narragansetts, however, under Sachem Hermon Garret, separated themselves from the alleged conspiracy to occupy a portion of the Narragansett territory at a distance from the possible scene of action.

Connecticut became alarmed, and apprehensive of danger to the colony, as well as the ruin of Uncas; and they despatched Thomas Stanton, with two other Englishmen, to the rendezvous of the belligerents, who were directed to obtain information as to their designs, and if such were hostile to the Mohegans, to make strenuous protest against their carrying out of that purpose. They found at Pocomtuck a large body of warriors who were making preparations for some sort of an expedition. The sachem received them politely. Stanton laid great stress upon the power of the English in war, their disposition to fairness, and finally declared that the English would defend Uncas with all the resources at their command. The reply of the sachem was that they were aware of these things, and had no desire to displease the English; and for that reason they would delay their purpose for a further consideration. This willingness on the part of the Pocomtucks to accede to the demands of the English messenger was not that they cared so much to oblige the English, as it was based upon a report brought in by a Mohawk runner that his tribe had been attacked by some eastern Indians, instigated by the French, and that they were obliged to keep their warriors at home as a matter of self-defence. This incident dissolved the league, nor was Uncas ever after "threatened by so formidable a combination." This conspiracy on the part of the Narragansetts resulted in their being ordered to make good their tribute, the arrears of which amounted to two thousand fathoms of wampum.

The feeling against Uncas, however, did not stop here; for the Indians of Rhode Island, convinced that Uncas was not to be disposed of by an open attack, began to plot for the riddance of their enemy after another fashion. The following year, 1649, numerous complaints of the Narragansetts were made by Uncas to the commissioners. He said they were plotting against him. They were trying to bring the Mohawks upon him. They were trying to put an end to his life by witchcraft. They had neither restored his canoes nor his prisoners. After this, Uncas boarded an English vessel which lay at anchor in the Thames. A Narragansett, Cuttaquin, who was also on the vessel, discovering Uncas, made a sudden attack upon the latter with a sword, by which Uncas got a wound in his breast which was at the time supposed to be fatal. Cuttaquin was arrested, and upon being interrogated by some of the English, among whom was John Mason, as to why he committed this assault, he replied to Mason: "I am a Narragansett; the Narragansett sachem is my sachem; they came to me and wished me to kill Uncas; they offered me a large quantity of wampum, and I accepted it; this wampum I spent, and was placed in their power; had I not fulfilled my bargain and attempted to kill him, they would have slain me."[1] The savage was thereupon delivered to the Mohegans, and was taken into the Mohegan territory, along with the sachem he had attempted to kill.

The statement of Cuttaquin so directly involved the integrity of the Narragansett sachems that Ninigret felt himself obliged to present himself before the commissioners at Boston, where he endeavored to clear himself and Pessicus. The commissioners, however, gave little credence to his arguments, and his protest that he was innocent impressed them but

---

[1] "A Narragansett Indian named *Cuttaquin*, 'in an English vessel, in Mohegan River, ran a sword into his [Uncas's] breast, wherby hee receeved, to all appearance, a mortal wound, which murtherus acte the assalant then confessed hee was, for a considerable sum of wampum, by the Narragansett and Nianticke sachems, hired to attempt.'"
Drake's *Book of the Indians*, vol. ii., p. 72.

WARS OF THE MOHEGANS

slightly. His assertion that the Mohegans had distorted the tale from Cuttaquin by torturing him was met upon the part of the commissioners by the reply that the savage gave his relation to Mason before he was delivered into the hands of the Mohegans. Ninigret was dismissed with numerous reproofs and threats, and a message was despatched to Uncas, who was on the high road to recovery, that his Narragansett prisoner was at his disposal. There is no record of his fate at the hands of the Mohegans.[1]

Notwithstanding the restrictions which the English had been continually putting upon the Indians since their settlement of the country, the independent spirit of the Narragansett sachems was not quelled in any degree. Whatever externals of submission might have been apparent, underneath was a current of unrest and a harboring of revenge. Ninigret[2] was one of those spirits whose yielding to the English was entirely superficial. It was now rumored that this sachem was about to bestow his daughter in marriage upon the brother of Sassacus, who had begun to exercise some influence upon the

---

[1] Hazard, vol. ii., pp. 129, 130.

[2] Ninigret, or Ninicraft, was the great-sachem of the Niantics, of the Narragansett family; he lived at Wekapaug [Westerly], R. I., and married a sister of Cashawashett [Hermon Garret].

Douglas-Lithgow, *Dictionary of American Indian Names*, p. 333.

wandering Pequods by collecting them about him, as if he intended to take up the mantle of his ancestors. The English surmised the object of this to be the weakening of the Mohegans by withdrawing from that tribe such Pequods as had made a common interest with them, which would naturally result in the building up of a new tribe, which could not be other than actuated by its ancient hatred for the Mohegans, and who for that reason might possibly become a formidable factor for war or peace. The English, taking this rumor for a certainty, with their usual celerity in heading off designs of this character, despatched messengers into the country of the Narragansetts and Nehantics, whose sachems were charged with the fact. They further purposed to carry on such inquiry of the matter as would afford them full knowledge of existing conditions, and, as well, to demand of the Narragansetts the tribute of wampum, which was greatly in arrears. Whatever basis there may have been for the origin of the report to the English as to the marriage of Ninigret's daughter, or the amalgamation of the Pequods, there is no further record to be had.[1]

Uncas had become to the English a necessary evil, and his complaints against the tribes neighboring upon the Mohegans had become almost continuous. In September of 1650 he complained to

---

[1] Hazard, vol. ii., p. 152.

WARS OF THE MOHEGANS

the commissioners that a sachem of Long Island, named Monhansick, had taken the lives of several of his people, and had bewitched others, among whom was himself. It was evident that the commissioners were not prepared to give much credence to the charge of witchcraft; but the killing of the Mohegans was a different matter, and proceedings were taken to ascertain the innocence or guilt of the Long Island sachem. If found guilty he was to give Uncas such satisfaction as he required; and if he refused the English were to resort to their usual method of intimidation by threatening him with their active displeasure.[1]

These incidents in the career of Uncas delineate his character with a singular completeness. Tyrannically ambitious, he was deeply suspicious; jealous of the prosperity of others, he was absolutely without honesty, mean to a nicety, and inordinately greedy. Hated by the sachems of the surrounding tribes, they neglected no opportunity of injuring him, the real cause of which was undoubtedly his secure standing with the English, whose dirty work he had performed without question. It was he who led Mason, under cover of the darkness of the night, to the fort of the Pequods. The accuser of Miantunnumoh, and his murderer as well, at the instigation of the English; the oppressor of such Pequods as had been allotted to him as his share of

---

[1] Hazard, vol. ii., pp. 150, 151.

the spoils; the abductor of Sequassen, by whom he was surrendered to the Connecticut magistrates; the unmitigated slanderer of every neighboring sachem who was too troublesome and too dangerous for him to attack openly; a brute, physically; thoroughly inoculated with the serum of cowardice; — this was the man to whom the English through all these early years lent their countenance and protection.

In 1651 Sequassen had returned to his own country, having been set at liberty, and the white settlers seemed to have done him some favor, which greatly grieved Uncas, who, after his usual fashion, carried his complaint to the commissioners. He said, "Sequassen was set up and they were going to make a great sachem of him; and yet he refused to pay their friend Uncas, an acknowledgment of wampum, which he owed him as his conqueror." The commissioners descended from their position so far as to avow to this low-bred sachem that they had no intention of lending to Sequassen any aid to greatness; and with their customary subservience to the whims of this fellow, they recommended to the government of Connecticut to see that Uncas received his rights, following this with the disclaimer that as to the tribute of allegiance claimed by Uncas they were wholly ignorant.[1]

Two years later, 1653, in the early spring, Uncas

---

[1] Hazard, vol. ii., p. 190.

made his way to the residence of Governor Haynes, at Hartford, to deposit a new complaint against the Narragansetts and the Nehantics, the burden of which was that the latter were confederating with the Dutch of New Netherlands against him. He said, "Ninigret has been to Manhattan and formed a league with the Dutch governor. He made the governor a present of a great quantity of wampum and the governor made him a present of a large box of powder and bullets. Then Ninigret went to a council of Indians over the Hudson River, and made a speech to them, asking their help against Uncas and the English."

He also related this circumstance, which is indicative of savage custom and superstition. He said that, two years before, Ninigret had made a gift of wampum to the Monheag sachem,[1] asking him to send him a man skilful in the use of poisons and magic. He promised one hundred fathoms of wampum additional upon the return of the sorcerer. Informed of this plot, Uncas set a watch both by land and by sea, by which the canoe containing the Mohican medicine-man was intercepted and that individual captured. With the savage empiric were six other savages, one of whom was a Pequod; another was a brother of the Monheag, whose name was Wampeag. The remainder were of the Narra-

---

[1] Probably the Mohican tribe whose habitat was along the Hudson River.

gansetts. The prisoners were carried to Mohegan by his men for examination. The Monheag and one of the Narragansetts confessed the plot; and upon identifying the sorcerer, the Mohegans, with unrestrained rage, killed him.[1]

The quarrel between Ninigret and the English continued through this year, 1653; until, in the following year, the commissioners declared war against this sachem, and a force of two hundred seventy infantry-men and forty good cavalry-men were raised to prosecute him. Major Willard was in command, and as he advanced into the Nehantic country the Nehantics made no defence, but left their dwellings and crops to the mercy of the English, in their flight taking refuge in a swamp for safety. Willard was accompanied by a number of Pequods. As a party of Willard's Pequods were going through the woods, while endeavoring to locate the hiding-place of the Nehantics, intending to use their persuasion with the Pequods who had found asylum among the Nehantics, and if possible cause their desertion, they came across three Pequods who were of Ninigret's party. After a parley between the Nehantic Pequods and those of Willard's force, seventy-three Pequods who had been allied to Ninigret came into Willard's camp, and the day after they were followed by sixty-three more. The character of this war was not marked

---

[1] Hazard, vol. ii., p. 211.

WARS OF THE MOHEGANS

by any particular energy, and the destruction of Ninigret and his people, as was intended by the colonies, was not consummated. Ninigret was allowed to become a party to a peace by which his power was practically broken, and the records of those times have very little more to mention of him.[1] It is evident that the Pequods who came over to Willard were not delivered to Uncas, as the latter complained of that fact to the commissioners, who, willing to please Uncas anew, remanded all arrears of tribute to such of the Pequods as should return to the Mohegan country.

In 1656 Uncas had made a compact of friendship with Sequassen, the same delivered by him into the hands of the English previously. A Podunk had killed a relative of Sequassen; he, taking umbrage at this outrage, made an effort to apprehend the murderer, which the Podunks prevented, whereupon Sequassen requested Uncas to assist him in the matter. Uncas, who was always open to opportunities which would enable him to get into a profitable broil with his neighbors, entertained the complaint of Sequassen, and bringing the matter before the English as a preparatory step in his aggression, the commissioners summoned all the

---

[1] For a relation of the various difficulties in which Ninigret became involved at one time and another with the English and the neighboring savage tribes, *vide* Hazard, vol. ii., pp. 308-381, *passim*.

parties interested. Webster was governor of Connecticut at that time, and when he sought to be informed of the character of the satisfaction required, Uncas's advocate, Foxon, alleged that the murdered sagamore was a great sachem; and, as well, that the man who killed him was a very "mean fellow." They insisted upon the surrender of the murderer and nine of the Podunk tribe. These latter entered a plea that Weasepano had done righteously, because the dead sachem had killed one of his uncles. The court was divided in its opinion; the governor laid down the law that the man who committed the crime was the only one liable to punishment, and urged upon the savages that a friendly settlement of the matter be had. The Podunks then offered wampum in settlement, which was refused by Uncas and Sequassen, who reduced their demand for victims by four. They insisted upon six Podunks being delivered to them for punishment. Wearied with the long and uninterpretable harangues of the contending parties, the commissioners urged Tontonimo, the Podunk sachem, to surrender the murderer. Pretending to consent, he evaded the immediate fulfilment of his promise by withdrawing himself and his followers, unnoticed by the magistrates, after which he hastened away to his fort.

This was not only displeasing to Uncas and Sequassen, but the commissioners regarded it as a deception practised upon themselves, and immediately despatched a messenger to Tontonimo with

WARS OF THE MOHEGANS

an order that they should observe their compact. Uncas finally was persuaded to accept of the murderer alone; but still denied by the Podunks, upon the plea that the friends of the criminal were so powerful, and there were so many of them in the fort, that he was unable to make this concession. After thinking the matter over, the commissioners came to the sensible conclusion that it was n't any matter of theirs; and, calling the complainants before them, they urged Uncas to take the wampum which had been offered. If he decided not to do that the Mohegans were to dispose of the matter among themselves, in accordance with their own ideas of justice — a license that was limited by a condition that none of the English should be interfered with, and that in case they should come into open conflict with the Podunks, no fighting should take place on the west side of the river. This was agreed to by the deputies, and the court adjourned.[1]

This was in accordance with Uncas's desire, whereupon he assembled a war-party with the purpose of invading the country of the Podunks. With his usual cowardice, being intercepted in the neighborhood of the Hockanum River by the enemy, whose numbers were apparently equal to his own, he decided that discretion was the better part of valor. After sending a message to the Podunk sachem that he would bring the Mohawks down

---

[1] *Colonial Records*, vol. i., pp. 304, 305.

upon him, Uncas made his way back to Mohegan. However, by means of a stratagem, he obtained the surrender of Weasepano.[1]

In the following year, 1657, Uncas again found himself threatened by the Narragansetts and the Nehantics, the number of whose fighting-men had been increased by detachments from the Pocomtucks and the Norwootucks, two Massachusetts tribes, who at the outset, with the assistance of some Pequods, surprised a canoeful of Mohegans and massacred them.[2] It was in this raid that Pessicus[3] made an invasion of the Mohegan country, and, driving Uncas into one of his fortresses, was in a way of finally getting him into his power.

---

[1] A Mohegan warrior supplied with Mohawk weapons was sent into the Podunk country, where he set fire to a wigwam under cover of the darkness. Dropping his weapons near the place, he quietly made his way back to his own people. The next day the Podunks left their fort to investigate the ruins, and possibly to discover some sign by which the incendiarist might be pursued. Seeing the weapons, they were at once satisfied that the Mohawks were out on a raid and that Uncas had begun to carry out his threat. They were so disturbed over the matter, and the possibility of having to maintain a dreaded war with the Iroquois, that they at once sent the murderer to Uncas and made peace with the Mohegans.

Dr. Dwight's *Travels*, vol. ii., p. 282.

[2] Hazard, vol. ii.

[3] Pessicus was a noted Narragansett sachem after the death of his brother Miantunnumoh. Before that, he was a Niantic sachem. Born in 1623, he was killed across the Maine border

WARS OF THE MOHEGANS

He probably would have succeeded had it not been for the appearance of a small party of English, which had been despatched by the Connecticut Colony to the relief of Uncas. Upon the approach of the English the Narragansetts at once retired; and the Mohegans, encouraged likewise, began a furious pursuit of the Narragansetts, overtaking many of them, whom they at once put to death.[1]

This quarrel grew out of the differences between Uncas and the Podunks, who were in a rage once they had discovered how easily they had been duped into surrendering Weasepano. Uncas again found himself in court to answer to the complaint of these two Massachusetts tribes, who alleged that Uncas had made war upon and driven their old friends the Podunks from their country. By the direction of the commissioners the government of Connecticut notified the Podunks to return to their country, and directed Uncas to let them alone. The Pocomtuck and Norwootuck sachems were informed of this proceeding, and were likewise enjoined from entering into any hostilities upon Uncas until the Court of the Commissioners should again convene.[2]

---

during the Indian wars which prevailed in that section of the country, by the Mohawks. He was known by the name of Pissacus, as well.
    Douglas-Lithgow, *Dictionary of American Indian Names.*
[1]*History of Norwich*, pp. 30, 31.
[2] Hazard, vol. ii., pp. 384, 385.

INDIAN WARS OF NEW ENGLAND

The result of this action could not but reveal to the English the futility of any attempt to harmonize these warring factions among the savages; for in 1658 the Mohegans were again invaded by practically the same confederation that had driven Uncas into his fort the previous year. The Mohegan sachem again took refuge in his fort,[1] while those besieging him made the serious mistake of committing some violence upon neighboring English settlements. Upon being informed that two of the settlers, Brewster and Thompson, had supplied the Mohegans with ammunition, and that Brewster, especially, had lent his house to some of the Mohegans as a temporary refuge, some musket-shots as well coming from the side of the river where Brew-

---

[1] "During the war between the Narragansets and Uncas, the former once besieged the fort of the latter, until his provisions were nearly exhausted, and he found that his men must soon perish, either by famine or the tomahawk, unless speedily relieved. In this crisis, he found means of communicating an account of his situation to the English scouts, who had been despatched from the fort in Saybrook to reconnoitre the enemy. Uncas represented the danger to which the English would be exposed, if the Narragansets should succeed in destroying the Mohegans. It was at this critical juncture that the greatest portion of the English troops in Connecticut were employed on an expedition abroad. A Mr. Thomas Leffingwell, however, a bold and enterprising man, on learning the situation of Uncas, loaded a canoe with provisions, and under cover of the night paddled from Saybrook into the river

WARS OF THE MOHEGANS

ster's house was located, their suspicions were aroused, and a few Pocomtucks forded the river to discover the source of these attacks. Not finding any one, they went to Brewster's house; and being balked in trying to gain entrance to the same, they repaid themselves for their trouble by carrying off a quantity of corn and some other property. The Pocomtuck sachem Annapecom reprimanded those engaged in this foray, and made them return the property so taken. Brewster, still dissatisfied, after the invading forces had retired, complained to the commissioners, who imposed a fine of forty fathoms of wampum upon the confederates. When that portion of the fine which was to be exacted of the Pocomtucks was levied upon their sachem, Annapecom made the following dignified response: "We desire the English sachems not to persuade us of a peace with Uncas, for we have experience of his

---

Thames, and had the address to get the whole into the fort. The enemy soon after, discovering that Uncas had received supplies, raised the siege. For this piece of service, Uncas presented Mr. Leffingwell with a deed of a very large tract of land, now comprising the whole town of Norwich."

Trumbull, *Indian Wars*, p. 62.

Trumbull states this as history. Drake quotes Rev. Wm. Ely, who regards it as a tradition of respectable origin, yet open to doubt.

Ely, *MS. Letter*.

Drake's *Book of the Indians*, vol. ii., p. 95.

falseness, and we know that if he promise much, he will perform nothing. Also, if messengers are sent to us from the English, we desire that they may not be liars and tale-bearers, but sober men and such as we can understand."[1] This last attempt terminates the invasions of the Mohegan country, and no more conflicts between the Mohegans and the Narragansetts are mentioned.

It is recorded that the restless spirit of Uncas would not allow him to observe a peaceful demeanor toward his neighbors for any length of time, and he was no sooner out of one complication than he became involved in another.

It was in August of this same year that some of his warriors killed a man and two women, savages of two Narragansett sachems who were tributary to the Massachusetts government. Other Mohegans made captive six Nipmucks, killing one and wounding another. The Narragansetts and the Nipmucks complained to the commissioners, before whom Uncas was ordered to appear at the next court; but with their usual compliance in all matters where Uncas was concerned, this was the last heard of that complaint.[2]

Possibly emboldened by this indifference of the commissioners, or impelled by a disposition for aggression, which seemed to have no bounds, in

---

[1] Hazard, vol. ii., pp. 396-423.
[2] *Ibid*, p. 388.

WARS OF THE MOHEGANS

1661 Uncas attacked the Quabaugs, a tribe of eastern Massachusetts, some of whom he killed and some of whom he made captives, despoiling their settlement and carrying off plunder which was estimated at thirty-three pounds sterling. The tribe attacked by Uncas was subject to Massasoit, who at this time was nearing the end of his career, having arrived at a ripe old age. Massachusetts, upon being informed of this raid, made immediate demand upon the Mohegans to restore the captives to liberty; and, as well, to return the property they had carried away. Uncas did not reply to this demand; and, the affair being some time after committed to the commissioners, John Mason was despatched to the Mohegans for satisfaction. Uncas, with his usual duplicity, responded that the previous order of Massachusetts had been received by him some twenty days before Mason's arrival, and he denied any knowledge of the Quabaugs being under the protection of the English, asserting that it was not a fact that they were tributary to Massasoit, but, on the other hand, they were the subjects of Onopequin, who was regarded by the Mohegans as one of their worst enemies. He excused himself with the assertion that Massasoit's people, along with Wamsutta, the eldest son of the Wampanoag sachem, had made many attacks upon the Mohegans, and that he had anticipated the demands of the English by giving the Quabaugs their liberty. This was the end of the matter; for it is evident that no further reparation was made upon the part of Uncas.[1]

In the years following, various regulations were adopted by the Connecticut government by which the intercourse between the Indians and the whites was to become more limited. The Indians were not allowed to live within a quarter of a mile of any English settlement; and if they brought their guns into the settlement they were to be confiscated. One tribe was not allowed to entertain wandering members of other tribes; and in no case was a strange Indian to be admitted to the settlements, unless fleeing from his enemy. Drunkenness prevailed among the savages, and the settlements were at times disturbed by their attempts to obtain liquor, and all Indians were forbidden to walk about the streets after nightfall, under penalty of a fine or flogging. The English were not allowed to take the property of an Indian for debt without consent, or upon legal warrant; and later it was enacted that such as trusted an Indian with goods were deprived of all right to appeal to law for the recovering of the same.[2]

It was during these years that the efforts for the Christianizing of the Indians were going on under the auspices of the Society for Propagating the Gospel in New England; and it is noted that at

---

[1] Hazard, vol. ii., pp. 450, 451.
[2] *Colonial Records*, vol. iii.

WARS OF THE MOHEGANS

this time the Mohegans, as well as the other Connecticut tribes, had little if any knowledge of Christianity, and were still to be regarded as among the heathen. Their practices were confined to their belief in God and other spirits. Charms, incantations, their dances and powwowings, were in conformity to their ancient superstitions. Under the teachings of Fitch, in 1674, the religious converts among the Connecticut Indians were estimated at thirty men and women and some few children. In 1671 Uncas was approached, and the permission of the sachems was gained, by which Mr. Fitch began his religious teachings at Mohegan, which was reported to the General Court of Connecticut. As an inducement to the Mohegans to receive Mr. Fitch, the General Court notified the Mohegans that all those who received the Christian religion would be especially favored, while those who opposed and rejected it would be afforded their displeasure — which is not suggestive of the meek and lowly spirit conveyed in the teaching of the Nazarene.

Whatever may have been the opinion as to the conversion of Uncas, the wish being doubtless father to the thought, contemporary writers upon this subject have held to the idea that the Mohegan sachem had a "theoretical belief in the doctrine of Christianity."[1]

---

[1] "In 1674, Daniel Gookin and John Eliot, while on a mis-

INDIAN WARS OF NEW ENGLAND

It is to be noted that in these last days of Uncas he was the leading spirit in all the warlike disposi-

---

sionary tour among the aborigines, came to a village of Christian Indians at Wabequasset in what is now the southeastern part of Woodstock. The two clergymen spent a great part of the night with the principal inhabitants praying, exhorting and singing psalms. There was one Indian present, a stranger, who took no part in the devotions, and for a long time remained silent. At last he rose and announced that he was a deputy of Uncas, sachem of Mohegan; and that in his name he challenged a right to, and dominion over, this people of Wabequasset. 'And,' he said to the two ministers, 'Uncas is not well pleased that the English should pass over Mohegan River to call his Indians to pray to God.'

"Gookin replied that Wabequasset was not subject to Uncas, but belonged under the jurisdiction of Massachusetts. And no harm need be feared, he continued, were it otherwise; for the only object of the English in preaching to the Indians is to bring them to a knowledge of Christ, and suppress among them the sins of drunkenness, idolatry, powwowing, witchcraft and murder. Gookin told the messenger to report this answer to his master; and he no doubt meant it, in part, as a lecture to the sachem upon his own habits and character. This circumstance took place nine years before the death of Uncas, and when he was already an old man of probably seventy summers. In another passage, Gookin mentions the Mohegan sachem as 'an old, wicked and willful man, a drunkard and otherwise vicious,' and tells us that he 'had always been an opposer and underminer of praying to God;' and he suspected him of being a great obstruction to the labors of Mr. Fitch."

DeForest, *History of the Indians of Connecticut*, pp. 276, 277.

WARS OF THE MOHEGANS

tions on the part of the Mohegans; that at the breaking out of King Philip's War, they, with the Pequods, remained loyal to the English. It was discovered by some of the settlers of Rhode Island, in the course of this war, that some of the Narragansetts disappeared at times, to return to their tribes wounded. Their conclusion was that the Narragansetts were friendly to Philip; and they were convinced of it upon the fact being made apparent that this tribe was sheltering Philip's old men, women, and children, and it was decided that an expedition should be made against the Narragansetts. A force of one thousand men was mobilized. One hundred fifty Mohegans and Pequods under the command of Oweneco and Catapazet, a son of Hermon Garret, went with this army against the Narragansetts. It was in mid-winter; and this expedition being entirely successful, the Pequods had the intense satisfaction of watching the Narragansett fortress disappear in fire and smoke, as their own had been destroyed years before.[1]

Canonchet was captured in this expedition; and of the Narragansetts, some fifty were killed and captured. Among these were the leading men of the Narragansetts. During the open season of this year the Narragansetts were practically driven out of their country.[2] Only the Nehantics remained,

---

[1] Hubbard's *Indian Wars*, pp. 129-144.

[2] Thus circumstanced and harassed by the Pequots, by the

INDIAN WARS OF NEW ENGLAND

by reason that they had taken no part in King Philip's War. It is recorded that of the Narragansetts in these various expeditions, two hundred thirty-nine were killed or captured; one hundred bushels of corn and fifty muskets were taken. The singular fact remains that not a single Englishman, Pequod, or Mohegan was killed or died of wounds in these various forays.

Among the prisoners taken by the Mohegans was a young warrior whose remarkable courage had singled him out for the torture, to which the English gave their consent. Hubbard says: "Lest their denial should disoblige their Indian friends, of whom they had lately made so much use; partly that they might have ocular demonstration of the barbarous cruelty of the heathen."[1]

English, who had evidently forgotten their aid in subduing the Pequots, the prey of the rapacious Mohegans, the Narragansetts appealed to the Crown. Charles II. received the agents of this unfortunate tribe, who besought the royal countenance and protection; nor was the appeal disregarded by the king, whose sympathies were not over-stirred in favor of his New England subjects. Instructions were despatched to the Royal Commissioners of New England to make a special inquiry into the case of the Narragansetts. They came, however, too late: the people over whom Canonicus had ruled were beyond relief. They had well-nigh ceased to exist; but their wrongs, by this appeal to the Great Father across the waters, had reached for them the court of last resort.

Freeman, *Civilization and Barbarism*, p. 79.

[1] "The young captive, unappalled by the dreadful fate

WARS OF THE MOHEGANS

Most of the captives were first given in charge of Uncas, but were finally withdrawn from his guardianship, to whom three hundred acres of land were assigned upon a point formed upon the junction of the Shetucket and Quinnebaug Rivers. Others were scattered among the Pequods; and it was about this time that one of the Shetucket Colony was killed, along with seven others who were employed by Mr. Fitch upon his Norwich farm. Uncas was suspected of the outrage, but, protesting

---

which awaited him, stood up, after the fashion of Indian warriors, and boasted his exploits. 'I have shot nineteen English with my gun. I loaded it for the twentieth. I could not meet another and let it fly at a Mohegan. I killed him and completed my number. Now I am fully satisfied.'

"The Mohegans formed a circle, and placed the victim in the center where all could gaze upon his tortures. They deliberately cut round one of his fingers at the joint, where it united with the hand, and then broke it off. They cut, in a similar manner, another and another, until only the stump of the hand was left. The blood flowed in streams, sometimes spirting out a yard from the wounds. Some of the English wept at the horrid sight, but no one interfered. The victim shrunk not from the knife and showed no signs of anguish. 'How do you like the war?' tauntingly asked his tormentors. 'I like it well,' he said; 'I find it as sweet as Englishmen do their sugar.' They cut off his toes as they had done his fingers, and then made him dance round the circle till he was weary. At last they broke the bones of his legs. He sank upon the ground, and sat in silence until they dashed out his brains."

DeForest, *History of the Indians of Connecticut*, pp. 284, 285.

his innocence, intimated that these crimes had been committed by some guerilla savages who occasionally were to be discovered wandering about the woods. In regard to this matter, Mr. Fitch wrote a letter to the General Court in which he said that Uncas "was even worse than before the war."[1]

This war with Philip was the ending of warfare upon the part of the Indians of Connecticut, especially among their own race. There may have been, here and there, some unimportant hostile actions, the last of which was in 1678, when the Mohawks made a raid upon the Mohegans. Several of Uncas's people were carried away captive, including one of his sons.[2] Mason died in 1672, and with his death seemingly passed away the necessity for further resort to force upon the part of the white people to keep the Indians within their proper bounds.

Uncas died in 1682 or 1683. Regarding this event very little is known. He was a man of

---

[1]*Indian Papers*, vol. i., docs. 32, 33.
[2]*Ibid*, doc. 37.

Uncas, one day conversing with Thomas Stanton of his own children, remarked that the three eldest were legitimate. "As for Ben Uncas, he *poquiom*," — is half-dog, his mother being a poor, beggarly squaw, not his wife. By common report, Ben's mother was the daughter of Foxon, his chief councillor.

Ibid, doc. 173, p. 57.

WARS OF THE MOHEGANS

marked and disagreeable characteristics, whose memory went back beyond the time when Adrian Block made his discovery of Rhode Island and Connecticut, and he died, doubtless, cherishing the traditions of his race.[1]

The Indian warriors in Connecticut in 1680 were estimated at five hundred, by which one infers that the total Indian population of Connecticut did not exceed, at that time, four to five times that number.

---

[1] "Mr. Washington Irving says, 'The Indian obeys the impulses of his inclination and the dictates of his judgment. The early records mention with great bitterness the doings of the Indians, and with strong approval the strides of civilization in the blood of the red man. They show us but too clearly how the white man was moved to hostility by the lust of conquest, and how merciless and exterminating was the warfare. Imagination shrinks at the idea how many intellectual beings were hunted from earth; how many brave and noble hearts of nature's sternest coinage were broken down and trampled in the dust. Treated by the colonists as if wild beasts of the forest, writers have endeavored to justify the outrage. The colonist found it easier to exterminate than to civilize; his apologists have found it easier to vilify the Indians than to discriminate. The appellations savage and pagan have been deemed sufficient to sanction hostilities; and thus the wanderers of the forest were persecuted and defamed, not because they were guilty, but because they were ignorant. . . . The rights of the savage have seldom been properly appreciated or respected by the white man. . . . A proud independence formed the main pillar of savage virtue; it has been shaken down, and the whole fabric lies in ruins.'"

INDIAN WARS OF NEW ENGLAND

It will be recalled that Trumbull, upon the coming of the English, estimates the Indian population of this section of the country from twelve to twenty thousand. This estimate, however, is not accepted by the conservative historian; and, as one writer has said, "It was founded in a large part upon tradition." DeForest notes that "on the death of Uncas all unity which our subject possessed, entirely disappears." Between the different tribes conflicts had ceased, and animosities were apparently buried; but the destruction of the Indians and the disintegration of the forces which combined to make these people a formidable obstacle to the settlement of the country were still perpetuated by the pandering of the English to their depraved appetites through the inordinate use of intoxicating liquors, despite all laws to the contrary; for the traders had the same liking for money that the savage had for rum. What the bullets of the English did not accomplish was ultimately arrived at in another and more reprehensible way.

How far the English race is responsible for the obliteration of the aborigine is not in question. It is more than probable that he would have fallen by reason of his own barbarism; and while the Indian never forgot a kindness or forgave an injury, his treachery and his cruelty to a conceived enemy were entirely consistent with his mode of living and his environment.

INDEX

INDEX

Abenake, 25, 31, 42, 45
Aborigine, estimation of, 176
Accomack, 111, note
Accomintas, 51, 174
Acquidneck (Rhode Island), 185, note
Acquidy, origin of name uncertain, 185, note
Adams on Indian titles, 63, note
Agamenticus, General Court of, 259, note
Agawams, attacked by the Tarratines, 170, note, 172, note, 348, note
    mentioned, 452, note
Agowaywam, 84, note
Agreement, tripartite, between Connecticut, the Mohegans, and the Narragansetts, 335
    with proviso, 337, 352
Ahab, mentioned, 287
"Akornes," dried for food, 104, note
Alden, John, 78, note
Alexander, 50; also 81, 121
Algonquin, 46, note
Algonquin trails, 264, note
Allerton, Isaac, 65, note
    at Pentagoët, 175
Alligwe, 26, note
Ameda, 32, note
Ammacongins, 42
Ancient and Honorable Artillery Company, 257, note
Androscoggin, 42
Anglo-Saxon, traditions of, 80
    folk-mote, 82, note
Annapecom, fined for raid on Brewster and Thompson, 469
    his reply to the court, 469
Ansantawae, 357
Antinomianism, 250, note, 424, note
Appanow (Epenow), see 129, note
Aramouchiquois, 42
Archipelagoes (Norwalk River), 184

[483]

INDEX

"Armour," 95, note
Arnold, Benedict, 434
Arrow-heads, 29, 106, note, 108, note
Ashquash, murders a woman at Fairfield, 427
Aspinet, 80, 125
Assacumet, 70, 73
Asson-neck, 30, note
Atherton, Lieutenant, 438, note
Attitude of English toward Indians that of spoilers, 175
Authorship of Mourt's *Relation*, 85, note
Awashonks, 50

Bagnall, Walter, 76; also note
"Barnes" of the Indians, 95
Barnstable, 51
Barricado, first built by Standish and his men, 95, 102, 103, 104, 105
Bashaba, The, 73, 264, note
Bay Colony, indifference of, to engaging in Pequod War, 245; also 227, 249, 290, 297
Bay-men, 239, note
Beacon Hill, 22, note
Beads, 98, 101
Beans, 41
Billington, John, 38, note, 124, 125
Bjarne, 29, note
Blackstone, William, 22, note, 102, note
Block, Adrian, Dutch explorer
    his vessel burned, 183
    builds another, 183
    names it the *Restless*, 183, note
    discovers Connecticut, 184
Block Island, 199, 208, 212, 216, 227, 228, 234, 249, 311, note
    expedition planned against, 227, 228
    Underhill's fight at, 228, note, 229, note
    could have but one result, 234
Blue Hills, 51, note
Bonighton at Saco, 174
Boston alarmed, 203, note, 410
    citizens of, armed and marched to Neponset, 203, note
    mentioned, 231, 232, 233
Boston Colony, as peace-makers, 203, note
Boston Harbor, Weston's party at, 134, 137, 143

INDEX

Boules, 98
Bound Brooke, 78, note
Bounty for Indian scalps, 170
Bow-strings, 32
Boyle, Robert, 371
Bradford, William, 62, 78, 89, 95, 102, 106, note, 193, 194, note, 210
    account of Hudleston's *Letter*, 139, note
    notes distress of Pilgrims in his *Journal*, 139, 140
    goes to Pemaquid for provisions, 140, note
    returns answer to hostile message of Canonicus, 142
    his and Winthrop's *Letters* on the Pequod War, 210-227
Branch, Arthur, 237, note
Brewster, Elder William, died, 65, note
Brewster, Fear, 65, note
Brewster and Thompson, settlers, attacked by Pocumtucks, 468
Bristol, Me., 77, note
Broches, 97
Brook, Lord, 205, note, 206, note, 251
Brown, John, 77, note, 110, note
    at Pemaquid, 174
Browne, James, 78, note
Bull, Lieutenant, at Fort Mystic, 275, note
Burdett, George, 259
Burial-places, 167
    Indian veneration for, 99, note
    mode of burial, 107, note
Burning at stake, 44, 45
Busheag, attacks a woman at Stamford, 427
    is surrendered to the English, 427
    executed, 428, note
Butterfield, Samuel, capture and torture of, 236, 237, 283, 295

Calendar, correction of, by Pope Gregory, 90, note
    Indian's, 31
Calumet, origin of, 158, note
Cambridge, Vane defeated for governor at, 250, note
Cammock, Thomas, at Black Point, 174
Cannibalism, 44, 45, note
Canonchet, 475
Canonicus, 21, 47, 48, 120, note, 129, 142, note, 192, note, 196, note, 208, 209, 231, 232, 233, 260, 416, 417

INDEX

Canonicus, sends message to Plymouth, 129
    declares war with English, 142
    afraid of English; accords them occult powers, 143
    breaks the sticks before Williams, 143, note
    goes to Boston, 233
    calls council of Narragansetts for extermination of English, 235, note
    reply to Roger Williams as to harboring Pequods, 320, note
    his entertainment of Williams, 321, note
    charges Uncas with duplicity, 321, note
    conference with Williams, Miantunnumoh, and Cassasinamon, 322, note
    disposition toward English, 347
    with Miantunnumoh, exonerated of Oldham murder, 347, note
    his warlike message to Bradford mentioned, 347, note, 416, 417
Capawack, island of, 84, note
Capawick, 71, 72
Cape Ann, Conant goes to, 192, note
Capemanwagen, 77, note
Capoge, 73
Carolinas, 318
Cartier, Jacques, 31, 32, note, 46, note, 69
Carver, John, 102
Casacke (blouse), 99
Casco Bay, 77, note
Cassasinamon, 447, 449
    with Obechiquod complains of Uncas, 449
Catapazet, 475
Caunacone, 129, note
Cellars, aboriginal, 94, note
Chabatewece, 326, note
Chalons, Henry, 70
Champlain, Samuel de, 38, note, 46, note, 124
Chapman, Robert, 237, note
Charity, The, and *The Swan*, in Plymouth Harbor, 143
    in interest of Weston, 143
Charles II., 250, note
Charlestown, 348
Charon's Ferry-boat, 292, note
Charter of Runnymead, 83, note
Chatham, 51

INDEX

Checatawbeck, 151
Chikatawbut, 106, note, 129, note
   his mother's grave, description of, 97
   his harangue to his people after the desecration of his mother's grave, 107, note
   instigates butchery of English, 155
Chimough, 431
Christian faith among Indians, meager influence, 369
Church commission, 232, note
Citackamuckqut, 326, note
Cleve, George, ejected from Spurwink, 174
Coddington, William, 325, note
Coins, ancient, found in Dorchester, 136
Coke, Sir Edward, 261, note
Collier, William, 403
Colonies, action of, in Pequod War, 248
Colonists, rejoice at destruction of Fort Mystic, 291
   frequently alarmed by rumors of savage raids, 348, note
Common House at Plymouth takes fire, 108
Conant, Roger, goes to Cape Ann, 192, note
Conbatant, 149
Coneconum, 72
Conectecott, 240, note, 241, note
Conightecute, 211, 213
Conightecutte, 220
Conighticutt, 226
Conjurors, 129, note
Connecticut, mentioned, 184, 186, 189, 193, 198, note, 204, 205, 206, 207, 227, 229, 244, 246, note, 290, 420, 467, 472
   estimated number of aborigines, 52
   settlers suspicious of Miantunnumoh, 381, note
   inclined to war with Narragansetts, 383, note
   advice of Massachusetts regarding, 383, note
   alarmed by the Narragansetts conspiracy, 454
   restricts intercourse with the Indians by legal enactment, 472
   Indian census of 1680, 479
Connecticut coast, 184, 197
Connecticut Colony
   comprised of Windsor, Hartford, and Wethersfield, 244
   settlers afflicted with poverty, 245, 246, 247
   decides war against Pequods, 246
Connecticut Court, 244

INDEX

Connecticut River, 186, 188, note, 190, note, 191, 192, 193, 194, 198, 199, 207, 228, 241, note, 248, 251, 281, 288, 311, 313, 343, 353, 364, 388
Connecticut River Indians, 343
Connecticut settlers, 282
Connecticut Valley, 186, 191, 196
Cook, Wequash. *Vide* Wequash
   betrayed Fort Mystic, 328
   described by Mather, 328, note
   supposed to have died of poison, 329, note
   captain under Miantunnumoh, 329, note
   a Pequod spy, 351
   his band broken up, 363
Copper knives, 41
Corbitant, 49, 126, 127, 129, note
   eludes Standish, 128
Corn of Indians, taken by Bradford and Standish, 94, 95, 102, note
   seed-ears, 94, note
Corstiaensen, Dutch explorer, 183
Cotton, Rev. John, 51, note
   his estimate of Roger Williams, 232, note
Court of Commissioners for United Colonies
   its personnel, 403
   aroused by a letter from Roger Williams, 437
   to despatch a company to Mohegan Garrison, under Mason, 438
   Drake's account of this expedition, 438, note
   sends two messengers to Pessicus, 438
Covenant of Works, 325, note
Cowate, 375, note
Cradock, Governor, message to Endicott, 165
Cromwell, Israel Stoughton commander under, 293, note
Cudworth, James, 78, note
Cullicutt, Serjeant, 441, note
Cummaquid, 38, note, 124, 125
Cushammakin, Cutshamequin, Cutshamoquen, 322, note, 347, note
Cutchamekin, 438, note
Cutshamekin, 173, note
Cutshamoquene, 322, note
Cuttaquin, attempts to kill Uncas, 456, note
   captured by John Mason, 456
   delivered to the Mohegans, 457

INDEX

Damariscotta, shell-heaps of, 27, 29
Dames, John, 434
Davenport, Lieut. Richard, 293, note
  on the march to Fairfield Swamp, 305
  engages the Pequods and is repulsed, 306, 307
Davenport, Nathaniel, 307, note
Davis, Sergeant John, 438, note
Death-song, 45
Deerfield, 270
Dehamda, 70
Delaware Bay, 183
Delawares, 26, note, 35
Denonville, 49
De Razier, the Dutch factor, 204, note
  visits Plymouth; opens a trade in wampum with Pilgrims, 204, note
Dermer, Capt. Thomas, 74, 93, note
  account of coming to Cape Cod, 74
  redeems Frenchman at Masstachusit, 122, note
Dighton Rock, 28, note, 29, note
Dike, Anthony, 238, note
Discovery, The, arrives at Plymouth, 144
Distance from Plymouth Harbor to Boston by water, 131, note
"Dogge," Indian, 90
Dogs, suggested for hunting Indians, 170
Donnacona, 69
Dorchester, 206, 208, note
Dorchester church removed to Windsor, 207
Dudley, Gov. Thomas, 380, note, 403
Dutch, The,
  navigators, 183
  fort at Hartford, 194, 195
  courage, 195, note
  oppose Holmes on the Connecticut, 198, note
  lose their trade on the Connecticut, 200, note
  mentioned, 200, 210, 242, 253, 254
  use stratagem to obtain two English girl captives, 261, note
  their traders cheat the Indians, 422
  savages retaliate; two Dutchmen killed, 422
  the Indians punished in turn; Dutch settlements attacked by Indians in force, 423
  expedition from New Amsterdam against Indians, 423

INDEX

Dutch, soldier kills Captain Patrick, 425, note
  war between, and Indians closed, 426

Eastham, 39, note
East River, Guilford, 377
Eaton, Governor, friendly to Indians, 359
Eaton, Theophilus, 403
Eencluys, Hans, of Manhattan, 185
Egyptians, mentioned, 97
Eliot, John, 124, note, 166
  his Bible, 271, note
  and Mayhew's efforts to Christianize the Indians, 370
  completes second edition of English Bible, 371
  writes Robert Boyle, 371
  his first attempt to Christianize the Indian, 372, note
  first meeting in Waban's wigwam, 373, note
  described by Drake, 373, note
  first mission at Natick, 373, note
  his work designated by Ellis, 376
  vide 473, note
Eltow, Jack, 316, note
Ely, Rev. William, 469, note
Embaulment, red Powder, 99
Endicott, John, 22, 63, note, 227, note, 228, note, 282, note
England, William, 77, note
English, begin career at Plymouth by robbing the natives, 93, note
  supposed by Indians to be in collusion with evil spirits, 129
  vindictiveness of the, 293
  their advantage over the savage, 295
  their incentives to retaliation, 295
  their characteristics, 296, 297
  determine upon the annihilation of the Pequods, 299
  prowess boasted of by Mather, 330, note
  capacity to drive a stiff bargain, 337
  sowing to the winds, 338
  enslaving the Indian a mania with them, 339, note
  Mather's fervor instanced, 339, note
  attitude of the Indians toward the, 343
  policy of, with Narragansetts, notes on, 343, 344
  their religious belief in "Divine Rights" to New England, 344, note
  causes of savage activities against, 344

INDEX

English, their alliances with the Indians of an entangling character, 344
    plot with Uncas the downfall of Miantunnumoh, 346, note
    have trouble at Sowams with the Narragansetts, 348, note
    timidity of, 408
    greed of, 411
    order Narragansetts, Mohegans, and Niantics before magistrates, 434
    plan a campaign against the Narragansetts, 437
    expedition against Narragansetts delayed until results of treaty are known, 440, note
    aroused by rumors of plotting of Narragansetts and Pequods, 458
    declare war against the Nehantics, 462
    give command to Major Willard, 462
    intend to destroy power of Ninigret, 463
Enslaving of the Pequods, 293
Epanow, Epenwe, Epenow, Gorges' account of, 72, 73, 74
    escape, 75
Escholl, 95
Etow, Jack, captures two Pequods, 303

Fairfax, Sir Thomas, 245, note
Fairfield, 289, 357
Fairfield Swamp, 177
Famine pinches Plymouth, 139
Farmington Stream, 194
Fenwick, John, 403
Finch, Abraham, 364, note
First Encounter, The, 105
Fisher's Island, 452
Fish-hooks, 138
Fitch, James, mentions Uncas, 247, note
Fitch, missionary, 473, 474
    efforts of, to Christianize Mohegans, 473
    writes General Court of Uncas, 478
Five Nations, 27, note
Florida, 264, note
Fort Mystic, attacked and destroyed by Mason, 177, 271
Fortune, The, 142
Foxon, a deputy of Uncas, 446, note, 450
    defends Uncas, 452

INDEX

Freeman, John, 77, note
French vessel cast away at Cape Cod, 92, note
Fresh River, 196, note
Frontenac, 15
Fryeburg, Me., 85, note

Gallop, John, 292, note, 339, note
    John, the son, 292, note
Gallup, "Skipper," 339, note
Gardener, Lion, 229, 230, 251, note, 252, note
    relation of attack on party at Saybrook Fort, 237, note
    relation of Miantunnumoh's plotting, 384, note, 385, note, 386, note
Gardener's Island, 252, note
Gardener's Manor, Lords of, 252, note
Gardiner, Richard, 87, note
Garret, Hermon, 454, 475
Gauntlet, running the, 47
Gibbons, girls of that name killed by savages, 242, note
Gibbons, Major, elected commander-in-chief of forces sent against the Narragansetts, 439
    his instructions, 439, note
Godfrey, at York River, 174
Gookin, Daniel, 473, note
Gorges, Sir Ferdinando, 70, 72
Gorton, Samuel, 350, note, 400; also 415
    driven from Plymouth, 400
    settled at Warwick, 400
    writes Uncas, 400
    effect of his letter, 401
    Winthrop's comment on same, 402
    his offence outside Massachusetts jurisdiction, 401, note
    entertained by Earl of Warwick, 401, note
    demands release of Miantunnumoh, 401
    vide, 402, note
    Parliament sustains his contention against the Puritans, 416, note
Gouch, John, 259, note
Gouch, Ruth, 259, note
Grampus, at Wellfleet Bay, 103
Graves of Indians desecrated by Standish, 97
Great Lakes, tribes about, 40
Great Patent of New England, 64

INDEX

Great Spirit, 445
Greenwich, 423
Gregson, Thomas, 403
Groton, 43, 246, note
Guilford Harbor, 302
Gulf of Maine, 34

Hampden, John, 205
Hanging of the weaver at Wessaguscus, 145
    Morton's account of same, 146-148
Harford (Hartford), 243, note
Harley, Henry, 72
Harlow, Captain Edward, 71
    kidnapped three Indians, 71
Hartford, 179, 186, 242, 244, 246, 249, note
    Indian fort at, 184
    General Court at, 243
    establishes quota for Pequod War, 245
Hartford Commission, 331
    Uncas and Miantunnumoh attend upon, 331
    its attempt to reconcile Uncas and Miantunnumoh, 334
Hawkins, the buccaneer, 99, note
    at Pamlico, 264, note
Haynes, John, 335
Head of the Mystic, 268
Heathen, savages so regarded by Puritans, 300, note
Heckwelder, 25, note
Hellegat (Hell-gate), 184, note
Hell-gate, 184, note
Heydon, William, 271
Hieroglyphic writings, 23, 29, note, 31
Higginson, Rev. Francis, 66, 67, note
    his book, 67, note
Hilton, at Piscataqua, 174
Hinckley, Thomas, 78, note
Hine, Thomas, 445
Hobbamocco, 58
Hobbomock's feat at Wessaguscus, 158
    vide 125, 126, note, 150, note
Hobbomok, 125, 126, 127, 128, 153, 155, 157
    warns the English, 84, note
Hobbomoko, 116, note

INDEX

Hobson, Captain, 73
Hockanum River, 186, 465
Holmes, William, 186
  goes to the Connecticut River, 193
  opposed by the Dutch at Hartford, 194
  erects a trading-house, 194, note
  his return to Plymouth, 196, note
  Pequods affronted by his purchase of land from their enemies, 197, 338
Hood, Robin, 64, note
Hopkins, Edward, 335, 403
Hopkins, Stephen, 36, note, 37, note, 89
  Samoset lodged with when at Plymouth, 112
House of The Good Hope, 187
Hubbard's account of the capture of a small body of Pequods by Stoughton, 292
"Hudibras," Butler's, 145
Hudleston's letter to the Plymouth Colony, 139, note
Hudson, Hendrick, 184, note
Hudson River, 183, 188, note, 318
Hunt, Captain, 39, note, 68, 114, note
  his kidnapping raid, 114, note, 116, note
Hurlburt, Thomas, 238, note, 316, note
Hutchinson, Ann, murdered by the Indians, 423
  her Boston house located, 423
  her banishment, 424, note
  lived at Acquidneck, 424, note
  removed into the Dutch country, 424, note
  her zeal, her friends, 425, note
Hutchinson set, 48
Hutchinson's account of the enslaving of the Pequods, 339, note
Huttamoida, 129, note
Hyde's account of the battle of Sachem's Plain and the capture of Miantunnumoh, 394, note

Increase of English population after 1626, 171
Indian, The, 22
  language, 22
  music, 22
  picture-painting, 23, 31
  his traditions, 24
  picture-writing, 24, note, 25, note

INDEX

Indian, The, arts, 26
    superstitions, 28
    literature, 30, 31
    letter-paper, 31
    character and attainments, 32, 176
    spun his thread from the spruce, 33
    mint-masters, 35
    habits, 36, 37, 40, 57
    physique, 38
    mood, 39
    implements, 40
    agriculture, 41
    laws, 42
    cannibalism, 44
    mode of torture, 45, 47
    scalping, 46, note
    government, 54
    Thomas Lechford's description of, 54
    weapons, 57
    religion, 58
    treatment of, by English, 63, note, 79, 82, 95, note
    land-titles from, 63, note, 64, note, 166-168
    absorption of lands of, by English, 67
    Indian "corne," 92, 93
    seed corn, 94, note
    burial-places, 99
    veneration of same, 100
    habitations, 103
    sold as slaves, 114, note
    garb, 121, note
    doomed race, 165
    their right to the soil, 166
    as to the rights of others, 196, note
    their highways, 264, note
    manner of fighting, 278
    attitude of the Church toward, 299, note
    a superstitious race, 369, note
    Christian faith among, 369, note
    traditions, transmission of, 369, note
    comity as to disposition of lands, 405
    habits were changing, 419
    laws for the restraint of; fines established, 420, 421, 472

INDEX

Indian, The, settlers forbidden to entertain, 420, 472
    inordinate appetite for liquors, 421
    penalty for selling liquor to, 422
    attack of, on Dutch settlers in 1642, 422
    curious instance of torture by, 445
    addicted to gambling, 448
    efforts to Christianize the, 472
Indian Bible, 371, note
Ingram, marooned at Pamlico, 264, note
Initial labors of New England colonists, 175
    their distribution, 174
Iroquois, 35, 44
Irving, Washington, description of the Indian, 479
Iyanough, 84, note, 125

James, the King, 118, 120
James-the-Printer, 371, note
    his descendants known in Grafton, 372
Janemoh, Janemo (Ninigret), 265, note, 323, note
    is entertained by Winthrop at Boston, 323, note
Jaques, Lieutenant, 24, note
Jeffery (and "Sargante Rigges"), 223
Johnson, Edward, 146
    mentioned, 229
Jones, Captain, 88, note, 144

Kennebec (River), 216
Kennebequi, 42
"Ketle," great, Standish takes it, after filling with corn, 94
Kichomiquim (Cutshamequin), 230, note, 312
Kievet's Hook, 185
    origin of name, 185, note
King Philip, 343
    his war, 476
    remarkable fortunes of English in Narragansett expedition, 476
    his downfall ended Indian troubles, 478
Kings, 58
Kiswas, captured by Uncas, 251
    who he was, 252, note
    tortured by the Mohegans, 253, note
Kitan, 58
Kithansh, 334

INDEX

Lalemant, 46, note
Laudonnière, 46, note
Laws enacted affecting Indian, 420
    fines established, 420, 472
    settlers forbidden to entertain Indians, 420, 472
    Uncas and Wawequa excepted, 421
    forbid Indians to trade with French or Dutch, 421
Lee, Lord, 226
Leffingwell, Thomas, 432, note, 468, note
Leif, 29, note
Leni-Lenape, 25, note
Lescarbot, 46, note
"Lether," Indian, 104, note
Levett, Christopher, 77, note
Little Compton, 50
Lobsters, 131
Lockett, Moll, 84, note, 85, note
Long Island Sound, 184, 188, note, 311, 318
Louis XIV., ambitious schemes of, 49, 75
Lovewell's Pond, battle of, 85, note
Ludlow, Deputy-Governor, receives Pequod messenger, 201
    demands the murderer of Stone, 202
    enters into a treaty with the Pequods, 202
    mentioned, 223
Ludlow, Roger, 64, note, 335

Maize, 41
Manana, 29
Manasconomo, his submission, 170, note, 175, note
Manhattan, 183, 204, 259, note
Manisees, 208, 292, note, 318
Manitou, 28
Manittos, 362
Manomet, 84, note, 159
Mascus, 350, note
Mashpee, 51
Mason, John, 164, 239, 241, note, 245, note, 312
    advances into Pequod country, 250
    commander-in-chief, 251, 255
    holds conference with his men, 257
    leaves decision to chaplain as to immediate advance, 257
    decides to march against Pequods, 257

INDEX

Mason, John, joined by Underhill, 257
    leaves Saybrook, 258
    interviews Canonicus, 260
    attitude of Miantunnumoh, 260
    renews march into Pequod country, 263
    at Nehantic fort, 264
    joined by the Narragansetts, 265
    discovers signs of the Pequods, 266
    fords Paucatuck River, 267
    camps at Porter's Rocks, 268
    plans advance, 270
    advance on Pequods at daylight, 269, note, 271
    the surprise and attack, 271
    Pequod fort given to the torch, 272
    massacre of the Pequods, 272; also note
    his dangerous position, 275
    saved by his helmet, 275
    attacked by Sassacus, 276
    describes manner of Indians in battle, 278
    joins Stoughton in final campaign against Pequods, 278
    retreat from Fort Mystic, 280
    joins Patrick on the vessels, 280
    return to Connecticut, 281
    criticised for his barbarous treatment of Pequods, 282
    his idea of punishment of the Pequods, 282, note
    his action justified, 284
    Johnson's relation of march to Fairfield Swamp, 304
    discovers Sassacus's hiding-place, 305
    fight at Fairfield Swamp, 306-310
    goes to the Nehantics, 323, note, 351
    sent to the Nehantics, 351, note
    ordered to march against the Nehantics, 438
    mentioned, 471
    died in 1672, 478
Massachusetts, 246, 249, note
Massachusetts, The, 51
    origin of the name, 51, note
    alleged plot of, against Plymouth, 149
Massachusetts Bay, 189, 197, 231, note, 290, note
    not averse to slave traffic, 319, note, 324, note, 350, note
Massachusetts Bay Colony, 83, note, 204, 205, 214
    notified of conditions in Connecticut, 246

INDEX

Massachusetts Bay Company, 175
Massachusetts Colony sends vessels to the Connecticut River, 191
    mentioned, 231, 248
Massachusetts Fields, 131
Massacre of French sailors at Peddock's Island, 136
Massasoit, 21, 36, note, 37, note, 47, 48, 51, 62, 66, note, 77, 81, 84,
    note, 96, note, 102, 116, note, 120
    gives land to English, 66
    gives hostages, 118, 123
    is entertained by the Pilgrim governor, 119
    described by Morton, 120
    his decease, 121, note
    leaves Plymouth, 122
    mentions no English as coming before Pilgrims, 122, note
    visited by English, 124
    mentioned, 125, 127, 128
    demands surrender of Squanto, 137, 138, note
    his friendship for the English cools, 141
    healed by Winslow, 152
    generous of his lands, 168
    vide 417
Massasoits, The, 112
Masson, Captaine (John Mason), 223
Masstachusit, 122, note
"Matchit" (evil), English manner of fighting, 279
Mather, Cotton, 39, note
    mentions fight at Fort Mystic, 274, note
Mather, Rev. Increase, 50, note, 81, 82, 84, note, 292, 299, note,
    300, note
    his perturbations of spirit, 299, note
    his comment on the Fairfield Swamp fight, 313, note
"Matt" found by Standish, 97
Mattabesett (Middletown), 359
Mattachees, 51
Mattachiest, 84, note
Maunamoh, 322, note
Mausaumpous, 334
Mavericke, Samuel, 22, note
Mawhawkes (Mohawks), 430, note
Mayflower, The, 39, note, 61, 64, 90, 93, note, 95, 123, 144
Mayflower Compact, 64, 65
May-pole at Merry-Mount, 172

INDEX

May-pole, revelries at, 146
Meanticut, 385, note
Mecumeh (Miantunnumoh), 349, note
Medicine-man, 28, 129, note
Mengwe, 25, note, 27
Menunkatucks, 52
Menunketuc, 301
Merchants' Adventurers' Company, 63, 137
Merrimacs, 382
Merry-Mount, 22, 86
    Morton, Thomas, of, 145
Metacomet, 48
Mettapoisett, 128
Mewhebato, 364, note
Mexam, 440
Mey, the Dutch explorer, 183
Miamis, 44, note
Miantunnumoh, 48, 120, note, 189, note, 192, note, 209, 233, 247, note, 248, note, 249, note, 260, 265, note
    complains to the Boston government of the Nehantics, 322, note
    his allotment of Pequods, 325, note
    sells land to Coddington, 325, note
    attends conference at Hartford, 331
    threatened by Mohegans, 332
    at Hartford, 332
    controversy with Uncas, 333
    invites Uncas to feast, 334
    described by Hubbard, 334, note
    has permission from Winthrop to right his own wrongs with Mohegans, 340
    and Canonicus exonerated of complicity in murder of Oldham, 347, note
    assumes leadership of Narragansetts, 348
    known as Mecumeh, 348
    generous with his lands, 349
    depredations by the Narragansetts, 349
    his errand to Boston, 350
    visits Boston, 1640, 379, 380, note
    summoned to Boston, 380
    his behavior and success, 381
    demands his accusers, 381, 382, note
    guest of Governor Winthrop, 383, note

INDEX

Miantunnumoh, takes suspected Pequod to Boston, 384, note
  latter's story disbelieved, 385
  ordered to deliver the suspect to Uncas, 385
  kills the Pequod on his way homeward, 385
  complains of aggression of Uncas to Governor Haynes; also to Governor Winthrop, 390
  plans to punish Uncas, 391
  attacks the Mohegans, 391
  number of his fighting-men, 392
  compelled to retreat, 394
  betrayed by two of his men, 395
  is captured, 395
  is silent before his captor, 396
  his attitude toward Uncas, 397
  taken to Hartford, 397
  to be disposed of as the Boston magistrates order, 397
  Drake's relation of his capture, 397, note
  has the sympathy of Connecticut settlers, 399
  appeals to Hartford authorities, 402
  his trial at Boston, 403
  court is inclined to shift responsibility, 403
  and leave question of guilt to clergy, 404
  final sentence characterized, 404, note
  its farcical character, 404-406, 407, note
  convicted under false pretenses, 406
  clergy declare his death necessary, 406
  decision of commissioners, 408
  Drake's review of the case, 409, note
  provision for safety of New Haven commissioners, 411
  delivered to Uncas, 412
  murdered by Wawequa, 413
  place of his murder and burial, 413
Michell, Mr., 243
Michell, old Mr., 237, note, 238, note
Micmacs, 31, 42
Middleborough, 50
Middletown, 359
Midnight alarm at Wellfleet Bay, 104
Minci (Monseys) The, 26, note
Minisink, 26, note
Mint-masters, 35
Mishawam, 22, note

INDEX

Mitteneague (Windsor), 206
Mohawks, 44, 52, 53, 311, 312, note, 318
    surprise and kill Sassacus and his party, 316
    send his scalp to the Massachusetts governor and council, 316; also note
Mohegans, 43, 169, 246, note, 247, note, 248, note, 318, 322
    acts of cannibalism doubted by Drake, 253, note
    at Fort Mystic, 273, 277
    release rights to Pequod lands, 337
    their wars, 343
    increased by Pequod accessions, 376
    their title to Pequod lands questioned, 378
    controversy over former conveyance by Uncas, 378
    maintain a guerilla warfare with the Narragansetts, 428
    the tribe weakened, 458
    have little knowledge of Christianity, 473
    mission work by Fitch among, 473
Mohicans (Hudsons), The, 26, note
Monchiggon (Morathiggon, Monhegan), sagamores, or lords of, 110, 138, 139
Monhansick, 439
Monheag, 461
Monhegan, 29, 68, 72
Monhiggs (Mohegans), 226
Monomoys, 51
Mononotto, 255, 288
    his wife and daughters, 225, 316
    escapes with Sassacus, 310
    Drake's account of this sachem, 310, note
    children of, 311
    known as Monowattuck, 313, note
    escapes from the Mohawks, 315
Monowattuck, same as Mononotto
Mon-taup, 14, note, 48, note, 84
Montowese, 357, note
Montville, 246, note
Monuments, 28
Morathiggon, a Mohegan sachem, 394
Morton, Thomas, 22, note, 76, 145, note; also 86, 98, note, 145
    his *New English Canaan*, 145
    account of Wessaguscus, 146
    its famous trial, 146

INDEX

Morton, Thomas, relates hanging of the weaver, 146–148
    mentioned, 172
Morton, William, complains of Uncas, 446
Morton's *Relation*, quoted, 87, 102, note
Mount Hope, same as Mon-taup, 14, note, 48, 84, 345, 372, note
Mourning, manner of, 55
Mourt's *Relation*, authorship of, 85, note, *et seq.*
Mowhakes (Mohawks), 226
Mugg, 76, note
Munisses (Manisees), 212
Mystic, the Indian a, 33
Mystic Fort, 312, 321, note
    site of, 287, note
Mystic River, exploration of, by Standish, 133

Nacook Brook, 159, note
Nahanada, 70, 74, 75
Nahicans (Nehantics), 184, note
Nahiggonticks (Narragansetts), 188, note
Namaskeags, 452, note
Namasket, 126, 128
Namaskets, 50
Nanasquionwut, 334
Nanepashemet, 132
    his grave, 132
    widow of, 132, 133
    power of, 133, note
    Standish finds his village deserted, 133, note
    his house at Rock Hill, 133, note
    killed by the Tarratines; house described, 133, note
Nanepashemets, The, 117, note
Nanohiggansets (Narragansetts), 387, 390, note
Nantasket, 192, note
Napoitan, 78, note
Nariganset Indians, 222
Narigansets (Narragansetts), 210, 211, 218, 219, 220, 226, 231
Narragansett, 256, 258, 260, 262, 265
Narragansetts, 34, 35, 43, 47, 48, 49, 129, 169, 187, 189, note, 199,
    note, 209, 229, note, 234, note, 235, note, 244, 248, 249,
    253, note, 257, 261, 263, 267
    rumored conspiracy of, against Plymouth Settlement, 127, note
    appear about Neponset, 203, note

INDEX

Narragansetts, afraid, at Fort Mystic, 270
    join in massacre of the Pequods, 274
    after fight, turn homeward, 275
    reëngage the Pequods, 277
    Mason aids them, 278
    Underhill, also, 279
    object to being left in the Pequod country, 281
    intentions of Pequods against, 285
    errand of Roger Williams to, 320
    English indifference to, apparent, 323
    radical difference between them and Mohegans, 331
    accuse Pequods and Mohegans of robbery, 332
    release rights of conquest to Pequod lands, 337
    jealousies between them and Mohegans, 344
    approval of Uncas by English arouses their suspicions, 346
    at Neponset, 347
    their disposition toward the English, 350, note
    natural foes of Pequods, 376
    defeated by Mohegans at battle of the Great Plain, 394
    their sachem captured, 394
    unsuspicious of duplicity of commissioners, 399, note
    trial and murder of Miantunnumoh, 403-413
    made annual pilgrimage to the scene of Miantunnumoh's death, 413
    their sorrow at the death of Miantunnumoh, 414
    the *particeps criminis*, 415
    notified not to molest Uncas, 416
    offer of peace, extended to, by English, 416
    threaten Uncas, 417
    hatred for Mohegans grows, 417
    Pessicus becomes leading sachem, 418
    their reply to Winthrop's answer to overtures of Pessicus, 418
    their resentment aroused, 418
    habits of Indians undergoing change, 419
    women and children of English fear the savages, 419
    English enact stringent laws to control the savages, 420
    at war with Mohegans, 428
    Pessicus summoned to Hartford to meet Uncas, 428
    complain to commissioners at Hartford, 429
    compelled to sign agreement not to molest Mohegans, 430, note
    hostilities again renewed against Mohegans, 431
    attack Mohegan fort on the Thames River, 432

INDEX

Narragansetts, attack abandoned, 432
    a later invasion stopped by appearance of English, 433
    conspire with Mohawks against Mohegans, 454
    conspiracy fails, 455
    friendly to King Philip, 475
    appeal to the Crown, 475, note
    as a nation practically destroyed, 476
    torture of a Narragansett warrior, 476, note
Narragansett Bay, 184, 188, note, 192, note, 196, note, 343
Nashacowam, 173
Nashuas, 51, 451, note, 452, note
Nassau Bay, 184
Natick, first mission established at, 373, note
    rules for conduct of converted Indians at, 374, note
Nations, The Five, 27, note
Nattawahunt, 129, note
Naumkeags, 51
Nauset, locality, 79, note, 84, note, 107, note, 129
Nausets, 38, note, 106, note, 125, 129
Nausibouck, 334
Nawaas, 184, note
Nawwashawenck, assaulted Pumham, 350, note
Nehantic, 264
    fort at, 264
    visited by Mason, 323, note
Nehantics, 52; also 184, note, 119, 319
    to avoid Patrick and Mason, abandon their village, 281
Nepaupuck, his trial and execution, 364, note
    accused of murdering Finch, 364, note
    jurisdiction of New Haven Colony questioned, 365, note
    convicted and beheaded, 365, note
Nepenett sachems, 225
Neponset, 203, note
Neponsets, 51
Nesutan, Job, 372, note
New Amsterdam, 256
    Thanksgiving at, 426
New Brunswick, 264, note
New Canaan, quoted, 146, 148, 161, note
New England Charter, 191
New England Coast, 197
New England Company, Endicott's *Letter* to, 63, note

INDEX

New Hampshire, 259, note
New Harbor, 71, 77
    Pemaquid Point, 70, 140, note
New Haven, 302
    settlers of, 356
New Haven Bay, settlement of, 353
    consideration for land about, 354
    settlers, 356
Newichawannock, 174
Newichawannocks, 51
New London, 188, note, 246, note, 287, 351, 352
New Netherlands, Manhattan to be capital of, 184, note
New Plymouth, 205
Newtowne, 206
    colonists go to Connecticut, 207
Niantics (Nehantics), 199, note, 246, note, 318, 319, 322, note, 324
Ninicraft, 457, note
    visits the Mohicans, 461
    solicits their aid against Uncas, 461
    continues his quarrel with the English, who declare war against him, 462
Ninigratt, 435, note
Ninigret, 199, note, 252, note, 264, 265, note, 319, 323, note, 351, 357, note
    his treatment of the government messengers, 436
    goes to Boston, 456
    denies Cuttaquin's charges, 456
    dismissed by magistrates with threats, 457
Nipmucks, 51, 52, 451, note
    located, 457
    raided by the Mohegans, 470
Nobsquassetts, 51
No-ke-chick ("parched-corn-meal"), 114
Nonantum, 375, note
Nonantums, 51
Norridgewock, 40
Norse Occupation, 29, note
North Shore, 290
North Stonington, 246, note
Norton, Captain, killed, 198, 207
Norwalk Indians, sell land to Roger Ludlow, 64, note
Norwalk River, 184

INDEX

Norwootucks, 466
Nyantick Peacots, 430, note

Obbatinewat, 132, 133, note
Obbatinua, 129, note
Obechiquod, complains that Uncas has taken his wife from him,
    446, note, 448, 449, 450
Obtakiest, 149, 160
    the fate of his people, 161
    his embassy to Plymouth, 162
Ocquamehud, 129, note
Oldham, John, 193, 209, 210, 212, 233, 235, note, 283, 295
    butchery of, 189, 192, note, 208, note
Oldom (Oldome, Oldham), John, 212
Oliver, Mrs., whipped, 425, note
Oneko, cannibalism of, 413, note
Onopequin, 471
Oompaum, 111, note
Osemequon, Oosamequin, Massasoit joins in conveyance of Rhode
    Island lands, 326, note
"Owanux! Owanux!" alarm-cry of Pequods at Fort Mystic, 271
Oweneco, 475

Pakemit, 375, note
Pakonokick (Pawkunnawkutt, Pokonoket), 124, note
Pamlico, 99, note
Paniese, 125, note
Panises, 157
    description of, 158, note
Pankapogs, 51
Paomet, 84, note
Parnall, William, 77, note
Passaconaway, 451, note
    died, 452, note
Passamaquoddy, 41
Passongesit, 100, note
Patackost (Patackoset), 111, note
Patrick, Captain Daniel, 223, 249, 261, 262
    march delayed by a curious incident, 249, note
    reaches Providence, 261
    joins Mason at Narragansett, 281
    too late for Fort Mystic fight, 281

INDEX

Patrick, Captain Daniel, goes to Saybrook by land, 281
   mentioned, 366
   killed by a Dutch soldier, 425, note
Patuxet, 111, note, 115
Paucasit, 326, note
Paucatuck River, 196, 267
   English at, 266
   Mason fords this stream, 267
   location of their forts, 267
   Narragansetts and Mohegans withdraw across, 268
Paugessets, 52
   sell land to the English; delivery by turf and twig, 357
Paugus, 84, 85
Paupasquat, 326, note
Pawkunnawkut, 48, note
Pawpiamet, 431, 435
Pawtucket (Petuhqui, Puttukque), 111, note
Peacott (Pequod), 247, note
Peas, given the Indians in payment for corn taken by Standish, 96, note
Pecksuot, 84, 85, note, 128, note, 155, 156, 157, 171
   massacre of, 148
   his message to Standish, 155
Peddock, Leonard, 98, note
Peddock's Island, 98, note
   Frenchmen wrecked on, 98, note
Peeters, Thomas, 433, 447
Pekoath, 191
Pell, Mr., mentioned, 238, note
Pemaquid, 70, 343
   destroyed, 16
   settlement at, 140, note
   considered, 141, note, 183, note
Pematesick, 328
Pennacook Confederacy, 451, note
Pennacooks, 51, 451, note
Penobscot Bay, 138
Pentagoët, 45, 175
Pentuckets, 452, note
Pequakets, 85
Pequents (Pequods), 210, 212, 213, 214, 215, 216, 219, 220, 221, 226
Pequin, Pequetan, 191, note

INDEX

Pequit, 241, note
Pequits (Pequods), 238, note, 240, note
Pequods, 34, 35, 43, 81, 169, 189, 194, note, 196, 197, 198, 200, 201, 203, note, 204, 207, 227, 228, 230, 232, 233, 234, note, 236, 237, 240, 242, note, 250, 252, 253, 254, 255, 257, 260, 267
claim country about Connecticut River, 186
by conquest, 186
sell to the Dutch, 186, 187
their treachery, 187
at climax of power, 197
open negotiations with English, 201
number of warriors estimated, 207
plot to exterminate the English, 231, 234, note
frustrated by Roger Williams, 231
conference with Narragansetts, 235, note
extent of the domain of, 246, note
disposition of women and children, 249
outwitted by the Dutch, 254
give up two English girls taken at Wethersfield, 255
protected by squaw of Mononotto, 225, 316
regard Uncas as a renegade Pequod, 267
hold a feast at Fort Mystic, 268
their fort attacked by Mason, 271
women and children massacred, 273, 274, note
grief at destruction of Fort Mystic, 276
Mason relieved by arrival of the English fleet, 276
described by Mather, 277
punishment inevitable, 279
method of fighting, 279
punishment of, regarded as merited by Endicott, 282, note
their destruction as a people considered, 284
their plans anticipated by the English, 285
hold council after destruction of Fort Mystic, 285, 286
determination to abandon country to invaders, 286
destroy the royal village, 287
its location, 287, note
revenge upon Uncas, 287, note
location of fort destroyed by Mason, 287, note
portion of nation go to the westward; their fate, 288
capture three colonists; the torture, 288
direction of their flight, 289
take shelter in Fairfield Swamp, 289

INDEX

Pequods, racial characteristics, 296
    an object of slender sympathy, 296
    a race of wanderers, 298
    harassed by the English, 301
    Sassacus's hiding-place betrayed by Pequod spy, 303
    surrounded at Fairfield Swamp, 307
    defy Mason, 308
    attempt an escape in the fog, 309
    make a night sortie against Patrick, 309
    repelled by Patrick's men, 309
    captured by Mason, 310
    power broken, 314
    feared by adjacent tribes, 314
    sold into slavery, 315
    end of the, as a nation, 317
    number taken and killed at Fairfield Swamp, 317
    their dispersion, 318, 319, note
    efforts of a portion to maintain independence, 329
    conference held at Hartford for their final disposition, 330
    their troubles exploited by Mather, 330, note
    their number agreed upon, 336
    their final disposition, 337
    their lands appropriated by the English, 357
    break treaty with English, 360
    attacked by Mason and Uncas at Paucatuck River, 360
    for locating on Paucatuck River, 360
    Mason plunders their village, 360
    attack Mason, 361
    the parley, 362
    their village at Paucatuck destroyed by Mason, 363
    last foray against, 363
    sequestration of Pequod lands, 367
    allotment of, among the neighboring nations, 376
    male children, how disposed of, 398, note
    dispersed by Uncas, 452, note
    refuse to return to the Mohegans, 453
    desert the Nehantics and surrender to Willard, 462
Pequod Harbor, Mason orders a landing at, 256
    mentioned, 257
    forts on the Mystic reënforced by Sassacus, 268
Pequod River (The Thames), 230, 263
    Mason is relieved by appearance of fleet, 274

INDEX

Pequod War, 164, 343
    English at Wethersfield the aggressors, 357, 359
Pequots, 34, 43, 81
    described, 188, note
Perkins, John, 173, note
Pessicus, sends gifts to Winthrop, 418, 466, note, 467, note
    warned not to war against Uncas, 418
    summoned, with Uncas, to Hartford, 428
    inspires fear among English, 430, note
    invades Mohegan country, 431
    destroys Mohegan villages, 432
    driving the Mohegans into their forts, 432
    messengers sent from Boston to, 434, note
    his reception of them, and his reply, 435, note
    explains non-appearance before magistrates, 435
    Roger Williams warns the Boston authorities of by a letter, 436
    commissioners send two other messengers, 439
    goes to Boston, 440
    English impose conditions, 441
    hostages demanded of; poll-tax levied on Narragansetts and allied tribes, 442
    enters into treaty with English, 443
    invades Mohegan country, 466, note
    killed across the Maine border, 466, note
Pettuck's Island, 136
Pewee (Kieveet), 185, note
Pharmacy, Indian, 31
Philip, King, 49, 50, 62, 75, 81, 84, 162
Phœnician navigators, 30, note
Picture-painting, 24, note, 31
Pierce, Mr., attends Sir Richard Saltonstall, 206, note
Pierce Patent, 65
Pierce, William, takes captured Pequods to Bermuda, 225
Pigwacket, 40, 42, 43
Pilgrim compared with Puritan, 82, note
Pilgrim Fathers, 22
Pilgrims, how they wrought with Puritans, 79
    first landing of, 90
    their perilous condition at Plymouth, 138
    apprised of Virginia massacre, build a fort, 142
    description, 142, note
    on verge of starvation, 142

INDEX

Pilgrims, believed Indian supernaturally endowed, 157, note
Pincheon, M., mentioned, 240, note
Pinnace, Oldham's, 292, note
Piscataquay River, 172
Piscataquis River, 130, 343
Piscataways, 51
Plague, The, 49, 66, note, 112, 130
    Squanto only survivor at Pawtuxet (Plymouth), 116, note
Plows in use in Connecticut, 1647, 368
Plymouth, population of, 1630, 72
    distance by water from Boston to, 130, note
    threatened with famine, 139
    fort built at, 142, note
    mentioned, 158, 159, 160, 161, 198, 246
    Winthrop's discouraging attitude, 193
    governor of, 234, note
Plymouth Colony, 248
Plymouth traders, 35
    settlers, 62
    people go to Nauset to buy corn, 79, note
    profit by Indian generosity, 164
    suggest to Winthrop to plant colony of Connecticut, 193
Pocanokit (Pokonoket), 122, note
Pocassets, 49
Pocumtucks, 466
Podunks, 52
    driven from their country, 467
Pokonoket, 176
    derivation, 124, note
Pokonokets, 48, 49
Policy of English with the aborigine, 169
Pomeroye, Eltwood, 265, note
Popham, Lord chief justice, 73
Porter's Rocks, where Mason camped night before attack on Fort Mystic, 268
Powahes, 56
Powows, 129, note
    meeting of, after fight at Nauset, 129, note
Powpynamett, 435
Prat (Pratt), Phineas, 159
Pratt, Phineas, 159
Praying Indians, 54, 370

INDEX

Praying Indians, attached themselves to Philip, 371
   census of, 375, note
   places of worship, 375, note, 376, note
   removal of, to island in Boston Harbor, 376, note
Presumpscot, 42
Prin, Martin, 71
Prophecy of the French sailor, 130
Providence, Roger Williams settlement at, 261, note
Puckanokick (Pokonoket), 149
Puddington, Mary, 259, note
Pumham, used by English against Miantunnumoh, 350, note
   claimed to be sachem of Narragansetts, 350, note
   killed by Nawashawenck, 350, note
   mentioned, 405, 434
Pummumshe, 431
Pumpions, 41
Pumumsks, 435
Puncapug, 375
Puppompogs, 334
Purchas, Samuel, 122, note
Puritan, 21, note, 62, 63, 64, 82, 232, note, 248, note, 282, note, 296, 298, 324
   bullets, 82, note
   his avowed purpose toward the Indian, 163
   why he failed, 164
   compared with the Pilgrim, 164
   his creed exemplified in John Mason, 164
   the opposite of the Indian, 165
   as a slave-catcher, 294, note
   government shows resentment against Miantunnumoh, 351, note
Puritans, expected to be missionaries of Christian religion, 166
   their conscience, 232, note, 294, note
   considered in relation to the destruction of the Pequods, 282, note
   their bigotry, 299
   claim Shawomet, 350, note
   of the New Haven Colony, 356
   their community considered, 411
   their influence on the Indian, 411
Puttaquppuunck, 321, 322, note

Quaboags, raided by Uncas, 471

INDEX

Quaboags, captives liberated, 471
Quadequina, 116, 117, 118, 129
Quahag, 35, note
Quame, 321, note
Quincy, 131
Quinepaug, 287
Quinipeac, 391
Quinnebaug River, 477
Quinnipiacks, 52, 289, 303, 353, 354
    sell land to the English, 354
    consideration, 354
    treaty with English, 356
Quonehtacut, 189
Qunnonigat, 326, note

"Racounes," 104, note
Ralé, Sebastian, 14, 23, note, 31
Raleigh, Sir Walter, 190, note
Ralph, of Nobscussett, 78, note
Red Island, The (der Rood Eylandt), 185, note
Relation of debarkation from *Mayflower*, by Morton, 87
Restless, name of Block's vessel built at Manhattan, 183, note
Rhode Island, mentioned, 47, 48, 233, note, 238, note, 246, note,
        261, note, 325
    discovered by Block, 185
    trade established there by the Dutch, 185
    origin of the name, 185, note
    alarmed by the Mohawks, 344
Richmon, George, 75, 76
Richmond Island, 75, 76, note
Rigges, Sargante (and Jeffery), 223
River of Red Mountain (Housatonic), 184
Robin, of Ipswich, 173, note
Robin, of Massachusetts, 78, note
Robinson, Rev. John, writes Captain Standish of the massacre at
        Wessaguscus, 162
Rock Hill, Medford, 132, 133, note
Rumble, Sir Thomas, 237, note

Sabino, 26
Sachem's Head, capture of Pequods at, 301, 302
Sachem's Plain, battle of, 394

INDEX

Sachem's Plain, Miantunnumoh captured at, 394
  Miantunnumoh killed at, 413
  his burial-place, heap of stones, 413
  pilgrimages of Narragansetts to, 413
Saco, 42
Saconet, 84, note
Saconets, 50
Sagadahoc River, 26, 70, 71, 109, note
Sagadahoc settlement, the first, 71
Sagamore, John, reveals plot of Narragansetts to Plymouth, 234, note
Salem, population of, 1630, 172
Saltonstall, Sir Richard, 205
  comes to Boston, 206
  made assistant; returned to England; the portrait, 206, note
Samoset (John Somerset), 21, 33, note, 47, 48, 62, 77, note, 96, note, 106, note, 112, note, 413
  his first visit to Plymouth, 109
  deed to John Brown of Pemaquid lands, 110, note
  entertained by the Pilgrims, 111
  gifts to, 112, note
  brings his friends to Plymouth, 113
  Mourt describes their garb, 113
  singing and dancing, 113
  their food, 114
  mentions the Nausets, 114, note
  remains at Plymouth, 115
  English give him a hat, etc., 115
Sampson of Nobscussett, 76, note
Sanaps, the wife of, and Uncas, 448
Sasco, 303
Sassacouse (Sassacus), 226
Sassacus, place of residence, 267, 286; *vide* 43, 188, 200, 201, 202, 226, 246, 254, 255, 263, 449
  attacks English at Fort Mystic, 276
  planned to invade Narragansetts, 285
  holds a council of war, 285
  abandons his home, 286
  Mason's attack unexpected, 286
  former power as a sachem, 287
  takes refuge in Fairfield Swamp, 288, 289
  betrayed by Pequod spies; their fate, 301

INDEX

Sassacus, escapes capture by the English, 310
    the swamp battle, 311
    his fame, 311, note
    his desertion of his people considered, 312, 314
    inveterate enemy of Pequods, 313
    flees to the Mohawks; surprised and killed by them, 315
    his scalp sent to the Massachusetts authorities, 315, note
    beheaded by the Mohawks, 318
Saugatuck River, Patrick buys land at mouth of, 366
Saukatucketts, 51
Saunders, John, 149
Say and Seal, Lord, 205, 206, note, 251, note
Saybrook, fort at, 235, 236
    mentioned, 228, 229, note, 235, 250, 251, note, 255, 256, 275, 281, 363, 432
    attacked by Pequods, 236
Scalping-knife, 46
Scalps, 46, note
Scarborough marshes, 75
Schegichbi (New Jersey), 26, note
Schenectady, 270
Scurvy-stricken followers of Cartier, 31, 32, note
Sebequanash, 377
Seekonk, 233, note
Seely, Lieut., 438, note
Seely, Sergeant, 241, note
"Sentinells" set, 93
    alarmed at Wellfleet Bay, 104
Separatists, 21, 62
Sequassen, sells Connecticut lands to English, 187, 247
    defeated by Uncas, 288, 289
    Uncas and, 379
    feud between Uncas and, 379
    plots against Uncas, 443
    summoned to Hartford, 443
    his capture and release, 443, 444, 453, 460
    vide 453, note
    relative killed by a Podunk, 463
    Uncas' deputy, Foxon, appeals to Governor Webster, 464
    matter settled, 465, 186, note
Sequeen, same as Sequassen
Sequen (Sequassen), 453

INDEX

Sequen (Sequassen), returned to his own country, 460
Sequin (Sowheag), 241, note
Settlers, two hung in trees on Connecticut River, 295
Shallop, the *Mayflower's*, 87, 88, 96, 101
    Standish sails with it to Cape Cod, 96
    also to Wellfleet Bay, 102
    mentioned, 112, 124, 131, 228, note, 236, note, 243, note, 251
Shantok Point, 432
Shawmut, 83, note
Shawomet, 350, note
    Miantunnumoh sells same to Gorton, and begets enmity of the English, 350, note
    claimed by Plymouth Colony, 350
Shell-heaps, 27
Shetucket Indian killed, 477
    Uncas accused of the crime, 477
Shetucket River, 391
Shoes of Indians, how made, 121, note
Shurts, Abraham, at Pemaquid, 110, note, 174
Sickenames (Mystic) River, 186, note
Six-mile Island, 237, note
Skeleton of Indian found at West Medford, 132, note
Skittwarroes, 70
Slaine, John, 116, note
Slave-traffic, Indian, 324, note
    Massachusetts Bay not averse to, 319, note, 324, note, 350, note
Slaves, Pequods sent to Massachusetts as, 293
Smith, Capt. John, 68, 72, 98, note, 111, note, 122, note, 135, 136
    his visit to Massachusetts Bay, 135
Smith, Mr., mentioned, 213
Smyth, Francis, 434
Snaphance, 105
Sochoso, 196, note
Sohegans, 452, note
Sokaknoco, 434, note
Sokoki, 42, 43
Solon, Me., rock-tracings at, 29
Sommers, Will, 151
Southport, Me., 77, note
Southworth, Constant, 78, note
Sowaams (Puckanokick), 149

INDEX

Sowgans, 452, note
Sowheag, 52, 241, note, 357, note, 358, 359
   cause of attack on Wethersfield, 357, note
Sparrow, The, at Plymouth, 144
   Weston's vessel, sails later for Wessagusset, 144
Spencer, John, 238, note
Spurwink, 75
Squanto, 36, note, 74, 75, 115, note, 116, 140
   comes into Plymouth, 115
   only survivor of plague at Patuxet, 116
   a plotter, 116
   as a pilot, 117
   as an interpreter, 117
   sent to Aspinet, 125, 126, note, 127, 128
   plots, 126, note
   rumor of his death, 127
   Standish goes to Nemasket to his rescue, 127
   Standish attacks Corbitant's village, 128
   wounded Indians taken to Plymouth, 128
   goes with Standish to Massachusetts Bay, 130
   suggests robbing the Massachusetts Indians, 134
   arouses anger of Massasoit, 137
   who demands of Winslow his surrender, 137 (Drake's note), 138, note
   interprets the message of Canonicus to Bradford, 142
Squantum Headland, 131
Squashes, 41
St. Bartholomew massacre, 296, note
St. Castin, 45
St. Charles River, 32
St. John's River, Ingram at, 264, note
St. Lawrence River, 42
Stadaconé, 31
Stamford, 259, note, 367
Stamford, outrage at, 427
Stamford village, Indian raid on, 423, note, 427
   Dutch at, 426, 427
   settlers call on Hartford for help, 427
Standish, Miles, 67, 79; also note; likewise notes on 80, 84, 89, 92, 102, 115, 118, 128, 129, 130, 134, 149, 153, 245
   experience in Low Countries, 80, note, 95, note
   discovers Indians, 92

INDEX

Standish, Miles, his party finds great "Ketle," 92
    also a basket of corn, 93
    description of same, 93
    his acts of vandalism, 99, note
    ghoulish curiosity, 100
    shoots his first Indian, 105, note
    given full authority in military matters, 109
    attacks Namasket, 128
    conveys wounded Indians to Plymouth, 128
    explores Massachusetts Bay, 130
    raids Wessaguscus; massacre of Wittuwamet and Pecksuot, 149-157
    disposition with savage, 152
    alleged valor, 153
    informs Weston's men of Indian's plot, 154
    derided by Wittuwamet, 156
    mentioned, 157, 160
    returns to Plymouth safely, 158
    died at Duxbury, 89, note
Stanton, Thomas, 224, 239, note, 240, note, 307
    parleys with Pequods, 224, 239, note, 240, note, 307
    sent by the Massachusetts Commissioners to the Narragansetts, 454
Stoddard, Rev. Solomon, his letter to Governor Dudley, 170
Stone, Captain, murder of, 188, 189, note, 197, 199, 202, 203, 207, 210, 211, 228
Stone, chaplain of Mason's company at Fort Mystic, 257
Stonington, 246
Stonington, North, 246
Stony Brook, 78, note
Stoughton, Captain Israel, sent into the Pequod country, 290
    mentioned, 225, 295
    his force reduced, 290
    his movements, 291
    lands at Pequod River, 291
    joined by the Narragansetts, 291
    captures a small party of Pequods, 292
    Hubbard remarks upon his disposition of, 292, note
    his letter to Winthrop, 292, note
    reserving some of the captive savages to his own use, 292, note
    Drake suggests his motive in this, 294, note
    joined by Mason in his pursuit of the fleeing Pequods, 298

INDEX

Stoughton, Captain Israel, extracts from *MS.* letter of, 312, note
Stratford Ferry, Mohawks at, 444
Straw, Jack, 190, note
Strong waters, 57, 117
Succonet, 150, note

Taretines (Tarratines), 133, note, 174
Tarratines, 42
    their foray against the Massachusetts, 132
    marauding excursions, 172, 173, note
Tassquanot, 448
Tatobam, 43, 246, note
Taunton, 30, note
Taunton River, 28
Thames River, 414
    Mason retires to mouth of, 275
Thanksgiving ordered on return of soldiers from fight at Fairfield Swamp, 313, note
    at New Amsterdam, 426
Thistle, totem, 26, note
Thompson's House raided by the Pocumtucks, 469
Thompson's Island, 131
Thorfinne Karlsefne, 29, note
Thorvald, 29, note
Tille, 243, note
Tilley, Edward, 89
Tilley, John, captured and tortured at Saybrook, 242, 244, note
    incensed with Gardener, 243, and note
    mentioned, 283, 295
Tilley's Folly, 243, note
Tisquantum, 70, 74, 115, note
Tobacco, 37, note, 41, 57, 114, 121, 258, note, 339, note
Tolland, county of, 246, note
Tomahawk, 46
Tontinimo, Podunk sachem, 464
Torture of victims, 44
    manner of, 46
Trask, Captain, 223
Treaty, between English and Massasoit, 119
    with Corbitant and other sachems, 129, note
    of October 8, 1640, source of litigation, 378

INDEX

Treaty, Mohegan title questioned, 378
    between Pessicus and English, 443
Trelawney, Edward, 76, note
Trumbull's account of torture of colonists captured by Pequods on Connecticut River, 288, note
Tunxis Conspiracy, 420
Turkey, totem, 26, note
Turner, Captain, his expedition against Block Island, 227

Unalatchgo, 26, note
Unamis, 26, note
Uncas, 43, 188, and note, 200, 226, 246, 248, 252, 263, 431, note
    character, 246, note
    feud between and Miantunnumoh, 247, note
    buried, 247, note
    exploit of, on march to Saybrook, 250
    his integrity doubted by Gardener, 251
    foray at Bass River, 251
    captures Kiswas, 251
    a renegade Pequod, 267
    wounded at Fort Mystic, 270, 273
    joins in pursuit of the Pequods, 300
    captures a party of Pequods at Sachem's Head, 302
    weakness of the Mohegans, 320
    goes to Boston, 325
    accused by Massachusetts authorities of deceit, 326
    his protestations of good faith, 327
    called to Hartford by English, 330
    his star of fortune in the ascendent, 330
    commanded to appear before Council, 333
    Stanton charges him with lying, 335
    prominence of, 345
    arouses suspicions of Narragansetts, 346
    claims leadership of Pequod country, 372
    married Sebaquanash, 377
    hatred of Narragansetts for, 379
    accuses Miantunnumoh of conspiracy, 379
    attempt upon life of, 382
    charges his injury to Miantunnumoh, 384
    complains to Massachusetts authorities, 387
    his duplicity suspected, 387
    alleged assailant killed by Miantunnumoh, 387

INDEX

Uncas, second attempt on life of, 388
    Governor Haynes investigates, 388
    his demands of the Narragansetts, 388
    other attempts to kill him, 389
    invades Sequassen's territory, successfully, 389
    is advised of march of Narragansetts against him, 392
    collects his warriors, 392
    surprises the Narragansetts by a ruse, 393
    the parley, 393
    fight at Sachem's Plain, 393, *et seq.*
    account of fight by Hyde, 394, note
    takes Miantunnumoh to Hartford, 401
    his fears, 402
    advised by Connecticut magistrates, 402
    character of, reconsidered, 407, note
    summoned to Hartford, 412
    agrees to kill Miantunnumoh, 412
    his alleged acts of cannibalism, 413
    Miantunnumoh murdered by Wawequa, a brother of, 413
        by direction of the Connecticut Commissioners, 412
    English appoint witnesses to the act, 412
    Pessicus and, summoned to Hartford to settle their differences, 428, 430, note
    besieged by Pessicus, 432
    released by Leffingwell, 432, 468, note
    appears at Stamford with his warriors, 445
    investigates murder of Whittemore, 446
    inclined to be troublesome, 447
    complained of by Peeters and Morton, 447
    defiles the wife of Sanaps, 448
    a child of, dies; custom, 448
    sends Wawequa to the Pequods, 449
    complained of by Obechiquod and Cassasinamon, 449
    is defended at Boston by Foxon, 450
    complained of by John Winthrop, Jr., 451
    involves Wawequa, 451
    reproved by magistrates and fined, 452
    authorized to reduce the Pequods to obedience, 453
    attacked by Cuttaquin, 456
    a necessary evil to the English, 458
    his character again under discussion, 459
    jealous of Sequassen, 460

INDEX

Uncas, visits Governor Haynes, 461
  is given powder and bullets, 461
  complains of Ninigret, 461
  makes a compact with Sequassen, 463
  assembles a war-party against the Podunks, 465
  driven into his fort by Pessicus, 466
  makes a raid upon the Narragansetts, 466, note, 467
  Canonchet notifies Uncas to let the Podunks alone, 467
  surrender of Weasapano demanded by, 467
  refused, he obtains Weasapano by a ruse, 467
  ordered into court, 470
  raids the Nipmucks, 470
  also the Quabaugs, 471
  ordered by John Mason to release Quabaug captives, 471
  Mason anticipated, 471
  last days of, 474
  described by Gookin, 474
  accused of murder of Shetucket Indian, 477
  protests innocence, 477
  described by Fitch, the missionary, 478
  death of, 478
Uncass (Uncas), 226
Underhill, Captain John, expedition against Block Island, 227, 228, note, 229, note, 230
  relieves Saybrook Fort, 240
  joins Mason's expedition against Pequods, 257
  a description of, 257, note
  reproved by Cotton, 258, note
  punished by the church, 259, note
  enters employ of the Dutch, 259, note
  settlers at Stamford, Conn., 259, note
  at Dover, 259, note
  assumes governorship of New Hampshire, 259, note
  delegate to New Haven Court, 259, note
  appointed Assistant Justice for colony, 259, note
  commanded Dutch against Indians, 260, note
  battle of Strickland's Plain, 260, note
  settled afterward at Flushing, 260, note
  delegate from Oyster Bay to Assembly, 260, note
  under-sheriff, Queen's County, 260, note
  died at Oyster Bay, 260, note
  mentioned by Hubbard, 260, note

INDEX

Underhill, Captain John, the attack of Fort Mystic, 270, 273
  described by Vincent as a poltroon, 279
  rescues the Narragansetts and Mohegans from Pequods, 279
  vide 425, note, 426
  destroys an Indian village, 426
Ungongoit, 77, note

Van Curler, Jacob, 186, 187
  builds fort on Connecticut River, 187, 293, note
Van Dyck, Ensign, 426
Van Twiller, Wouter, 186, 191
Vane, Gov. Harry, defeated by Winthrop, 249, note
  mentioned, 208, 214, 226, 238, note, 246
  the election, 293, note
Vane, Sir Henry, 380, note
Verrazano, Foster's story of capture of a boy, 69
Vincent, description of Underhill, 279
Vines, Richard, 174
Virginia settlers, massacre of, 141

Waban's wigwam, Eliot held first church service among the Indians at, 373, note
Wabequasset, 474, note
Wachusett, 171, 174 note
Wagonckwut, 322, note
Wahginacut, a Podunk sachem, 190
  makes overtures to Winthrop, 191
Waiandance, 252, note
  his daughter captured by Ninigret, 262, note
  betrays Miantunnumoh's purpose to Gardener, 385
Walford, Thomas, 22, note
Wamesits, 452, note
Wampanoags, 48, 121, note, 125, 126, 128, 163, 323, note, 324
Wampan-oke, 124, note
Wampas, 373, note
Wampeag, Monheag medicine-man, captured by Mohegans, 461
Wampompeag (wampum), 203, note
Wampum, wampumpeag, 35, note, 56, 64, note, 203, 204, note, 211, 383, note, 386, 405, 449, 452, 456, note, 464, 469
  Plymouth buys, 204, note
  how made, 205, note

INDEX

Wampum, given to Uncas to ransom Miantunnumoh, 398
    also to commissioners, 399, note
Wamsutta, 471
Wanape, 73
War declared against the Massachusetts, 149
Wars of the Connecticut Indians ended, 478
Warwick, Earl of, 205, 401, note
Wassamaquin (Massasoit), 173
Wassapinewat, 149
Waterford, 246, note
Watertown, 192, note, 411
Watertown Mill, 372, note
Wattone, 365
Wawequa, 412, 413, 449
    depredations on neighboring Indians, 446, 451
    complained of by Nipmucks, 452
Way, Thomas, 77, note
Waymouth, Captain George, 115, note, 140
Weasapano, 466, 467
    kills relative of Sequassen, 464, 466, note
Weaugomhick, 328
Wecapaug Brook, 196
Wedgewood, John, 307, note
Weeks family, murdered, 207, note
Weetamoo, 81, 84
    death of, 50, note
Weetowisse, 429, 431
Wekapaug (Westerly), 265, note
    seat of the Nehantics, 199
Welde, Rev. Thomas, 424, note
Wellfleet Bay, 102
Wepawaugs, 289
Wequash, 189, note, 270, 287, note; also, note in full, 328; 351, 363, note
    various estimates of his character, 270, note
Wequaumugs, 328
Wessagusset (Wessaguscus), 22, note, 128, note, 143, 144, 145, 146, 149, 153, 155, 170
Wessagussets, 51
West India Company, 185
Westerly, 199, note, 265, note
Weston Settlement, 22, note

[525]

INDEX

Weston, Thomas, 135, 138, 144, 151
    his connection with the Plymouth Settlement, 135
    sails along North Shore, 135
    terminates his connection with Plymouth venture, 136
    his shallop puts into Plymouth, 138
    sends a colony to Wessagusset, 143
    his company made up of profligates, 144
    hanging of the weaver, 144
    Hubbard denies the fact, 148, note
    his plantation at Wessaguscus, 146
    disposition of Plymouth toward his colony, 150, note
    suffering of his men at Wessaguscus, 153
    threatened by Indians, 153
    sell their clothes for corn, 153
    doubts Standish's story of plot, 154
    betrayed Standish's confidence, 154
    his colony, and its dispersion, 158
Wethersfield Colony, 241, 244, 254, 258, 283, 316
    settlement warned, 242, note
    man killed at, 242, note
    surprised, 242, note
    quota for Pequod War, 245
    mentioned, 283
Weymouth, at Sagadahoc River, 70
Wheelwright, antinomian pretender, 250, note
Whittemore, John, murdered at Stamford, 445
    his body found, 446
Wigwams, 57, 103, 167, 229, note, 241, note
    interior of, 103, note, 104, note
    burning of, at Fort Mystic, 271, 272; also, 272, note, 283, 316, note, 360, 382
Willard, Major, despatched against the Nehantics, 462
Williams, name of family massacred near Hartford, 207, note
Williams (Williamson), John, 118, note
Williams, Roger, 41, note, 48, 124, note, 143, note, 188, note, 208, 209, 261
    visits Canonicus in behalf of Plymouth, 231, 232, 234, note
    banished from Plymouth, notes on 232 and 233
    his career, 261, note
    compared with the two Mathers, 261, note
    forbidden the jurisdiction of Massachusetts, 262, note
    finds asylum in Rhode Island, 262, note

INDEX

Williams, Roger, the prophet of his time, 262, note
    employed by Winthrop as ambassador to Narragansetts, 319, note, 320, note
    vide, also, 327, 328, 329
    accompanies Narragansetts to Hartford, 331
    goes to Boston with Miantunnumoh, 380, note
    sends a letter to the magistrates, 436
    warning them that war is imminent, 437
Williamson, Master, 118, note
Willson, Mr., 225
Winchester, 132
Wincombone, wife of Mononotto, 316; also note
    Hubbard's relation of her, 317, note
Windsor's quota for Pequod War, 245
    vide, 194, 207, 244
    settled, 207
Wine, 57
Winge, John, 78, note
Winnepesaukees, 452, note
Winslow, Edward, 36, note, 37, note, 62, 84, note, 102, 149, 193, 194
    compensates Massasoit for corn taken by Standish, 101
    meets Massasoit first time, 117
    gifts to, 117
    his entertainment of, 117
    his display, 119
    visits Massasoit, 124
    refuses to surrender Squanto to Massasoit's messengers, 137, 138, note
    plays Esculapius, 152
    Relation referred to, 154
    his narrative of the precarious existence of Obtakiest and his people, 161
Winter, John, 76, note
Winthrop, John, Gov., 22, note, 81, 83, note, 190, 191, note, 194, note, 198, note, 203, note, 212, 218, 222, 226, 229, 293, note, 403, 452
    at Salem, 174
    protests against the Dutch settling on the Connecticut, 191
    claims country under New England Charter, 191
    discourages settlement of the Connecticut lands, 193
    his and Bradford's *Letters* on the Pequod War, 210-227, 294, note

INDEX

Winthrop, John, Gov., interest in Mononotto's wife and children, 225
    convicted of leniency to Roger Williams, 232, note
    his disposition of Miantunnumoh, 248, note
    engineers his own election, 249, note
    the son of a lawyer, 262
    Barry's description of, 262
    his acquiescence in enslaving Pequods, 294, note
    his guiding hand in affairs, 297
    attitude toward the aborigine, 324, note
    description of Miantunnumoh before the court at Boston, 382, note
    after death of Miantunnumoh threatens the Narragansetts, 415
    his reply to Pessicus, 418
Winthrop, Jr., John, of New London, 207, 433
    complains of Uncas, 451
Witchcraft, 57, 459, 461
Wittuwamet, 84, note, 85, note, 129, note, 150, note, 156, 160, 171
    massacre of, 149-158
    boasts of his knife to Standish, 155
    his head set up on Plymouth fort, 158
"Wolves unkennelled," 339, note
"Woman," used in contumely, 37
Wongungs, 52
Woodstock, 474
Woosamequin, 120, note
Wopigwooit, a Pequod sachem, 186, 188, 200, note
    sells Connecticut lands to the Dutch, 186
    the price given, 187
    his death, 189, 200
Wopowags, 52
Wunnashowhatuckoogs, 331, 333
Wunnaumwauonck (faithfulness), 143, note
Wurregen, 387, note
Wuttackquiackommin, 328, note
Wuttamaoug, 41

Yarmouth, 51
Yotash, 321, note, 361

www.ingramcontent.com/pod-product-compliance
Ingram Content Group UK Ltd.
Pitfield, Milton Keynes, MK11 3LW, UK
UKHW021301180426
11947UKWH00015B/954